D0906439

CURRENT PERSPECTIVES IN SOCIAL THEORY

Volume 1 ● 1980

CURRENT PERSPECTIVES IN SOCIAL THEORY

A Research Annual

Editors: SCOTT G. McNALL
GARY N. HOWE
Department of Sociology
University of Kansas

Associate Editors: ALAN SICA
University of Kansas

RICHARD APPELBAUM
University of California, Santa Barbara

JEFFREY HALLEY
SUNY—Purchase

JOHN SEWART
University of Santa Clara

JONATHAN TURNER
University of California, Riverside

VOLUME 1 ● 1980

 JAI PRESS INC.
Greenwich, Connecticut

CONTENTS

LIST OF CONTRIBUTORS

Stanley Aronowitz — Department of Sociology, University of California—Irvine

Janet Saltzman Chaftez — Department of Sociology, University of Houston

Saul Feinman — Department of Sociology, University of Wyoming

Sang Jin Han — Department of Sociology, Southern Illinois University

David L. Harvey — Department of Sociology, University of Nevada—Reno

Elizabeth Safford Harvey — Department of Sociology, University of Nevada—Reno

Gary N. Howe — Department of Sociology, University of Kansas

Barbara Hockey Kaplan — Department of Sociology, American University

Douglas Maynard — Department of Sociology, University of Wisconsin—Madison

John O'Neill — Department of Sociology, York University

Paul Piccone — Department of Sociology, Washington University

C.G. Pickvance — Urban and Regional Studies Unit, University of Kent at Canterbury

John Sewart — Department of Sociology, University of Santa Clara

Alan M. Sica   Department of Sociology, University
                                        of Kansas

Lawrence Smith   Department of Sociology, University
                                        of Nevada—Reno

Charles Tilly   Center for Research on Social
                                        Organization, University of Michigan

Lyle G. Warner   Department of Sociology, University
                                        of Nevada—Reno

Morton G. Wenger   Department of Sociology, University
                                        of Louisville

Thomas P. Wilson   Department of Sociology, University
                                        of California—Santa Barbara

Mayer N. Zald   Center for Research on Social
                                        Organization, University of Michigan

INTRODUCTION

This volume is intended to present a sample of current social theorizing. We make no attempt to select papers consistent with our own theoretical concerns and perspectives. Rather, the concern is to make accessible a variety of work based in quite diverse theoretical traditions, representing what we consider to be significant points in a sociological field marked by increasing differentiation and antagonism. As such, the collection does not contain a representative cross section of sociology. For example, there is nothing in this volume to suggest that structural functionalism is alive and well, and the theoretical assumptions underpinning the every-day practices of the large group of sociologists mired in abstracted empiricism are not articulated here. Included here are works which indicate the *problems* of sociological theorizing in a more or less explicit fashion.

This volume and those which will follow reflect the times and a pre-vailing crisis in the social sciences, a crisis which transcends the issue of the validity of this or that theory to root itself in such basic concerns as the nature of theorizing and the epistemological status of what is termed science. A collection of essays devoted to illuminating the contemporary state of social theory produced 20 years ago would have looked very different both in regards to form and content. Such a collection would have been negligibly concerned with what theorizing is, and the totality would probably have been much more coherent than the totality encountered here. The age of consensus lies interred in the past; today, the general crisis of legitimacy in American society is reflected in American sociology, where the ultimate reconcilability of theoretical means and ends has become, to say the least, problematic. The Balkanization of politics in the 1960s and 1970s finds its professional intellectual reflection in the fragmentation of sociological theories and practices.

Any collection of theoretical essays produced 20 years ago would surely have included somewhere a call for synthesis, an indication that we would all learn and improve ourselves by attempting to absorb the insights of others into our own work. Such a call would not have been merely a pious hope, for the shared ultimate grounds of most sociological theorizing in that period offered at least the possibility of integration into a single "scientific" thrust. The editors do not call for synthesis. Even the most sublime piety strains at the prospect of a synthesis between the ethnomethodological current discussed by O'Neill and the geneticist-evolutionist perspective offered by Feinman. Equally, the rigorous Marxist critique of theories on international economic and political relations offered by Howe and Sica is not compatible with Aronowitz's perspective on the shortcomings of Marxism-as-science. Wilson and Maynard do suggest some ways in which ethnomethodological and Marxist explanations might be fused, but only after both sides have undergone redefinitions that some Marxists and ethnomethodologists would consider unacceptable. There seems to be no real possibility of a total synthesis, and there is no expectation that anyone should undertake such a thankless task. Certainly, this introduction will make no attempt to square the circle.

If we do not present materials for a new, unified science, the essays do, one hopes, inform. If the various currents represented here are mutually antagonistic they are *not* in the same measure doomed to mutual ignorance. While the "sectarianism" of currents is dictated by the temper of the times, and while close attention to one's own theoretical assumptions represents a welcome return to self-conscious intellectual activities, there is no reason for this involution to involve indifference to what is being done and thought in the rest of the sociological world. Any polemic is made more persuasive by an accurate representation of antagonists, and we can all learn from Moliere's remark that we embrace our enemy all the better to strangle him. For example, the critique of positivism is a very common feature of much sociological theorizing, but the frequent absence of any real understanding of the problematic vitiates critique. The point is that development of any problematic involves dialectical antagonism in which weaknesses in the elaboration of the thesis must necessarily weaken the antithesis. In this and future volumes the editors intend to present the antagonistic protagonists of the debate in sociological theory. This intent had very real consequences for the contributors, and in fairness to them the consequences should be made explicit.

The intent informing the volume is to make accessible a variety of forms of sociological theorizing to a general audience who might be expected to have uneven knowledge of the various fields involved. Recognizing this, we stipulated that contributions should include significant overviews of major developments within their respective fields, and that their arguments be stated in a language intelligible to the nonspecialist. The latter stipulation is a necessary part of any endeavor to inform, but its costs have to be recognized. Language plays a dual function: one of identifying the speech community (or theoretical group) to which the speaker-writer claims affiliation; and one of imposing a unique system of classification upon the world. The former is part of the social dynamic of the theorist-as-professional; the latter is an aspect of any form of theorizing. It is generally accepted that the "totemism of language" is a part of all sociological theorizing today, and it is generally deemed reprehensible—though it is necessary to observe that the standard of intelligibility commonly applied is nothing more than the specialized discursive rule of the dominant fraction within the discipline. Admitting the occasional extravagance in the use of language as social identifier is not, however, tantamount to condemning all special languages in theory. Special terms indicate the unique way in which a theoretical group divides and constitutes reality. For example, the use of the term *surplus value* by Marxists is not merely a way to indicate a theoretical persuasion while discussing profit, for surplus value is not equivalent to profit—rather, it relates to the difference between value expended on productive labor and value produced by labor, not to the difference between income and total costs. On the other hand, there may be terms which are common to different theoretical groups but which have fundamentally different meanings in their respective discourses. For example, the term *theory* has quite different connotations in positivist sociology than it has in Althusserian Marxism. Language is important, and the attempt to impose a common, everyday language upon contributors would represent the suggestion that synthesis is possible, that there does exist a common metatheoretical base. The result is an uneasy compromise, involving an attempt to maintain the language of a field or perspective to the extent compatible with its intelligibility to the outsider. All involved in the production of this volume recognize the costs of any concessions to everyday langauge. All equally hope that this will not be taken to indicate that theoretical differences are less than they really are.

The editorial hand lies, and will lie in the future, lightly upon the content of the contributions. The aim is to present what *is* rather than to editorialize within the papers themselves. The result is contradictions among contributions, which are selected less for their "truth" content than for the way in which they represent common theoretical perceptions within the discipline. This having been said, some of the major lineaments of the ideal informing this volume should be explicated. A major preoccupation is a clarification of what theory and "science" is and can be. The collapse of the American theoretical consensus has inscribed within it the problem not only of the content of theory, but also of what theory itself is. This problem is hardly confined to American sociology; it is also found, for example, in the French structuralist debate over the epistemological status of theory and its proper role with regard to practice and pragmatics. This problem suggests analysis along two dimensions: discussion of epistemology and ontology; and clarification of the meta-assumptions behind existing theory. These preoccupations give contemporary theory a peculiar complexion, for it tends to be theory about theory rather than about the "real" world. Repudiation of the classical relation between practice and theory in positivism, particularly of the necessary pragmatism of any theory constituted as a means of practical domination, opens the question of what a "scientific" theory really is—when "science" is defined as a purely theoretical and nonpragmatic exercise. In their very different ways Howe and Sica and Aronowitz emphasize the distortions suffered by theory when influenced by conjunctural political pragmatics, though they differ radically in their evaluation of the significance and meaning of Althusser's conception of Marxist science. In a slightly different vein, both Piccone and Sewart discuss the possibilities of theory *not* grounded in a discourse constituted in terms of categories expressing the contingent interests of bourgeois domination. Piccone is less sanguine about the prospects of development of a positive position out of Critical Theory, expressing the continuing difficulty of the Frankfurt School in establishing rational grounds for its own critique. Sewart, on the other hand, illuminates Habermas's attempts to do precisely that through establishing the claims implicit in discourse itself, thus giving a naturalistic justification for a theoretical position. This question of the relation between discursive formation and the logic of social structure is further pursued by Han in an essay offering a synthesis of Althusser, Foucault, Offe, and Habermas. Again, at issue is not so much a convergence of answers as a certain convergence in the sort of questions asked, e.g., about distortions introduced by the submission of theory to the question and actuality of power, and about the general form of a theory which is a theory rather than a means of domination and mystification. Such questions are necessary in the wake of the collapse of a consensus which engendered a systematic silence in regard to these issues, and their appearance is less a product of a voluntaristic "turn to philosophy" than of an objective crisis in the organization of intellectual practice.

In this context it is imperative that the real methodological and philosophical issues in sociological theory be clearly exposed, a task involving, *inter alia,* an archaeology of the sociological classics to reveal some of those basic choices obscured by precrisis interpretations. It is in this light that Wenger's piece on Weber and the *Stand* should be seen as a contribution to thinking about theorizing. Textual exegesis and "reexcavation" can appear not merely as ends in themselves, but as recognitions of some of the fundamental choices and issues besetting sociology when it was still in the critical stage before it was transformed into a transparent ideology serving the ends of the powers that be. Kaplan's biting statement on World System Theory plays precisely this role in denouncing a theory group claiming to represent, but simultaneously obscuring, one of the most coherent critical traditions in the armory of social science. If Kaplan and Howe and Sica decry the abuse of Marxism by practical and theoretical empiricists of various persuasions, Harvey and his colleagues indicate that more or less pure Marxist theory (in this case the theory of alienation) does explain and predict empirical realities even though it is inspired by a concretely abstract theory of capitalism in general rather than by direct induction from observed "facts." Pickvance, too, shows the direct relevance of general theorizing for the explanation of the particular in demonstrating how competing Marxist theories of the state and crisis necessarily involve different approaches to urban fiscal crises. Implicit in Pickvance's contribution is the further radical theoretical question of whether it is possible or legitimate to postulate any *general* theory of social institutions, or whether it is more legitimate to offer theories of epochs and conjunctures. This is a particularly appropriate question in the context of the Marxist commitment to a dialectical and historical form of analysis, but it also lies at the heart of the debate over positivism. In this sense, Sewart's discussion of the development of Habermas's theory is a valuable illustration of the dangers any theory runs in seeking to establish itself on grounds which transcend particular structures of domination, i.e., the risk of falling into a nondialectical universalism which is *not* saved by invoking the principle of the historical unfolding or evolution of the dominant principle or relation.

It would be inaccurate to represent the whole of sociological theorizing as embroiled in the task of seeking dialectical alternatives to positivism. One of the responses to the current crisis is less to change the form of positivism than to change its content. This is clearly visible in the empiricist wing of World System Theory, whose response to the accusation of the absence of a totalizing vision in conventional positivist sociology is to constitute the whole world as one great data set. That is, one response to the critique of positivism is to constitute the crisis as one involving what conventional sociology has typically correlated in its search for reality rather than the method itself (and its mode of representation and explanation). Chafetz's contribution falls more or less within this sort of response, attempting to establish cross-cultural relationships between the nature of work and sexual stratification. Again, however, there is an attempt to disarticulate the theory from the grossest forms of empiricism by separating factors in total status position which are contingently rather than necessarily intertwined. Implicit in this procedure is precisely the question addressed by the structuralist epistemologists, i.e., the extent to which theoretical categories should stand in a relation of direct reflection to the world of common practice. In a somewhat different fashion, Zald's discussion of the internal development of social movement theory presents a similar picture of shifts within an established branch of theory, involving movement closer to political sociology and a more formal and abstract model of social movements revolving around the issue of competition over scarce resources. While such formalization is redolent of a positivist orientation, Zald does introduce an important qualifier to the effect that the importance of the resource allocation issue corresponds to the preoccupation with wealth in American society. That is, the formalization is not carried over into a general theory, but is specified as appropriate to a particular social formation.

Precisely this caution with regard to mechanistic and universalistic theories in historical sociology and the study of social change is encountered in Tilly's overview of a field in which he is a prominent figure. Tilly charts the rather recent attraction of history for sociology, emphasizing the substantial caution with which more traditional general theories of rise and fall are currently treated, and the variety of paths between sociology and history. While it is clear that historical sociology is not *necessarily* grounded in dialectical and critical vision, the general enterprise might be represented, in part, as the posing of a formal question in substantive terms—as asking not whether general theory is possible, but whether general theory makes good sense of particular cases. If more critical and dialectical theory attacks conventional positivist sociology head-on, some parts of historical sociology might be pictured as engaging in a war of attrition.

Finally, Feinman's piece on genetic theory represents an attack on conventional theory from an entirely different direction. More or less explicit in all the other contributions is criticism of conventional positivism for its misrepresentation of theory and science and, of course, the reality perceived through those prisms. Notwithstanding the heat of the debate, some minimal consensus does exist, i.e., that a *social* theory of society is both possible and mandatory. Feinman does not engage in a critique of science; what he does suggest is that social theories are inadequate to understand society, that the natural (i.e., genetic) base of existence plays a role in social action and organization. In comparison to the extravagant claims of the sociobiologists Feinman's claims are engagingly modest, but the implicit criticism nonetheless asserts itself, i.e., that there is nothing wrong with science—the problem lies in the categories of analysis. This problem is not that categories are not "abstract" enough but that they are too abstract, divorcing man from his physical materiality. In a certain limited sense such a position joins hands with structuralism—in their joint repudiation of methodological individualism and voluntarism. The difference, of course, lies in the fact that structuralism locates the "objective" organizing force on the level of *social* structure, whereas the metatheory behind Feinman puts it on the level of *natural* structures and imperatives. Paradoxically, there exists a commonality between the naturalist position and the ethnomethodological project outlines by O'Neill. The latter argues for a more direct connection with the natural properties of everyday discourse and interaction, postulating in a manner more explicit than Feinman that the socially situated ideological models of sociological theorizing falsely obscure certain universal characteristics of the organization of social life.

All of the contributions to this volume involve reflections upon what sociological theorizing is and should be, and this is the unifying thread that justifies their juxtaposition. Present here is less a fundamental common basis for theorizing about theory than a common discomfiture with the operations and assumptions of a nonreflexive theoretical consensus only now in the phase of real disintegration. We do not offer a path out of chaos, and that was never our intention. What we do assert is that theorizing about theory is important, that without theorizing a sociological practice is impossible. Our contributors differ radically in their opinions about what correct theorizing is. We all have to make our own choices with regard to what constitutes legitimate modes of representation, but to make such choices without knowledge of the alternatives is, as Sartre has informed us, a form of bad faith with ourselves and the essence of intellectual work. It is precisely this reasoning that makes collections of essays on current theory a justifiable and valuable type of sociological product. We hope we have created the conditions for a more discursive and dialectical sociological self-clarification through exchange.

Gary N. Howe and Scott G. McNall

PART I

THE STATE OF THE ART

ON WORLD SYSTEMS THEORY

Barbara Hockey Kaplan

In these few pages I have been asked to identify *world systems theory*, distinguish its general problematic from that of other approaches, and delineate trends in its development. Clearly, I can only assert what could, in my view, be systematically demonstrated.

There is as yet no unified theory of world systems. There is a world system concept, a world system perspective "which [officially] recognizes the primacy of analyses of economies over long historical time and large space, the holism of the socio-historical process, and the transitory (heuristic) nature of theories" (Wallerstein, et al., 1977). All these are the work of Immanuel Wallerstein, his close collaborator Terence Hopkins, and a group of colleagues who have also founded a "school" of world system studies and an intellectual movement. It is Wallerstein's choice of the world system concept and its effect on his attempt to construct a theory that are of particular interest to social theorists as an attempt to break out of the Utopia of structural function-alist theory. He is, however, tackling Marx's problem without Marx's

Current Perspectives in Social Theory, volume 1, 1980, pages 3–5.
Copyright © 1980 by JAI Press Inc.
All rights of reproduction in any form reserved.
ISBN: 0-89232-154-7

problematic and working within an epistemology which will not allow the kind of explanation he seeks.

A decade ago Wallerstein began his study of social change—the process of transformation of enduring social structures—specifically, the genesis and dynamics of capitalism as a world economy and its potential transformation to socialism. At that point, the process of change was clearly central to his work. But Wallerstein believed that "one could only speak of change in social systems" (1974:7). Influenced by Gramsci's concept of totality, he missed or dropped its dialectical content and translated it into empirical scope and chose the world market as the appropriate "unit of analysis." It was, for him, the smallest whole system with a single division of labor identified as organized around the exchange of essential goods. This "natural" first choice has been crucial for all the rest. Attention shifted from the dynamics of change to the structure and functioning of the system, as if it must be constructed theoretically before change to it or from it could be studied.

Wallerstein was sharply critical of bourgeois social science, particularly modernization theory, for its level of abstraction, its ahistorical dichotomies of opposites, its focus on values rather than their material base, and its disciplinary fragmentation. He sought to replace it with something quite different and better—"to look reality in its face." The reality he saw in his earlier work on colonialism in Africa was inequality on an international scale. Although this had been addressed theoretically in the work of Lenin and others on imperialism, Wallerstein chose Gunder Frank's reductionist analysis of unequal international exchange without tracing Frank's concept of trade as the nexus of inequality to its origins in Marx's theory of capitalism. He thus omitted the production process where can be found not only exploitation but the nexus of both the class struggle, as the determinant of the direction of change, and the structural contradiction which contains the dynamic for capitalist development. This was another in the long series of choices which inexorably, but unknowingly, led him back to the kind of theory he explicitly opposed.

A careful examination of Wallerstein's method suggests that he is equally unaware of its derivation from the theory that he set out to replace. Without this awareness, a kind of pragmatic empiricism guides him away from what might be fruitful for his purpose and leads him unerringly to what is not. For example, consider another statement: "This led me into two great debates. One was the degree to which 'all history is the history of the class struggle.' Phrased another way, are classes the only significant operating units in the social and political arenas?" (1974:3). Shorn of the dialectic classes become simple units operating in his system.

The materialism to which Wallerstein turned is the mechanistic materialism of the eighteenth century *before* its fusion with the dialectic—one of the roots of functionalism. This is evident in the way he proceeds to theorize about the world system. He assures that the core and periphery, the opposite and distinct zones of international inequality, fall naturally into place while the contradictory semiperiphery needed to balance and stabilize this system still causes difficulty. With transformation implicitly theoretically limited to terminal stages or "epochs" of the system, rather than inherent throughout its development, change here becomes motion, e.g., displacement of particular nation stages up and down from these zones in a form of transposition of traditional models of social mobility from individuals to states in the international arena. In short, the terms periphery and semiperiphery suggest motion and cause the world system theorist to cease looking for causes of change. There is a circulation of elite (strongest) states at the core. Most recently, after attempts to replace the lost dynamic with concepts such as "proletarianization" and "bourgeoisification," attention has turned to cycles.

So, although the world system perspective does indeed deal with the exploitative reality of international capitalism, and although some of those working within this perspective have made the epistemological break to dialectical materialism, world system theory has made no such moves. Confined by its metaphysical methodology the empirical referent may be vast, but the theory remains constricted by its ahistorical empiricist method, its fragmented concepts and the underlying systems model. A theory of the dynamics of social change did not need to be invented.

REFERENCES

Kaplan, Barbara Hockey (ed.)
    1978   Social Change in the Capitalist World Economy. Beverly Hills, Calif.: Sage. (Contains bibliographic material on this perspective).
Wallerstein, Immanuel
    1974   The Modern World-System. New York: Academic Press.
Wallerstein, Immanuel, et al.
    1977   Review 1(2):inside cover.

FROM PHENOMENOLOGY TO ETHNOMETHODOLOGY:

SOME RADICAL "MISREADINGS"

John O'Neill

Phenomenology has always had a relation to the sciences (Husserl, 1970) and among these sociology, whatever its own difficulties with scientific method, merely continues and deepens the occasion for phenomenological reflection upon the institution of rationalized scientific practice and its relation to the everyday life-world. By the same token, sociology, at least among its classical theorists, has always been concerned to reflect upon the tradition of rationality within which its own methodic practice has achieved such efficacy, while remaining as much a symptom of as a cure for the troubles it diagnoses.

It is clear that the program of Husserlian phenomenology, like any other cultural artifact, has been appropriated with rough justice accorded to Husserl's intentions and for the rest made to accord with what philosophers and sociologists needed from it in relation to their own contexts of

Current Perspectives in Social Theory, volume 1, 1980, pages 7–20.

reflection and practice. Husserl has been the subject of radical "misreadings" (Bloom, 1975), whose significance cannot be ignored by phenomenologists or sociologists. These misreadings are the source of what we have in mind when we speak of work (which we cannot survey in all its detail) that passes as phenomenological sociology (Psathas, 1973), social phenomenology (O'Neill, 1970), existential sociology (Douglas and Johnson, 1977), cognitive sociology (Cicourel, 1973), and ethnomethodology (Garfinkel, 1967). We refer to:

1. (a) Schutz's reading of Husserl and Weber, and (b) Schutz's reading of Parsons
2. Merleau-Ponty's reading of Husserl
3. Garfinkel's reading of Parsons and Schultz

I am not suggesting that anyone's intellectual biography is to be recounted in strict accordance with such a schema. Rather, I take it that many of us have followed only part of these tales, losing interest in different places, picking up again according to different moods, some especially affected by the political and professional climate of the 1960s, others drawn in the light of shifting analytic and methodological interests. A lot will depend upon the degree to which particular thinkers have followed developments in such bodies as the Society for Phenomenology and Existential Philosophy, the American Sociological Association, and the Ad Hoc Group on Phenomenological Sociology which met at the World Congress of Sociology in 1974 and 1978. In these places, there is a growing, if at times grudging, recognition of the working interests of phenomenological (Schutzean) sociology and of ethnomethodology, especially in the direction of conversational analysis. Similarly, there has been a fairly steady flow of journal articles and a small number of textbooks and anthologies which testify to the institutionalization (however controversially it is rendered) of sociological work whose practice courts legitimation in a phenomenological legacy of some sort (Mehan and Wood, 1975; Turner, 1974; Schwartz and Jacobs, 1979). In any case, it would not be easy to adjudicate between insiders and declared outsiders in the conduct of terminological, conceptual, and programmatic disputes that govern much of the literature in this area.

With this in mind, I shall try now to recover what I can of the effective developments, relations, and lost trails that have shaped the practical history of the encounter between phenomenology and sociology in North America.

We cannot forsake at least a bare sketch of the ideas in Husserl that were to be taken up and transformed by Schutz and others. We do so with desperate brevity:

1. Husserl claimed for phenomenology a method of suspension (*epoche*) which was thoroughly "critical" in that it grasped objects in a

mode absolutely intrinsic to their perceived status and therefore without further unexamined/unexaminable presuppositions.

2. "Later" Husserl turned away from the critical program of a "pre-suppositionless" phenomenology to a phenomenology of objects and relations given in "co- and pre-knowledge" whose horizons unfold through our interpretative being-in-the-world (*Welt-Bewusstseins-Leben*).

3. The "life-world" (*Lebenswelt*) is therefore not a simple correlate of consciousness, nor is it thematically present to us; we are present to it as "already-meaningful" (*Anschaulich*). Every goal of ours presupposes the concrete meaningfulness of the life-world as the ground of all specific thematizations, as well as of all our "doxic acts," "intentions," "relevances," and "regional" sciences.

4. Theorizing stands in contrast not only to the concrete givenness of the life-world, but also to the *practical world* in which we conduct ourselves in respect of the things and persons around us, trading upon past-accomplishments (*Erhandeltes*) as well as striving to expand upon them. The practical world therefore is not to be confused with the life-world of which, no less than theorizing, it stands as only a province of meaning and action.

5. The life-world is a world of co-given persons present to us as subjects and partners (*Genossen*) as well as objects of interaction. It is as partners that we share in a common world (*Vergemein-schaft*). The commonality of the life-world is constituted through the mutuality of *comprehension* and *communication* whereby co-subjects seek to be understood by one another and to reach reciprocal agreements.

6. The world of our everyday experience (*Alltagsleben*) is the historically given cultural, political, socioeconomic world—the real world for us. This everyday world has for its horizon the universal common world (Brand, 1973).

SCHUTZ'S READING OF HUSSERL AND WEBER

I propose a similarly brief encapsulation of the places where Schutz took his stand with respect to Husserl and Weber. This involved "moves" in the direction of a phenomenological sociology which set itself off from transcendental and egological phenomenology. In the first place, Schutz considered a number of Husserl's ideas as positive contributions to the analysis of the subjective meaning of action:

1. Meaningful action is conduct motivated in terms of a *project*, i.e., rehearsing a future course of action in fantasy.

2. The relation of the fantasied project to its prior motives and its ensuing action is intelligible only through Husserl's analysis of *inner time*

consciousness. Schutz thought this a significant omission in Weber and later in Parsons.

3. Husserl's analysis of the *theory of signs and symbols* and of meaning-endowment could be applied to the analysis of larger symbolic institutions, language, art, religion, and myth.

4. Husserl's analysis of the pre-predicative experience and the nature of *types* can be extended sociologically to analyze how we interpret the action of fellow men in terms of course-of-action types and personal types, and why we in turn self-typify in order to establish the universe of communicative comprehension.

What Schutz definitely rejected in Husserl, is summarized in the following general remark:

> In summing up, we may say that the empirical social sciences will find their true foundation not in transcendental phenomenology, but in the *constitutive phenomenology of the natural attitude.* Husserl's signal contribution to the social sciences consists neither in his unsuccessful attempt to solve the problem of the constitution of the transcendental intersubjectivity within the reduced ecological sphere, nor in his unclarified notion of empathy as the foundation of understanding, nor, finally, in the interpretation of communities and societies as subjectivities of a higher order the nature of which can be described eidetically but rather in the wealth of his analyses pertinent to problems of the Lebenswelt and designed to be developed into a philosophical anthropology (Schutz, 1972:149, my emphasis).

Such secondary knowledge of Husserl is more than likely all most phenomenological sociologists have to trade upon. One can be more certain that phenomenological sociologists and ethnomethodologists have read Schutz. This is because his writings are easier to understand, more accessible, and more directly related to the American sociological tradition, inasmuch as they deal with Weber, Parsons, Mead, Thomas, Cooley, Scheler, Sartre; and with identifiable issues of sociological concern, such as the stranger, the problem of mutual understanding, and the relation between common sense and scientific knowledge. Schutz had no political position to speak of, yet his ideas have as often as not been taken in a radical sense. This is because Schutzean phenomenology seems to offer a defense of the commonsense, everyday world—the life-world, as most sociologists understand it—against the expropriations of professional expertise and administrative control (O'Neill, 1978).

In addition to *The Phenomenology of the Social World* (1967), and the *Collected Papers,* Vols. I–III (1962, 1964, 1966), Schutz had the benefit of a systematic presentation in Berger and Luckmann's *The Social Construction of Reality* (1966). In a period of profound crisis, Schutz became a basic tool for anyone trying to be reflective about the practice of sociology (Gouldner, 1970; O'Neill, 1972). Moreover, he had the benefit of being creatively "misread" by Garfinkel to produce a deep radicalization (phenomenologically speaking) in the theory and practice of sociology. Garfinkel's *Studies in Ethnomethodology* (1967), while surpassing Schutz, served equally to bring him to everyone's attention.

Once again, therefore, we present only the barest schema of Schutz's ideas, focusing on the issues that have made his work central to the concerns of phenomenological sociologists and to the initial concerns of ethnomethodologists.

1. All human actions, interests, motives, and relevances are subject to *typification*.

2. Person and action typifications shape and are shaped by *institutions*.

3. Persons ordinarily possess in common and without question a *stock of knowledge* that provides taken-for-granted orientation in everyday contexts of social interaction.

4. A person's *natural language competence* is the same thing as his or her *knowledge of social structure*.

5. The *sociological attitude* creates a province of meaning distinct from the attitude of everyday life.

6. Although the attitudes of sociology and everyday life differ, the sociologist's attitude is never entirely cut off from *a natural language user's knowledge of social structure and personal action*.

7. These ties can be formulated in terms of *three postulates of adequate sociological description and explanation:*

   a. *The postulate of logical consistency*—the intersubjective validity of the sociologist's concepts within his own community of science requires that they be constructed in accordance with the principles of formal logic *or the principle of rationality*.

   b. *The postulate of subjective interpretation*—in the social world, as opposed to the world of nature, in order to explain an action as a result of a subjectively meaningful relation, the sociologist must construct an ideal-typical actor.

   c. *The postulate of adequacy*—every term employed in a sociological explanation of human action ought to be so constructed that it would be reasonable and intelligible to the actor and his fellow men.

SCHUTZ'S READING OF PARSONS'S THEORY OF SOCIAL ACTION

Schutz's place in American sociology was not always so secure. Although he had already published in Vienna 1932 his *Phenomenology of the Social World*, his encounter with Talcott Parsons, whose *The Structure of Social Action* had appeared in 1937, made it look as though Schutz would never find any intellectual home in the United States. In view of the recent publication of this exchange of correspondence, edited by Grathoff

(1978), and its recent review (Coser, 1979; Giddens, 1979; Wagner, 1979), it may be useful to consider the issues that set apart Parsonian theory and Schutzean phenomenology, not to speak of ethnomethodology which Parsons seems to have bracketed with the same reserve he maintained for over 40 years in respect of Schutz.

1. Parsons and Schutz were divided over *the relation between philosophy and sociology*. Parsons's neo-Kantian philosophy of science left him with no approach to *the lived experience of subjective action,* whereas Schutz's Husserlian phenomenology made the analysis of subjectively meaningful action the first task of sociology.

2. Parsons refused to be taken in the direction of phenomenological sociology because he was committed to the *analytic construction of a general theory of action*. Parsons distrusted the scientific value of what he took to be the *ontological direction in the subjective approach* and considered subjective phenomena meaningful only in terms of the categories of external observation.

3. Parsons rejected Schutz's sharp *separation of the rationality of the commonsense actor and the observing scientist* and stressed the continuity between the attitudes of science and daily life. Parsons's own critique of positivist science, while not opposing a substantially different conception of rational action, added an emphasis upon the *normative dimension* in order to resolve the praxeological problem.

It is not our task to resolve these issues. As we shall see, they were taken up again by ethnomethodologists who sought to render Parsons's concerns with the problem of order (O'Neill, 1976) in terms of a radical phenomenological analysis of the commonsense knowledge of structures of practical action and reasoning.

MERLEAU-PONTY'S READING OF HUSSERL

While it is not possible to point to any definite group of phenomenological sociologists working directly from Merleau-Ponty, his seminal influence cannot be overlooked. It is from him that Garfinkel (1967), O'Neill (1977), and Sudnow (1978) have drawn their emphasis upon the features of *incarnate* or *embodied action,* and their critical remarks upon the specific vagueness of sociological theorizing predicted upon the expectations of disembodied actors.

Merleau-Ponty's *Phenomenology of Perception* (1963) is, of course, a rich source for the rejection of the conceits of constructive analytic theorizing through a patient analysis of the already meaningful structures of mundane perception, sense, and reason (O'Neill, 1970; Pollner, 1974).

Once more, then, we shall present the merest sketch of the arguments and issues to be found in Merleau-Ponty's work from which in various ways phenomenological sociologists and political scientists have drawn:

1. The rationality of the world is not primarily the constructive analytic achievement of a *disembodied, atemporal cogito.*

2. There is a *pre-reflexive perceptual* and *sensory world of meaning* which is the communal and historical ground of all other rationalities.

3. There is no finished synthesis of meaning and rationality—only a radically *situated sense* that carries with it its own *non-sense.*

4. Philosophical interrogation, like all other forms of expression, is riddled with *historical contingency,* which is the very ground of intelligibility and not its sheer relativisation.

5. *Language* and the *body* are operative schemas of our being-in-the-world—of our *primordial institution*—upon which all other social and political institutions are grounded.

6. The rationality of social and political institutions is equally distorted by historicist and Platonist conceptions of reason and discourse.

7. Our social and political life is grounded in vast sedimentations of traditional and anonymous achievements of sense and non-sense which cannot be overhauled by any rationalist, or voluntarist fiat.

8. Marxist materialism, scientism, and historicism need to be rethought in the light of the phenomenological approach to language, embodiment, and institution.

As we have said, it is not easy to trace any direct following of Merleau-Ponty among sociologists, beyond the few we have mentioned. Nevertheless, one's sense of the development of phenomenological sociology and ethnomethodology makes it impossible to overlook his work as a seminal influence.

GARFINKEL'S READING OF
PARSONS AND SCHUTZ

We have already considered the failed encounter between Parsons and Schutz. As history would have it, it fell to Garfinkel, a student of Parsons, to radicalize the Parsonian problem of order (O'Neill, 1976) in terms of an equally radical reading of Schutz's conception of commonsense and scientific knowledge of social structure (Garfinkel, 1967:76–103).

We derive our knowledge of Garfinkel's reading of the Parsonian program from his unpublished but circulated manuscript, *The Parsons Primer.* In keeping with our previous procedure, we shall sketch the essential features of Garfinkel's reading of Parsons—remarkable for its already considerable grasp of the problem of adequate description of commonsense interpreted social structures of action. We hope that a discerning reader will find in the several sketches we have drawn up, the resources for reading back and forth propositions relevant to issues raised but not treated at length in our basic formulations of the individual positions that make up the history we are covering.

Garfinkel's Reading of Parsons

1. The sociological theorist is faced with *the problem of adequate description* of the data of society known in any way whatsoever to members as perceivedly accountable normal reality.

   a. What kind of limit can be placed upon the enumeration of properties that a perceived environment can show under any method of enumeration and description available to sociologists?

   b. How are the categories of objects and courses of judgment and perception employed by the actor to be made comparable to the categories and courses of judgment and perception that the sociologist employs as correct scientific procedcure?

2. Parsonian theory can be conceived to consist of procedures whereby a society that is known to its members in a more or less commonsense way is idealized in accordance with the rules of procedure known as "the rules of scientific inquiry."

3. With respect to the social actor's rules of reasoning regarding his environment, Parsons's correspondence theory is beset with the problem of the empirical adequacy of the actor's constructs. Because of the separation between the real world and the actor's perceptions, the correspondence theorist treats his concepts as empirical ideal types, designating probable conducts. On a congruence theory, the actor's perceptions, taken by him to be objective, are regarded by the observer as a construction of what at any particular stage he knows and is interested in.

4. Parsonian theory consists of a set of rules whereby a "society" that is initially known in any way whatsoever (i.e., relevance structure, multiple realities) is progressively transformed into a description of a theoretically possible society. Members of society are everyday theorists of the socially organized settings of their own affairs which range from the practical to the conjectured, dreamed and fantastic, moral, religious. Their first-order "accounts" are transformed in their sense through the methods of sociological theorizing and inquiry. The result is a transformed description to which sociologists give the status of *real social structures*.

According to Garfinkel, then, three basic problems beset the Parsonian theory of social action:

A. The Problem of the Logical Status of the Subjective Categories

The problem consists in the question of whether adequate description of a source of observable action is possible for the sociological theorist if he does not presuppose some reference to the interests of persons, their knowledge of their environment, their treatment of these environments—albeit without the sociological theorist making reference to or invoking the scientific adequacy of these interests in order for the theorist to decide what the real features of the environments are to which the person whose actions are being described is responsive. Schutz argued that Parsons assumed without analysis the phenomenon of the constitutive expectancies whereby things are "known and valued in common with others."

B. The Problem of Rationality

A question arises as to how the actor's everyday knowledge can be taken as a basis for the scientific observer's anonymous descriptions, themselves regarded as independent of the observer's own biography. It is at this point that the rationality assumption enters in order to produce communality between the actor's and the observer's knowledge of social structure. For the Parsonian correspondence theorist it is then possible to evaluate the actor's knowledge in the light of his own wider knowledge of the actor's environment and to render it corrigible in the light of instrumentally rational appraisals held in common by the observer and the actor. On a congruence theory, the actor's rationality is not subject to such ironic comparison. It is taken as a course of action reasonable for all practical purposes within his life situation.

Parsons's solution to the problem was to stipulate the *rule of adequate means* as a definition of rationality in conduct. This means that an action will be called rational if, in the selection of alternative means for achieving a future goal, the selections accord in content and procedure with those of empirical science.

C. The Problem of Social Causation Versus Naturalistic Causation

To continue with Garfinkel's critique of Parsons, given the property of the normative regulation of action, any attempt to relate conditions and consequences in the manner of natural causal sequences has to confront the troublesome fact that persons could, and do, treat theories of action as maxims of conduct. Because this is the case, causal explanations must presuppose the compliance of persons with some normative theory of their society as a set of rules of morally adequate conduct. The sociologist has to devise methods for discriminating normative from descriptive theories of conduct.

Garfinkel concludes that the problem of adequate description of related social structures, then, is resolved by Parsons into the following:

1. The *problem of social order*
2. The rules of procedure that define the *sociological attitude*:
   a. rules at level of unity of science and
   b. rules specific to scientific study of human actions.

Parsons's social system is a solution of the problem of adequate description consisting of *two theorems of social order*:

1. Real social structures consist of institutionalized patterns of normative culture.

2. The stable properties of the real social structures are guaranteed by motivated compliance to a legitimated order.

GARFINKEL'S READING OF SCHUTZ: ETHNOMETHODOLOGY

It would be highly misleading to suggest that Garfinkel's disco͟ practice of ethnomethodology was intelligible solely as an ex "misreading" Schutz—or Parsons, for that matter. We do not find the sense of ethnomethodology in its literary past—a "misreadin͟ intelligible only through its product. Keeping in mind, then, that we have employed a certain documentary method of retrospective/prospective inclusion in sketching our previous readings, in order to display their ties to issues arising from the encounter between phenomenology and sociology, we now sketch certain basic formulations of ethnomethodology:

1. The *methods of commonsense understanding* and *commonsense knowledge of social structure* and *action* are uniquely ethnomethodology's phenomenon.

2. Every feature of the logic, sense, facticity, objectivity, and accountability of action is to be analyzed as the *contingent, locally organized achievement of vulgar practices*.

3. The recognized/recognizable sense of action is unavailable to the invariant categories of constructive-analytic theorizing which *misses essentially* the situated, local production of naturally organized activities.

4. Any reading of the documentary organization of the norms, rules, and practices of an institution, so far from revealing the order of the institution, *presupposes a member's knowledge of its commonsense, accountable order* to remedy its intrinsic glosses and specific vagueness of sociological reconstructions.

5. A member's sense of an interaction is *progressively elaborated* in-and-over the course of interaction, in the same way that co-conversationalists improvise the sense of their talk in-and-over the course of conversation as a naturally competent display of talk.

The Linguistic Turn in Ethnomethodology

The natural order of social life may be displayed in the use by members of linguistic competences that are synchronous with identifying an orderliness and its repair. The sense of any stretch of conversational interaction requires the speaker to constrain and the listener to analyze its topic for the sense it will come to have and cannot possibly have from the very start—the latter being a Cartesian requirement of ideal languages. This is a basic competence—involving back and forward ties—analytic to all other conversational practices. Here we wish to signal a further set of propositions, an extension of the above five, in which the work of Harvey Sacks and Emmanuel Schegloff (Sacks et al., 1974) is of considerable importance.

6. Ethnomethodology claims that *constructive analytic social theorizing is itself only achievable through an unthematic reliance upon the* ~~   ~~ *'s natural language competence* whereby he bridges indexical ~~ ~~ns and their idealized descriptions.

~~   ~~ *self-explicating features of natural colloquy* are achieved the work of participant formulations which provide the structure ~~ ~~erliness of everyday activities in that

a. they exhibit upon analysis the properties of uniformity, reproducibility, repetitiveness, and typicality;
b. these properties are independent of particular production cohorts;
c. particular cohort independence is a phenomenon for members' recognition, i.e., "exhibited *in* the speaking"; and
d. phenomena *a–c* are every particular cohort's practical, situated accomplishment.

8. Above all, formulating is an *account-able* phenomenon this is to say that it is a phenomenon that members make happen; that they can observe; and that they can *do.*

9. "Doing" formulations consists of glosses which are methods for producing observable and reportable understanding within discursive interaction of which they are themselves determined phases. Glosses are the "machinery" whereby members remedy the problematic features of indexical expressions in order to achieve adequate sense, topic, relevance, and the like. Glosses are *essentially contexted phenomena,* of a sort that then

a. constitute what a member is doing on the occasions he does and recognizes;
b. are done invariably;
c. constitute the work of members for which [practices of cogent, rational talk] is a proper gloss;
d. meet the criteria *a–c* by satisfying the following "essential" constraints.

They are proper grounds for members' remedial actions—and complaints. Nevertheless, they are without remedy since every corrective action necessarily preserves the specific features it seeks to remedy, which means they are entirely unavoidable.

10. In more recent years, Garfinkel's insistence upon the problem of adequate description has led him to draw a distinction between *natural theoretic accounts* of orders of action and the *local, endogenous produc-*

tion of the orderliness of naturally organized activities.[1] Included in the naturally available sociologies are numerous analytic arts and sciences of practical action.

11. This distinction serves to locate the following *identifying issues of the problem of social order*:

    a. the *natural accountability,* i.e., available to vulgar competence, of the problem of social order;

    b. the *in situ* production of the identifying orderliness of the interior course of ordinary activities;

    c. the *ignored orderliness* of ordinary activities *consists* of their conversational practices;

    d. the problem of the *radical how* of ordinary *organizational things.*

12. Methods for study of naturally organized activities are constrained to a *unique adequacy requirement.* A method is adequate to the phenomenon it finds in the way that the method is *already* an organizational feature of the object it finds. Thus the unique adequacy requirement of methods prohibits the administration of methods external to the settings of practical inquiry and observation. It therefore rejects the idealizing practices of correspondence procedures of scientific method. That the organizational methods of objects are always and already there means that the produced orderliness of ordinary objects is for members a real fact and *not* a professional construct.

CONCLUSION

We have sketched the central elements of *natural language accounts* in order to show that the ethnomethodological and conversational analytic use of this notion must be understood as a phenomenon of uniquely *local order production.* It is therefore not reducible to the dramaturgical concept of a "line" (Goffman, 1959), nor can it be restricted to practices intended to repair infractions of routine practice (Scott and Lyman, 1968), since this misses what is accountably routine as well as what is relevantly specific in routine repairs. By the same token, accounts are not simply a theorist's device for the construction of practical actors (Blum and McHugh, 1971). Such artifacts of constructive analytic theorizing are themselves dependent upon the local, contingent, and natural orders of practical activity whose cogency is not open to formulation in abstraction from the empirical materials of situated and embodied linguistic practices. We think that Garfinkel's early notion of accounts remains central to the practice of ethnomethodology and conversational analysis. He has progressively tied the analysis of the rationality of accounts to locally produced endogenous orders of naturally organized activities. This move has deepened ethnomethodology's rejection of constructive analytic theorizing. By the same token, the *recipient-design* of locally managed conversational structures offers a strong sense of the local accountability which ethnomethodological descriptions seek to reproduce. Apart from these technical issues, any general talk of ethnomethodology is rendered hopelessly vague.

NOTE

1. The account here draws upon conversations with Garfinkel and draft versions of his forthcoming *Manual for Studies of Naturally Organized Activities*. London: Routledge & Kegan Paul.

REFERENCES

Berger, Peter L., and Thomas Luckmann
  1966 The Social Construction of Reality: A Treatise in the Sociology of Knowledge. Garden City, N.Y.: Doubleday.
Bloom, Harold
  1975 A Map of Misreading. New York: Oxford University Press.
Blum, Alan F. and Peter McHugh
  1971 ''The social ascription of motives.'' American Sociological Review 36:98–109.
Brand, Gerd
  1973 ''The Structure of the Life-World According to Husserl.'' Man and World 6:143–62.
Cicourel, Aaron V.
  1973 Cognitive Sociology. Harmondsworth: Penguin.
Coser, Lewis A.
  1979 ''A dialogue of the deaf.'' Contemporary Sociology 8:680–2.
Dallmayr, Fred R.
  1973 ''Phenomenology and Marxism: a salute to Enzo Paci.'' Pp. 305–56 in George Psathas (ed.), Phenomenological Sociology. New York: Wiley.
Douglas, Jack D., and John M. Johnson
  1977 Existential Sociology. New York: Cambridge University Press.
Garfinkel, Harold
  1967 Studies in Ethnomethodology. Englewood Cliffs, N.J.: Prentice-Hall.
Giddens, Anthony
  1979 ''Schutz and Parsons: problems of meaning and subjectivity.'' Contemporary Sociology 8:682–5.
Goffman, Erving
  1959 The Presentation of Self in Everyday Life. Garden City, N.Y.: Doubleday.
Gouldner, Alvin W.
  1970 The Coming Crisis of Western Sociology. New York: Avon.
Grathoff, Richard
  1978 The Theory of Social Action: The Correspondence of Alfred Schutz and Talcott Parsons. Bloomington: Indiana University Press.
Husserl, Edmund
  1970 The Crisis of European Sciences and Transcendental Phenomenology. Evanston, Ill.: Northwestern Univerity Press.
Mehan, Hugh, and Houston Wood
  1975 The Reality of Ethnomethodology. New York: Wiley (Interscience).

Merleau-Ponty, Maurice
  1963   The Phenomenology of Perception. London: Routledge & Kegan Paul.
O'Neill, John
  1970   Perception, Expression and History: The Social Phenomenology of Maurice
         Merleau-Ponty. Evanston: Northwestern University Press.
  1972   Sociology as a Skin Trade: Essays Towards a Reflexive Sociology. New York:
         Harper & Row.
  1976   "The Hobbesian problem in Marx and Parsons." Pp. 295–308 in Jan J. Loubser,
         Rainer C. Baum, Andrew Effrat, and Victor Meyer Lidz (eds.), Explorations in
         General Theory in Social Science: Essays in Honor of Talcott Parsons, Vol. 1.
         New York: Free Press.
  1977   "Mind and Institution." Pp. 98–108 in Don Ihde and Richard M. Zaner (eds.),
         Interdisciplinary Phenomenology. The Hague: Nijhoff.
  1978   "Merleau-Ponty's critique of Marxist scientism." Canadian Journal of Social and
         Political Theory 2:33–62.
Parsons, Talcott
  1973   The Structure of Social Action. New York: Free Press.
Pollner, Melvin
  1974   "Mundane reasoning." Philosophy of the Social Sciences 4:35–54.
Psathas, George
  1973   Phenomenological Sociology. New York: Wiley.
Sacks, H., E. Schegloff, and G. Jefferson
  1974   "A simplest systematics for the organization of turn-taking for conversation."
         Language 50:696–735.
Schutz, Alfred
  1962   Collected Papers. Vol. I: The Problem of Social Reality. The Hague: Nijhoff.
  1964   Collected Papers. Vol. II: Studies in Social Theory. The Hague: Nijhoff.
  1966   Collected Papers. Vol. III: Studies in Phenomenological Philosophy. The Hague:
         Nijhoff.
  1967   The Phenomenology of the Social World. Evanston, Ill.: Northwestern University
         Press.
Schutz, Alfred, and Thomas Luckmann
  1973   The Structure of the Life World. Evanston, Ill.: Northwestern University Press.
Schwartz, Howard, and Jerry Jacobs
  1979   Qualitative Sociology: A Method to the Madness. New York: Free Press.
Scott, Marvin B., and Stanford M. Lyman
  1968   "Accounts," American Sociological Review 36:46–62.
Sudnow, David
  1978   Ways of the Hand: The Organization of Improvised Conduct. London: Routledge
         & Kegan Paul.
Turner, Roy
  1974   Ethnomethodology. Harmondsworth: Penguin.
Wagner, Helmut
  1979   "Theory of action and sociology of the life-world." Contemporary Sociology
         8:685–7.

THE FUTURE OF CRITICAL THEORY

Paul Piccone

Although during the 1930s it was essentially a code word for Marxism at a time when it was suicidal to refer to such things by their proper names (Arato, 1978:3ff.; Jay, 1973:41–85) critical theory rapidly became a distinct theoretical perspective by the outbreak of World War II. On the other hand, as has also often been pointed out, notwithstanding Horkheimer's leading intellectual role, universally acknowledged by all those associated with the Institute for Social Research (Marcuse, et al., 1978–79:127ff.), there has never been a *single* critical theory but only a variety of positions whose differences were often more significant than their obvious similarities (Piccone, 1978:xivff.). Yet, all of the works of the major figures of the Frankfurt School share one fundamental objective: to come to terms with the new emerging forms of organized capitalism and to radically reconstitute the project of human emancipation that in traditional Marxist theory had been projected as the proletarian revolution.

Already at the turn of the century, the "Revisionism Debate" had revealed major theoretical flaws with the predominant Second International interpretations of Marxism (Piccone, 1977–78) and, of course, the

Current Perspectives in Social Theory, volume 1, 1980, pages 21–30.
Copyright © 1980 by JAI Press Inc.
All rights of reproduction in any form reserved.
ISBN: 0-89232-154-7

full political bankruptcy of that whole generation of Marxists became obvious at the outset of World War I with the end of the myth of "proletarian internationalism." Class struggle gave way to the old nationalist chauvinisms, and social democracy openly became nothing more than another means to manage social conflicts and thus reinforce capitalist relations of domination. Both the Third International and Hegelian Marxism sought to counter this state of affairs. Very soon, however, failure of revolutionary efforts all over Europe and the rise of Stalin again eclipsed all attempts to revitalize Marxism, (Piccone, 1972, 1974, 1978), which thereafter degenerated to the level of an official "science of legitimation" for totalitarian regimes with dubious "socialist" credentials. Contrary to Anderson's claim that Western Marxism as a whole was the result of political defeat and of "the structural divorce of this Marxism from political practice" (Anderson, 1976:29,42), Western Marxism in general, and critical theory in particular, became academic and philosophical enterprises because of the very impossibility of engaging in concrete politics in the late 1920s and 1930s, and, consequently, of the need to rethink some of the fundamental assumptions of Marxist theory itself.[1]

Nothing short of a detailed reconstruction of the theoretical trajectory of each leading member of the Frankfurt School would provide a satisfactory account of the extent and the direction of this process of structural reconstitution. Yet, a sketch of the intellectual path followed by one of its major exponents such as Marcuse can indicate both the strengths and the limitations of the whole collective effort while also suggesting future prospects now that, with Marcuse's death, the work of the original school can be considered a relatively completed chapter in the history of radical social theory.[2] The following will seek to locate the fundamental problem in that version of critical theory developed by Marcuse with various references to other members of the original group, so as to show both the centrality of the issues as well as alternative ways to deal with them (Piccone, 1976; Piccone and Delfini, 1970). In fact, if critical theory is to survive as a viable enterprise in the future,[3] these alternatives will need extensive elaboration in order to provide new ways to interpret social reality and reformulate the traditional Marxist project of human emancipation in ways that either the first generation of critical theorists never fully succeeded in doing or have once again been rendered obsolete by the changed character of social relations.

While educated in a tradition somewhat different than that of Adorno and Horkheimer, Marcuse's main problem—from his very first essay in 1928 to *The Aesthetic Dimension* (1978) published almost half a century later[4]—is typical of the whole school: the problem of the foundation.[5] Born in 1898, Marcuse came of age around World War I and, along with the best minds of the time, he soon realized that an age was coming to an end with nothing ready to replace it. Although he initially saw Marxism as a viable alternative and thus joined the Social Democratic party, he quickly became disenchanted with its policies after the murders of Rosa Luxemburg and Karl Liebknecht. Unlke Lukacs, Korsch, or Gramsci, who, likewise disenchanted with social democracy and the vulgar positivism and/or evolutionism of the Marxism of the Second International, sought to reinterpret Marxism in Hegelian terms rather than the prevailing economistic ones, the young Marcuse simply dropped out. He could not identify with the Bolshevik Revolution and the rising Third International, so he went to work in a second-hand bookstore and a publishing house in Berlin (Marcuse, et al., 1978–79). He eventually drifted to Freiburg where Heidegger had just published *Being and Time* and seemed to provide a way out of the general social decay with a concrete philosophy addressing the problems of the time.

Having never really rejected his basic Marxist convictions, however, he readily saw the possibility of transposing Heidegger's phenomenology and Dilthey's related philosophy of life as foundations for the general Marxist framework, which, in its rush to grasp the logic of the totality, had lost touch with the immediacy and urgency of everyday life. His first sophisticated work in 1928 (Marcuse, 1959a) dealt with the possibility of Heideggerian phenomenology providing an anthropological–ontological foundation for historical materialism and, conversely, historical materialism solving the problems that existential phenomenology could not generalize from the individual to the sociohistorical level. Revolution was no longer seen as resulting from the necessary unfolding of an economistic logic, but as the only way out of the dejected social existence (*geworfenes In-der-Welt-Sein*) unveiled by existential phenomenology (Marcuse, 1929).

In an historical context characterized by the consolidation of Stalin's dictatorship in Russia, Mussolini's fascism in Italy, and the rapid disintegration of the Weimar republic, Marcuse's project would only remain empty speculation buried in relatively inaccessible academic journals and well hidden beneath a practically impenetrable philosophical jargon. That it was a highly original contribution can be seen from the fact that roughly similar ideas were developed, wholly without any knowledge of Marcuse's long-forgotten works, by some of the best Marxist minds one generation later: Sartre and Merleau-Ponty in France, Kosik (1976) in Czechoslovakia, the *Praxis* group in Yugoslavia, Vajda (1971, 1978–79) in Hungary, Paci (1972) in Italy, and even some American New Left groups in the United States after 1968 (e.g., Piccone, 1970). The overwhelming theoretical weight of the official Marxism-Leninism of the various Communist parties, however, has succeeded in reducing all these efforts to politically useless exercises in a world divided into allegedly irreconcilable power blocs.

Between 1928 and 1932, Marcuse continued to elaborate his thesis in the pages of the *Archiv für Sozialwissenschaft und Sozialpolitik* and Hilferding's *Die Gesellschaft*—two of the most powerful intellectual organs of late Weimar Germany. Two major events, however, shook Marcuse out of his existential–phenomenological position and led him to join the Frankfurt School: Heidegger's capitulation to Nazism after Hitler's rise to power, and the publication of Marx's *Economic and Philosophical Manuscripts of 1844* (see Kellner, 1973). Marcuse not only recognized that Heidegger could not provide an answer to the problems of concrete everyday life, but he also discovered that what he had sought in Heidegger was already much better developed in the young Marx. Given that his Jewish blood was now considered "impure," Marcuse rapidly completed his dissertation on Hegel's ontology and emigrated to the United States to join Horkheimer's Institute for Social Research, working in exile at Columbia University.

The break with Heidegger, however, was never as sharp or as definitive as Marcuse subsequently claimed. The basic concepts of existence (*Dasein*) and life (*Leben*) that had been located as the moving force in Hegel's ontogenetic reconstruction of philosophy—and, therefore, located in Marx's philosophy of history—did become suspect. They could be easily instrumentalized and recycled as the concept of *Volk* by Nazi ideologists and turned into repositories of irrationalism, thus justifying the racism and barbarism typical of Hitler's policies. But Marcuse did not simply jettison these concepts. Rather, he sought to reinterpret them by means of Freudian categories. Although in his *Reason and Revolution* (1960) he reworked his interpretation of Hegel without the help of Heidegger and Dilthey to establish an unbroken continuity between Hegel and a dialectical sociology while refuting right-Hegelian interpretations that presented Hegel as the father of modern totalitarian regimes (cf., Popper, 1963; Cassirer, 1946), there is not yet any mention of Freud in that work. Only in *Eros and Civilization* (1955) do Freudian categories fully displace "life" and "existence" and provide what became the definitive and mature account of Marcuse's philosophical vision.

Unlike his friend Adorno, whose interpretaton of Hegel (*Drei Studien zu Hegel*) was always tempered by a flight back to Kantian philosophy and art whenever the all-encompassing tendencies of the system (the principle of identity) seemed to suffocate the irreducible particular, or his contemporary Ernst Bloch, whose *Subjekt-Objekt* presents Hegel as "the master of living motion in contraposition to dead being" while ontologizing the principle of hope as the system's rational kernel preventing totalitarian closures, Marcuse's account of Hegel remains singularly insensitive to the questionable outcome and presuppositions of the whole philosophical framework. The problem of the closure had been successfully avoided in his earlier Heideggerian work on *Hegels Ontologie und die Theorie der Geschichtlichkeit* by grounding the dialectic in phenomenology. In *Reason and Revolution,* however, this phenomenological grounding is removed so that the dialectic remains hanging with neither a Heideggerian experimential foundation nor an Hegelian absolutist viewpoint: it simply translates into a Marxist social theory which, lacking any agency of change, ends up engaged in a rearguard defensive maneuver against positivism and right-Hegelianism. It was an untenable position. Marcuse must have seen this fairly early, for after World War II he rapidly proceeded to reground his dialectic on a Freudian foundation.

The introjection of orthodox Freudianism does successfully prevent the totalitarian closure, but at too high a price: it also prevents that qualitative change which was the goal of Marcuse's entire theoretical reflection.[6] The objectivism implicit in the Freudian gambit strengthens the criticism of advanced industrial society by providing a theoretical bastion from which to launch the attacks, but also traps the critic in a naturalistic position restricting all changes to qualitative ones. The historicization of nature—which also allows Marcuse to call for a qualitatively new science—is not a way out of this dilemma, for the foundation of this historicity can only be a more basic permanence whose objectivistic character necessarily poses unacceptable ontological limits (as Adorno cleary saw in his innumerable attacks on "First Philosophy").[7]

This problem becomes all the more clear in *One-Dimensional Man* (1964), where the very character of the critique rules out any possible alternative beyond a vague "great refusal." Grounded in biology, this "great refusal" can be articulated by any oppressed group not yet fully integrated into the predominant logic of domination. It is not difficult to see how this vision could be appropriated by middle-class students dissatisfied with the plastic life style of their parents, appalled by the glaring injustices of racism, and vitally threatened themselves by the Vietnam War. That the "great refusal" could be readily turned into a "grudging acquiescence" need not even be argued here. What is problematic, and what ends up being Marcuse's Achilles' heel, is the convincing argument—put forth best by the Frankfurt School itself—that contemporary social structure creates a type of individuality whose wants tend to correspond to those that the system can satisfy and whose existence guarantees the uninterrupted reproduction of existing relations of domination. Marcuse's "Outsider" does not have a ghost of a chance in this situation: either he ends up successfully integrated or else he is summarily destroyed. Marcuse's own position becomes understandable as that of a living intellectual antique whose very distance from the everyday life surrounding him gives him the vantage point and proper distance from which to launch his critique.

This explains why Habermas, Wellmer, Apel, and other members of the new generation of Frankfurt School followers took a "linguistic turn," and, rather than reconstitute critical theory along Freudian lines, sought to integrate communication theory with the school's more traditional concerns (Wellmer, 1976). Having himself convincingly shown the disappearance of bourgeois individuality in his *Die Strukturwandel der Oeffentlichkeit*, Habermas in the middle 1960s was caught in the same quandary as Marcuse: what was the use of talking about emancipation if there was no chance of the problem even being understood, much less of there being the possibility of carrying out the revolutinary transformation necessary to achieve emancipation? The linguistic turn that he took in the middle 1960s guaranteed an a priori foundation, thus rendering irrelevant the search for the nonexistent agent of social change.[8] If emancipation is assumed by the very intersubjective structure of communication, then even repressive systems presuppose it, and, in the long run, their very survival will ultimately rest on its realization. That Habermas has not the faintest idea of *how* this will take place in advanced industrial society is not seen as a major problem. In fact, having shown further in his *Legitimation Crisis* that the technocratic and bureaucratic character of late capitalism precipitates crises of motivation, rationality, economy, and legitimation that cannot be solved by means other than the democratization of the societies involved. Habermas goes on to elaborate a theory of evolution to support the metaphysical inevitability of emancipation rather than focusing on the specific historical dynamics within which this emancipation is to take place (Habermas, 1979). When all is said and done, Habermas's linguistic answer not only is just as suspect as Marcuse's,[9] but it is also less radical, inasmuch as it is no longer able to deal effectively with ecological problems, to question the nature of modern science, or to speak of a qualitatively new individuality.

What critical theory needs to successfully pursue its emancipatory aims is an adequately grounded dialectic. Such a grounding cannot be provided by recycled versions of Hegel's Absolute Spirit, Heidegger's existential phenomenology, Freud's biologism, or Habermas's communication theory. In the first case the outcome can only be totalitarian and reactionary—as Marx and his followers never tired of pointing out. In the second the result is a pseudo-concreteness that not only fails to penetrate to the level of existing social relations but also entails all of the problems so well described by Kosik (1976: 1–35) and Adorno (1973a). With Freudianism and communication theory the dialectic disappears altogether in linear naturalism (Marcuse) or in a philosophically flat transcendental scheme

(Habermas). As Paci (1972:275–86) has shown, the only viable foundation can be provided by *Husserlian* Phenomenology. But this exacts a relatively heavy price. It requires the forfeiture of the objectivistic notion of the totality in favor of a nomological one whose validity cannot thereby be guaranteed metaphysically but will have to be vindicated in everyday practice.[10]

Without at this point entering into a detailed theoretical elaboration, which would obviously involve a number of complex philosophical issues well beyond the scope of the present discusssion, it is sufficient here to indicate how such a reintroduction of the dialectic in critical theory solves the previously discussed quandaries.[11] First of all, it would allow the *historicization* of both traditional marxism and the various versions of critical theory developed by the first generation of Frankfurt School thinkers. Second, once understood as the necessarily inadequate expressions of periods that they described from an explicit viewpoint of emancipatory possibilities, it becomes possible to retroactively criticize them in terms of the objective historical results which have subsequently invalidated them, thus revealing what precipitated them into obsolescence. And, third, this allows their reformulation in terms of the new historical conditions, but in accordance with the same emancipatory spirit that initially animated them.

This historicization of traditional Marxism as the theory of entrepreneurial capitalism and of classical critical theory as that of the transition period (the New Deal, Stalinism, and fascism) opens the way for an understanding of the present as the age of fully developed monopoly capitalism (see Piccone, 1978a). In the same way that, in the particular case of American society, the New Deal meant the successful integration of significant parts of the Marxist sociopolitical program, not by destroying capitalism but by revitalizing it, the integration of the core ideas of critical theory is now being translated into a process of social reconstruction meant to guarantee the capitalist weathering of today's social and economic crisis (cf., Piccone, forthcoming). If the displacement of the market by state interventionism was the most important result of the New Deal strategy, this was accomplished by the destruction of any lingering bourgeois individuality by means of the culture industry and the redesigning of the productive process. But this strategy also destroyed any remnant of that public sphere providing both the goals and the regulatory mechanisms that make bureaucracies the rationalizing agencies that Weber described. No longer directed or regulated, the resulting inefficient and repressive bureaucratic apparatus necessary to carry out the New Deal strategy becomes *the* problem once monopoly capital becomes predominant. It is at this point that the state itself, in order to help regulate its Frankenstein-like bureaucracy, must undertake the task of reconstituting that individuality that it had previously annihilated. In so doing, however, it changes the entire character of organized capitalism, making critical theory in its earlier versions no longer capable of comprehending it.

Today the future of critical theory hangs on whether it can successfully reconstitute itself by articulating a phenomenological dialectic, and thus begin to both understand new and otherwise incomprehensible phenomena and reformulate the emancipatory task in terms of the new possibilities that they offer.

NOTES

1. Perry Anderson's (1976) efforts to contrapose a healthy Trotskyist tradition to Western Marxism's alleged scholasticism fail to take into account both the political irrelevance and intellectual sterility of the various sectarian versions of Trotskyism that have proliferated over the last half century. For an excellent critique of all this, see Peter Beilharz (1979).

2. Although significant figures such as Erich Fromm, Karl Wittfogel, and Leo Lowenthal are still alive, it is unlikely that their future work will provide bold new departures.

3. Hitherto major studies of the Frankfurt School, such as Jay's *The Dialectical Imagination* (1973), Susan Buck-Morss's *The Origin of Negative Dialectics* (1977), Phil Slater's *Origin and Significance of the Frankfurt School: A Marxist Perspective* (1977), and even Arato and Gebhardt's *The Essential Frankfurt School Reader* (1978), have tended, wittingly or unwittingly, to present critical theory as a subject for intellectual archaeology rather than a living tradition—even if a minoritarian one within contemporary social thought. For strong rejections of this approach, see Russell Jacoby's review of Jay's book in *Theory and Society* (1974), the Jacoby–Jay exchange in *Theory and Society* (1975), as well as Jacoby's review of Slater's work in *Telos* (1977).

4. In this last major work, Marcuse is concerned with the problem of the foundation of the autonomy of art: "The radical quality of art, that is to say its indictment of established reality and its invocation of the beautiful image of liberation, are grounded precisely in the dimensions where art *transcends* its social determination and emancipates itself from the given universe of discourse and behavior while preserving its overwhelming presence" (1978:6).

5. In Adorno, of course, the problem of the foundation takes exactly the opposite direction: the absolute and uncompromising rejection of any foundation whatsoever as ontology (i.e., reification) or First Philosophy. See Theodor W. Adorno (1978–79). As I have argued in "Beyond Identity Theory" (1978–79:140–42), Adorno's rejection of any foundation leads him to his weak position in *Negative Dialectic*, where his efforts to trace out the logic of the *essence* lead him to eternalize his own historical predicament and preclude the possibility of qualitative change itself once those same historical conditions—i.e., those of the New Deal, Stalinism, and Nazism—themselves become obsolete.

6. Thus, Marcuse (1978:72) grudgingly acknowledges this limitation: "Socialism does not and cannot liberate Eros from Thanatos. . . . It is the struggle for the impossible, against the unconquerable whose domain can perhaps nevertheless be reduced."

7. Thus, Marcuse (1969b:10ff.) finds himself forced to present morality as a disposition of the organism—an instinct—whose changes "may 'sink down' into the 'biological' dimension and modify organic behavior." Such a naturalistic answer at best avoids the problem and at worst plunges the whole discussion into a fatalistic philosophy of history where "freedom" and "will" turn out to be irrelevant and illusory attributes in a human predicament that allows only for gradual improvements.

8. Despite his excellent exposition of Habermas's ideas, Thomas McCarthy (1978:385) fails to see this important consequence of Habermas's "linguistic turn" and insists on seeing the lack of an agency of change as the "familiar embarrassment" of Critical Theory. For a critique of it, see Jean Cohen (1979:74ff.).

9. As Whitebook (1979:47ff.) has put it, however, Habermas's linguistic turn does not really succeed in providing a philosophical foundation, for "the terrain that Habermas wants to stake out for his transcendental foundational discourse thus lies somewhere between empirical science and first philosophy." Either way, no satisfactory solution is possible and Habermas, among other things, ends up regressing to the Enlightenment position that his teachers and colleagues in the Frankfurt School had so violently rejected. Consequently, he is not able to deal with crucial problems such as the reconciliation with nature.

10. The category of the totality has been central in Marxism at least since Lukacs, who considered it essential, or Adorno, who rejected it in favor of the "false totality." For an elaboration of the problems involved, see Martin Jay (1977). In an otherwise interesting account, Jay ends up paradoxically collapsing Adorno's and Althusser's accounts.

11. The phenomenological dialectic discussed here has little to do with Adorno's negative dialect which, in order to avoid identity theory, cripples the universal to save the integrity of the particular: "Dialectics unfolds the difference between the particular and the universal, dictated by the universal." Cf. Theodor W. Adorno (1973:6). Thus, to prevent this domination of the concept, Adorno dismantles the dialectic and restricts it to a negative role. A phenomenologically grounded dialectic avoids this quandary by privileging the *Lebenswelt* over and above any dialectical reconciliation, and by constantly returning to the lived dimension. Adorno's phobia of this dimension as the repository of Romantic reaction prevented him from ever fully understanding phenomenology, even though Husserl is a constant reference point in his work. For a very positive account of Adorno, which mildly criticizes him for his Eurocentrism, see Susan Buck-Morss (1977).

REFERENCES

Adorno, Theodor W.
  1973a The Jargon of Authenticity. Evanston, Ill.: Northwestern University Press.
  1973b Negative Dialectic. New York: Seabury Press.
  1978–79 "Metacritique of epistemology." Telos 38:77–103.
Anderson, Perry
  1976 Considerations on Western Marxism. London: New Left Books.
Arato, Andrew, and Eike Gebhardt (eds.)
  1978 The Essential Frankfurt School Reader. New York: Urizen Books.
Avinieri, Shlomo
  1968 The Social and Political Thought of Karl Marx. New York: University Press.
Beilharz, Peter
  1979 "Trotsky's Marxism—permanent involution?" Telos 39:137–52.
Buck-Morss, Susan
  1977 The Origin of Negative Dialectics. New York: Free Press.
Cassirer, Ernst
  1946 The Myth of the State. New Haven, Conn.: Yale University Press.
Cohen, Jean
  1979 "Why more political theory." Telos 40:70.
Jacoby, Russell
  1974 "Review of the dialectical imagination." Theory and Society 1:231–33.
Jay, Martin
  1973 The Dialectical Imagination. Boston: Beacon Press.

Kellner, Douglas
1973 "Introduction to Marcuse's 'On the Philosophical Foundations of the Concept of Labor in Economics.'" Telos 16:2–8.
Kosik, Karel
1976 The Dialectic of the Concrete. The Hague: Mouton.
McCarthy, Thomas
1978 The Critical Theory of Jürgen Habermas. Cambridge, Mass.: M.I.T. Press.
Marcuse, Herbert
1929 "Ueber konkrete Philosophie." Archiv fur Sozialwissenschaft und Sozialpolitik 62:111–28.
1955 Eros and Civilization. Boston: Beacon.
1960 Reason and Revolution. Boston: Beacon.
1964 One Dimensional Man. Boston: Beacon.
1969a "Contributions to a critique of historical materialism (1928)." Telos 4:3–34.
1969b An Essay on Liberation. Boston: Beacon Press.
1978 The Aesthetic Dimension. Boston: Beacon Press.
Marcuse, Herbert, et al.
1978–79 "Theory and politics: a discussion with Herbert Marcuse, Jürgen Habermas, Heinz Lubasz and Telman Spengler." Telos 38:124–52.
O'Neill, John (ed.)
1976 On Critical Theory. New York: Seabury.
Paci, Enzo
1972 Function of the Sciences and the Meaning of Man. Evanston, Ill.: Northwestern University Press.
Piccone, Paul
1970 "Phenomenological Marxism." Telos 9:3–31.
1972 "Dialectic and materialism in Lukacs." Telos 11:105–34.
1974 "Gramsci's Hegelian Marxism." Political Theory 2:32–45.
1975 "Korsch in Spain." New German Critique 6:148–63.
1976 "Beyond identity theory." In John O'Neill (ed.), On Critical Theory. New York: Seabury Press.
1977–8 "Labriola and the Roots of Eurocommunism." Berkeley Journal of Sociology 23:3–44.
1978a "The crisis of one-dimensionality." Telos 35:43–54.
1978b "Introduction." In Andrew Arato and Eike Gebhardt (eds.). The Essential Frankfurt School Reader. New York: Urizen Books.
Forth- "The future of capitalism." In Adolph L. Reed, Jr. (ed.) The Circle in Spiral.
coming
Piccone, Paul, and Alexander Delfini
1970 "Marcuse's Heideggerian Marxism." Telos 6:36–46.
Popper, Karl
1963 The Open Society and Its Enemies. Boston: Routledge & Kegan Paul.
Slater, Phil
1977 Origin and Significance of the Frankfurt School: A Marxist Perspective. Boston: Routledge & Kegan Paul.
Vajda, Mihaly
1971 "Marxism, Existentialism and Phenomenology: a dialogue." Telos 7:6–29.
1978–79 "Lukacs' and Husserl's critique of science." Telos 38:104–18.
Wellmer, Albrecht
1976 "Communication and emancipation: reflections on the linguistic turn in critical theory." In John O'Neill (ed.), On Critical Theory. New York: Seabury Press.
Whitebook, Joel
1979 "The problem of nature in Habermas." Telos 39:41–69.

THEORIES OF THE STATE AND THEORIES OF URBAN CRISIS

C. G. Pickvance

INTRODUCTION

Any understanding or urban fiscal crises in those countries where they occur, and of their absence elsewhere, depends on theories of three objects:

1. A theory of economic and political crisis which would define crises in a scientific rather than a journalistic manner, and would identify the processes leading to such crises.

2. A theory of the territorial division of labor which would explain the geographic pattern of economic activity and changes within it in terms of basic economic and political processes.

3. A theory of the state which would explain the distribution of state functions vertically between levels of the state and horizontally between different ministries, between elected and appointed bodies, in terms of attempts to assist the accumulation process.

Current Perspectives in Social Theory, volume 1, 1980, pages 31–54.
Copyright © 1980 by JAI Press Inc.
ISBN: 0-89232-154-7

Clearly these three theories are not necessarily distinct and the great appeal of Marxism is that it offers the prospect of three theories making use of a single set of concepts and explanatory statements.

The aim of this paper is not to set out definitive Marxist theories in each of these three cases, for reasons of ignorance and space. What I wish to do is, first, examine the relation between economic crisis and urban fiscal crisis, and, second, identify some issues in the Marxist theory of the state which are crucial to an understanding of urban fiscal crises (or their absence).[1] The rationale for this paper derives from a sense that increasingly new theoretical contributions in the three areas above (and in others) cannot simply be added to existing ones, but that there are very real incompatibilities among them. To take an example, the idea that by adding Miliband, Poulantzas, and Offe together, figuratively speaking, the result is superior to any one of the component elements, seems to me completely mistaken. The parts are no more compatible than oil and vinegar and, what is more, the idea that they can be interrelated does a serious injustice to each of the authors concerned.[2]

The argument here will be that our understanding of urban fiscal crises (or their absence) can be no more sure than the foundations on which our theoretical edifice is built, and that the use of an eclectic set of building materials for the foundations is no longer adequate (if it ever was). My concern is that we should confront the very real differences of view which lie *within* a Marxist theoretical framework. The paper is divided into two parts, dealing first with theories of crisis and then with theories of the state.

THEORIES OF CRISIS

Our aim in this section will be to examine the link between theories of economic crisis and analyses of urban fiscal crisis. Our conclusion will be that the link is very weak, and that the occurrence of urban fiscal crises is primarily due to the character of political institutions in a society.

How frequently one is exposed to "crises" depends on what country one lives in. The French press reports a very large number of crises whereas British newspaper readers have to be content with a more meager diet. Sometimes one has the impression that academic debates build on journalistic notions of crisis. I will assume, however, that scientific concepts of crisis are distinct from journalistic notions.

Among academics, Marxist and liberal views of crisis differ fundamentally. For liberals (and journalists) an economic crisis is a

"dysfunctional" stage or moment which interrupts, suddenly or by a stroke of fate, the essentially harmonious functioning of the "system," a necessarily temporary stage (a bad patch to be gone through) ending with the necessary restoration of "equilibrium" (Poulantzas, 1976:20).

Or in the British context as Fine and Harris (1976:18) write of Denis Healey (Chancellor of the Exchequer),

> it is clear that he does not see crises as endemic to capitalism, but that the recent crisis and current depression are to be understood in terms of the *difficulties* associated with the balance of payments, inflation and budget deficit. (Emphasis added.)

By contrast, for Marxists

> the open outbreak of economic crises . . . cannot be looked upon as "a deviation" from "the normal course" of accumulation. Rather, it signifies the sharpening and manifestation of a fundamental contradiction propelled by the accumulation of capital. It can be deduced from the law of the tendency for the rate of profit to fall that this contradiction cannot remain dormant but that the latent crisis of capital must repeatedly be transformed through the disruption of the accumulation process into open crisis (Hirsch, 1978:70).

In a sense capitalism is in permanent crisis, but to use the term in this loose sense—as, for example, in refering to the present (and last?) phase of capitalism as a phase of "general crisis"—is to deprive it of any specific meaning. As Poulantzas (1976:22) puts it, it is necessary to distinguish between the "generic elements of crisis" which are always present and the specific use of the term to refer to a "particular situation of condensation of contradictions." Poulantzas argues that economic crises do not necessarily lead to political crises and that political crises (i.e., those in which political class struggle vis-à-vis the state apparatuses is overt) can also exist on their own. He proposes the term "structural crisis" for those cases where both types of crisis have broken out.

So far we have mainly been concerned with labels. Let us now examine briefly the factors which in Marxist theory explain the outbreak of crises. We shall follow Hirsch's concise account. In order to increase relative surplus value, capitalists introduce more advanced technology into the production process. This generally reduces the demand for labor into the immediate production process and thus increases the industrial reserve army (unless demand increases). But this attempt to accumulate faster by raising labor productivity leads to a fall in the *average* rate of profit, i.e., to a fall in the global mass of surplus value relative to capital advanced. Therein lies the permanent possibility of economic crisis.

However, whether overt crisis breaks out or not depends upon the operation of countertendencies: (1) higher labor productivity reduces the cost of constant capital (in embodied labor time) and hence limits the increase in the organic composition of capital; (2) it also reduces the value of labor power (consumption goods embody less labor), thus increasing relative surplus value; and (3) technological progress can also increase the rate of rotation of capital (see Lamarche, 1976, and Lojkine, 1976). Apart from technological innovation are other factors: (4) the continued use of old techniques and continued role of sectors with below average organic composition of capital; (5) the destruction or devaluation of capital by war, cyclical crisis, or by new inventions—which raise the average rate of profit; and, (6) the means of increasing absolute surplus value: longer working days, faster pace of work, depressed real wages. Finally, the *distribution* of profit (but not its average rate) depends on reducing the shares taken in ground-rent and, by circulation of capital (which increase the share for industrial capital); on reducing the unproductive sections of the population (state workers, the military, and so on); on the strength of monopolies (able to secure above-average rates of profit); on the state financing of unprofitable but necessary spheres of production; and on "unequal exchange" with the Third World (Hirsch, 1978:68–73).

Before returning to these countertendencies we must first indicate effects (or "functions") of crises—when they are not prevented by the countertendencies. The symptom of crisis is an excess of capital advanced in relation to the mass of profits available, i.e., an "over-accumulation of capital." The crisis can only be overcome by a change in the parameters of the situation, viz. by a *reorganization of the conditions of production and relations of exploitation (which include a change in the state functions)*. Hirsch identifies three main cases: (1) Crises facilitate capital concentration and centralization via bankruptcies and mergers—through the credit system and the joint stock company. This may reduce the total value of capital advanced (and hence raise the average rate of profit) and will certainly increase profitability differentials between monopoly and competitive sectors. (2) Crises lead to an expansion of the market and an export of capital to restore profit rates. (3) Finally, economic crises intensify the rate of technological advance.

As far as state functions[3] are concerned, Hirsch notes how economic crises (1) threaten the material basis of the "welfare state" which will be dismantled if working-class weakness allows it; (2) oblige the state to intervene in new ways to preserve bourgeois rule in new circumstances, e.g., giving priority to the general conditions of production needed by monopolies, foreign policies to support economic expansion, industrial subsidies and incentives to help nonmonopolistic firms survive, promotion of mergers, economic management to protect firms against cyclical disturbances including incomes policy, and anticyclical state expenditure, especially on infrastructure and nonreproductive goods (these policies are subject to contradictory demands and translate themselves into conflicts over tax rates and tax shares and the nature of state expenditure, particularly in crisis and slow growth conditions); and (3) also increase the range of general conditions of production which individual capitalists will call on the state to provide—a range which is expanding anyway as the socialization of production proceeds—in health, education, transport, energy development, city-building and renewal, and scientific and technological research.

To turn now to a specific example, Gutman (1976) and Fine and Harris (1976) have both examined in detail the way the British state coped with the economic crisis of late 1973 to early 1975. Gutman emphasizes the long-run weakness of the British economy and the inability of British capitalists to raise productivity as fast as their competitors. This long-term weakness can be linked to the ending of the benefits of imperialism as new competitors emerged on the world market after 1900 (restricting expansion possibilities); the strength of the working class, which was not destroyed by fascism and has hindered the raising of relative surplus value; early industrialization which meant that there was a greater investment in older equipment which hindered modernization; and the lack of any agricultural labor reserve to draw on. This led to the vicious circle of low investment–out of date equipment–slow productivity growth–weakening export share–low economic growth. Attempts to modify this sequence were jeopardized by the government's simultaneous aim of preserving the role of sterling as a reserve currency (and London as a world financial center) with the notorious "stop-go policy" result.

The failure to raise productivity adequately has been associated with the postwar "profit squeeze" identified by Glyn and Sutcliffe (1972) who show a secular fall in *gross* company profits over the post-1945 period. More recent evidence, however, emphasizes how corporate taxes have been lightened to leave *net* company profits unchanged, thus counteracting the trend in gross profits (Field et al., 1977). Clearly, however, as Hirsch points out such countertendencies are bought at a price, namely, higher personal taxes or decreasing state expenditure.

Fine and Harris's discussion of the British state's response to the economic crisis of 1973–1975 mentions many of the features referred to by Hirsch as crisis responses that reorganize the conditions of production and relations of exploitation: financial aid for the restructuring of private capital; further nationalizations; restructuring schemes for existing nationalized industries (all in 1975); massive corporate tax relief on stock appreciation and cuts in state *social* expenditure (but not industrial aid or nationalized industries expenditure) (November 1974); the gradual restoration of an incomes policy (by 1976)—which was impossible earlier since it was on this issue that the Conservative government was defeated in February 1974. Fine and Harris (1976:2) conclude that

> the breaking of the circuit of capital in the crisis phase has been followed by far-reaching plans for the restructuring of capital so that the conditions have been laid for raising the rate of exploitation in value terms.

What relevance does this discussion of economic crisis have for an understanding of urban fiscal crises? Very little. The significance of its irrelevance is considerable since if urban fiscal crises are more than superficial phenomena, i.e., if they correspond to some inherent tendency in modern capitalist societies, then our discussion of crisis theory should have revealed such a tendency. In fact it did not. Now this may be because the discussion is incomplete, but if it is not (as I would claim) our conclusion must be that those countries in which urban fiscal crises occur experience them due to the nature of the "adjustment" between their political institutions and the economy.

On the other hand, our discussion of crisis theory did touch on a tendency to *general* fiscal crises. I would argue that such a tendency only becomes manifest at the municipal level due to the particular political structure of the country concerned. If this is the case, then it must be concluded that there is no general tendency to urban fiscal crisis. The latter is rather a culturally specific phenomenon. In addition to these theoretical considerations we shall refer to some empirical evidence for our argument:

1. the British case, where, despite the unarguable evidence of economic crisis presented above, there has been *no urban fiscal crisis;*
2. the United States case, where the important finding is that there is *no general urban fiscal crisis.*

As Gordon (1977:108) puts it:

> [the] current urban crisis is not a general urban crisis at all. Some cities are undergoing a crisis, like New York and Detroit, while others are not.

To explain this in more detail, the British case shows that although the local economy in any area is affected by the economic crisis, the system of municipal financing acts as a buffer shielding the municipality's finances from its local economy. The essential elements in this buffering arrangement are: (1) the range of municipal functions which exclude unemployment benefit and welfare payments, two of the expenditure categories most sensitive to economic fluctuations; (2) the high proportion of central grants—which represent some 65 percent of municipal expenditures; and (3) the importance of the equalization element within these central grants, an element which is paid to the poorest 85 percent of local authorities measured in per capita rateable value (property assessment) terms. These latter two features like the first reduce the dependence of municipal finances on the local economy. Finally it should be mentioned that municipal borrowing is dependent upon central approval, and municipal bonds are backed by central government. Some of the necessary conditions of the New York fiscal crisis are thus absent. Having said this it should be noted that the economic crisis has led to two important changes in municipal financing. First, as a major field of state expenditure, central grants to local authorities have been held by a "cash limits" policy (1975) which effectively means that they cover one or two percentage points of municipal expenditure less than in 1974. Second—a change whose significance has not been generally appreciated—the equalization or "resources" element in central grants is now (after 1974) calculated *after* (rather than before) the "needs" element (i.e., based on objective measures of numbers of children, of over 65s, etc.) and the "domestic" element (i.e., a general subsidy to domestic ratepayers introduced in 1967 to cushion them against rising local expenditure). Despite these two changes the British system acts as an effective buffer between the local economy and municipal finances. (As a corollary, the relative equalization of service provision this system permits may facilitate industrial location choices insofar as local authorities with weak local economies will, nevertheless, be able to provide the necessary services for industries wishing to locate in the area.) In sum, the British case demonstrates that economic crisis is not necessarily translated into urban fiscal crisis. Any link depends on the state structures and financing systems in place. The question for research then becomes why has the British state set up the buffering mechanism we have described.[4]

We now return to the U.S. case. If, as I have argued from the British example, there is no necessary connection between economic crisis and urban fiscal crisis, what implications does this have for an understanding of American urban fiscal crises—assuming that we are seeking "an explanation of urban fiscal strains commensurate with their perennial and widespread occurrence" (Friedland et al., 1977:448) rather than mutually exclusive explanations for each country?

To start with it is welcome to find confirmation of our argument in a study of urban fiscal crises in the United States. As Hill (1977:77) writes:

> It is tempting to suggest that the current fiscal crisis facing central cities in the United States is a result of the steep economic downturn in the economy during the past few years and the fiscally conservative policies of a Republican administration in Washington. Yet, while exacerbated by our latest economic slump, the urban fiscal crisis of the 1970s is actually an intensification of a post-World War II trend. With the exception of the Great Depression in the 1930s, *more defaults were recorded in the expansionary 1960s than during any other decade since the middle of the nineteenth century.* (Emphasis added.)[5]

While our argument that urban fiscal crises were not necessarily connected with economic crises was based on a case of the absence of the former in the presence of the latter, Hill's conclusion shows the reverse combination (i.e., urban fiscal crisis *outside* conditions of economic crisis) and gives us greater confidence in the general validity of our initial statement.

Our conclusion is thus that it is not possible to use arguments about tendencies for *general* fiscal crisis of the state (O'Connor,[6] Hirsch) to explain the existence of *urban* fiscal crises. From the evidence we have cited it is clear that mediating political structures are of the essence in determining at what state level any fiscal crisis tendency becomes manifest.

The question for research is therefore why different countries have developed different state structures, some of which result in urban fiscal crises, and others of which prevent them only to see the fiscal crisis tendency (when economic crisis conditions are present) appear at the central level of government. This does not mean recourse to a political explanation because the object is differences in *political* institutions, but one in which both political and economic factors take their place in the explanation.[7] (And as we indicate in the next section we do not expect an explanation which shows a tight functional fit between economic and political interests and institutional "solutions.")

THE MARXIST THEORY OF THE STATE AND THE STATE OF THE MARXIST THEORY

We now turn to theories of the state, which is the field most marked by eclecticism, as noted earlier. Our aim in this section will be to point out some of the contrasting alternatives in this area from which *choices* must be made. Failing this our understanding of urban fiscal crises—and their absence—will have no coherent basis. Four topics are selected for consideration:

1. the relations between economic and political spheres;
2. the legitimation function and the role of democracy;
3. state interventionism—Habermas and Offe;
4. state intervention and "system performance,"

The Relations Between Economic and Political Spheres

We shall approach this question via the debate reported in Holloway and Picciotto's (1978:6) recent collection *State and Capital: A [German] Marxist debate*. Whatever one's views on the detailed issues discussed in this collection it is abundantly clear that to think there is any single body of writing which deserves the term "Marxist theory of the state" is to live in cloud-cuckoo land. Holloway and Picciotto's (1978a:3) comment on the

Poulantzas–Miliband debate illustrates the scale of the divide they see. "[F]or all their real differences, that which [they] have in common is at least as significant as that which separates them." By contrast, they argue the German state deprivation debate argued in their book falls outside this constricting framework, viz. the illusory polarity between instrumentalist and structuralist approaches.

The essential difference according to Holloway and Picciotto is that whereas Miliband and Poulantzas (and Offe and Habermas) "focus on the political as an autonomous object of study," Hirsch and several writers in the German debate emphasize the "unity in separation" of the economic and political. (It should be noted that the contributions in Holloway and Picciotto [1978b] represent only one side of the debate. The two major writers whose works are omitted—Offe and Habermas—both belong to the other side). Clearly this *is* a fundamental difference of approach even if Poulantzas (1976) in his latest articles does seem to be beating a retreat from his previous position. The only conclusion is that there is no (single) Marxist theory of the state, and that the starting point for any analysis of urban fiscal crises is correspondingly unclear.

The essential argument of Hirsch and the other contributors to Holloway and Picciotto (1978b) is that the functions of the state cannot be taken as given and that to treat state functions in a vacuum or to start from the "content" of state activity is to miss the fundamental point that it is the *state "form"* which needs to be explained. The prior question is thus why do the relations between classes "appear in separate forms as economic relations and political relations" (Holloway and Picciotto, 1978a:18), e.g., why does class domination take the form of state domination? The two main answers given in the German debate are that the state form is necessary either:

1. to ensure the reproduction of capital as a whole given that the anarchic activity of individual capitals cannot secure it (Altvater, 1978), or
2. to secure bourgeois domination given that individual capitalists cannot achieve this and require a separate agency to do so. The separation of political and economic spheres thus removes relations of force from the immediate production process (Hirsch, 1978).

What is striking about these two arguments is their essentially parallel character: both assert that individual capitals cannot themselves secure the performance of a "functional need." In my view, however, Holloway and Picciotto (1976) make some serious mistakes in their analysis of the debate. First, whereas in an earlier (and very effective) article criticizing Gough they used *both* arguments to explain the structural autonomy of the state, they subsequently wrote (1977:98), with some embarrassment, that this "combination of the two derivations of the state . . . now seems to us eclectic." However they give no reason for this new judgment. In my view the two derivations are in fact not only parallel but are also *completely compatible:* since the two "functional needs" concerned mutually imply each other, e.g., it is difficult to see how the "reproduction of capital as a whole" (argument 1) could occur without the "ensuring of bourgeois domination" (argument 2). (Lojkine [1976] in his analysis of the role of the state in urbanization in fact uses both arguments.) In my view there is no basis for Holloway and Picciotto's description of the use of the two arguments together as "eclectic."

Second, Holloway and Picciotto favor the second argument (Hirsch) against the first (Altvater). They list "three strong objections" to Altvater but none to the Hirsch. This is very kind to Hirsch but their reasoning does not withstand scrutiny. In effect the main argument they use *against* Altvater is the same one that they use in *favor* of Hirsch. How is this contortion achieved?

Quite correctly they object to Altvater on the grounds that the first derivation explains the *need* for an institution capable of ensuring overall social reproduction but does not show how such an agency necessarily comes into existence or, if it did, how it would be certain to fulfull stated needs. However, the parallel objection which can be made against Hirsch, i.e., that he does not show how the state necessarily comes into existence or how it secures capitalist domination, is in fact quoted as an argument in favor of Hirsch's view! As Holloway and Picciotto (1978a:25) write:

> The earlier contributors assume that within the scope allowed it by the exigencies of capital accumulation, the state can act in the interests of capital in general. For Hirsch the structural relation of state to society makes even this extremely problematic, for he sees the contradictions of capitalist society as being reproduced within the state apparatus, thus making it questionable where the state can ever act adequately in the interests of capital in general.

Ignoring Holloway and Picciotto's sometimes bizarre judgments, what can we conclude from this German debate? In my view the attempt to divide form and content of state activity, and to make the former subject to logical analysis and the latter subject to historical analysis is not successful. Basically the failure is epistemological: to separate out "form" as somehow logically related and outside history is mistaken. Holloway and Picciotto (1978a:27) sense this since they rightly "see Marx's categories as simultaneously logical and historical categories," but do not draw the conclusion that the attempt to separate logical (form) and historical analysis is mistaken. They are embarrassed to find even their German contributors raising doubts about form analysis, e.g., Hirsch (1978:66) writes that "the general derivation of form cannot go beyond trivialities," and admonishes them saying "that a realization of the limits of the approach should not lead to scepticism about its value" (1978a:30).

In view of the limits to "form analysis" admitted by Hirsch, and my doubts suggested above as to whether it is a correct form of abstraction, can we learn anything from the debate reported in Holloway and Picciotto's collection? In my opinion, we certainly can—and the editors may in fact have done a disservice by emphasizing the form analysis question. To my mind, the great value of the work of Hirsch is that he really does offer an attempt to analyze the emergence of state functions in relation to the exigencies of capital accumulation and crisis. His discussion is admittedly pitched at a somewhat abstract level as we saw in the last section, i.e., he examines the *general* links between economic crisis and a range of state functions designed to remedy it, but he nevertheless demonstrates very effectively that there *is* fundamental division within Marxist theory of the state between those writers who treat the political sphere as autonomous (in practice if not in principle) and those who do not. For those who see the political sphere as autonomous, it is meaningful to start from a list of precise state functions, whereas for those who deny this view, state functions are not permanent and unchanging but activities imposed by the prerequisites of capital accumulation in specific conditions and are thus continually open to change.

The Legitimation Function and the Role of Democracy

The implications of the Hirsch position can best be seen in the field of legitimation and democratic institutions. In particular his position leads to the conclusion that it is fallacious to posit a legitimation function as an eternal function and hence to make it a starting point of analyses appealing to the need for legitimation. The crucial point is made clearly by Hirsch (1978:97).

> The bourgeois state . . . must be understood in the determination of its concrete functions as a reaction to the fundamentally crisis-ridden course of the economic and social process of reproduction. *The developing state interventionism represents a form in which the contradictions of capital can temporarily move: but the movement of capital remains historically determining.* (Emphases added.)

In other words, the very existence of the interventionist state, the welfare state, is not permanent. "The state apparatus is itself a moment of the movement of capital and of the struggle of the classes" (Hirsch, 1978:99).

And in the case of democracy, Gerstenberger (1978:149–150) writes that:

It is not ideology that is the most important stabilizing factor, but rather the naked force that lurks behind the forms of appearance. Thus, it is not definitely settled that the capitalist mode of production *requires* formal equality, universal suffrage and democratic structures.

From a different starting point Mingione (1977a:30–31) reaches the same conclusion

that the democratic format is not at all a natural aspect of capitalist political domination . . . [but] is a working-class gain and is typical only of historical cases where the working class is involved in a coalition which aims to eliminate a common and powerful enemy or where it has become too strong to be dominated by open repression.

It can be seen that the assumption that capitalist states take democratic forms in order to implement some eternal legitimation function is based on a treatment of the political sphere in isolation. The realization that this function may not be eternal is largely conditioned by the economic crisis situation of today which is revealing the dependence of this function on a particular set of economic and political conditions (strong economic growth, a militant working class) which are disappearing.[8] It should be noted that the legitimation function has been under attack from another angle.

Mann (1975:276) has shown that the assumption of the legitimation function, namely, that citizens have strong orientations to the rationality of the state, is highly dubious:

Most citizens of the West do not normally possess any very coherent set of norms, values, or beliefs. *Such beliefs as they have are contradictory in their tendency, can change rapidly and almost randomly, and appear to be of a very low salience to them.* (Emphases added.)

He explains any legitimacy crisis as an occupational disease of intellectuals whose raison d'etrê is the search for rationality and who are thus the most aware of contradictions and hence expect crises to break out at any moment. I find Mann's position very plausible.

Offe's (1975a:258) comment on Mann's view is extremely interesting. He is forced to admit that "there is no functional need for explicit legitimation as long 'as everything goes well' "—though he argues that this cannot be assumed to be the normal case. However the paradox of Offe's view is evident in that it implies that the legitimation function is not *necessary* in conditions of stable economic growth, whereas many writers have argued that this is the *only* occasion when it is *possible* since in times of economic crisis repression is likely to be resorted to. The examples of the legitimation function and of democratic institutions illustrate the fundamental analytical difference entailed by treating state institutions and functions as moments of, or as contingent on, economic processes, rather than as autonomous.

State Interventionism: Habermas and Offe

The same difference can be traced through in the analysis of state interventionism. To show this we shall examine some of the writings of Offe and Habermas.[9] The fundamentally opposed positions regarding the analysis of state interventionism can be illustrated by two quotations:

> [S]tate interventionism represents a *form* in which the contradictions of capital can temporarily move: but the movement of capital remains historically determining (Hirsch, 1978:97).

> today the state has to fulfill functions that can be neither explained with reference to prerequisites of the continued existence of the mode of production, nor derived from the imminent movement of capital (Habermas, 1976:52).

The contrast could not be clearer. In one case, as we saw earlier, the state is understood as a form of class relations which remain determinant. In the other case the state has surmounted the economic conditions which give rise to it and now constitutes an independent political force—hence the possibility of treating it as an autonomous entity. Since we have already discussed the former view we will consider briefly the latter view which can be found in the work of Habermas and Offe and, at one remove, in that of Pahl (see Pahl, 1977; and Pahl and Winkler, 1974).

The essential distinction made by Habermas is between the state's "market-supplementing" functions and the state's "market-replacing" functions. This closely parallel's Offe's (1975b) distinction between allocative and productive modes of state action. For Habermas (1976:51) the *market-supplementing* functions of the state refer to the system of civil law, control of the worst side effects of market functioning, provision of general conditions of production (human and material), national defense, and policies to support the domestic economy. In these cases the state acts as a "non-capitalist who vicariously asserts the collective capitalist will."

By contrast, Hirsch argues that late capitalist states have further functions which *replace the market* and thereby prevent the law of value from operating. He mentions as examples "indirectly productive" government spending on education, science and technology which increases the production of surplus value, the "political" character of wage negotiation (in contrast to its one-time "market" character) and the distribution of use values administratively rather than by the market in response to growing legitimation problems (free health services?).

For Habermas and Offe these new forms of state intervention in late capitalism mean that "any attempt to explain the political organization of power through the categories of political economy becomes implausible" (Offe, 1972:81). For Offe (1972:81) orthodox Marxist theory is only applicable to liberal capitalism in which "the economic system was institutionalized as a domain beyond *the authority of the state*" (emphasis added).

In addition to these new state functions Offe sees further changes which for him throw doubt on the applicability of orthodox Marxist analysis. First, the " 'vertical system' of class inequality has largely been replaced by a 'horizontal system of disparities between vital areas'; only minor inequalities [are] still directly due to economic causes" (Offe, 1972:95). Second, Offe (1972:96) denies the link between class power and state power: "[T]he pluralistic system of countervailing powers [makes it] difficult to conceive how any particular interests could attain a position of permanent dominance within such a system" (emphasis added).

Offe's analysis of the state is that it pursues a *"cautious crisis management and long-term avoidance strategy"* with respect to three system problems (economic stability, trade and defense, and mass loyalty) whose management "has become an objective imperative transcending particular interests"[10] The way this strategy benefits or deprives social groupings is described thus: *"structually determined privileges* in functional areas accrue to certain interest groups, which *because of their functional indispensability*, if not on the basis of commonly proclaimed and commonly prosecuted interest, are favoured in the enjoyment of political subventions" (1972:101, second emphasis added). Conversely groupings that are "incapable of generating dangers to the system as a whole" are structurally curbed.

Any similarity between this conclusion and structural-functionalism is *not* accidental. Classes have been dissolved and class interests replaced by objective system needs transcending particular interests. It is the state as system manager which defines the system needs which generate the new pattern of social inequality. The state has only a contingent relation with capitalism—it *happens* that the economic system responsible for prosperity is capitalist—but the analysis is not in principle limited to capitalist societies.

It hardly needs to be said that Habermas's and Offe's work represents an *alternative* to Marxist analysis. It starts from the new functions of capitalist states and argues that they are no longer compatible with Marxist theory. But where Habermas and Offe part company with writers like Hirsch, Altvater, and Lojkine is not in their observation of new state functions but in their conclusion that these prevent the application of orthodox (or any) Marxist theory.

The fundamental question they raise is that posed earlier: Is Marxist theory only applicable when the economy is removed from state influence? I am unconvinced by their answer. In my view the existence of classes is not contingent upon the conditions of liberal capitalism. And to my mind the analysis of state policies is largely possible in terms of class interests—though as I will argue in the next section a "tight-link functional" model, which makes a mechanical connection between class interests and policies, is untenable. Offe and Hirsch, from different starting points, both insist on the difficulties of state interventionism but I prefer to conclude with Hirsch (1978:97–107) that these are necessary consequences of the conditions in which the state operates rather than with Offe that we are forced back to a pluralist picture of power and a structural-functionalist view of society. Whatever one's judgment on this question, one conclusion seems inescapable: Offe's and Habermas's work on state interventionism represents an original alternative to Marxist analysis and thus excludes their being added eclectically to Marxist writers.[11]

State Intervention and System Performance

In this section we shall consider the question of the functionality of state intervention.

> It is questionable whether the commonly assumed *degree* of dependence of the capitalist accumulation process on *certain definite* state measures would stand up to fundamental analysis. We can equally suppose that for some state activities no direct connection can be shown with the conditions for valorization of capital. If such considerations are taken seriously and not just put down to historical accident, this poses problems for the materialist analysis of the state which we have not yet even begun to think about (Gerstenberger, 1978:159).

It is extremely refreshing to come across a quotation such as this since it poses a question which is rarely posed, the tightness of the links between the different elements of a society, and in particular the degree of integration or *functionality* of state interventions. In my view, two models of the relation between state and society[12], are possible and our implicit model has a very great bearing on our understanding of urban fiscal crises. To summarize them we can use the terms *tight-link functional model*, which assumes a tight link between social (mal)functioning and (remedial) state intervention, and *loose-link functional model*, which assumes only a loose link between social functioning and state intervention (Pickvance, 1978).

To illustrate the tight-link model we may quote from O'Connor or Boccara. For O'Connor (1973:30), "The state sector expands because state agencies and contractors *must* supply capital to the monopoly sector and because monopoly growth in turn *require* that the state devote even more funds to social expenses.'' (emphasis added). A parallel argument is made by Boccara (1971,I:53–54) et al.:

> The progress of productive forces *makes* certain types of health education and scientific research expenditure *indispensable.* . . . But these expenditures are regarded by monopoly groups as costs of production which are unprofitable in the short term and whose useful effects appear only over the long term. For the monopolistic bourgeoisie these expenditures are a burden on profits. Hence it seeks to relieve itself of them as soon as it can, while reserving the right to complain later of their insufficiency. . . . The state is thus *pushed* to take charge, indirectly or otherwise, of a large part of these expenditures. (Emphases added.)

In both of these quotations a tight-link functional model of the state–society relation is implicit. In both cases the assertion of the *functional need* for a type of state intervention is taken to be a sufficient explanation of its occurrence. The political processes by which this need is mediated are ignored. In other words these statements share the same weaknesses as the form analytic approaches to the state examined earlier which sought to explain the existence of the state by the functional need for it.

In contrast, the loose-link model places in question the ease with which functional needs are met (once identified). Consequently it implies that some needs may not be met, or may be met partially, and that in general the adjustment between needs and interventions will be slow and problematic. (We should make clear that even if all such needs were met this would not ensure a smoothly functioning society since this would imply a functionalist image of the state as safety valve. Since the state is not neutral its interventions are inherently marked by the class contributions of the society).

My (1977) reasons for thinking that a loose-link model is more accurate are the following. First, as just indicated, the state is not an independent entity, and hence will be subjected to contradictory demands by different classes, or fractions of capital, placing in doubt its ability to further any single demand (and a fortiori any collective need which hinders individual capitals). (The conflicts between these various classes and class fractions will often appear as interministerial conflicts.) Second, many branches of the state develop strong patron–client relationships with their corresponding fractions of capital (e.g., defense, housing and transport ministries, with arms manufacturers, house and road building industries) and these prevent rapid changes in priorities from being effected. Strong client fractions of capital also hinder the meeting of *collective* needs, on behalf of which there is no single client.[13]

Third, it is often assumed that different demands for intervention are mutually compatible. In fact as the scale of intervention grows the chance of incompatibility increases. Numerous examples can be given to illustrate this, e.g., in Britain, the conflicts between the promotion of economic growth (irrespective of spatial implications) and regional policy (demanding particular spatial patterns), and more recently between land use planning (which gives local authorities the responsibility for "rational" town planning) and their obligations under the 1975 Community Land Act (which gives local authorities a direct interest in maximizing their profits as buyers and sellers of development of land). Similarly state intervention has a potentially politicizing character since once the "invisible hand" of the market is removed, the state acts as a lightning conductor for opposition (Castells, 1975:179).

The final and most controversial reason for thinking that the loose-link model of state–society relations is more accurate lies in the fact that the state's resources are limited and prevent the performance of functions (Lojkine, 1976; Holloway and Picciotto, 1978a:25). This reflects one of the ways in which the state is dependent upon the rate of capital accumulation and level of real wages.

This raises the whole question of state finance which in my view remains one of the most murky areas of Marxist analysis. In order to understand this question better we need to distinguish between sources of finance and the beneficiaries of intervention. Some writers claim that all state expenditure is a deduction from surplus value, in which case the interest of capital in keeping it to a low level is fairly clear. However this position is untenable since if we start from the notion that wage levels tend toward the cost of reproduction of labor power then it is clear that an increasing part of these reproduction activities is mediated by the state, which means that part of state expenditure comes from direct taxes.

Obviously we can make no simple equation between the sources of taxes (corporation taxes versus direct taxes) and the uses to which they are put (to benefit corporations versus to benefit workers). However the crucial point of argument is the assertion that while many state activities (Type I) benefit corporations alone, and many (Type II) benefit both corporations and workers, some (Type III) benefit workers only. This is not intended as a universal statement: it applies to those capitalist states which under working-class pressure have undertaken the second and third types of activity rather than just the first. It implies a rejection of the view that the welfare state consists solely of activities I and II (cf., Mingione, 1977b:375). From this analysis, we can conclude that capital as a whole seeks state activities of Types I and II, and their financing from direct taxes. Conversely the working-class interest is in activities II and III and in their financing by corporate taxation. In response to the economic crisis the burden of taxation is in fact shifting toward personal taxation (Field and Pond, 1977; Wolfe, 1977), and as we saw earlier state expenditures on industrial assistance and restructuring Type I is rising, while expenditures on health, welfare, and education (which falls in Types II and III) is falling. Thus we can see how the balance of the class struggle today compared with the more affluent 1950s and 1960s is reflected in procapital state policies.[14]

If the above analysis is correct then struggles for Type II state activities will be easier to win than Type III, but the earlier analysis of certain Type II and III activities as forming part of the value of labor power provides the necessary theoretical link between struggles in the workplace and struggles over collective consumption. As Evers (1976:54) puts it: "the conflicts in the cities and the plants are elements of one and the same problem: the struggle over the value of labour-power."

After this discussion on state finance, let us return to our two models of state–society links and their implications for our understanding of urban fiscal crises. *On the tight-link model any difficulty in state financing of activities I or II would necessarily lead to a decline in the performance of the capitalist sector.* If this was found as a consistent result it would provide empirical support for this model. However, as Gerstenberger's quotation at the head of this section suggests, and as our discussion of the theoretical reasons for preferring the loose-link model also suggested, *it seems extremely unlikely that a failure to finance activities in cases I or II would have an immediate impact.* The loose-link model would suggest a far looser structuring of the system with far more "leeway" and "play" between the parts.[15] Whichever model is correct, one important methodological point must be made: *the study of state intervention (and of how it is affected by urban fiscal crises) is impossible in the absence of measurements of "system performance."*

It may be that Marxist writers, in making the break with structural functionalism, thought they were also breaking with a systemic model of society. This is not the case, as our discussion shows, and I would go so far as to say that *without any methodology for measuring system performance Marxist analysis is empty.* The problem is this. The various capitalist nations have shown themselves exceptionally durable, i.e., socialist revolutions have not taken place in such societies. Thus in one sense capitalism has continued to function in those societies, and history deprives us of the contrast between successful and failed capitalist societies. The contrasts which are available historically must be in the *degree* to which a capitalist society functions effectively.

My point is that unless we devote attention to ways of measuring "degrees of success" in "system performance" we have no idea where to look for the possible effects of changes in the amount of state intervention.

By definition, the tight-link model of state–society relations prevents this question from being posed since on this model the state acts as a homostatic device providing "exactly that which can be regarded as functional at the time for the concrete conditions of capital accumulation" (Gerstenberger, 1978:159). There can be no conception of inadequate performance since the actual level and nature of state intervention is always the necessary one.

However, as soon as we adopt the loose-link model the question of the adequacy of system performance becomes crucial. It should lead us to seek a methodology for assessing the adequacy of state activities from the point of view of the capitalist interests involved. Habermas (1976:49) is one of the few to recognize the problem when he writes: "whether performances of the subsystems can be adequately operationalized and isolated and the critical need for system performance [to be] adequately specified is another question. This task may be difficult to solve for pragmatic reasons." But it is a sad reflection on the state of Marxist theory that no systematic attention has been given to this issue.[16] If as most recent writers[17] agree (Castells, Poulantzas, Hirsch, Offe, and Habermas), "the guiding idea we should adopt . . . is that of a state plunged up to the neck in economic and social contradictions" (Vincent, 1976:100), than surely the omission of the study of the impact of such a state on the functioning society is a glaring one.

CONCLUSION

We hope to have demonstrated that certain mutually exclusive choices must be made within the Marxist theory of the state if eclecticism is to be avoided, and that analyses of urban fiscal crises, for which an understanding of the state is critical according to the argument that urban fiscal crises were *not* reflections at the municipal level of general fiscal crisis tendencies, cannot escape from these choices.

To summarize, the main choices identified appear to be:

whether the political realm can be treated as autonomous, in which case state functions can be isolated, or whether there is a necessary dependence between the economic and political spheres, in which case state functions can only be treated in relation to the accumulation process;

whether the legitimation function and the need for democratic institutions can be treated as necessary to the capitalist state, or whether their presence is due to a particular stage in the accumulation process (and its political consequences);

whether the state has developed such power and autonomy relative to the economic sphere that it is now outside the control of any particular class fraction (Offe and Habermas) or whether despite its vastly increased role it is still subject to the laws of motion of capital; and, finally,

whether state intervention is completely "functional" (tight-link model) or whether its functionality is limited (loose-link model), in which case a first priority is the analysis of its effects—in terms of limited performance levels.

ACKNOWLEDGMENT

This paper was prepared for the Conference of the Research Planning Group on Urban Social Services, Bielefeld University, W. Germany, August 1978.

NOTES

1. For reasons of space we shall not discuss the second area here. For excellent recent treatments of this question see Castells and Goddard (1974) and Lojkine (1977:149–159).

2. I would like to thank John Mollenkopf for unintentionally suggesting this theme.

3. It is important to the argument that follows that Hirsch derives these functions of the state in terms of crisis-imposed needs, i.e., that he treats the state as reflecting the imperatives of the economy.

4. This is the current object of research at the Urban and Regional Studies Unit, University of Kent.

5. It should be noted that several contributors to the Alcaly and Meremelstein collection place considerable emphasis on the economic crisis as a factor in urban fiscal crises, e.g., Alcaly and Bodian (1977) and Edel (1977).

6. A reading of Alcaly and Mermelstein's *The Fiscal Crisis of [some] American Cities* indicates that surprisingly few contributors make use of O'Connor's theory for this purpose. In two cases the theory is used in its original context in discussions of the growth of government activity (Alcaly and Bodian, 1977:41, and Edel, 1977:231) and ironically in the single case where it is applied to municipal activity the author *denies* its relevance (Zevin, 1977:20).

7. So far this largely remains to be done, though Piven (1977) has argued that federal grants were used from the early 1960s by the Kennedy and subsequent administrations to secure democratic votes among urban blacks, and that following the rise of provider group demands state and federal aid was used first to bail out the cities and subsequently to restrict city spending. Similarly Castells (1976) has documented a number of the crucial economic and "urban" trends, but without drawing the conclusions for the character of the state apparatus in question here.

8. It is worth noting that Lojkine's (1976:139) treatment of the state makes no reference to a legitimation function, but only to a domination function—whose form (repression or legitimation) presumably varies according to economic and political conditions.

9. Due to the conditions of production of this paper I was unable to refer to other writings of these authors.

10. In a later article Offe (1975:144) has argued that capitalist states have overwhelming difficulties in playing allocative and productive roles, i.e., market-supplementing and market-

replacing functions, and that they are "capitalist" only in their attempts and not in their success in finding a strategy which embraces these two functions.

11. In a recent discussion of state policy formation Hirsch (1976:119) uses the term "structural selectivity" and makes reference to Offe, but his use of it is quite different from that in Offe (1972).

12. I do not imply here that the state is outside society.

13. As in the case of the "logical" need for a planning ministry which integrates housing, town planning and transport, which is however never met due to the respective power of the client capitals and the absence of any capital with a direct interest in rational planning.

14. It will be noted that we have deliberately avoided the debates about whether state activities are productive or not. Unfortunately these debates create more heat than light since they assume that only productive labor (i.e., which is involved in commodity production, and which takes place within a capital-wage relation) is necessary and hence can lead to startling paradoxes like the statement that, "if all state activities are unproductive then the modern capitalist state, given its size, must be a large impediment to capital accumulation" (Rose, 1977:32).

In fact three relations of state activity to productive labor can be distinguished. First, though by definition state workers' labor is not productive of surplus value it is nevertheless *in Types I and II necessary to the production of surplus value in the capitalist sector.* (In the same way, labor in the circulation and consumption spheres is necessary but unproductive.) This reflects the socialization of production and reproduction.

Second, when state activity takes the form of transfers or purchases it enables surplus value produced by productive labor to be realized. This is true also of purchases in connection with activity III (Preteceille, 1977:120). Third, Type III is apart from this link unrelated to productive labor—and is precisely the type of state activity most under pressure in time of crisis.

15. Our threefold typology of state activities leads us to expect Type III activities to be the first to be sacrificed. They can be seen as responses imposed by popular pressure which may be eliminated due to a lessening of this pressure. In the cases of Type I and II activities the interest of fractions of capital is involved and their survival depends on the strength of these fractions. In the case of Type II activities there is some scope for common opposition between fractions of capital and workers.

16. A project at the Urban and Regional Studies Unit, University of Kent, for which money has been applied will tackle this issue.

17. The sole exceptions are probably adherents of the "state monopoly capitalism" school for whom the ability of the state to engage in planning activities is guaranteed by the support of the monopolies.

REFERENCES

Alcaly, R.E., and H. Bodian
1977 "New York's fiscal crisis and the economy." In R.E. Alcaly and D. Mermelstein (eds.), The Fiscal Crisis of American Cities. New York: Vintage.
Alcaly, R.E., and D. Mermelstein (eds.)
1977 The Fiscal Crisis of American Cities. New York: Vintage.
Altvater, E.
1978 "Some problems of state interventionism: the participation of the state in bourgeois society (1972)." In J. Holloway and S. Picciotto (eds.), State and Capital: A Marxist Debate. London: Arnold.
Boccara, P., et al.
1971 Le capitalisme monopoliste d'état: Traité marxiste d'économie politique, 2 vols. Paris: Editions Sociales.

Castells, M.
   1975   "Advanced capitalism, collective consumption and urban contradictions: new
          sources of inequality and new models for change." In L.N. Linberg, et al. (eds.),
          Stress and Contradiction in Advanced Capitalism. Lexington, Mass.: Lexington
          Books.
Castells, M., and F. Godard
   1974   Monopolville. Paris: Mouton.
   1976   "The wild city." Kapitalistate 4–5:2–30. (Also in Castells, M. 1977, The Urban
          Question. London: Arnold).
Edel, M.
   1977   "The New York crisis as economic history." In R.E. Alcaly and D. Mermelstein
          (eds.), The Fiscal Crisis of American Cities. New York: Vintage.
Evers, A.
   1976   "Urban structure and state interventionism." Kapitalistate 4–5:141–57.
Field, F., M. Meacher, and C. Pond
   1977   To Him Who Hath. Baltimore: Penguin.
Fine, B., and L. Harris
   1976   "The British economy, May 1975–June 1976." Bulletin of the Conference of
          Socialist Economist 14:1–24.
Friedland, R., F.F. Piven, and R. R. Alford
   1977   "Political conflict, urban structure and the fiscal crisis." International Journal of
          Urban and Regional Research 1:447–71.
Gerstenberger, H.
   1978   "Class conflict, competition and state functions." In J. Holloway and S. Picciotto
          (eds.), State and Capital: A Marxist Debate. London: Arnold.
Gordon, D.M.
   1977   "Capitalism and the roots of urban crisis." In R.E. Alcaly and D. Mermelstein
          (eds.), The Fiscal Crisis of American Cities. New York: Vintage.
Glyn, A., and B. Sutcliffe
   1975   British Capitalism, Workers and the Profits Squeeze. Baltimore: Penguin.
Gutman, R.
   1976   "State intervention and the economic crisis: the Labour government's economic
          policy 1974–5." Kapitalistate 4–5:225–70.
Habermas, J.
   1976   Legitimation Crisis. London: Heinemann.
Hill, R.C.
   1977   "State capitalism and the urban fiscal crisis in the United States. International
          Journal of Urban and Regional Research 1:76–100.
Hirsch, J.
   1976   "Remarques théoriques sur l'état bourgeois et sa crise." In N. Poulantzas (ed.), La
          crise de l'etat. Paris: P.U.F.
   1978   "The state apparatus and social reproduction: elements of a theory of the bour-
          geois state." In J. Holloway and S. Picciotto (eds.), State and Capital: A Marxist
          Debate. London: Arnold.
Holloway, J., and S. Picciotto
   1976   "A note on the theory of the state." Bulletin of the Conference of Socialist Econo-
          mists 14:1–9.
   1977   "Capital, crisis and the state." Capital and Class 2:76–101.
   1978a "Introduction: towards a materialist theory of the state." In J. Holloway and S.
          Picciotto (1978b), below.
   1978b (eds.), State and Capital: A Marxist Debate. London: Arnold.

Lamarche, F.
1976   ''Property development and the economic foundations of the urban question.'' In
C.G. Pickvance (ed.), Urban Sociology: Critical Essays. London: Tavistock.
Lindberg, L.N., et al. (eds.)
1975   Stress and Contradiction in Advanced Capitalism. Lexington, Mass.: Lexington
Books.
Lojkine, J.
1976   ''Contribution to a marxist theory of capitalist urbanization (1972).'' In C.G.
Pickvance (ed.), Urban Sociology: Critical Essays. London: Tavistock.
1977   Le marxisme, l'état et la question urbaine. Paris: P.U.F.
Mann, M.
1970   ''The social cohesion of liberal democracy.'' American Sociological Review
35:423–39.
1975   ''The ideology of intellectuals and other people in the development of capitalism.''
In L.N. Lindberg, et al. (eds.), Stress and Contradiction in Advanced Capitalism.
Lexington, Mass.: Lexington Books.
Mingione, E.
1977a   ''Pahl and Lojkine on the state: a comment.'' International Journal of Urban and
Regional Research 1:24–36.
1977b   ''The crisis, the corporations and the state.'' International Journal of Urban and
Regional Research 1:370–8.
O'Connor, J.
1973   The Fiscal Crisis of the State. New York: St. Martin's Press.
Offe, C.
1972   ''Political authority and class structure: an analysis of late capitalist societies.''
International Journal of Sociology 2:73–108.
1975a   Introduction to Part III. In L.N. Lindberg et al. (eds.), Stress and Contradiction in
Advanced Capitalism. Lexington, Mass.: Lexington Books.
1975b   ''The theory of the capitalist state and the problem of policy formation.'' In L.N.
Lindberg et al. (eds.), see above.
Pahl, R.E.
1977   ''Managers, technical experts and the state.'' In M. Harloe (ed.), Captive Cities.
New York: Wiley.
Pahl, E.E., and J.T. Winkler
1974   ''The coming corporatism.'' New Society 10(Oct.):72–6.
Pickvance, C.G. (ed.)
1976   Urban Sociology: Critical Essays. London: Tavistock.
1977   ''Marxist approaches to the study of urban politics: divergences among recent
French studies.'' International Journal of Urban and Regional Research 1:219–55.
1978   ''Explaining state intervention: some theoretical and empirical considerations.'' In
M. Harloe (ed.), Proceedings of the Conference on Urban Change and Conflict,
Jan. 1977. London: Centre for Environmental Studies.
Piven, F.F.
1977   ''The urban crisis: who got what and why.'' In R.E. Alcaly and M. Mermelstein
(eds.), The Fiscal Crisis of American Cities. New York: Vintage. (Orig. publ. in
R.A. Cloward and F.F. Piven, The Politics of Turmoil. New York: Pantheon,
1974).
Poulantzas, N.
1976   ''Les transformations actuelles de l'état: crise politique et la crise de l'état.'' In N.
Poulantzas (ed.), La Crise de l'état. Paris: P.U.F.

Preteceille, E.
1977 "Equipments collectifs et consommation sociale." International Journal of Urban and Regional Research 1:101–23.

Rose, S.
1977 "On classifying state expenditures." Review of Radical Political Economies 9:31–42.

Vincent, J.M.
1976 "L'état en crise." In N. Poulantzas (ed.), La crise de l'état. Paris: P.U.F.

Wolfe, D.
1977 "The state economic policy." In L. Panitch (ed.), The Canadian State. Toronto: University of Toronto Press.

Zevin, R.
1977 "New York City crisis: first act in a new age reaction." In R.E. Alcaly and M. Mermelstein (eds.), The Fiscal Crisis of American Cities. New York: Vintage.

HISTORICAL SOCIOLOGY

Charles Tilly

Historical sociology, as a field of inquiry, hangs together by negation and contradiction. If we date the emergence of sociology from Comte or Spencer, then "historical sociology" once constituted nearly the whole of the sociological enterprise. During sociology's first century, sociologists dehistoricized the field. The separation of sociology from history operated, curiously enough, through both abstraction and concretization: abstracting social processes from the constraints of time and space, concretizing social research by aiming it at reliable observation of currently visible behavior. Live individuals, properly studied, would reveal universal social laws. Or so many sociologists hoped.

The flight from history was more massive among the followers of Mill or Durkheim than among those of Weber or Marx (to attach convenient figureheads to the four main vessels of sociological thought). By World War II, the discipline—especially its enormously influential North American branch—had succeeded in wrenching itself away from history. Even then the lonely practitioners of historical analysis were united

Current Perspectives in Social Theory, volume 1, 1980, pages 55–59.
Copyright © 1980 by JAI Press Inc.
All rights of reproduction in any form reserved.
ISBN: 0-89232-154-7

chiefly by negation. For a wide variety of reasons, they rejected the main trends of sociology.

As the disparate coalitions that make revolutions always learn after the revolutions are won, shared opposition to a common enemy is a poor guarantee of agreement on other gounds. In the heyday of ahistorical sociology, the discipline's seekers after history ranged from a Sorokin (with his massive tabulations of the whole of Western experience) to a Heberle (with his efforts to puzzle out the electoral patterns of Schleswig-Holstein at the end of the Weimar Republic). Perhaps the most important areas of historical effort in sociology during the 1940s were (1) the history of civilizations, à la Sorokin or Kroeber; (2) the history of social thought—Barnes or Becker; (3) the appropriation of historical settings or cases to contemporary sociological analysis—Homans or Firey; (4) the attempt to solve specific historical problems via sociological methods—Merton or Heberle. Since then the variety has increased, although the history of civilizations has lost its erstwhile popularity.

The big changes have occurred in the last decade or so. Sociology as a whole has moved back toward history. Why and how? The most important single reason for the shift, I believe, was increasing dissatisfaction with developmental models of large-scale social change. Models of modernization, industrialization, social mobilization, political development and related processes had grown up to accompany the economists' apparently powerful models of economic development. In fact, the sociological models were weak, the processes hypothetical.

Considering that they presumably dealt with processes which unfold in history, the developmental models were strangely timeless. Their time was the stereotyped, repetitive, mechanical time of clockwork; wind it up, and the same sequence begins again. Such models would eventually have burst apart as a result of their own internal tensions, and smashed as a result of their collision with an unyielding social reality. The bursting and smashing occurred sooner than one might have expected, because the model's political grounding became controversial. Spokesmen—real and imagined—for the Third World lambasted both the substance of developmental theories and the programs of change they embodied. The international movement against American warmaking in Southeast Asia promoted skepticism, and sometimes anger, in both regards.

Historical work was a natural response to the new skepticism, for the following reasons:

1. There was the emergence of the notion that the conditions which representatives of rich countries called "underdevelopment" were actually consequences of colonialism, imperialism, and other forms of

domination by those very rich countries; that notion led easily to a re-examination of the paths by which poor countries had reached their present condition. Willy-nilly, the reexamination was historical.

2. A reasonable way to attack the developmental models being proposed to forecast and guide Third World experience was to show that the models applied poorly on their home grounds, the historical experiences of "developed" countries.

3. Poor countries became less attractive sites for research on large-scale social change, as Western scholars developed qualms about their political and intellectual roles, and as local scholars and politicians began to resist academic colonialism; it became more comfortable for all concerned if the Western scholars aimed their studies of large-scale social change at the past. (I am least sure of this third point, since in areas such as demographic analysis there has been no obvious decline in the involvement of Western specialists in research on the Third World; the most one can claim there is that some of the energy which might have streamed into Third World studies has instead flowed into historical analysis of Western population processes.)

At the same time (and for some of the same reasons), Marxist historical work began to flourish as never before. As a result, different sorts of Marxist analyses became the strongest current in the reaction to developmental theories. These factors provided strong incentives for sociologists concerned with large-scale social change to dig into history as never before.

Trends within the historical profession reinforced the swing toward historical work in sociology. In several distinct branches of history, professional historians began trying to solve old problems by adopting models and methods drawn from the social sciences. Studies of political elites, of elections, of economic growth, the social mobility, of class structure, and of population processes are the obvious examples. The results of the kind of work done by a Louis Henry, a Lawrence Stone, or a Robert Fogel attracted a great deal of attention, and some emulation, from historians. Eventually the results came to the attention of sociologists as well. The sociologists recognized two opportunities: first, to influence sociological thinking through the study of historical settings and materials which sometimes yielded conclusions different from those routinely encountered in analyses of contemporary social processes; second, to make an impact on historical practice. Very few sociologists acquired the full array of historians' professional skills, including mastery of the relevant texts and archives. But the sociologists were often ingenious and energetic in squeezing systematic, even quantitative, evidence from sources which historians had regarded as of secondary importance: biographical dictionaries, old censuses, parish registers, and the like.

Let me not exaggerate. Among the fifteen to twenty thousand professional historians currently practicing in the United States, no more than a few hundred maintain an active, daily involvement in the social sciences. Outside the United States, the proportion is surely lower. Of some six to ten thousand professional sociologists in the United States, only a few score are doing research which historians recognize as a contribution to their own field; over the rest of the world, the ratio is similar. In the United States, the rest of the 300–400 sociologists seriously involved in "historical sociology" either address problems which, for all their interest to fellow sociologists, stand low on the historical agenda, or do their work by glossing and synthesizing the publications of historians, rather than dealing with the texts which historians regard as their raw material. Some do both at once.

The sociological historians and the historical sociologists, furthermore, are not working on a unified set of problems. Within history, sociological work falls into at least three distinct clusters: (1) studies of cities and other communities; (2) studies of population processes, families, and marriage; and (3) studies of elites, stratification, and social mobility. In addition, scattered students of popular culture, of collective action, of industrialization, and of agrarian change use sociological models and procedures. On the whole, these varied investigators maintain closer ties to sociologists who are dealing with similar problems and with other historians who are interested in the same times and places than they do with each other. Within sociology, the fragmentation is equally great: some family sociologists do historical work, a number of political sociologists do historical work, and so on. Their common ground is shaky. When these sociologists get together, to be sure, they can swap tales about dealing with the historians in their areas of study. But their unity is fundamentally negative; it consists of not doing what most other sociologists do.

There is, then, no coherent field called "historical sociology," only a number of separate paths between history and sociology. Yet there are possible grounds for discussion and collaboration among sociologists who share an interest in historical work. First, most of them aim their attention at large structures and big processes: urbanization, the development of capitalism, the origins of democratic politics, the creation of world systems. Work on such structures and processes presents some common problems—problems of theory, method, and substance. Second, different sorts of historical materials raise common technical problems: the inference of processes and structures from data produced routinely by those very processes and structures; identifying and correcting the biases of the authorities, bureaucracies, and elite observers that produced the bulk of the documents available for our use; negotiating between the categories people of a given time and place used in their everyday lives and the categories we need to make effective comparisons with other times and places, and so on. Finally, theories and models vary significantly in the extent to which they are historically grounded.

"Historically grounded" theories and models assert that where and, especially, when a process occurs significantly affects its character. Some sociologists, for example, propose models of industrialization in which the process is essentially the same whenever it occurs; the developmental models we discussed earlier tend to take that form. Others insist that early industrialization differs from late industrialization, because the presence of relatively industrialized countries constrains the industrialization of the latecomers. The latter models—whether correct or not—have the greater historical grounding. Sociology as a whole can only gain, I believe, from an increased historical grounding of its models and theories. So if the diverse investigators working at the edges of sociology and history band together to promote a systematic appreciation of the significance of time and place for social processes, I suppose it will do no harm to call their common effort "historical sociology."

ISSUES IN THE THEORY OF SOCIAL MOVEMENTS

Mayer N. Zald

In recent years, social movements theorists and researchers have loosened their ties to collective behavior analysis and moved closer to political sociology. The sources of this shift have been several: (1) the events of the 1960s led both participant and observer to highlight the interaction of political process and change with social movement processes; (2) empirical studies testing individualistic assumptions about personal strain and deprivation, assumptions which underlie some version of collective behavior theory, have been found wanting; and (3) the development of resource mobilization theory provided tools of analysis more compatible with politicosociological and politicoeconomic assumptions and guiding metaphors.

Resource mobilization theory comes in several forms. In McCarthy and Zald (1977) it has an economistic slant, with a good deal of emphasis on the infrastructure of societal support, industry competition, cost benefit of modes of mobilization, and the like. In its more political guise (cf.,

Current Perspectives in Social Theory, volume 1, 1980, pages 61–72.
Copyright © 1980 by JAI Press Inc.
All rights of reproduction in any form reserved.
ISBN: 0-89232-154-7

Tilly, 1978), social movement activity is a continuation of political activity directly affected by the political structures and processes of the larger society, social movement activity is nested among the moves of individuals and groups contending power.

Whatever their form, resource mobilization approaches move to center stage macroscopic issues of the organization of movements and their place in larger societal processes. Micro issues central to collective behavior and psychological analysis, such as the nature of grievances, interpersonal processes, the recruitment of members, and the joys of participation, are not dismissed, but are moved to a supporting rather than central role. Emphasis is given to external structures and processes of political regimes and of the larger society.

Although resource mobilization theory has received much attention in recent years and has opened up a number of issues for research that were barely touched in earlier work, it is by no means a finished or well-developed theory. The work of Tilly, Oberschall, and of McCarthy and Zald suggests a number of theoretical issues that require development. I would like to briefly sketch three macro issues that deserve detailed treatment: the study of movement–countermovement interaction, the dynamics of social movement industries, and the shape, size, and orientation of the social movement sector.

Let me identify the central problematic for each issue, and then sketch the relevant units of analysis or major dimensions.

1. *Movement–Countermovement.* The typical strategy of social movement analysis has been to examine the adherents and organizations comprising a social movement. Often the focus has been upon one segment of a movement—an SMO and its adherents. Resource mobilization theory leads one to focus upon the relations of movement organization and adherents to authorities and their agents. Yet such a focus ignores a central aspect of almost any movement: that a movement very often generates a countermovement that may become independent of the authorities. Much of the mobilization potential of a movement, its tactics, and its ultimate fate stem from its battles with a countermovement; that is true for pro- and anti-abortion, the abolition movement, and nuclear and anti–nuclear power. The theoretical issue is how best to describe this interaction.

2. *The Structure of Social Movement Industries.* We (McCarthy and Zald) introduced the concept of a social movement industry as an analogue to the economist's concepts of an industry, a group of organizations (firms) offering similar products to a market of buyers. Social movement industries are all the SMOs striving for a similar change of goals in a society. It should be immediately apparent that the concept alerts us to

aspects of movements largely ignored. Few movement are dominated by a single organization; and any sophisticated movement leader recognizes the continuing tension of cooperation and conflict with other units of the industry. Yet to date we have not had explicit models or propositions to deal with the issue.

3. *The Social Movement Sector.* The social movement sector has been defined as the combination of all social movement industries in a society. We (McCarthy and Zald, 1977) introduced the idea to get at the issues of the generalized readiness to support movements for change in a society. Because of their economistic bias and because they largely focus upon the American case, they concentrate on how levels of affluence, discretionary time, communication facilities, and repression act as inhibitors or facilitators of the sector. This is, however, an incomplete approach. Casual inspection would lead one to note that other societies, seemingly as open and rich as ours, have fewer social movements, and these are differently integrated into the political structure of society. The issue to be posed is: how does the social movement sector articulate with the social and political structure of society? This is a problem for cross-national and historical analysis.

MOVEMENT AND COUNTERMOVEMENT

A social movement can be defined as a set of mobilized preferences for social change in a society. Using this very inclusive definition leaves open to question how much change is sought and how the preferences manifest themselves in organized activity. Preferences for change without manifest behavior or mobilization will be called a *latent* social movement. A countermovement is a set of preferences opposed to those changes. No specific direction is implied by these definitions. Movements can be "backward" looking or forward looking, left or right. Countermovements occur in response to movements. The concept of a *latent* movement and countermovement is useful to combat a possible ahistorical use of the concept of movement and countermovement. For instance, it would be a mistake to see the antiabortion countermovement as *just* a response to the abortion movement. The beliefs opposing abortion were well in place, indeed institutionalized. They become mobilized, transformed into an active countermovement, in response to the successful actions of pro-abortion movement and authorities.

Both movement and countermovement can be described in terms of the usual components of social movement analysis—support bases, movement organization, tactics, SMO interaction, and the like. What, however, are the major problematics of SM–CSM interaction?

Conceptualizing Movement–Countermovement Interaction

I believe that the best metaphor for thinking about SM–CSM interaction is to think of them as nations at war. SMs and CSMs command pools of resources to be used in a variety of battlefields. Just as one nation may be stronger at sea and weaker on land, so an SM may be stronger on the streets and weaker in the courts. Moreover, a victory or defeat in one arena or battlefield shifts the locus of attack, the nodal point for the next major battlefield. For instance, once the proabortion forces won the Supreme Court to its side, anti's shifted to the issue of use of federal funds. I presume that antiabortionists would like to gain Supreme Court support. Yet until new constitutional grounds are found, or a different reading of the biology of "life" is convincingly presented, this battlefield is moot.

The war metaphor has several limitations. First, the metaphor implies relatively unified antagonists, yet SMs are best described in terms of congeries of groups and MOs (since wars are often fought by coalitions, this is a matter of degree). Second, the nature of the battle, tactics, and resources are quite different in war and in social movement. Wars always imply the use of physical coercion; some social movements may battle only with persuasive techniques. Third, the state may act as arbitrator and guide where no third party constrains wars, at least not between major powers.

Yet the advantages of using the metaphor are quite striking. At each point in time, it sets a frame for weighing the advantages and disadvantages facing each party to the conflict. Moreover, it opens up social movement analysis to the powerful analysis of tactics and tacit bargaining stemming from game theory and analysis of strategic bargaining (Schelling, 1963).

Mobilization Processes

Thinking about social movement–countermovement interaction as groups at war highlights an important process central to any intergroup conflict; mobilization of one part heightens or affects the mobilization of other parties. The emergence of a conflict issue polarizes or increases cleavage in a community, and the mobilization of one side in a conflict issue creates the conditions for the mobilization of the other side (Coleman, 1957).

The idea of a spiral of conflict or increased polarization as a cause of mobilization is attractive, but too simple. First, we need to have a better understanding of the counterpart processes of demobilization and de-escalation; and second, we need to consider the possibility that under some conditions, mobilization of a movement or countermovement decreases the mobilization of the other side. Finally, the role of the mass media in mobilization and demobilization must be better undestood. Do they operate as score keepers, calling the signaling trends in mobilization and demobilization?

Location in the Social Structure

Just as nations at war can be described in terms of their geopolitical and economic resources so, too, can SMs and CSMs. Movement and counter-movement are described by: (1) the number and social characteristics of adherents, (2) the number and kinds of MOs, (3) the tactics of MOs (which link to resources), (4) ideology, and (5) the expectations of supporters. Since SM and CSM have different organizations and locations, their tactical and strategic opportunities vary. For instance. the anti–nuclear power movement has characteristics of a mass movement, while the pro–nuclear power movement resembles more an institutionalized pressure group with one or two peak associations. It is hard to imagine the pro–nuclear power movement mobilizing a march on Washington, while the antinukes have. On the other hand, the pros have enormous resources of technological expertise, far outweighing the antis.

The relative resources of each side affect the battlefield on which SM and CSM meet.

Relation to Authority

At any point in time and on different issues, SM and CSM stand in different relation to authorities. Conceive of authorities as the set of pivotal and public agencies (national, state, and local) that command or control authoritative allocational decisions. In one situation, authorities may be coterminous with the CSM, speaking for it, guiding its activities, restricting the SM. In other situations, authorities may be relatively neutral or immobilized (see Mayer, 1971, for a discussion of counterrevolutionary movements). National authorities may favor the SM and local authorities the CSM, as during the height of the civil rights movement in the South.

When an SM wins, it either captures authorities, now utilizing them and their resources as agents of the movement, or change their decision premises. The CSM then faces a different set of tasks, has a lower command of authority resources, must choose a different set of targets, and has a lower legitimacy with authorities.

One of the advantages of the SM–CSM analysis and the analogy to war is that it forces a dynamic interactional and over time analysis. It forces us to examine a movement in an historical process, not as a social curio, an artifact of a particular movement.

INDUSTRY STRUCTURE AND MO INTERACTION

We (McCarthy and Zald, 1977) have introduced the concept of a social movement industry (SMI) as the organizational analogue to a social movement. The SMI is all of the SMOs oriented toward SM's change goals. Drawing upon the analogy between an SMI and industry as defined by economists, we developed a number of hypotheses about the growth of industries, the survival and growth potential of specific MOs within an industry, and the internal differentiation of the industry.

In our forthcoming paper (Zald and McCarthy, 1980) we develop a number of propositions about cooperation and competition within an industry. We develop our hypotheses out of two bodies of theory: economic models of competition, and organizational theories about the dynamics of interorganizational relations. I do not want to repeat the analysis here, but examples of some of the hypotheses are:

> *Hypothesis 2.* The range of appeals and the variety of organization is partly related to the heterogeneity of potential supporters (p. 12).
>
> *Hypothesis 8.* The more the (board) interlocks, the greater the cooperation among SMOs.

I am persuaded by logic and empirical cases that we are on the right track. Here I want to raise two issues we didn't discuss: (1) What determines whether an industry is locally based and fragmented or has a more nationally oriented focus? (2) How does an MO dominate an MI?

Local and National Structures

In our 1977 and 1980 papers, we ignore an issue that deserves explicit treatment. We nod in the direction of Gerlach and Hine (1970), but in practice ignore them; Gerlach and Hine focus upon local ideological and solidarity groups while we are more interested in the garnering of resources and influencing authorities. Integration of the two perspectives, however, may provide a clue to the determinants of industry structure. Let me simply summarize how an integrated perspective would approach the study of movements.

The structure of an SMI is shaped by: (1) the amount of demand for its products; (2) the organizational–technological requirements to deliver its product; and (3) the amount of ideological and organizational hegemony of the goals leading SMOs. "Products" or goals are varied but may be either individual or collective. To the extent that a movement offers individual satisfaction and change, solidarity, and interpersonal satisfaction, it *must* have small units delivering rewards at the location of potential numbers. That is, SMOs cannot deliver solidarity through the mails or over radio or TV. The "product" entails a local unit. To the extent that an SMO works at changing national or state laws, it must have units aggregating demands and resources and lobbying or pressing at those levels. An SMO with national level political goals can do without local units. It could collect resources and support from isolated individual constituents or from major centralized funding sources and have a centralized lobbying and media development unit. An SMO or industry pressing for state acts must develop state level constituencies and vehicles for representing it.[1] Thus, as movement goals include both political and individual aspects, we would expect a more complex national and local structure.

Elsewhere, we (1977) have argued how increased market size (increased demand) leads to the entrance of new competitiors in an industry. There are few barriers to entry to social movement organizations: the major barrier seems to be the necessity to differentiate products/goals or tactics sufficiently to *warrant* competition. (Where competition is its own justification amongst businesses, competition amongst SMOs in a supposedly altruistic SMI requires justification.) So as the movement grows so will the number of MOs in the indsutry. But we have little knowledge of how MI growth at the national level relates to MI growth at the local level.

MO Domination of an Industry

How is domination over an industry achieved? Economists treat the problem in their discussions of market share and leadership in concentrated industries. (Interestingly, economists are better at describing the *effects* of domination, than the reasons a particular firm comes to dominate. The latter issue is discussed by management theorists.) What are the factors that lend a movement industry to be monopolized or dominated by one or two MOs? Two answers have traditionally been given, and, for shorthand purposes, they can be labeled charisma and coercion. A third answer is survival of the fittest.

Charisma and Symbolic Hegemony

One path to industry domination is through the capture of key symbols. The MO and its leaders articulate the vision and the pathway or program to the vision that seems to give the most hope to sympathizers. The articulation of the vision and the pathway lead energy and money to flow toward the rising MO. Other MOs begin to copy the dominant MO or to pattern their program and vision partly to differentiate themselves from the dominant MO, partly to find a mode of accruing resources that comes only by cooperating with or fitting into the dominant penumbra.

Coercion

The second mode of acquiring a dominant position is through coercion. The church militant and the revolutionary party are alike in believing there is only one true answer and it is theirs. SMOs are in the business of acquiring power. Where the MO neither grants the legitimacy of alternative pathways nor foreswears the use of coercion, MOs may systematically destroy opposition, including MOs committed to similar goals but maintaining autonomy.

Survival of the Fittest

Finally, where the MI exists in a very inhospitable environment, especially extreme repression, the MO that goes underground, that adopts a conspiratorial cell structure, may survive as other MOs disappear. They dominate by default. When repression lifts, other MOs may flourish again, but the surviving MO has the advantage of a working leadership and an organization in place. Even so, other MOs may more clearly link to the preferences of the latent social movement. And, as repression lifts, the MOs in place may not capture the new wave.

The concept of a social movement industry raises a number of questions that have been largely ignored by students of movements. It helps us to think about the relationship of a movement to all MOs in the movement. It helps put boundaries around the question of inter-MO relations, and it raises questions about industry structure, entry, domination, number, and local and national relations that have not been systematically treated. It does not, however, deal with one issue that begs for analysis: Why do some societies have more social movement activity than others?

THE SHAPE OF THE SOCIAL MOVEMENT STRUCTURE

The social movement sector is defined as the aggregate of all social movement industries, that is, all of the SMIs (and CSMIs) working for social change. Descriptively, sectors differ in the number of SMIs that are active, the amount of activity across the industries, the extent of articulation of SMIs with each other, and the ideological distribution and dominant orientation of the movements. (By ideological distribution, I mean the range of change goals that are articulated. For crude, heuristic purposes, the distribution can be described on a left–right continuum or on the distribution of extreme–moderate goals and tactics.)[2]

I am not prepared at this time to offer a systematic set of propositions in which some aspect of the SM sector is seen as dependent or caused by some aspect of political or class structure. But some illustrative propositions and observations are in order.

1. The size and range of issues in the SMs are inversely related to the costs of mobilizing. Where social control and repression are high and systematic and discretionary economic resources are low, social movement activity will be low.

2. In modern times, the relation of class organization to the party system is a major determinant of the degree to which social change preferences are highly articulated by the parties. In particular, where the labor movement "owned" or grew up in close relation with mass parties, change preferences have had an acceptable institutional vehicle. On the other hand, a more autonomous social movement sector develops where either the political party structure is not articulated with the class structure, because the parties are omnibus vehicles, or because they excluded groups.

3. The social movement sector is shaped by the structure or political decision making in a society. As a general rule, the greater the decentralization and disarticulation of levels, the more the opportunity for social movement organizations to make claims.

4. The predominant *issues* of the social movement sector are shaped by the stages of economic and political development. When the emerging Western nation states attempted to extend their power and control over local economies and populations, the characteristic rebellion of the sixteenth and seventeenth centuries was the tax rebellion. Although taxes continue to provide grist for political and social movement actions, the tax *rebellion*, with local communities or regions using violent tactics as a source of resistance, has disappeared. At a later stage of capitalist economic development, issues of political and organizational rights for the lower classes and then of economic security and working conditions become dominant issues.

5. The social movement sector also responds to major national and international forces. The history of major parties found in European countries—the Christian Democrat, the Socialist, and the Communist parties—cannot be written without major attention to the international political scene or to the specific fate of counterpart parties in other countries.

The "action" in understanding the social movement sector will come on the macro and institutional side, largely because behavioristically oriented social scientists have focused on the social psychological side. Preferences for change are related to an active stance on the part of members of a society, and there is a well-known literature on citizen attitudes, mobilization, and political participation, from De Tocqueville to Verba and Almond, that gives a social psychological explanation for the size of the sector. The macro perspective heightens our awareness of how social structure effects the options for participation, the costs of participation, and the shape and orientation of social movement activity. At some point, we may be able to combine the findings of the earlier literature with a more structural perspective.

CONCLUSIONS

I have examined three major areas where fruitful theorizing and research need to take place: the relation of movement to countermovement; the structure and process of industries; and the shape, size, and orientation of the social movement sector. For each of these large issues, I have suggested some answers or at least the line of analysis which I think will be fruitful in providing answers.

These three issues grow out of my preoccupation with the resource mobilization perspective and the analysis of social movements as part of political sociology. But they are hardly the only important problem. Indeed, the most important problem may lie at the very different level. Earlier I used the phrase symbolic hegemony. But American analysts of social movements have shied away from serious attention to ideology, to symbol systems, their internal socio-psycho logic. Recent developments in semiotics, hermeneutics, and culture systems, however, may soon make it possible to bridge that gap. Without attention to meaning systems, analysis of macrostructural factors may risk missing the shaping content of concern of social movement action; with only symbolic analysis we risk analysis empty of cost, constraint, and opportunity.

ACKNOWLEDGMENTS

This paper was delivered at the annual meeting of the American Sociological Association, Boston, Massachusetts, 1979. I am indebted to Linda Koboolian, Daniel Steinmetz and John D. McCarthy for their critical comments. Production of this paper has been aided by a grant from the Univerity of Michigan's Phoenix Project for research on the peaceful uses of atomic power.

NOTES

1. Much of the literature of political science dealing with state and national politics and pressure group structure may be relevant to the analysis.

2. Recently I have been working with Roberta Garner who has taken the lead in writing a long theoretical paper that addresses the determinants of the changing shape of the social movement sector.

REFERENCES

Abendroth, Wolfgang
1972   A Short History of the European Working Class. New York: Monthly Review Press.
Coleman, James S.
1957   Community Conflict. Glencoe, Ill.: Free Press.
Dahl, Robert A.
1966   Pp. 332–402 in R.A. Dahl (ed.), Political Opposition in Western Democracies. New Haven, Conn.: Yale University Press.
Duverger, Maurice
1963   Political Parties. New York: Wiley.
Gerlach, Luther, and Virginia Hine
1970   People, Power and Change: Movements of Social Transformation. Indianapolis, Ind.: Bobbs-Merrill.
Hobsbawm, E.J.
1962   The Age of Revolution: Europe, 1789–1848. London: Weidenfeld & Nicolson.
Mayer, Arno J.
1971   Dynamics of Counterrevolution in Europe, 1870–1956: An Analytic Framework. New York: Harper & Row.
McCarthy, John D., and Mayer N. Zald
1977   ''Resource mobilization and social movement: a partial theory.'' American Journal of Sociology 82:1212–39.
Rokkan, Stein
1970   Citizens, Elections, Parties. Approaches to the Comparative Study of the Processes of Development. Oslo: Universitetsforlaget.
Thompson, E.P.
1963   The Making of the English Working Class. London: Gollancz.
Tilly, Charles
1978   From Mobilization to Revolution. Reading, Mass.: Addison-Wesley.
Zald, Mayer N., and Roberta Ash
1966   ''Social movement organizations: growth, decline and change.'' Social Forces 44(Mar.)'327–42.
Zald, Mayer N., and John D. McCarthy (eds.)
1979   The Dynamic of Social Movements: Resource Mobilization, Social Control and Outcomes. Cambridge, Mass.: Winthrop.
Zald, Mayer N., and John D. McCarthy
forth-   ''Social movement in industries: cooperation and competition among movement
com-   organizations.'' In L. Kriesberg (ed.), Research in Social Movements, Conflicts
ing   and Change, Vol. 3. Greenwich, Conn.: JAI Press.

ADDITIONAL REFERENCES

Boulding, Kenneth
1962   Conflict and Defense. New York: Harper & Row.
Heirich, Max C.
1971   The spiral on Conflict: Berkeley, 1964. New York: Columbia University Press.
Killian, Lewis
1972   ''The functions of extremism.'' Social Problems 20(1):41–8.

Oberschall, Anthony
   1973   Social Conflict and Social Movement. Englewood Cliffs, N.J.: Prentice-Hall.
Schelling, Thomas C.
   1963   The Strategy of Conflict. New York: Galaxy Books.

PART II
CURRENT PERSPECTIVES

SCIENCE AND IDEOLOGY

Stanley Aronowitz

INTRODUCTORY REMARKS [1]

While some tendencies within Marxism have observed that some features of late capitalism are anomalous with respect to the Marxist theory, official Marxism has been prone to invent categories that integrate these features into the theory (example: relative autonomy to explain the disjuncture between economic bases and elements of the superstructure), rather than challenge the underlying assumptions of Marxism itself.

Marxism's defense of the concept of an ideology-free science is an aspect of its self-defense. If adjustments must be made in particular features of the theory, these are held to be a response to new developments within the capitalist order, or new knowledge produced by the experience of the revolutionary movement, or even the results of more penetrating work either in the natural sciences—by bourgeois social scientists who are acknowledged to be capable of good results in specific areas, but not in theory—or by Marxist research.

In Thomas Kuhn's (1967) terms, the paradigm, that is, the general framework of the theory, remains intact. Marxism holds that as long as

Current Perspectives in Social Theory, volume 1, 1980, pages 75–101.
Copyright © 1980 by JAI Press Inc.
All rights of reproduction in any form reserved.
ISBN: 0-89232-154-7

capitalism exists its self-critique must be limited to particular historically transcended aspects of the theory for there can be no other general theory of capitalism. These limits are no less severe than those imposed upon physical or chemical research. Since the seventeenth century, Newtonian physics has remained hegomonic, even if relativity physics was introduced to correct some of its obvious deficiencies (although most scientists would argue the reverse thesis: Newtonian science is made a special case by the more general theory—relativity physics). Marxism's adherence to the fundamental category of the dialectic of labor, as the explanatory framework for understanding the configuration of social relations, has been as little disturbed as the general methodological as well as theoretical framework of classical mechanics, its way of looking at the world. To challenge the mode of production of material life as the determining instance of all social life is to depart from the essential presupposition without which Marxism is not possible.

To challenge the concept of the separation of science from ideology at all levels is to challenge Marxism itself. Since it partakes in the assumptions of all science since the enlightenment, it is the only possible true way of looking at the social world. For this reason, contemporary Marxism cannot look at the social relations of science from the *inside,* that is, has never been able to locate the scientific world view, the mechanization of the world picture, the experimental method, the form of its results, and the legitimating weight of the scientific community to sanction that which is called science, within the framework of the critique of ideology. This duality of science and ideology in Marxist debate is the subject of the next section.

SCIENCE AND IDEOLOGY: HABERMAS

It is by now well known that challenges to the orthodox Marxisms of the past abound. Perhaps the central points during which these challenges appeared in the twentieth century were World War I and its aftermath, and after Khruschev's famous revelations concerning the crimes of Stalin. These events prompted naturally not only a reexamination of the political practice of the Communist movement, but a searching probe into the theoretical presuppositions of Marxism itself. Not the least of these efforts was the movement back to Marx in search of sources that might have given rise to Stalinism or, alternatively to rescue Marx from those who had distorted his ideas while acting in the name of Marxism (cf., Kosik, 1976).

The critique of Marxist practice inevitably led to a critique of Marxist theory. What I want to examine are two varieties of this critique. First, I will render a reading of the relation of Herbert Marcuse's critique of science and technology to Jurgen Habermas's effort to simultaneously preserve its implied critique of Marxism while trying to reformulate and transcend the categories of Marxism. Second, I will examine Louis Althusser's defense of Marxism against those who tried to extract from the early Marx paths to the renovation of social theory. In both Habermas, the Marx-critic, and Althusser, the staunch defender of Marxist orthodoxy, we will find an almost identical reaffirmation of the traditional conception that science is incommensurable with ideology, however their routes differ. I will contend that, unless Marxism is able to understand itself as both a theory of the actual development of capitalism *and* as a type of ideology that both expresses the particular interests of the working class within capitalist society and contains ideological elements within its own theoretical formulations, it cannot provide a significant critique of science as social relations.

The title of Habermas's (1970) essay "Technology and Science as 'Ideology'" already contains the clue to its meaning; ideology is put between quotation marks because Habermas intends to show that this formulation contains an ambiguity. Habermas deals with Herbert Marcuse's attempt to show that, contrary to the pervasive belief that technology and science are neutral aspects of the forces of production and may be regarded as part of the legacy of a new socialist society, they are, in fact, repositories of domination.

According to Marcuse, "domination perpetuates and extends itself not only through technology, but *as* technology and the latter provides the great legitimation of the expanding political power, which absorbs all spheres of culture." Moreover

> science, by virtue of its own methods and concepts, has projected and promoted a universe in which the domination of nature has remained linked to the domination of man—a link which tends to be fatal to this universe as a whole. Nature scientifically comprehended and mastered, reappears in the technical apparatus of production and destruction which sustains and improves the life of individuals while subordinating them to the masters of the apparatus. Thus the rational hierarchy merges with the social one (Marcuse, 1964:86).

The implication of Marcuse's judgment is that what Max Weber calls rationality is a self-contradictory phenomenon within late industrial capitalism. That which is called rational contains the progressive organization and subsumption of all human action by criteria that subordinate action to the purposes of the organization of domination—corporate, state, and ideological. The penetration to all areas of society by criteria of rational decision increases production, makes the functions of the state less arbitrary and increasingly subject to bureaucratic rules, and harnesses science and technology.

Habermas accepts Marcuse's reading of Weber's theory of rationalization, but rejects his interpretation of the significance of the subordination of science and technique to economic development and political domination. For Marcuse, humans have been forced to cut a deal in order to gain material comfort. They have been obliged to surrender their individual and collective control over their own destiny. Or, to be more accurate, the promise of freedom made by the old bourgeoisie has now been refurbished by the new apparatus of capitalist domination to mean the *freedom to consume*. Marcuse finds that this apparatus of domination appears rational, that is, the apparatus appears in the form of science and technology, and, becomes virtually immune from attack.

According to Habermas, the central error in Marcuse's formulation of the problem is that he has retained a concept of ideology appropriate to an era long surpassed by the new capitalist apparatus. In the old concept, the ideological was linked to the world view of a definite social class. Ideology represents not only a self-justification of its legitimacy within bourgeois society, but also the class striving for a new society. That is, the old model of ideology always contains a utopian element as wish fulfillment, delayed gratification, or repressed desires. Ideology was not only a form of false consciousness, in Habermas's reprise, but a political weapon that yielded practical results.

Technology and science are no longer types of ideology in this meaning of the term, because in modern society the apparatus lacks a normative basis for decision making. The normative belongs to traditional society where classes vie for political power over a centralized state, where myths and religion are legitimating ideologies, and where the distribution of economic rewards has a class basis. Under these anterior conditions, classes were faced with *practical* problems, defined here as problems that are solved according to a priori normative rules. Habermas contends that these characteristics no longer obtain in modern society which he refuses to call "civilization." Classes have not disappeared in contemporary society, but have been irreversibly integrated into the apparatus. Although the class struggle has not disappeared, it is suppressed and only appears as a factor in the technical, rational procedures of the apparatus.

Technology and science cannot be called "ideology" in the old sense of the word, for they are neither mythic nor religious in the way that science was regarded in the seventeenth century. They have been fully subsumed and instrumentalized by a system of rational-purposive action which, in Habermas's (1970:99) words "makes permanent the extension of subsystems of purposive rational action, and thereby calls into question the traditional form of legitimation of political power," i.e., ideology. The traditional distinction between means and ends has been reversed: means are no longer determined by, or subordinated to, ends as they were in traditional societies. The collapse of the two, in Habermas's view, is irreversible since the old normative systems that obeyed different logical principles have been permanantly laid to rest.

Habermas proposes nothing less than the reformulation of the theoretical framework of Marxism, in which he finds Marcuse still caught. Marcuse's attempt to show technology and science as ideology was predicated on the assumption that people still obeyed the rules of *interaction* rather than the rules of what Habemas has called *rational-purposive action*. The trouble with this assumption, according to Habermas, is that history has surpassed traditional societies. The old distinction between forces and relations of production on one hand and the base and superstructure on the other in which ideology functioned had to be reassessed.

Rational-purposive action and interaction are the two new a prioris of Habermas's theoretical system. Human societies in all epochs require labor in order to master nature and survive. But traditional societies rigorously separated *work* from other activities, having to do with intersubjective communication, relations that are mediated by language, social norms, the construction of institutional frameworks that embody the moral development of children and the maintenance of conventional authority.

Late capitalism, with its integration of the state with the economy, its nearly complete subsumption of science and technology, and its suppression interaction, has attempted, in Habermas's description, to inform institutional frameworks for human action with the standards of technological and scientific rationality. For Habermas, Marxism has been suppressed precisely because it has occluded interaction as a separate category from its discourse; the hegemony of technocratic consciousness may not be overcome; it must be taken for granted.

For Habermas, Marxism's program for overcoming the problem of domination is anachronistic since the establishment of new "relations of production" to unleash the suppressed forces of production has already occurred within the framework of domination. Technology and science are at once the new hegemonic forces of production *and* the institutional framework for social life. Emancipatory practice must focus on the restoration of that which has been suppressed by late capitalism: the richness of intersubjective communication informed by social norms, in short, the moral life.

When Habermas calls for the abandonment of the critique of technology and science as ideology it is not a sign of his celebration of their ascendancy; he recognizes that they have become forms of domination as well as emancipation from deprivation and arduous labor. However, since the entire framework of economic and political power is intertwined with the very canon of technical rationality, Habermas sees Marcuse's critique of rationality as a futile, romantic effort that is grounded in the confusion between purposive rational action bound up in *work* and the ethical life bound up in *interaction*.

By this reformulation we are asked to accept the technical-scientific structure of social relations as eternal and impenetrable. Habermas conflates work and science/technology in a single term—"rational-purposive action." The ideological disappears from their processes. Science and technology have become the historically evolved *form* of the relations of humans to nature and to that part of social relations having to do with work. The task for Habermas is to extricate a part of social relations that may be subject to normative rules from the province of rational-purposive action.

Habermas proposes to deny the dialectic of labor its internally contradictory character. Only labor's binary "interaction" may be the scene of ideological analysis and debate. Instrumental reason, a term coined by Max Horkheimer (1947), has so enveloped the world of work that the project of its transformation into emancipatory activity which, in Marx, depended on the contradictory unity of work and interaction, now becomes impossible when the rationality is entirely subsumed by the apparatus. This is not the place to explore the philosophical implications of taking science and technology for granted, that is, of returning to the Weberian critique of rationality in order to shed its Marxist formulations. Suffice it to say that Habermas has reintroduced the Kantian distinction between reason and judgment and tried to make politics a new aesthetic. At the same time, the sundering of the unity of human activity paves the way for political quietism or, to be more exact, advances a theory that ends by accepting the ontological neutrality of science and technology, despite its acceptance of Marcuse's linking of these with domination. For Habermas, domination is merely the price one must pay for material comfort. Since class struggle no longer constitutes the dynamic of historical change, but has been replaced by rational-purposive action appearing as technology and science, any effort to maintain their ideological character, which must always be predicted on the existence of social classes as significant social actors, is doomed to failure.

Habermas is right to point out that Marcuse stopped short of carrying his critique to its logical conclusion: Marcuse fails to posit alternatives to technology and science even hypothetically. Marcuse's refusal is grounded, not in some intellectual acceptance of the new technocratic framework of modern society as desirable, a conclusion that must be drawn from Habermas's position despite his gesture to the theory of domination, but from his belief that the working class as historical subject, the only material basis for ideology-critique, had failed, at least for the time being. Moreover, Marcuse has a deep-seated Marxist suspicion of efforts to construct alternatives as logical exercises before the material conditions for their realization are manifest.

Perhaps the most blatant and archaic duality retained by Habermas is the mind–body split implied by the distinction between work and interaction. For Habermas wishes to separate communications and normative judgments from the labor process, and presents this conclusion as an empirically given proposition. The confusion of this thought results from the assumption that the exploitation of nature for human survival, both in terms of material subsistence and protection against natural forces, requires the repression of communication free of domination. The labor process, then, is defined as hostile to human reflection—social practice which may be mediated by historical development. But, for Habermas, it can never be part of an emancipatory *praxis* because it already contains two forms of the domination of Nature as well as domination of one's internal nature.

Habermas asks Marxism to abandon the "dream of the whole man," that slogan adapted by Marx from Feuerbach's effort to bring humankind down to earth (Marx, 1964). In renouncing the possibility of a dialectical totality in favor of systems, he has ratified the technical division of labor by producing a new ideology of human nature in which these divisions are elevated to a structural concept. The "mind" is always rational and directed toward natural and human domination while the body is the sensuous, affective side of that species called human. In this metaphoric construction, the body is surrendered to the mind in the labor process, or, more exactly, indulges its desire for freedom, through fantasy or privatization.

In late capitalist culture one's private life is colonized by technologically mediated culture, which now regards the problem of alienated labor as a technical issue, one subject to administrative manipulation, scientific investigation, and negotiation. Therefore, Habermas wishes to remove the body from the mind, a step made necessary by the totalizing force of technical reason in the labor process, and made possible by the end of material scarcity, except for marginal groups in late capitalist societies. To the extent that Habermas has a political program his aim is to constitute an institutional framework that allows the fantasy life of individuals to become part of social life free of technological domination.

But this is no political program at all because politics is no longer free to contravene technological and scientific domination in Habermas's own conception of the repressive totality of late capitalism. To argue for a noninstrumental system of interaction advanced and legitimated by an institutional framework whose force derives from technological domination is to admit that what Habermas calls the sociocultural phase of human development has no material base. Having ceded to technological consciousness the entire sphere of rational-purposive action, Habermas is left with a constituency of university, college, and high school students whose political force derives precisely from their disjoined relation to the labor process and their freedom from rational-purposive action. Since they are not workers, technicians, or scientists (yet), Habermas believes that the legitimating processes of late capitalism, i.e., its ability to "deliver the goods" by mobilization of science and technology, are not operative among students because "their protest is directed against the very category of reward itself."

Habermas's general theory of the centrality of interaction and work is unable to cope with changes in Western capitalism in the 1970s, in part because the material condition he posits as the presupposition for the struggle for a public sphere unburdened of distorted communication and mediated by technical reason, no longer obtain. The postulate of the end of material scarcity is now only a partial description of the social and political environment confronting the apparatus. Its failure to sustain growth beyond the Vietnam War and the early 1970s in Western Europe has challenged the legitimacy of the apparatus of domination and produced new problems for the political directorate and opens the space for a critique of technology and science as ideology.

Since we have learned that the apparatus can fail to deliver the goods the theoretical possibility of creating an opposition has returned even among the workers. Recent studies of the labor process, showing their class-based character, have exposed the extent to which rational-purposive activity has a specific history. Its character has been revealed to be temporal and structural only in terms of a particular mode of production (Braverman, 1974).

Although Habermas does not claim that technology and science are neutral in their origins, he makes an historical argument that says that the reified appearance as immutable "things," as instruments, must now be accepted as "natural" facts. For those who follow Habermas in insisting upon the absolute opacity of rationality, its relegation to the labor process and the treatment of work as instrumental activity, the only solution to the disappearance of classes and class struggle as relevant conceptual categories of social analysis is to insert interaction as an autonomous category of the social process.

SCIENCE AND IDEOLOGY: ALTHUSSER

The virtue of Habermas's work is to remind us of the indissolubility of the Marxist framework. It is not possible to disassociate the theory of ideology from classes and class struggle, any more than science and technology may be regarded as either historically or logically independent of social relations. But that is exactly what Louis Althusser (1968) and his school have attempted to do. Their assertion that Marxism is a science is specifically linked to the concept that in order to become a science its theoretical system or discourse must separate itself from ideology. Althusser regards the critique of ideology as the first and crucial step in the development of science and claims that the early Marx may be partitioned from the late Marx on the basis of his critique of idealism. Althusser distinguishes science from ideology in three ways: (1) The object of knowledge is different. The scientific object of knowledge, while different from the "real" world, is no longer informed by religious abstract essences. (2) It cannot be said that science and ideology are separated by a Chinese wall; science emerges out of its critique of ideology and constitutes itself in and through this critique. For Althusser, scientific knowledge is marked by its mode of production of knowledges (the plural here refers to Althusser's insistence that the knowledge modes of production, e.g., chemistry, physics, Marxism, are distinct practices that comprise science. The use of the singular is ideological because it connotes a totality that is more than the ensemble of material practices.) This mode of production, according to Althusser, may be linked to the labor process. The specific object of knowledge for each science is the raw materials from which the theoretical means of production (the methods of science including theory, experiments, and techniques) derives a result. (3) Althusser acknowledges that the historical relations ("both theoretical, ideological and social") form the context of scientific labor. But these historical relations are accorded no real weight in the production of scientific knowledge. Althusser (1970:67) holds that scientific knowledge is "concerned with the real world through its specific mode of appropriation of the real world . . . the mechanism that insures it." This mechanism, the process of the production of knowledge, enables "the grasp of the concept." For even though the object of knowledge and the real world are distinct, science can, in Althusser's view, appropriate the real object or the real world through both a critique of the ideological object and its ability to form a mechanism of knowledge.

At this point is is necessary to caution against the apparent homology between Althusser's concern with the process of the production of knowledge, its theoretical conditions so to speak, and traditional concerns of epistemological inquiry. For he not only distinguishes his approach from the school of Marxist humanism—in which appear (in his account, at least) the a prioristic notions of appearance and essence, of the abstract totality climaxing in an idealistic ideology that must be banished from Marxist science—but also from Husserl and his school, which proceeds from the problem of whether knowledge is possible (Althusser, 1970:52). Althusser implicitly agrees with the view that knowledge and its mode of acquisition are the object of philosophical inquiry, but not the question of how a subject can know the object. For Althusser, this is the wrong question since it ignores the real progress of science, a mode of production that has already established the possibility of science free of ideological determinations by its grasp of the real world through its mechanism and its means of production.

Althusser places himself within one tendency of Marxist thought, a Marxism that makes a decisive break with reflection theory, according to which knowledge is "reflection" of the real world where ideas correspond to material processes as a matter of simple causality. Althusser recognizes that the mechanism of scientific practices only yields a "knowledge effect" from which theory must make inferences. Althusser's theory of truth retains the traditional notion of the existence of an external world "independent of the process of knowledge" but makes no claim for the correspondence of ideas derived from scientific practice with this world as some kind of mirror image.

> We can say, then, that the mechanism of production of the knowledge effect lies in the mechanism which underlies the action of the forms of order in the scientific discourse of the proof. . . . In fact these forms of order only show themselves as forms of the order of appearance of concepts in scientific discourse as a function of other forms which without themselves being forms of order, are nevertheless the absent principle of the latter. [T]he forms of order (forms of proof in scientific discourse) are the diachrony of a basic synchrony. . . . Synchrony represents the organizational structure of the concepts in the thought-totality or system (or as Marx puts it "synthesis") diachrony the movement of succession of the concepts in the ordered discourse of proof (Althusser and Balibar, 1970:67–78).

But the proof is not in the eating. The proof is found in the internal structure of science. The famous criterion of practice as the verification of a theory means the distinct scientific practice to which any specific discourse refers. For Althusser, theoretical "practice" is contained by its own structural unity, a logical order that grasps the real "in thought." There are no guarantees of scientific truth except the norms established by the scientific community.

We arrive, then, at a convergence between the work of Kuhn, Althusser, and, as we will see, Peirce. Kuhn (1967) locates scientific revolutions in the contradiction between the old paradigm and the anomolies of its experimental practice. The dominance of the new paradigm takes place when it is able to explain phenomena considered anomalous by the older one. The new paradigm may change the substance of science, but the norms of theoretical validity remain those accepted by the scientific community. For Kuhn change is a process occurring within science; it takes place on the basis of the willingness of those whose work is "normal" science to accept the new paradigm. The scientist is equipped with a series of concepts, a theoretical framework that is capable of grasping the real world in thought. Knowledge is not derived from observation, but is only confirmed by it. This is similar to Althusser's belief that the predicate of any true affirmative proposition lies, implicitly or explicitly, in its subject. This relation between subject and predicate resides in the grounded connection between the two, or in their unity in structure. Althusser has evolved a theory in which the forms of thought, the correspondence among the various elements, and the logical principle of order constitute the proof of theory. Here verification through practice, labeled by Althusser rank empiricism, is subsumed by the logical principle or order. The "absent" link in Althusser is the relation of thought to nature.

The sphere of empirically grounded knowledge is found in the realm of ideology. Politics, indeed all the sciences whose subject is "man," must be ideological. According to Althusser the subject of social science is social structure (the synchronic) and its ordered discourse which is prior to verification. Here, the reconstitution of the object of knowledge from "man" to "society" as a social fact irreducible to individuals, their subjectivity, and their ideological relations to each other and the social structure within which they live, combines with the ordered discourse to constitute science itself.

Althusser thus introduces a dualism in the study of the social world. There can be no science of social relations, unless these are treated as a determinate ordered discourse, obeying definite laws already specified by the Althusserian canon that makes structures the true object of any science. Nevertheless, people do study interactions and social norms and record their experiences of the social world unmediated by structural analysis. These studies are called ideology by Althusser and defined pejoratively, although accorded the status of legitimate, ideological discourse, but not science. This is the sphere of "lived" experience, or the "imaginary" relation of persons to the real—imaginary because people are not theoretically grounded; they lack the apparatus of true knowledge and cannot grasp the real except as ideology.

Class struggle, either at the level of trade union practice or practical revolutionary politics, can only be ideological since these arise from the lived experiences of the workers. Science is separate from the class struggle, even though class and class struggle may be the object of knowledge of scientific investigation provided they are viewed from the perspective of structuralist analysis.

In the end, Althusser claims that Marxist science like any other science can be value-neutral. It has overcome the "iron cage" of the imaginary relation with the real within which all ideological discourse is imprisoned. Its language machine is capable of assimilating any raw material, chopping it up into discrete objects, ordering it according to logical principles named, and mapping in advance and "producing" knowledges that take on the aspect of a predicate of which the mechanism itself is the subject.

Althusser's metaphor of production and of the machine is not arbitrary. His Marxism turns out to be an almost conscious adaptation to the age of mechanical reproducibility, one in which the machine is both form and content, or, to be more exact, the form produces the content.

Althusser's attack on the search for origins as ideological is an attack on the effort to insist on the validity of knowledge before the Enlightenment, just as Copernican science criticized its forebears as mysticism. For at heart, Althusser is a rationalist; anything that refuses his mechanical idea grinder is labeled irrational or ideological. A science of politics or of art is possible only on condition that these are treated as idological discourses since they are premechanical.

Among other problems, the Althusserian theory of science seems incapable of finding the new features of social, economic, and political development since, in his own metaphoric analogy (Althusser, 1971), these are part of social unconscious, and Althusser views the unconscious as the seat of the irrational, the structural origin of all ideology. Following the metaphor, the process of scientific knowledge acquisition may be compared to the process by which the patient makes conscious the irrational, unconscious desires and needs in order to control them. The congruence of Althusser's conception of science and the instrumentalization of reason that has been integrated harness the unconscious and make it part of the conscious life, transform it from alien nature to raw materials for the theory machine.

I do not believe that this comparison of Althusser's separation of science and ideology with the unbridgeable parts of the psychic structure in Freudian theory is farfetched. Just as Freudian psychology has a side which seeks to subordinate anarchic, irrational human nature to rational-purposive action, so Althusser wishes to restrict ideology to certain spheres of human activity, or, if possible, to progressively subordinate them to Marxist science, considered here sovereign because untrammeled by lived experience.

John Mepham (1974), a British philosopher, has likened the relation of science and ideology to two different generative sets having a different matrix of internal relations. Both are considered structured discourses that may be understood as separate languages. In Mepham's conception "social life is structured like language" arranged on a semantic field that is, in the main, beyond the scientific comprehension of those who participate. In Mepham's (1974:107) words, "The natural self-understood meanings encountered in social life form a text which we need to decipher to discover its true meaning." The comparison with Freud's theory of dreams comes to mind. Just as the dream speaks a language which is different from that of the conscious life and defies literalization, so people in everyday life speak an unconscious language that can only be translated by means of other, more scientific categories. The structure of Freud's thought entailed a "generative set" of concepts through which the dream work could be deciphered. These were grounded in the mechanism of the psychic structure and certain processes that followed from the contradictions among its elements. Freudian–Lacanian psychoanalysis constitutes itself much like the Althusserian definition of science. The unconscious speaks a language whose meanings are hidden to ordinary comprehension. It can only reveal itself through slips of the tongue, jokes, gesture, and dream-work, which must be "transcoded" into the language of science in order to be understood. The "real" is a set of relations constituted as a structured discourse which is invisible to ordinary cognition but presents itself in a "phenomenal form." Social life perceives this phenomenal form and translates perception into the structured discourse of ideology which is constituted as an imaginary relation to the real, maintaining the real as opaque, that is, concealing its generative set of relations.

In Freud's (1966) theory science as ordered-discourse-deciphering is necessary, but not sufficient for cracking the hidden code of the unconscious. The unconscious constructs mechanisms of defense (condensation, displacement linear causality, clues that lead to blind alleys) just as the real masks itself to cognition. Thus the Althusserian attack against the possibility of gaining scientific knowledge through observation, since the "data of experience" only yield the real in its phenomenal form. Science must treat the observed perception of things with scepticism, treating these data as ideology, the critique of which will constitute the first step in the development of science. The transformation and subsumption of the data of experience into the raw material upon which the knowledge producing machine will labor is the way Freud hoped to make the manifest text of the dream part of the process by which the latent text is revealed.

In Mepham's reading of Althusser's theory of the relation of science and ideology the latter is not produced by erroneous, or even class-bound, beliefs or value systems. If this were so, ideology would disappear with the end of class society. But the Althusserian variety of Marxism insists that ideology is structured discourse of lived experience whose variance from the "real" is not subject to historical change. The particular phenomenal form of real relations will surely change with the transformation of capitalism into socialism. But the gap between real relations and phenomenal forms is transhistorical, that is, ideology as "lived experience" does not disappear because its source is not the distorted values and beliefs of bougeois society; it is not false consciousness.

Ideology transcends the mode of production because it is a structure of the relations between lived experience and the real.

Science arises from the critique of ideology in every society. The theory machine will always be necessary to prevent the phenomenal form of real relations from rendering all reality opaque. Here, then, is the inevitable privileging of science, the necessity of its separation from ideology, the heart to the concept of its transhistoricity. While Kuhn does not in principle exclude social and historical determination, or at least influence of the process and structure of scientific knowledge (indeed his analogy between scientific and political revolutions is explicitly drawn), he has brought none of these relations inside the process of scientific development. The implication of this exclusion from the discourse of Kuhn's investigation of the history of science is close to Althusser's attempt to separate science from ideology. Both would agree, to be sure, that historical, ideological, and social considerations are part of the context of science, but the insistence on the autonomy of normative practices, such as criteria for validity, and constitution of the scientific object, tends to neutralize the ideological influence/determination of science itself.

Kuhn is, of course, much more critical of the category of scientific truth than Althusser whose insistence on the discontinuous, with his categories of relative autonomy, and on the primacy of structure renders his complex argument philosophically naive. While he does not go as far as Paul Feyerabend (1976) in claiming that the dominance of a scientific paradigm in any historical period is arbitrary, that it has no historical necessity, Kuhn (1967) does argue that scientific "progress" remains "in the eye of the beholder." But what puts Althusser and Kuhn in the same theoretical camp is the notion that the relative autonomy of the scientific community from the "laity and everyday life" is the foundation of the insularity of science from ideology and the guarantee of "truth."

In this respect, Kuhn's ascription of insularity to the separateness of science in social terms from everyday life, its institutional autonomy, has the virtue of leaving the door open for an empirical investigation of whether this assertion holds for contemporary science, if it ever did for earlier periods. I shall examine below the thesis that such autonomy of science from ideology could never be successfully argued, at least up to the present. Althusser, on the other hand, in his desire to show the scientificity of Marxism (an antiempiricist and antipositivist science to be sure), has been constrained to hermetically seal both Marxism and other "scientific" practices from interaction with social, ideological, and historical relations that determine, in any measure, the internal relations of scientific activity, except insofar as science emerges at the intersection of the epistemological break from ideology in terms of the constitution of the object of knowledge. But, for Althusser, the paradigms of science are debated, decisions arrived at, new theoretical norms agreed upon, entirely *within* the scientific community.

Consider the words of the philosopher Charles Sanders Peirce. Referring to the concept of truth Peirce (1955) said, "The opinion which is fated to be ultimately agreed to by all who investigate, is what we mean by truth, and the object represented in this opinion is the real." Peirce viewed the object as independent of the processes of knowledge, but remained fixed on the ideal of one necessary result of investigation by all those competent to conduct this work. For Peirce, as much as Althusser, the mechanics or methods of science are the road to knowledge. It is their infallibility that must be relied on to yield truth. If these could be challenged, the relativity of scientific truth, its fallibility, and thus its ideological character, would be a logical result.

Althusser has worked himself into a cul de sac on the road to asserting the scientificity of Marxism. Since he can only admit that Marxism may be an ideology from the point of view of the revolutionary movement, but not in the rigorous terms in which scientific discourse is cast, and because he rejects the reflection theory of knowledge and the correspondence theory of truth, he finds himself caught in a very unMarxist idea: the possibility that a sphere of social activity may be free of what he considers ideology to consist of—the imaginary relation between humans and their objective world. In his conception Althusser has posited a privileged mechanism that saves science from historical, political, and social determination. Althusser's "mechanism" is the category of structure or system of concepts that are ordered in a certain way, in a type of hierarchy where the succession of one concept by another has a specific form that is said to be scientific.

Althusser even finds the concept of mediation ideological, since this is not a material concept and, by its insertion into the process of the production of knowledge, undermines the certainty of knowing and reintroduces the question about the problematic relationship between science and its object. We find ourselves in the curious position (especially for a Marxist theorist) of asserting that the mechanisms of scientific knowledge are ideologically neutral. This implies that technique, the experimental method, and technology as such are neutral as well since, in Althusser's conception of the history of science, scientific knowledge gives rise to technology. Consequently, Althusser equates science and technology with the labor process as the sum of human relations to nature, constituted as material practices that are entwined with the structure of production.

Elsewhere I have argued that the doctrine of the neutrality of technology is untenable (Aronowitz, 1978). We must now demonstrate that the ideological neutrality of science is similarly untenable. One cannot help but notice that both Habermas and Althusser, despite their antagonistic theoretical frameworks, deny that technology and science are ideology. But where Habermas's argument rests on his conception of the permanence of reification after the universalization of commodities by capitalism and has conflated reification with the new given of rationality, Althusser has attacked the category of reification as such. For Althusser, science is a self-legitimating discourse whose ordering of proof, apparatus of theory, method of discovery are *unproblematic*. His task is to show that Marxism is scientific because it orders its concepts in a structural unity that is homologous with other sciences, a theoretical practice whose history consisted in the overturning of the ideological. In Althusser's hands, Marxism is now a social theory whose determinations may be said to be independent of its social, historical, and ideological context, since science cannot refer to its origins or its context, but is ultimately self-justifying. (This, of course, opens the path for the party theoreticians and the separation of science and politics.)

The importance of Althusser's contribution to the Marxist theory of ideology is his insistence that ideology is situated within the forms of social life rather than within the realm of ideas alone. The freeing of the concept of ideology from the label of "mere illusions" was originally accomplished by Lukacs (1967), who found the basis of ideology, not in Weberian values and beliefs or the earlier Marxist idea of "false consciousness," but in the ordinary apprehension of the forms of appearance of things. But Lukacs's argument stems for his theory of reification within capitalist society. In the measure that the commodity becomes dominant in the process of production, historically, relations among persons (the "real relations" within the capitalist mode of production) are enshrouded in a fog of mystification. Their form of appearance is relations between things, an exchange of equivalents that seem to be grounded in the intrinsic properties of objects rather than in social relations. In this conception the source of ideology, which is universal among all those who live within the capitalist mode of production, is the commodity form. The opacity of the material world is not a property of perception, but a "natural" cognitive result of the transformation of use value into exchange value, the process of production into the process of exchange and the subsumption of the labor process under capital.

For Lukacs, class relations *mediate* these fundamental sources of the production of ideology by giving ideology a specific character. But the values and beliefs of a class are necessarily variants of bourgeois beliefs, not because of the imposition of these ideas by concrete persons, who may be their bearers, but because the configuration of commodity production subsumes the concrete into the abstract, both at the level of labor where labor time as a unit of measurement replaces the specific kind of labor (weaving, carpentry, cooking, or waiting on tables) and at the level of the commodity where use value is subsumed under exchange value. Thus we measure ourselves in terms of how much in wages the sale of our labor power will bring. We are "worth a definite quantity of money" (Mepham, 1974:108). Mepham points out that the transformation of the value of labor power (the amount of socially necessary labor time embodied in the commodities necessary for the reproduction of the worker and her family) into wages is a prime example of how the form of appearance of real social relations leads to ideology. The worker believes that his wages represent the number of hours for which he has sold his labor power. The ideological category of the "value of labor," is treated as if the exchange of a certain quantity of labor power for wages was an exchange of equivalents. In turn, this mystification hides the source of capitalist profits that now appear to originate in the marketplace, the risk factor in investment, or in eternal morality. The form of appearance of the commodity, in this case labor, hides the source of profit, the difference between the value of the commodity and the value of labor power. Marx uses the terminological transformation to point to his distinction between appearance and reality. The value of labor power becomes wages, surplus value becomes profits, and production becomes a series of market exchanges. It is not that the perception of the social reality is false, but that the reality has two forms: its appearances and its real relations, or essence.

Lukacs locates the appearance/reality problematic within a definite historical stage of development: the capitalist mode of production. Althusser, on the other hand, transforms Lukacs's insistence on the historicity of the category of ideology into a structural principle. That is, he posits the imaginary relation of humans to the real and the *opacity* of the real relations as transhistorical, since this relation is rooted not in the commodity form but in the structural distinction between the language of appearances and the language of reality. Since these languages are ordered discourses that obey their own inner laws and are quite separate from each other, the deciphering task is finally a cognitive rather than a social and historical problem. The consequence of formulating the problem of ideology in these terms is to establish science as the only possible means by which ideology may be overcome. There are, for Althusser, no circumstances that may render social relations transparent to lived experience. We are *always* destined to live our lives ideologically, regardless of the social system.

Thus the ideological is *naturalized* by Althusser's structural binaries. On the one hand, he has abolished the myth of the "integrated civilizations" that for Lukacs was the basis for his critique of late capitalist society. The critique of ideology in Althusser's hands no longer relies on the assumption that transparent social relations may be experienced under any circumstances. Our relation to the real will always be problematic because of the incommensurability of symbolic order as discourse with the real; only science, by constructing a mechanism of knowledge ordered in the manner of the real by its structural, rather than empirical, homology may grasp the real. On the other hand, the implicit assertion of Althusser's theory of science is that what is real in *appearance* is rational.

As we have seen, Habermas, too, subscribes to a view that precludes a clear understanding of the ideological character of science and its methods. It is by returning to Gramsci's (1971) contributions that we can correct the limitations of Habermas and Althusser. Nevertheless, it is important to recognize the similarity between Gramsci and the structural conceptions of ideology advanced by Lukacs and Althusser. Gramsci's polemic is directed against those who would see ideology as a "reflex" of the economic base, a distorted image in the minds of persons and groups of underlying processes which have no effect on the base of society. Gramsci is attacking the pejorative use of the concept of ideology by insisting that it is "*necessary* to a given structure," not only because "ideologies mobilize human masses" but also because they create the terrain on which men move and acquire consciousness of their position. For Gramsci, ideology is the form of which material forces are the content of social structure, although this distinction between form and content has "purely didactic" value in his opinion since both are necessary and inconceivable without the other. So Gramsci refuses to see ideology as simply superstructural. At the same time he situates the ideological in the process of social life, in the sinews of politics and revolutionary action. But he also situates science within the same context:

> If it is true that man cannot be conceived of except as historically determined man—i.e., man who has developed, and who lives in certain conditions, in a particular social complex or totality of social relations, is it then possible to take sociology as meaning simply the study of these conditions and the laws which regulate their development? Since the will and initiative of men themselves cannot be left out of account, this notion must be false. The problem of what "science" itself is has to be posed. Is not science itself "political activity" and political thought, in as much as it transforms men and makes them different from what they were before? If everything is "politics" then it is necessary—in order to avoid lapsing into a wearisome and tautological catalogue of platitudes—to distinguish by means of new concepts between on the one hand the politics which correspond to the science which is traditionally called "philosophy" and on the other between the politics which is called political science in the strict sense. If science is the "discovery" of formerly unknown reality, is this reality not conceived of in a certain sense as transcendent? And does the concept of science as "creation" not then mean that it too is "politics"? Everything depends on seeing whether the creation involved is "arbitrary," or whether it is rational—i.e., "useful" to men in that it enlarges their concept of life, and raises to a higher level develops life itself. (Gramsci, 1971:244–245)

Much of Gramsci's conception of science was developed in a polemic against Bukharin's (1928) "popular manual" of Marxist "science" published in the Soviet Union in the 1920s. Here, Gramsci opposes Bukharin's repetition of the now orthodox view that science and ideology can be clearly separated, by showing that neither can the methodologies of the natural sciences be mechanically applied to the social sphere nor can science itself be abstracted from the totality of social relations that produce it. For Gramsci there is a distinction between ideology as the false conceptions of a few individuals and ideology and science as different sides of the material forces of historical change. According to Gramsci, science is a form of politics, i.e., an ideologue which "discovers" a formerly unknown reality, not as a discourse separate from the social and historical context that gives rise to it but as a function of that context.

Consistent with one line of Marxist theory of ideology, for Gramsci, every class that contends for political and social power generates ideologies that compete for "hegemony" within civil society and the state. The dominant class establishes its region over intellectuals who contend for moral and intellectual leadership in society with those of other classes, because no class may rule without the "spontaneous consent" given by the great masses to the general direction of social life which is shaped by the dominant social group. A class does not gain ascendancy arbitrarily, but because of its dominant position in production. While the proletariat cannot gain power, or achieve hegemony over the producers of ideologies, it can offer up its science against bourgeois science whose adequacy may be measured by the degree to which it can "uncover" reality (Gramsci, 1971).

In the sense in which ideology is deeply political, its close relation with science, which is also political, is evident. Since for Gramsci science is a *praxis*, that is, a set of material practices infused with the political ideologies of social classes which seek political, social, and economic hegemony over other social classes, the idea of the neutrality of science is simply not tenable. The proletariat, through praxis produces an ideology that becomes scientific because it unmarks the coercive basis of power. Gramsci locates the possibility of a Marxist science that can "transcend" the opacity of social reality in a praxis that is "interested" in emancipatory discoveries. But this creative process of discovery may not be construed as nonideological. Even if it arises as a critique of the dominant ideology, it is a type of political discourse, one that has a teleological element, and is limited by its historical and social circumstances.

The theory of hegemony—according to which systems of ideas are produced by dominant social groups or groups seeking power whose object is to create a new terrain "on which men move" to mobilize masses to struggle or not—I call the *general* theory of ideology. Ideology is not *only* produced by the metonymic extrapolation from the forms of appear-

ance of "real relations," which in Althusser's theory become materialized in social institutions that are self-reproductive (the famous concept of
ideological state apparatuses—religion, education, trade unions, the family). It is also produced by the process by which the ruling class or the
oppositional class in capitalist society gains hegemony over a group of
intellectuals who generate a language, a cognitive apparatus of investigation and understanding which expresses its specific relation to the world
and tends to reproduce it as "natural." The degree to which its language
and apparatus successfully penetrate the material world of society and
"nature" is an aspect of its collective relation to social life.

It remains for me to show *how* science is a form of social relations, for
even if Marcuse has already argued for the ineluctability of the relation
between science and technology and social domination, he has not provided us with a systematic, detailed explanation of the way in which its
own "methods and concepts [science] have promoted a universe in which
the domination of nature is linked to the domination of man" or the *way* in
which science is a form of ideology.

SCIENCE AND SOCIAL RELATIONS

If Althusser is correct that the theories, experimental method, and technique comprise the core of scientific knowledge, then one of the crucial
tasks for an argument that wishes to oppose the separation of science and
ideology is to show the ideological character of the *experimental method*
itself. The Copernican Revolution has been supposed by most writers on
the subject to consist in the first place of taking account of the observation
of nature in the development of scientific theory. Its *sufficient* contribution to the history of science has traditionally been understood as the
insistence that a scientific proposition can only be verified (falsified) by
means of experiment. However, as we will see, the experiment is an
ambiguous activity.

The presupposition of all science, according to Karl Popper (1936), is
that no scientific proposition may be said to be true unless it can be
falsified. This, a priori, is part of the apparatus of modern science and is
closely linked to what contemporary sciences means by theory: a theory
is a proposition that can be verified (falsified) by experiment/observation.

Now, observation is not the same as experiment in the commonsense
use of these terms. Observation usually implies the reception by the
senses of external phenomena. But for science, the term observation is
linked to experiment; the scientist observes effects of experiments or, to
be more exact, records results of experiments in statistical form. A theory
is an hypothesis that can be quantified by means of observing effects
recorded in numerical form. In this sense, the scientific observation of

human behavior, no less than the observation of microparticles, is concerned with effects which are presumed to be accurate reflections of the intrinsic properties of the object (which, it will be recalled, was exactly Althusser's definition of science in action).

The ambiguity of the experimental method becomes apparent when we remember that its preconditions include decisions about how the object of knowledge is to be constituted, not only by its classification according to levels and fields but also in the design of the experiment. It is commonplace among scientists to reduce the number of variables to be observed to the *least number possible* because the accuracy of the results is understood to be a function of this reduction. Thus, the second condition, after limiting variables, is to limit the observational field by decontextualizing the object so as to facilitate the project of predicting and controling behavior. I do not wish to dispute this procedure for the moment, but simply to point out that such decontextualization implies that the category of accuracy has already changed the concept of observation to conform to the requirement of prediction and control. What are observed are the effects of an experiment on an object under condition determined by the scientist. Of course, the scientist knows that decontextualization limits the claims resulting from the experiment, or its generalizability.

Experiment is a type of human activity, then, that is an *intervention* by the scientist (subject) into "objective" social processes. The forms of intervention entail the establishment of the context within which the object is observed, i.e., the machinery employed to produce the effects from which inferences are made according to theoretical presuppositions and from the rational-purposive basis of all modern knowledge. Heisenberg's (1958) indeterminacy principle attempted to preserve the objectivity of scientific theory by inserting the observer into the observational field and arguing for a science which recognized the problematic character of the results and included these in its calculation procedures as results. The instrument of observation must be taken into account in the measurement of the object as well as the determination of its position.

The philosophical implications of this argument have disturbed scientists and philosophers because of the revelation that the object of knowledge may be our relation with the object, not the thing itself. Most physicists have now been obliged to acknowledge that nature offers more than one option, depending upon the theoretical framework in which the experiment is conducted. Largely because of the development of quantum theory, modern theoretical physics, at least, has been forced to work with uncertainties. The experiment is one valid means of knowing the external world *provided* we understand that knowledge depends upon its theoretical presuppositions, which are taken as no more than possible explanations for the characteristics of matter.

A crisis in science has occurred because of the challenge posed by Heisenberg and others to its positivist assumptions, particularly the notion that the relation of the observer to the observed was unproblematic. When Heisenberg reduced to mathematical language the simple notion that what is observed depended on the apparatus of observation (the experiment), the scientificity of science was thrown into question.

Since we can only calculate effects and infer causes, control and predict behavior by constituting the object of knowledge theoretically and changing it in the process of our intervention, I would argue that the so-called "laws of nature" are better described as *laws of science*. Scientific theory describes the relation of humans to the object of knowledge, not necessarily the objects themselves. Further, our knowledge of effects is always mediated by the logic of scientific discovery, e.g., by its concepts of causality as a part of the apparatus of discovery.

The implications of modern developments in theoretical physics have called into question the positivist tradition since new ideas such "as co-existent states," "uncertainty of possibilities," and so on seem incongruous with the loss of contradiction and mutual exclusion. Heisenberg asserted that the logical principles that underly mathematical symbolization were no longer in a relation of simple correspondence to nature. This is evident in the concepts deriving from the theoretical ambiguity of physics, its noncorrespondence with nature, which Heisenberg has called the "limits of the correlation" between the older language of classical physics and the new concepts, soluble only if

> one confines the language to the description of facts, i.e., experimental results. However, if one wishes to speak of the atomic particles themselves one must either use the mathematical scheme as the only supplement to natural language or one must combine it with a language that made use of a modified logic or of no well-defined logic at all (Heisenberg, 1958).

When science digs into the area of "potentialities or possibilities" it has left the world of experimentally adduced facts or things, and the old logic must be abandoned.

If natural language is filled with meanings that defy precision and thus make control and prediction difficult, the language of control, mathematics, contains within it, a limit on science. The questions within scientific theory that imply a logic that defies the formal categories of space and time, and have renounced, however implicitly, the purposively rational, i.e., experimental basis of investigation, discover that ordinary language, precisely because of its undecidability, is more suited to these issues. Experimental methods whose results are formulated in purely quantitative terms may not be abandoned, but must be placed in a subordinate position to speculative science frankly concerned with a reconceptualization of all the fundamental presuppositions of the old science.

CONCLUSION

It is time to summarize the discussion of the relation of science and ideology. I will follow it by a discussion of the problem of the truth in relation to ideology.

My central thesis that science may not be considered a separate discourse from ideology depends on the following propositions:

1. The concept of the science/ideology antimony is itself ideological because it fails to comprehend that all knowledge is a product of social relations. Within capitalism, and particularly late capitalism, these relations are organized according to a division of labor (principally the division between mental and manual labor). The rational-purposive basis of social production under both capitalism and state socialism means that science as an aspect of the division of labor is subsumed under capital and/or the state. That is, its purpose, albeit unconscious, is to participate in reproducing the system of domination of the larger social order. This ideological function is revealed in at least five ways:

a. The choice of the object of knowledge or inquiry is determined by the complex of economic and political institutions such as corporations and the state, since these have a virtual monopoly of the means of scientific production and dictate, more or less completely, those projects that may be supported. This monopoly does not preclude funding occasional projects that depart, in one way or another (although never in toto) from the canon of normal science. But these are always relegated to exceptions whose function is to legitimate normal, incremental science. Kuhn's structure of science revolutions ascribes paradigmatic change to internal developments within science, particularly the relation of experimental results to accepted scientific laws. Since science as well as technology are entwined with the relation of power, these changes will always be constrained and configured by social and political influences.

b. But the end of corporate and state domination over science and technology is a necessary, but not sufficient, condition for an emancipatory scientific theory and practice. As Marcuse (1964) has reminded us, after centuries of reproduction of society according to division of classes and division of labor, we have internalized, even introjected, domination. Specifically, this means that the *object of knowledge* has been constituted according to the social division of scientific labor (physics, chemistry, biology, psychology, and human sciences) and these are considered separate objective levels of natural and social realtiy, rather than necessary, but partial, abstractions from the totality of social existence and have been historically formed. The object is constituted by a technical division of labor where specialization of tasks within a field determines the perception of the investigator, such that a fragment is defined as the object, taken out of its natural context for the purposes of study. The result of this fragmentation is to impute characteristics to an object, discovered under certain circumnstances but taken as intrinsic to the object.

c. Ways of knowing in contemporary science are ideological. The experimental method is not an "observation of nature" free of presuppositions. It assumes (1) that the abstraction of the object from its natural context is unproblematic and (2) that the intervention of the observer into the observed both by means of measurement which produce certain "effects" from which inferences are made, and producing "causes" of the effects such as electrical charges of certain frequency and magnitude in physics, inoculations into animals to produce symptoms from which causes are inferred, etc. The assumption of *intervention* is only part of the reflexivity of science to the extent that it tries to "correct" for its ingression. But the experimental method must be recognized as informed by its presupposition of rational-purposive action—that is, the control of nature and humans so that their action may be predicted. Its claim to value neutrality is vitiated by the degree to which behavioral hypotheses or symptomatic readings are endemic to scientific inquiry.

d. *The form of the results* of science are historically located in the formal logic of Aristotle which tried to understand forms of nature irrespective of their particular content. Galileo's doctrine that the "book of nature" was written in the language of mathematics was the logical culmination of this attempt to reduce nature to a form that permitted its predictability and control. But mathematics as the hegemonic form of scientific discourse constitutes a boundary of science. To the extent that knowledge is inextricably linked to language discourse, it generates a set, an internal unity that excludes those questions that require the language of ambiguity and that do not rationalize anomalies in terms that reduce *significations* to their technological dimensions. The separation of quantity from quality is linked to the divorce between means and ends. A society wishing to *use* the results of science to serve class-determined or class-mediated human ends requires science to take a form in which it may be infinitely fungible. Even if the ostensible purposes of research are not instrumental in the immediate uses of results, the quantification of results lends technical significance to the research. Under present conditions such technical uses are almost always connected to social and natural domination or profit.

e. The development of conventions that are legitimated and reproduced within the scientific community determines what is called truth and what is acceptable as science. These conventions are not separate from the paradigms of scientific knowledge which may be seen as both the presupposition and the outcome of the systematic requirement that certain traditions of inquiry, methods and forms of results be followed. The observance of the conventions are just the other side of the rituals and credentials that are precondition for entrance into the scientific community. No less than any other specialization in the division of labor, the scientific community regulates entrance requirements, conditions for membership maintenance, and power relation within the community. Since the entire machine of scientific investigation presupposes the social relations of the prevailing mode of production, the project of transforming science must be consonant with the project of transforming social relations.

2. The struggle for the transformation of ideology into science is a critical project in our period of late capital society. It proceeds on the foundation that the critique of all presuppositions of science and ideology must be the only absolute principle of science. A reflexive science is radically opposed to "normal science" that takes its epistemological and methodological foundation for granted.

Gouldner (1976) has offered a searching critique of Marxism, claiming that, while Marxism has been the reflexivity of bourgeois society, it has failed to be self-reflexive. This judgment is only partially true. Since the turn of the century, when it became apparent that capitalism had undergone a fundamental transformation in its structure and material and ideological practices, those who wished to preserve Marxism as a living socialist philosophy and critique of capitalist society have tried to comprehend the character of the changes and to discover their implications for Marxism itself. The Frankfurt School, which tried to integrate Freud and Weber within a Marxist framework, made a serious effort to challenge the theoretical presuppositions of Marxism in the light of historical changes. More recently, others have claimed that the historical condition that produced Marxism have been surpassed by the integration of the working class into late capitalist society. As I have shown above in my critique of Habermas, such positions do not constitute a critique of Marxism from within, but abolish its foundations by constituting a new scientific object. At the same time, whether in its French (the new philosophers) or German ("post-Marxian") manifestations, since it cannot identify the motive force of history (because it has abandoned the category altogether), it is left with a new positivism. For those who have abandoned class as a vital historical category, there are no conditions for the transformation of society. All critical theory may do is refine the categories of the eternal, reified present and wait for the "will" (or the learning capacity) of man to take care of the rest. But, Gouldner is right to point to the historicity of Marxism and its nineteenth-century insistence on the autonomy of science. For a revolutionary theory cannot be critical of itself if its highest aspiration remains to achieve scientificity in the traditional sense. It is this aspect of Marxism that has generated the post-Marxist antinomies as much as the changes of social condition within late capitalism and the deformations of state socialist societies.

3. Science and ideology have the same object—the material world that has been produced by social labor considered historically. All relations with this world are mediated by material and social structures and the concept of unmediated relations that may produce knowledges that are independent of the social processes by which they were acquired is the ideology of science that draws its inspiration from the bourgeois protest against feudalism. Since the relationships of science, magic, and religion are internal to one another because they all purport to offer adequate explanations for natural and social phenomena, it is rank ethnocentrism to claim that one may be privileged over the others without specifying the sociohistorical setting which under capitalism tends to subsume all discourse under its system of rational-purposive action. Within this framework, modern science becomes a partner of industrialization, whose social consequences have both liberated us from the brute struggle with nature and imprisoned us in a logic of domination and degradation.

4. If science is ideological, what is truth? My argument leads to the conclusion that truth is the critical exposition of the relations of humans to nature within a developing, historically mediated, context. Within this critical project, the form of appearance of social relations is a unidimensional rationality that implies particular conceptions of space and time, and causality, and construes the object of knowledge by socially determined criteria. The laws of science *are* the laws of nature providing one specifies the system of ratonality within which they are discovered. Their reified "natural" appearance remains opaque without the weapons of criticism: we can discover the external world as a product of the collective labor of centuries, not by observation, but by the construction of a series of concepts that are contradictory to the certainty of the senses that only report the surfaces. I am not claiming that Marxism is the only critical science. Normal science, particularly the study of microphenomena, has also contained a critical dimension but is not, in itself, critical. For example, the discovery of the atom, which was theoretized long before it was "observed," or the hypothesis of the psychic structure whose existence could only be inferred from a "reading" of symptoms. In the study of society Marx's theory of surplus value is, above all, a logical discovery.

NOTE

1. This article is extracted from a chapter of *Science, Technology and Marxism* (Boston: South End Press, forthcoming).

REFERENCES

Althusser, Louis
1968   For Marx. New York: Pantheon Books.
1971   Lenin and Philosophy. London: New Left Books.
Althusser, Louis, and Etienne Balibar
1970   Reading Capital. London: New Left Books.
Aronowitz, Stanley
1978   "Marx, Braverman and the logic of capital." Insurgent Sociologist 8:126–46.
Braverman, Harry
1974   Labor and Monopoly Capitalism. New York: Monthly Review Press.
Bukharin, Nikolai
1928   Historical Materialism. Moscow: Foreign Languages Publ. House.
Feyerabend, Paul
1976   Against Method. London: New Left Books.
Freud, Sigmund
1965   Civilization and Its Discontents. New York: Norton.
Gouldner, A.
1976   The Dialectic of Ideology and Technology. New York: Seabury.
Gramsci, Antonio
1971   Selections from the Prison Notebooks. New York: International Publ.
Habermas, Jurgen
1970   Toward a Rational Society. Boston: Beacon Press.
Horkheimer, Max
1947   Eclipse of Reason. New York: Oxford University Press.
Kosik, Karel
1976   Dialectic of the Concrete. The Hague: Mouton.
Kuhn, Thomas
1967   The Structure of Scientific Revolutions. Chicago: University of Chicago Press.
Lukacs, Georg
1967   History and Class Consciousness. London: Merlin Press.
Marcuse, Herbert
1964   One Dimensional Man. Boston: Beacon Press.
Marx, Karl
1964   The Economic and Philosophical Manuscripts. Moscow: Foreign Languages Publ.
        House.
Mepham, John
1974   "Theory of ideology in capital." Working Papers in Urban Studies.
Pierce, Charles S.
1955   "The fixation of belief." Selected Writings of C. S. Peirce, Justin Buehler (ed.).
        New York: Dover.
Popper, Karl
1936   The Logic of Scientific Discovery. London: Routledge & Kegan Paul.

TOWARD A MACRO-LEVEL THEORY OF SEXUAL STRATIFICATION AND GENDER DIFFERENTIATION

Janet Saltzman Chafetz

In recent years there has been a growing body of theoretical literature, largely the result of work by anthropologists and sociologists, that attempts to explain differences in the status of women relative to men cross-culturally and over time. Concurrently, a substantial body of literature has developed, produced primarily by psychologists and sociologists, which is oriented to the masculine and feminine gender roles. This literature is typically more ethnocentric and descriptive and less theoretical than that which concerns sexual stratification or the differential status of women and men. It is the intent of this paper to develop, on the basis of literature from both approaches, a unified, macro-level theory that has as its dependent variables both gender role differentation and sexual stratification.

The ideas presented in this paper draw heavily from ideas and data

Current Perspectives in Social Theory, volume 1, 1980, pages 103–125.

presented by Martin and Voorhies (1975), Blumberg (1978), and Nielsen (1978). The Nielsen and Blumberg books are short texts on social and sexual stratification which review a large number of anthropological and sociological studies pertaining to status differences between males and females. Each suggests a number of general propositions, either implicitly or explicitly, pertaining to the determinants of sexual inequality cross-culturally. Likewise, the anthropologists Martin and Voorhies suggest a number of such propositions in their monograph based both on ethnographies and on statistical data from the Human Area Relations File. Indeed, this work forms one important basis for the texts by both Blumberg and Nielsen. However, despite the fact that many of the components of the theory to be presented in this paper can be found in some or all of these works, nowhere are they pulled together and presented systematically, as one integrated theory. This project is oriented to just such a synthesis.

The theory to be presented treats men and women as internally undifferentiated general categories. Clearly, in any given society males and females may be sharply differentiated by class, ethnicity/race, and other social stratification variables. A wealthy woman, for instance, is in most ways superior in status to a poor man. Nonetheless, it is appropriate to compare the sexes as categories, ignoring other stratification variables, to the extent that women in any given society tend to share approximately the same position relative to men who are their peers in all ways except sex. Although this assumption underlies the theory presented here, its use is only heuristic. Generally, in class-stratified societies women in the upper strata are more sheltered, i.e., denied freedom of movement and contact outside the family, than women in the lower strata. Women in poor families often cannot afford to be absent from economically productive activities. In turn, as will be evident later, such activity contributes heavily to enhancing women's status relative to men's. As Van den Berghe (1973:98) states:

> [T]he status disparity between men and women in the upper class is frequently much greater than among the peasantry and working classes. Notwithstanding stereotypes, and an etiquette of "gallantry" to the contrary, upper class status for a woman is often a gilded cage in which she may share the material comfort and the leisure of the males of her class, but few of the freedoms enjoyed either by lower class women or by her male class equals.

In fact, women of high social class (and, in modern industrial, capitalistic societies, middle class women as well) often serve the function of symbolizing their male kin's (father's or husband's) social status through conspicuous leisure and conspicuous consumption (Veblen, 1953:229ff.). Ironically, such a role deprives them of power and status because of their male class peers, rendering them totally dependent on male support. To reiterate, however, despite such class differences in the status of women relative to men, for heuristic purposes the theory presented in this paper will focus on the sexes as two, and only two, categories, ignoring for the most part internal differentiation along class lines.

SEXUAL STRATIFICATION AND GENDER DIFFERENTIATION DEFINED

When a large number of different societies are examined, it is clear that there is extensive variation in the degree to which men and women within each have access to the scarce values of their community (Nielsen, 1978; Martin and Voorhies, 1975; Blumberg, 1978). These scarce values include political power and authority, consumer goods, services, social prestige, knowledge (education), freedom from restrictions not placed on all societal members (especially those concerning sexual expressions and physical movement), and opportunity for psychic enhancement and gratification (Nielsen, 1978:11–13). In all known human societies males are advantaged relative to females in their access to at least some of these values. Nowhere in human societies do we find that females are fully equal, not to mention superior to males in overall status (Nielsen, 1978: 39; Van den Berghe, 1973:53). The reason for this is not known but has been much speculated about (for reviews of such speculative "theories," cf., Hartmann, 1976; Martin and Voorhies, 1975:Chap. 6; Leibowitz, 1978). In this paper it is simply taken as a given, thus truncating the logically possible stratification range. However, societies do vary on a continuum between those that approach sexual equality and those in which males are vastly superior to females in their access to most of the scarce values of their community. Sexual stratification refers to the extent of difference between the overall status of women and men within a society.

Given the number and types of scarce values which may be entailed in the determination of overall status, precise measurement is probably not possible. One can measure with substantial precision such aspects of stratification as access to material rewards, educational opportunities, and formal political authority. However, other aspects, such as degree of access to psychic enrichment and gratification, and informal power, can at best, be roughly approximated. Thus, the composite measure of the gap between female and male status is, of necessity, loosely measured in each society. This lack of measurement precision, however, does not preclude gross comparisons. It is, in other words, possible to roughly categorize societies as approaching either equality or inequality or at a limited number of intermediate points on that continuum.

Societies also differ on the extent and degree to which males and females are *expected* to differ, regardless of whether or not they do in fact, on traits of behavior, personality, interest, and intellect. Gender stereotypes have been loosely lumped together under the rubric "gender roles" which, while probably a misnomer (cf., Chafetz, 1978:Chap. 1), is a conventional and convenient term. It is important to note, however, that the variable "gender differentiation" does not include the *specific* social roles assigned to men and women (e.g., particular work roles). Social roles, as contrasted with general expectations concerning behavior and psychic and intellectual traits, are treated in terms of other variables in this theory. It would therefore be tautological to include them in this dependent variable. In all known societies adult males and females confront different social expectations concerning their personal behavior and characteristics. There is, of course, wide variation cross-culturally in the definition of appropriate masculine and feminine traits and behaviors, with particular traits defined as masculine in one society and feminine in another, or as the province of neither or both sexes (cf., Mead, 1935, for examples of this). Moreover, and more importantly in this context, societies differ in the degree to which gender differentiation exists. At one extreme a society may assume very few categorical differences between the sexes (e.g., the Arapesh studied by Mead, 1935), while at the other extreme, the sexes are considered "opposite" each other (e.g., Victorian England).

Measurement of gender differentiation is, in fact, measurement of stereotypes (not necessarily real behavior) and, while precise information is lacking for many, if not most, cultures, the methodology is available potentially to measure this variable with considerable precision. It is important to note that the concept gender differentiation does not imply inequality. It is *logically* possible to talk about "separate (different) but equal." *Empirically,* it appears that "different" is strongly associated with unequal, that is, that degree of gender differentiation and degree of sexual stratification are highly correlated (Sanday, 1974). Conceptually, however, they are distinct variables and the fundamental theoretical issues involve explaining variations in each and the interaction between the two. The remainder of this paper is oriented toward those tasks.

ECONOMIC ORGANIZATION AND SEXUAL STRATIFICATION

The theory to be discussed in this paper is presented schematically in Figure 1. The linkages depicted in this chart and discussed in this paper are those thought to be of most importance in explaining the dependent variables. Clearly, most of the variables discussed are indirectly or directly related to one another. Many of these linkages are ignored for purposes of parsimony and comprehensibility.

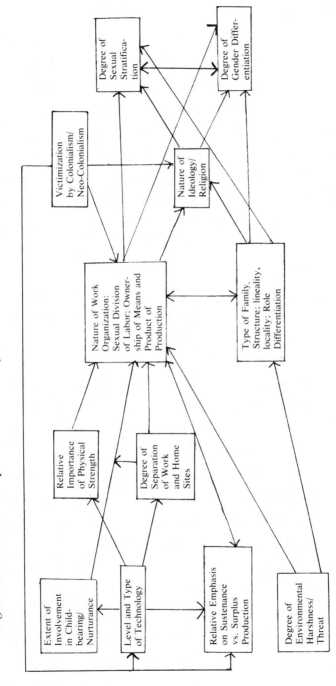

Figure 1. The Main Components of a Theory of Sexual Stratification and Gender Differentiation.

The most important variable in the entire theory is, in fact, a set of intervening variables which pertain to the manner in which the economic or productive activities of a society are organized. This composite variable includes three components: the sexual division of labor, ownership or control of the means of production, and ownership or control of the products of production.

The first, the division of labor by sex, concerns societal definitions of men's work versus women's work. The specific tasks are less important than two other features of labor division. First, in societies which produce little or no surplus, the extent of the contribution of each sex to acquiring or producing basic sustenance is important. Second, in societies which produce a surplus, the extent to which the activities of each sex contribute to that surplus, or exchange goods, is important. For reasons currently unknown, exchange (surplus) production is typically more highly valued everywhere than sustenance production (Neilsen, 1978:19). Thus, the sexual division of labor results in differential status in a three-tiered fashion. Women experience very low status relative to men if they produce little or nothing toward sustenance or exchange. They tend to receive almost equal status compared to men when their labor produces either half or more of the sustenance products in nonsurplus producing societies or a considerable proportion of the exchange goods in surplus producing societies. Other combinations tend to place women in an intermediate category of relative status. As Engels (1968:490) noted nearly a century ago:

> Peoples whose women have to work much harder than we would consider proper often have far more real respect for women than our Europeans have for theirs. The social status of the lady of civilisation, surrounded by sham homage and estranged from all real work, is socially infinitely lower than that of the hard-working woman of barbarism.

The other two components of the organization of work, which are highly interrelated, involve the ownership or, more importantly, the control of the means (including land as well as capital) and the products (including salaries or wages in cash-based societies) of production. In societies where labor involves sustenance production only, the degree to which women control the distribution of the products (mostly food) their labor produces will strongly influence their relative status. The means of production are typically simple (e.g., a stick, a container) and potentially available to all. The ability to grant or withhold the product, namely, the necessities of life, will therefore strongly influence the relative status of each sex. Where surplus production is developed, those who profit will be those who can choose the manner in which the surplus will be distributed, namely, the product owners. Often, the means of production involved in surplus production are elaborate and/or scarce (e.g., privately owned land, expensive machinery). There will be a strong tendency for those who are able to gain control over the means of production to also be able to control the product, regardless of whether or not their labor is involved in production (Nielsen, 1978:39). Thus, to the extent that the economic (and, as will be discussed later, family) organization places control of the means and/or product of production disproportionately in the hands of men, women's status will tend to be very low, while it will approach equality where women control the means and the product of their labor. Control over work products can mitigate the effects of the division of labor. Specifically, even if women produce most of the goods, if they do not control their distribution women's relative status will tend to be low (cf., Blumberg, 1978:Chap. 3; Van den Berghe, 1973:72).

These three components of work organization—sexual division of labor, control of the means of production, and control over the products of production—are influenced by several other factors. One of the important influences on the degree to which sex (if either) controls the means and products of production is family structure. This will be discussed in a later section. (Figure 1 shows several other direct and indirect influences on the composite variable work organization.)

CHILDBEARING AND NURTURANCE AND WORKSITE LOCATION

Societies differ in the average number of pregnancies women experience and the amount of time during which women are bound to the care of very young children, though the "breeder-feeder" roles are reserved for women in all societies (Boulding, 1976). Although in no known society have women ever averaged the biologically maximum number of births possible, at one extreme there are societies in which women are frequently pregnant and/or nursing children who, therefore, cannot be left by the mother for very long. Traditional agrarian societies often exemplify this extreme. At the other end of the continuum in societies such as our own today, women average few children, wean them early or bottlefeed them, which allows them to leave children in the care of others. At issue here is the average amount of the life cycle women in general devote to the care of their own children in a given society. Where the birth rate is high, that will usually be the bulk of the adult life span. Where it is low, a few adults, almost always women, can take care of the children of many women, allowing most to spend the bulk of their adult years in productive labor.

Societies also differ on the extent to which worksites are separated physically from homesites. At one extreme, in simple horticultural societies for example, the worksite may be contiguous with the residence. At the other extreme, many miles may separate the two, such as in modern industrial societies. To the extent that women are often pregnant and/or nursing, it is difficult for them to work *efficiently* long distances from their domicile. Some individual mothers may leave their offspring in the care of others, but women as a category will be curtailed in their productive efforts by their maternal responsibilities. Therefore, the greater the distance between worksite and home, *and* the greater the average number of pregnancies and/or breastfeeding children, the less involved women as a group are in productive activities (cf., Blumberg, 1978:26). To the extent that they are less involved in production, they are also less likely to control the means of production or the products that result. These phenomena, of course, lead to their lesser status relative to men.

Several authors (Nielsen, 1978:36–37); Martin and Voorhies, 1975: Chap. 9; Blumberg, 1978:50–52) have observed that women's status takes a severe plunge when agriculture replaced horticuture as a dominant economic activity of a society. Part of the reason for this is that the large fields characteristic of agricultural production, unlike horticultural plots, are typically far from home (Blumberg, 1978:50). It is interesting to note in this connection, the evolution of women's roles on Israeli kibbutzim. The initial effort to avoid a sex-based division of labor in these agrarian communities gradually failed, and over time the agricultural activities became increasingly male, the domestic and childrearing ones female. Presumably, pregnancy and lactation combined with distance between fields and nursery do produce this change (Van den Berghe, 1973:56). In turn, this change in women's productive role appears to have contributed to a decrease in their involvement in kibbutz political roles, and in their status generally.

TECHNOLOGY, PHYSICAL STRENGTH, AND WORKSITE

It is apparent that changing techpology directly influences the degree to which worksite and homesite are physically separated. Just as agriculture removes plant growing from proximity to domicile, industrialization removes the production of other products (e.g., clothes, processed foods, furniture) from home to factories. In fully industrialized societies there is almost total separation of the two sites.

Technological changes also affect the degree to which physical strength, of which men as a category possess more than do women, affects the organization of work. In hunting and gathering societies, the bulk of the food supply (as much as 80 percent) is often furnished by women gathering fruits, nuts, and grubs, and hunting small game (Boulding, 1976:96; Blumberg, 1978:6–7; Martin and Voorhies, 1975:Chap. 7). These activities, unlike the male job of pursuing large game with projectile weapons, require relatively little physical strength. Likewise, producing food with a digging stick or hoe, characteristic implements of horitcultural societies, requires no more strength than women typically possess. Heavy jobs, such as felling trees and clearing land, are typically masculine pursuits in such societies. With the development of the plow and the use of draft animals, physical strength becomes quite important to the basic production of food (Martin and Voorhies, 1975:282ff.; Nielsen, 1978:36). This, combined with the separation of home and work sites, accounts for the fact that with the development of agriculture, for the first time in human history men take over the vast proportion of production activities, hence control of the means and products of production. Women's status relative to men's is lowest in this type of society. With industrialization, the premium on physical strength diminishes and becomes largely irrelevant for most work activity. However, the effect of this on women's status is not great as long as women are tied to the vicinity of the domicile by frequent pregnancy and lactation. The development of an effective birth control technology and bottle feeding combine to begin a reversal in the trend that separates women from productive labor and thereby guarantees them a very low status relative to men.

ENVIRONMENT AND WORK ORGANIZATION

Degree of environmental threat or harshness is a compound variable consisting of two components. First, there is the physical environment: what level of exertion does it require for a group to "earn its living" in a given environmental niche? Clearly, as technology advances, difficult environments become less onerous, but at least when considering technologically simple societies this variable must be included. For instance, it is patently more difficult for a group lacking sophisticated technology to survive in the tundra or desert than in temperate climates and moderately vegetated terrains. The second component of this definition refers to the social environment: the extent to which a group is threatened by other groups of people.

The chief impact of environmental threat and harshness on sexual stratification is related to the effects on family structure. However, independent of that, environmental harshness does directly affect work organization. In cases of a harsh physical environment the search for food may entail extensive travel from homesite. While such groups tend to be nomadic (e.g., the Bedouin), there is nonetheless a premium on unfettered, rapid mobility in pursuit of game and/or grazing lands.

Males, who as discussed earlier have greater general mobility, would tend to monopolize the major productive activities. This in turn serves to increase the status difference between males and females (Martin and Voorhies, 1975:341).

FAMILY STRUCTURE AND SEXUAL STRATIFICATION

The chief components of family structure relevant to this theory are lineality and locality. In the final section the division of labor or degree of role specialization within the family is also considered. As a general proposition, it is safe to assert that women's relative status tends to be highest in cases of matrilineality and matrilocality (Blumberg, 1978:43–44; Martin and Voorhies, 1975:224–225; Schlegel, 1972:98, 101–102) and very low in cases of patrilineality and patrilocality (Nielsen, 1978:30). It is primarily under patrilineality, for instance, that women's sexuality is severely controlled in great excess of the control exercised over men's. Restricting women's sexuality to marriage insures known and "proper" paternity, necessary to patrilineality. Moreover, restrictions on women's sexuality are closely related to restrictions on their physical movement in public, which are designed to further insure premarital virginity and marital faithfulness. Other aspects of family structure and functioning, such as the institutions of bride price and dowry, and polygyny versus single wives, may be related to the status of women, but they are not central to explaining it. Indeed, they are probably better viewed as partial indicators of women's relative status rather than as causes of it.

In general, it also appears to be the case that the more women are involved in the important productive activities of their society, and the more they control the products of their labor, the less likely the family structure is to be patrilineal and patrilocal, hence the higher their relative status. All of the variables already discussed, which impact women's place in the organization of work, tend to also indirectly impact on family structure. Likewise, the variables discussed in this section pertaining to family structure shape the organization of work by sex. However, as will be evident in the next section, the main causal direction posited in this theory is from work organization to family structure.

TECHNOLOGY, SURPLUS, THE ORGANIZATION OF WORK, AND FAMILY STRUCTURE

The potential of a collectivity for producing an economic surplus, i.e., goods over and above those needed to sustain the lives of group members, is in large measure a function of its technology (Lenski, 1966). Following

Lenski's general schema, hunting and gathering societies lack the technological capacity to produce a surplus; horticultural societies may be able to produce a small surplus; agricultural societies can produce a larger one; and industrial societies produce still more. However, merely being technically able to produce surplus goods does not automatically mean that a society will do so. At least among horticultural societies, some "take life easy" and produce only that which is necessary to survive.

Sahlins (1972:Chap. 1) suggests that even hunting and gathering societies may produce little because they desire little, rather than because they are incapable of producing more. Other societies, however, work harder and produce a surplus (Blumberg, 1978:14, 35). As will become evident shortly, the reasons for such differences in cultural values pertaining to productivity versus leisure are under debate. However, irrespective of why, the fact that some societies pursue surplus production does have implications for work organization, family structure and consequently sexual stratification.

In hunting and gathering societies there is no strong emphasis on lineality and no consistent pattern of locality (Martin and Voorhies, 1974:186; Leibowitz, 1978:15). There are few, if any, goods to be passed on between generations and no compelling reason for either sex to typically dominate residence patterns (Nielsen, 1978:25). For instance, of 90 such societies studied by Martin and Voorhies, 56 were bilateral (1975:185). In such societies not only is there little social stratification, as Lenski (1966) points out, but there is minimal sexual stratification as well (Leibowitz, 1978; Martin and Voorhies, 1975:189; Boulding, 1976:96; Nielsen, 1978: 22, 25–26; Van den Berghe, 1973:73).

Among horticultural societies that do not produce a surplus, most are matrilineal and matrilocal. This type of society has the highest proportion of that family structure of any societal type (Blumberg, 1978:42; Schlegel, 1972:17). This results from the fact that women develop horticulture from their gathering activities and become the gardeners (Nielsen, 1978:26). Men's work in such societies consists of periodic hunting, the provision of political and religious leadership, and such occasional and relatively heavy horticultural tasks as those involved in clearing the land for new gardens to replace plots depleted by cultivation (Boulding, 1976:97). As the primary productive force and suppliers of much of the food supply, women have a presumptive right to control the means and products of horticultural production. This, in turn, encourages matrilineality, based on passing the land down through the line that uses it—women (Aberle, 1974:655–730). Moreover, women work collectively in gardening and the most cohesive work groups are those based on blood kinship and lifelong acquaintance. This encourages matrilocality, a structure which keeps related women together (Martin and Voorhies, 1975:220ff.; Nielsen, 1978:30).

Family structure is more diversified among horticultural societies which produce a surplus, especially for trade. Sahlins (1972:Chap. 3) suggests that more complex family structures create the impetus for surplus production for purposes of trade. Regardless of the direction of causality, to produce a surplus with a relatively simple technology, men must often become involved more directly in food-raising. Stated otherwise, the more a society wishes to produce, the less it can afford idleness by either sex (cf., Sahlins, 1972:Chap. 2). With the greater involvement of males comes the lesser justification for matrilineality and matrilocality and an increase in the number that are patrilineal and patrilocal or organized in an intermediate fashion (Nielsen, 1978:29–30). In some cases women may be reduced to mere laborers. They work their husband's (or father's) land and turn the produce over to the male line for distribution. In such cases polygyny also becomes highly advantageous. Men with several wives have several laborers working to produce a surplus which will belong to them and their kin. In these societies wives create wealth for husbands (cf., Blumberg, 1978:37; Boserup, 1970; Nielsen, 1978:31). Regardless of whether or not they go to this extreme, the emphasis on surplus production decreases matrilineality and matrilocality, hence the relative status of women who no longer have a monopoly control over the means and products of production (cf., Schlegel, 1972:80; Martin and Voorhies, 1975:233ff.). On the basis of less information, Engels concluded in a similar vein that lineage patterns changed from female- to male-dominated as the wealth of the community increased (1968:495).

Sahlins (1972:Chap. 3) argues that in horticultural societies, the development of political authority which overarches individual domestic units contributes to an increased emphasis on surplus production. The chief, or "big man," and other leaders use their authority to encourage the development of a surplus to be used for their further status aggrandizement. Political authority appears to be nearly universally a male-dominated activity; the existence of ancient matriarchy has yet to be demonstrated empirically and thus remains in the status of the mythical (Van den Berghe, 1973:53). The theoretical question here is a classic chicken-and-egg issue: which comes first, surplus production which involves males to a greater extent, thus creating male-dominated lineage and political structures, or male-dominated political and kin structures which encourage surplus production? From the point of view of the theory presented in this paper, Sahlins's argument offers no mechanism to explain the evolution from nonsurplus, matrilineal, matrilocal horticultural societies to patriarchal, surplus producing, politically more complex societies. To the extent that males do not control, and indeed are relatively secondary in the productive activities of their society, upon what basis would they be able to develop kinship and political authority? In other words, the theory presented here reverses Sahlins's causal chain. While agreeing that surplus production is related to more complex and male-dominated family and political structures, it is postulated that such structures arise as a result of greater male participation in production activities which, in turn, arises from efforts to produce a surplus. However, once in existence, it is altogether likely that the new structures further spur surplus production. Why a society pursues surplus production initially is still not known, however.

With the advent of agriculture comes a much increased emphasis on surplus production. As a result, men replace women as producers of basic commodities and as traders of surplus in the cities (Blumberg, 1978:50–52; Nielsen, 1978:35–37; Martin and Voorhies, 1975:283). Due to economic considerations not directly relevant to this theory, the family structure tends to become neo-local and bilateral, but women do not benefit in status from the decline of strict patrilineage and patrilocality (Nielsen, 1978:37). In fact, it is in agricultural societies that women's relative status is lowest, with practices such as foot-binding, veils and masks, purdah, suttee, and dowry (Blumberg, 1978:52; Nielsen, 1978:37; Martin and Voorhies, 1975:29ff.). In agricultural societies women, like men, may be isolated from kin, but women alone are isolated from productive labor and public life. Of course, such isolation is most severe among the wealthy. Poor women are often required to play a more productive role if their families are to survive. Be that as it may, in agrarian societies women's function comes closer to being limited to that of "breeder-feeder" and domestic than in any other type (cf., Martin and Voorhies, 1975:294–296). It is interesting to note that Lenski (1966) argues that agricultural societies are also the most highly class stratified.

While industrialization further increases the emphasis on surplus production, it also produces countervailing tendencies which are, in toto, stronger in their effects on the status of women. Geographical mobility of the family becomes important, increasing the tendency to neo-locality and the separation of both males and females from kin. Bilateral descent is further strengthened by the fact that most members of industrial societies do not accumulate goods directly related to the discharge of their offspring's work (e.g., land for farmers, tools for artisans); they accumulate liquid assests. They are more able to pass along a substantial part of their inheritance to daughters without endangering their son's class position. In addition, access via kinship to some forms of material wealth, or to educational opportunities, is typically greater for women in industrial societies than in agricultural ones. Moreover, declining birth rates and the decrease in emphasis on physical strength in productive activities enable women to increase their contribution to the production of an economic surplus. In fact, in advanced industrial societies such as our own today, the labor power of a substantial proportion of adult women is required in service occupations, which are highly labor intensive.

Stated otherwise, in highly advanced technological societies, there is increased demand for female labor power to supplement male labor (cf., Oppenheimer, 1970). Just as males were "pulled into" more productive labor to supplement female labor when horticultural societies began to produce a surplus, females are "pulled into" more productive labor as industrialized societies increasingly devote more resources to the production of services for exchange value. The same principle applies in both cases: the push to produce additional wealth requires additional labor power which, in turn, is drawn from the heretofore less economically productive sex.

As a result of these factors, women's relative status is somewhat higher in industrial societies compared to agricultural—at least after a "lag time" during the early stages of industrialization. This partial reduction in the degree of sexual inequality parallels an overall reduction in class stratification posited by Lenski (1966). However, like classes, the sexes remain highly unequal. In terms of sex stratification, this is because, at least in large measure, their dual roles as surplus producers and "breeder-feeders" prevent women from competing on an equal basis with single-role males, who can devote full attention to their productive role (Nielsen, 1978:61). Irrespective of the type of political economy ("communist," "socialist," "capitalist") women in industrial societies remain unequal to men in status (Martin and Voorhies, 1975:402–405; Van den Berghe, 1973:73).

Before continuing with an explication of the theoretical model developed in this paper, a point of clarification is in order. At least since Engels wrote his famous essay on "The Origin of the Family, Private Property and the State" in 1884, communists, socialists, and today many radical feminists as well, have argued that the root of sexual inequality is to be found in private property and the development of class stratification. As a logical corollary to this assertion, the abolition of private property, the institution of class inequality, should eventuate in sexual equality as well. The logic of the argument developed in this paper does not totally contradict this position. Rather, it views sexual inequality as more complex in origin. It is posited that a major factor in the development of sexual inequality is indeed the development of economic surplus (i.e., "wealth") which is closely related to the development of class systems. However, this model postulates a number of other important factors related causally to sexual inequality, independently of this one. The logic of this approach is that the abolition of private property is certainly not *sufficient* to result in sexual equality, a stance supported to date by the empirical evidence from socialist/"communist" societies. Whether or not the abolition of private property is even a *necessary* precondition to sexual equality today is not clear.

ENVIRONMENT AND FAMILY STRUCTURE

It has already been noted that in some cases the physical environment affects sexual stratification because of its impact on the organization of work by sex. Both harshness of physical environment and social threat directly shape the structure of the family, and thus again the relative status of women.

In physical or social situations, where group survival is threatened or problematic, there seems to be a premium on male group cohesiveness (Martin and Voorhies, 1975:222–223,234). Just as matrilocality and matrilineality enhance female group solidarity, so too do patrilineality and patrilocality enhance male group solidarity (Nielsen, 1978:30). In other words, males tied together by blood kinship and lifelong acquaintance work together more cooperatively and with less competition and hostility than nonkin males. Whether for purpose of waging war (overwhelmingly a male task), or doing strenuous labor to gain sustenance or produce a surplus, cohesive male groups, hence patrilineality, patrilocality, and a relatively low status for women, seem to be necessary (Martin and Voorhies, 1975:223). One can only speculate as to why male solidarity is required in these cases. On the one hand, one can suppose that the greater physical strength and mobility of males contribute strongly to this phenomenon. This is probably the case in terms of a harsh physical environment, as suggested earlier. On the other hand, and especially in terms of males monopolizing warfare, one could posit greater innate aggressiveness on the part of males. Whatever the reason, cross-cultural data provided by Martin and Voorhies (1975) demonstrate that in conditions of chronic threat or harshness, the family structure is typically male-dominated and the overall status of women low.

It is interesting to note that even in a nation where women do participate in the military and where the government sponsors a general ideology of sexual equality, war resulted in a temporary decline in the status of women. In their study of the impact of the Yom-Kippur War on the status of Israeli women, Bar-Yosef and Paden-Eisenstark (1977) note that females, who are not permitted to participate in actual combat, were temporarily forced into traditional roles and suffered a short-lived setback in the quest for equality. A much more extreme example of the negative impact of militarism and war on the relative status of women can be seen in the case of Nazi Germany, where official government doctrine explicitly rejected extrafamilial roles for women, excluding them from virtually all positions of power or influence (Rupp, 1977). Perhaps the most striking indicator of the status of women during war is the treatment of them by victorious armies. In her classic book on rape, Brownmiller (1975:25–26) argues:

> War provides men with the perfect psychologic backdrop to give vent to their contempt for women. The very maleness of the military—the brute power of weaponry exclusive to their hands, the spiritual bonding of men at arms, the manly discipline of orders given and orders obeyed . . . confirms for men what they long suspect, that women are *peripheral, irrelevant to the world that counts,* passive spectators to the action in the center ring. (Emphases provided)

It might be noted also that the bulk of the major empires that have existed historically have been rooted in agrarian societies (e.g., Greek, Roman, Chinese, Spanish). Empire-building societies are fundamentally militaristic. This fact may contribute further to the other factors, already noted, which result in agrarian societies being characterized by the lowest relative status for women of any societal type.

The degree of sexual stratification is largely explained by the variables already discussed, primarily the organization of work as it is shaped by a number of variables, and secondarily by family structure as it results from work organization and other variables. Two other sets of variables may directly or indirectly influence sexual stratification as well, and it is to those that attention is now turned.

IDEOLOGY AND RELIGION

The model posits the view that the thought system of a society will tend to support both its basic organization of work and its characteristic family structure, thus indirectly supporting the degree of sexual stratification. In addition, perhaps typically, the dominant political and/or cultural ideology and religion will explicitly support the sexual stratification system with rules pertaining to the rights, obligations, and prescribed and postscribed behaviors and rewards of each sex. In this they explicitly reinforce gender differentiation as well as sexual stratification.

There is one general type of case in which the dominant religion and/or ideology may not reflect basic family and economic structures, hence the relative status of women. This type of case exists where a society is dominated by an external force which imposes its religion and ideology, among other things, on the dominated group. In recent centuries the most obvious cases of this were colonialism of Third World societies by Western nations. It also seems apparent that in societies where work organization and family structure are in the process of change, the religious and ideological systems may lag, thereby contradicting rather than reflecting current socioeconomic realities. Finally, in recent years there is an increasing tendency for official government ideologies to support sexual equality, often without sufficient strutural change to bring about such equality. The experience of the Soviets demonstrates that such an ideology does not, in and of itself, insure equality (Lapidus, 1976; Martin and Voorhies, 1975:371–381).

COLONIALISM AND NEOCOLONIALISM

When Western nations colonized much of the rest of the world, they brought with them a religion and set of beliefs which reflected the agrarian social structure which spawned Christianity and which had recently characterized their own societies. Regardless of the particular brand of Christianity, women were defined as distinctly different from and inherently unequal to men. Male dominance of the world of work, indeed all aspects of public life, was assumed by Westerners (cf., Martin and Voorhies, 1975:297–300). Female sexuality was sharply controlled, placing a premium on such things as modesty, premarital virginity, and marital monogamy. Depending on the particular society colonized, these views may or may not have had the same relationship to the status of women as the indigenous belief system. Where the colonized group was hunting and gathering or horticultural, there was probably considerable discrepancy; where it was agricultural there probably was not. Regardless, in many instances (e.g., Latin America) the religious and ideological system of the colonizers was forced on the indigenous population. In virtually all instances substantial missionary work oriented to voluntarily converting the local population was conducted with greater or lesser success.

Had only the belief system been exported to colonized nations it is possible that their sexual stratification systems would have changed little. However, many societies in which women had relatively high status compared to men (especially in Africa where many societies were horticultural) experienced a sharp decline in the relative status of women. This resulted from the impact of the Westerners on the local technology, emphasis on surplus production, and organization of work (Boserup, 1970; Martin and Voorhies, 1975:297ff.).

The primary motivating force behind colonization was profit-seeking. Western nations sought cheap raw materials, food, and new markets. Clearly, to meet these purposes the colonized society had to produce goods for export. Many subsistence societies were converted into producers of surplus or exchange foods which, as discussed earlier, typically entail a decline in women's status. Horticultural societies were encouraged to adopt the technology and productivity of agricultural production, often to the detriment of women. Moreover, on the basis of ethnocentric beliefs, the new technology was given by Westerners to males, who may never have worked the land. This left the female horticulturalists to continue lower status subsistence activity while men gained status through exchange production, or to withdraw from production thereby experiencing further status loss. The new occupational opportunities created by the colonizers, in the mines, on large plantations, in the military, and in the cities, were overwhelmingly given to males, who thus became part of the modernized, Westernized sector of the economy and were in an advantaged position to dominate when independence came. In short, the division of labor changed in many cases of colonization, mostly to the disadvantage of women, because of the direct activities of the colonizers, the impact of technological changes introduced by the colonizers, and often because of the shift from sustenance to surplus production (Martin and Voorhies, 1975:298ff.; Boserup, 1970; Draper and Cashdan, 1975). It is interesting to note an exceptional case where colonization did not serve to reduce the status of women. In Java, both women and men were recruited by the Dutch into export production, thus maintaining their equal economic contributions from precolonial days (Stoler, 1977).

The impact of neo-colonialism on sexual stratification is more subtle but depends basically on the same types of phenomena evident under colonialism. Neo-colonialism entails an asymmetric relationship between economically and technologically more advanced and less advanced societies. The asymmetry involved is twofold. First, it is in the form of dependence of the less advanced nation on the more advanced for markets for relatively inexpensive raw materials, foodstuffs, and labor-intensive finished goods. Second, it entails dependence by the less advanced nation on the more advanced for the provision of relatively expensive, sophisticated, manufactured goods and technology. According to dependency theorists, the effect of neo-colonialism is general poverty for most members of the less advanced society. Moreover, women, and especially working-class and poor women, typically fare much worse than their class equals among men in such societies (Boulding, 1976:104; Elliott, 1977; Arizpe, 1977).

In order to export enough to begin to keep up with the costs of imports, such societies must do two things: maintain low wages in labor-intensive production, and become maximally efficient in the production of exportable raw materials and foodstuffs. The low paid, insecure, low prestige, labor-intensive jobs are open to women (e.g., clothing manufacture in Taiwan, cf., Kung, 1976). Other positions in the formal economy often become the preserve of men who, under colonialism, had been preferred and trained for them and which, at any rate, sometimes require strength and mobility (e.g, military, mining, and large-scale agriculture). Urbanization often outpaces industrialization in these societies. Jobs being relatively scarce, women's opportunities are kept very limited, especially in white-collar positions, males being assumed to need the income more (Papanek, 1977:16). The only other major economic opportunities for most women in these societies are those in the "informal economy"

(Arizpe, 1977; Chinchilla, 1977)—prostitution, street-vending, domestic service, bar-girl—which are low in status and pay (and often are not counted in the GNP or employment figures), or as subsistence, rural horticulturalists in a economy which is increasingly urbanized and based on cash. In any case, women are largely removed from, or prevented from entering, the central productive roles, if indeed they are able to fill any economic role at all. Vasquez de Miranda (1977), for instance, demonstrates the decline of female labor force participation in Brazil which has accompanied development, while Arizpe (1977:31) documents the increasing unemployment rate of women relative to men in Mexico.

DEGREE OF GENDER DIFFERENTIATION

To this point, except to mention the effects of ideological and religious systems on gender differentiation, this dependent variable has been ignored. Nielsen (1978:120–121) suggests that gender "roles" may not be stable traits of personality, as they are often viewed by psychologists and sociologists alike. Rather, they may more fruitfully be viewed as the situational results of the performance of specific social roles. "Although socialization and its effects may set outer limits to behavior, the social role being played may dictate which learned behaviors are expressed at any given time" (Nielsen, 1978:120–121). From this perspective, mothers aren't nurturant because of a deep-seated trait of nurturance that females learn (or have innately); rather, women act in nurturant fashion when they play the concrete role of mother. Likewise, men may act competitively because they are in a competitive role at work or in sport, but would not necessarily do so when fathering.

Given this approach, one can assume that the extent to which women and men do different tasks, play widely disparate concrete social roles, strongly influences the extent to which the two sexes develop and/or are expected to manifest widely disparate personal behaviors and characteristics. Two of the most important potential sources of role specialization are the family and the organization of work. The less differentiated the roles of men and women in these contexts, the less one would expect to find gender differentiation, as well as ideological or religious support for such differentiation. Moreover, it is likely that the more that men, relative to women, play the major productive roles in a society, the more role differentiation there is within the family, which becomes defined as exclusively the woman's "sphere." For instance, where both sexes are expected to participate in production, you would not be likely to find women (but not men) defined as passive or dependent, as you do in any societies where women are seldom involved in productive work. An example of this are the fewer stereotypes of women as passive and dependent among American blacks where more married, as well as single, women are expected to work outside the home, compared to white married women (Ladner, 1972; Yorburg, 1974). Similarly, where men and women have similar parenting roles, such as among the Arapesh (Mead, 1935), both are viewed as nurturant, a trait thought to be weak or lacking in men in those societies where they don't care for children, such as our own at least until recently.

In addition to social role structures influencing gender differentiation, so too does differential status. Students of social stratification and of minority–majority relations have often posited a series of personality and behavioral consequences of subordination. Unger (1977:17) has argued that differences in degree of power or status are a better predictor of behavior than sex (see also Henley, 1977; Meeker and Weitzel-O'Neill, 1977; Kanter, 1976). However, by definition the greater the sexual stratification, the more males and females are differentiated in relative status and power, and the greater their behavioral differences. In short, the greater the sexual stratification, the greater the gender differentiation.

Finally, a system of relatively sharp gender differentiation will tend to buttress a high degree of sexual stratification. The traits which result from inferior status tend to weaken the ability of those who have them in terms of fulfilling social roles that result in higher status. Even if those of lower status do not possess such attributes, they will be assumed to and will be treated as if they in fact do. In such manner a self-fulfilling prophecy is created. Degree of sexual stratification and degree of gender differentiation are mutually interacting and supporting phenomena.

CONCLUSIONS

A general, macro-level theory explaining variation in sexual stratification and gender differentiation has been presented. The model is not exhaustive. Undoubtedly, other variables could have been included. For instance, nothing has been said concerning access to educational opportunities, a variable that might be expected to be important in both industialized and contemporary "developing" societies. This omission is predicted on the assumption that differential access to education *reflects* (and subsequently reinforces) the existing organization of work and gender differentiation patterns of a society. Therefore, it is not an important *causal* variable to be included in the theory. Indeed, access to educational opportunities was mentioned as one among many components of the dependent variable sexual stratification. It would thus be tautological to include it as a separate variable.

This theory, as noted, treats men and women as internally undifferentiated categories. It is important to emphasize that, as a result, the theory is not relevant to explaining intrasocietal differences in the statuses and roles of men and women. For instance, one should not deduce from the theory statements such as: employed wives will have higher status relative to men than their nonemployed counterparts in a given society. Regardless of the veracity of such a statement, it is not related to the substance of this macrotheory, which addresses relative sexual status and gender differentation among total societies.

This model is equally applicable to studying change in the dependent variables over time and to examining differences cross-culturally. It serves to summarize a considerable amount of literature from anthropological studies of simple societies, sociological studies of industrial and Third World societies, and social psychological studies of gender role stereotypes. Finally, it has clear ramifications for public policy oriented to the achievement of sexual equality. Equal status and the minimization of gender differentiation, themselves inseparable, cannot be achieved without first creating the demographic and technological conditions and family structures necessary for women to participate equally with men in the productive enterprises of their society. In the absence of such basic structural changes, no amount of rhetoric, no amount of value or attitude change, no quantity of antidiscrimination laws will achieve sexual equality.

ACKNOWLEDGMENTS

I would like to thank Rosalind Dworkin and Helen Ebaugh for their helpful comments on earlier drafts of this manuscript.

REFERENCES

Aberle, David D.
1974 "Matrilineal descent in cross-cultural perspective." Pp. 655–730 in David M. Schneider and Kathleen Gough (eds.), Matrilineal Kinship. Berkeley: University of California Press.
Arizpe, Lourdes
1977 "Women in the informal labor sector: the case of Mexico City." Signs 3:25–37.
Bar-Yosef, Rivka Weiss, and Dorit Paden-Eisenstark
1977 "Role system under stress: sex roles in war." Social Problems 25:135–45.
Blumberg, Rae Lesser
1978 Stratification: Socioeconomic and Sexual Inequality. Dubuque, Iowa: Brown.
Boserup, Ester
1970 Woman's Role in Economic Development. London: Allen & Unwin.
Boulding, Elise
1976 "The historical roots of occupational segregation." Signs 1:94–117.
Brownmiller, Susan
1975 Against Our Will: Men, Women and Rape. New York: Bantam Books.
Chafetz, Janet Saltzman
1978 Masculine/Feminine or Human? Itasca, Ill.: Peacock.

Chinchilla, Norma
   1977   "Industrialization, monopoly capitalism, and women's work in Guatemala."Signs
          3:38–56.
Draper, Patricia, and Elizabeth Cashdan
   1975   "!Kung women: contrasts in sexual egalitarianism in foraging and sedentary con-
          texts." Pp. 77–109 in Rayna Reiter (ed.), Toward an Anthropology of Women.
          New York: Monthly Review Press.
Elliott, Carolyn M.
   1977   "Theories of development: an assessment." Signs 3:1–8.
Engels, Frederick
   [1884] "The origin of the family, private property and the state." Pp. 455–593 in Karl
   1968   Marx and Frederick Engels, Selected Works. New York: International Publ.
Hartmann, Heidi
   1976   "Capitalism, patriarchy, and job segregation by sex." Signs 1:137–69.
Henley, Nancy
   1977   Body Politics: Power, Sex and Nonverbal Communication. Englewood Cliffs,
          N.J.: Prentice-Hall.
Kanter, Rosabeth Moss
   1976   "The impact of hierarchial structures on the work behavior of women and men."
          Social Problems 23:415–30.
Kung, Lydia
   1976   "Factory work and women in Taiwan: changes in self-image and status." Signs
          2:35–58.
Ladner, Joyce
   1972   Tomorrow's Tomorrow: The Black Woman. Garden City, N.Y.: Doubleday.
Lapidus, Gail Warshafsky
   1976   "Occupational segregation and public policy: a comparative analysis of American
          and Soviet patterns." Signs 2:119–36.
Leibowitz, Lila
   1978   Females, Males, Families: A Biosocial Approach. North Scituate, Mass.: Duxbury
          Press.
Lenski, Gerhard
   1966   Power and Privilege: A Theory of Stratification. New York: McGraw-Hill.
Martin, M. Kay, and Barbara Voorhies
   1975   Female of the Species. New York: Columbia University Press.
Mead, Margaret
   1935   Sex and Temperment in Three Primitive Societies. New York: Dell.
Meeker, B.D., and P.A. Seitzel-O'Neill
   1977   "Sex roles and interpersonal behavior in task-oriented groups." American Soci-
          ological Review 42:91–105.
Nielsen, Joyce
   1978   Sex in Society: Perspectives on Stratification. Belmont, Calif.: Wadsworth.
Oppenheimer, Valerie K.
   1970   The Female Labor Force in the United States. Berkeley: University of California
          Press.
Papanek, Hanna
   1977   "Development planning for women." Signs 3:14–21.
Rupp, Leila J.
   1977   "Mother of the Volk: the image of women in Nazi ideology." Signs 3:362–79.
Sahlins, Marshall
   1972   Stone Age Economics. Chicago: Aldine-Atherton.

Sanday, Peggy R.
1974   "Female status in the public domain." Pp. 189–206 in Michelle Zimbalist Rosaldo and Louise Lamphere (eds.), Women, Culture and Society. Stanford, Calif.: Stanford University Press.

Schlegel, Alice
1972   Male Dominance and Female Autonomy. New Haven, Conn.: Human Relations Area Files, Inc.

Stoler, Ann
1977   "Class structure and female autonomy in rural Java." Signs 3:74–89.

Unger, Roda K.
1977   "The rediscovery of gender." Paper presented at the Eastern Psychological Association Meetings, Boston.

Van den Berghe, Pierre
1973   Age and Sex in Human Societies: A Biosocial Perspective. Belmont, Calif.: Wadsworth.

Vasquez de Miranda, Glaura
1977   "Women's labor force participation in a developing society: the case of Brazil." Signs 3:261–74.

Veblen, Thorstein
[1889] The Theory of the Leisure Class. New York: Mentor Books.
1953

Yorburg, Betty
1974   Sexual Identity: Sex Roles and Social Change. New York: Wiley.

THE UTILITY OF EVOLUTIONARY THEORY FOR THE SOCIAL SCIENCES

Saul Feinman

Recently, popular publicàtions have noted that adults who were adopted as children seek to find out the identity of their biological parents. Social scientists might attribute this desire to the effects of social influence that is applied by nonadopted individuals who wonder out loud how the adoptee could live without such knowledge. Or, the search might be seen as part of the quest for self-knowledge and self-identity. Alternatively, its motivation might be assigned to curiosity.

In contrast, an evolutionist might say that the adopted child's behavior increases inclusive fitness, which is the combination of one's own and one's relatives' reproductive and rearing success. Knowledge of the identity of consanguinal relatives is a prerequisite for adaptive (i.e., inclu-

Current Perspectives in Social Theory, volume 1, 1980, pages 127–159.
Copyright © 1980 by JAI Press Inc.
All rights of reproduction in any form reserved.
ISBN: 0-89232-154-7

sive) fitness, inducing patterns of kin altruism. The adoptee is seeking the identity of those persons upon whom he could more adaptively bestow altruism. Terms such as *inclusive fitness* and *kin altruism* are central concepts in the evolutionary analysis of human social behavior, although they are rather alien to contemporary social science.

Genetic evolutionary theory focuses on the reproductive and rearing consequences of behavior. Other social science answers for the adoptee's behavior—curiosity, self-identity, social construction of reality, and social influence—would not be rejected, but rather, would stimulate questions of how these motivations affected reproduction and rearing. For evolutionary theorists, social science explanations beg rather than answer the central questions. The invocation of curiosity as a motivator might lead the evolutionist to wonder whether curiosity is present because it gave its bearers greater reproductive and rearing success than did a non-curious approach to the world. If curious people know more, and if knowledge increases reproductive and rearing chances, then curiosity may have become more common than disinterest because curious adults produced and reared more curious children than disinterested adults produced and reared disinterested children.

The interest in reproductive and rearing consequences is based on the assumption that behaviors are influenced by mechanisms that either are genetic or function as if they are. A behavior increases in relative frequency if its bearers reproduce and rear more offspring with that behavioral trait than do individuals with alternative tendencies. The concentration on reproduction and rearing success is unusual in contemporary social science theory. Therefore, is genetic evolutionary theory a useful perspective for social scientists?

Genetic evolutionary theory, the synthesis of Darwinian concepts of natural selection and adaptation with modern genetics, is a major paradigm in biology, but it has rarely been applied to humans. In the last five years, some biologists (Barash, 1977a; Wilson, 1975) have suggested that human social behavior could be fruitfully considered within this perspective. Wilson (1977) suggests that this perspective is more profitably applied to nonliterate societies than to the large complexes of industrial states, while others (Dawkins, 1976) believe that human behavior's large cultural component removes it from the realm of evolutionary theory.

While social scientists generally ignore or are critical of this evolutionary approach, others not only advocate it (Barkow, 1978; Van den Berghe, 1974) but have also engaged in evolutionary research on various social behaviors. These studies have focused on nonindustrial societies, considering territoriality (Dyson-Hudson and Alden-Smith, 1978), primitive warfare (Durham, 1976a), food sharing (S. Feinman, 1979), human kinship (Van den Berghe and Barash, 1977), inheritance patterns and lineage (Greene, 1978; Hartung, 1976; Kurland, forthcoming), conformity (Barkow, 1977), and social status (Irons, 1979).

In addition to general criticisms of evolutionary theory, e.g., comments in the *American Sociological Review* in the wake of Van den Berghe's (1974) "Bringing Beasts Back In," more pointed criticisms have been made. Sahlins (1976) has criticized the evolutionary explanation of how altruistic behavior might become prevalent. Altruistic behavior is behavior which increases the reproductive and rearing success of the recipient at the expense of the donor. The selection for altruistic behavior lies in the assumption that altruistic individuals are more likely to help their kin and other individuals. Thus, altruistic behavior is selected for because of the beneficial consequences for relatives of altruists (who also are likely to be altruistic), which outweigh the deleterious outcomes for the individual (Hamilton, 1964). Sahlins suggests that human altruism is often directed at nonrelatives or at socially defined relatives under conditions where social definitions do not coincide with biological relatedness. Other criticism has come from social scientists (Mazur, 1976) and biologists (Peters, 1976) who have argued that evolutionary theory is tautological.

This debate has continued apace in recently published collections of papers (Caplan, 1978), and has been well analyzed by Ruse (1979) from his vantage point as a philosopher of science. While awareness of the debate is helpful in considering the merits of human applications of evolutionary theory, the present paper takes the position that much of the debate judges evolutionary theory without fully delineating its concepts, propositions, assumptions, and scope conditions. Such a full delineation is attempted here in order to give the question of whether evolutionary theory is useful for social science a fair consideration.

SOCIAL SCIENCES THEORIES OF CHANGE AND CONTIUITY

Many social science theories focus on how and why relative frequencies of alternative responses to the same enviornmental condition, e.g., individuals' behavioral strategies, or societal types, change or are stable over time. The "why" component usually focuses on the differential adaptiveness of alternative forms in given environments. Genetic evolutionary theory has a similar focus and, as such, can be considered to be a member of this family of change and continuity theories that provide guidance for social scientists.

From a cultural ecological perspective, Harris's (1974) analysis of how the taboo against pork became prevalent in ancient Middle Eastern societies uses a change and continuity approach which conceptualizes selection and adaptation as occurring at the societal level. Harris notes that pigs compete with humans for food low in cellulose, which is scarce, and, in addition, are poorly adapted to the hot and arid climate of the region. In such an environment, it would not be particularly functional for a society to raise and consume pigs. Hence the taboo. Similarly, structural functionalism examines both individual and societal consequences of phenomena such as types of deviance and conformity (Merton, 1968). The basic logic of such theory formulation lies in first describing the prevalent responses and then attempting to answer the question of "why" these forms are most common. While much of this research is based on cross-sectional observations, there is an implicit assumption that alternative responses to the same environmental conditions that were less successful were consciously abandoned, or increased their bearers' vulnerability to forces antagonistic to survival.

A similar approach is taken by reward theorists who study the ways in which reinforcement modifies the ratio of alternative responses to stimuli. The impact of reinforcement on children's responses to requests for altruistic behavior, the effects of parental behavior on the formation of racist and sexist attitudes in young children, and the modification of individuals' expectation states by others' evaluations, all consider changing ratios of alternative responses. Many reward theorists study change over time, in contrast to cultural ecologists and structural functionalists who explain the relative success of common forms by implicit comparison to hypothetical alternative forms which diminished in frequency because they were not as effective in meeting environmental demands.

Reward theory, too, has a cross-sectional version—the rational actor theory—in which one assumes that actors deliberately select maximally rewarding behaviors. Rational actor theory is generated by delineation of strategies that should have a maximum payoff in various settings. It is assumed that less-than-optimal forms were once employed, but that individuals' ratios of maximal to less-than-maximal responses decreased over time.

Evolutionary theory, like structural functionalism, cultural ecology, reward theory, and rational actor theory, focuses on change and continuity of response ratios (the how) and explanations of why such changes do or do not occur (the why). It is important to remember that the criticism of circularity that has been directed at evolutionary theory has also been made for other change and continuity theories. An evaluation of the utility of evolutionary theory for social science needs to be carried out in the larger context of all change and continuity theories. Problems that are characteristic of the theory group as a whole, then, should not arouse greater concern for a specific type, e.g., evolutionary theory.

However, evolutionary theory possesses some features which distinguish it from other change and continuity theories. It is these features which provide one with a different means of analyzing social phenomena. Three key characteristics can be briefly identified. First, the theory assumes that genetic or genetic-like mechanisms influence both the production of behavior and its transmission to offspring. Second, in common with reward and rational actor theories, it focuses on adaptation at the level of the individual rather than of larger social groupings. Third, while other change and continuity theories take a broad view of survival and adaptation, evolutionary theory focuses on the reproduction and rearing of offspring who have similar behavioral tendencies.

PREVIOUS WORK IN EVOLUTIONARY THEORY

As a preliminary to a more formal explication of evolutionary theory, several examples of how this approach has been applied by social scientists will be given. By illustrating the basic nature of this theory, variations in its uses, and potential problems, these examples can serve as a guide to the explicit formulation of the approach.

Barash's (1976, 1977b) investigation of male mallard ducks' reactions to their mates' "rape," and of male mountain bluebirds' reactions to their mates' apparent "adultery" is typical of many evolutionary studies of animal behavior. In the male bluebird's absence, Barash placed a stuffed museum replica of a male blue bird near the nest, and assumed that this would indicate to the male subject that his mate had been adulterous. The relevant dependent variable was the mated male's behavior upon return to the nest and discovery of the "intruder." Males were commonly observed to attack the female and chase her from the nest. It was assumed that the male then sought out a new mate.

In observing naturally occurring behavior of maillard ducks, Barash noted that forced sexual intercourse by nonmated males was common. What does the mated male do when he discovers that his mate either is being raped or has just been raped? In the former case, the male will usually attempt to interrupt the copulation, although the probability of interference is reduced if there are multiple rapists. If copulation has already been completed, the mate is likely to engage in forced sexual intercourse with the female.

Barash's analysis of these behaviors illustrates how evolutionary theory aims to explain the adaptive functions of observed behaviors, i.e., how they might enhance the male's reproductive success in each case. Although the ideal form of evolutionary theory utilizes longitudinal data, Barash's use of data collected at *one* point in time is a common practice. His assumption that the observed behaviors represent highly adaptive responses that are the products of a long selection period and that less adaptive behaviors have earlier been reduced in frequency is also typical.

Once he assumes that the modal patterns observed in each species primarily represents adaptive individual behavior, Barash attempts to delineate a model of how the behaviors confer reproductive and rearing advantage upon their users, and have therefore been preferentially selected over time. The analysis focuses on *consequences,* viewing rape and adultery as having the same consequence, i.e., increasing the probability that the male will invest in the rearing of offspring that are not his own. Males who provide such care to the offspring of adulterous or raped mates are likely to decrease in frequency since such effort detracts from their ability to invest in genetically similar offspring. Rejection of the bluebird female and the protection or rape of the mallard female are seen as functionally similar behaviors that decrease the likelihood of male parental investment in offspring which are not his.

How can rejection, protection, and rape be functionally similar? One important factor is that the mallard male is committed to staying with his mate. Rejection of a raped mate is not an adaptive strategy, since female mallards are not abundant. The male is making the best of a poor situation, either protecting his mate prior to the completion of the rape, or introducing his own sperm to compete with that of the rapist. On the other hand, the male bluebird is likely to find another mate since the male/female ratio is lower. The difference in male responses to functionally similar female behavior is due to variation in the sex ratio.

These examples illustrate a number of features of evolutionary analysis. First, while evolutionary theory ideally studies changes over time, much research considers a single point in time. Second, researchers usually assume that observed behaviors are produced by a long and consistently directed period of selection in which the ratio of more to less adaptive behavior has increased. The researcher assumes that observed behavior is adaptive, i.e., that it contributes to reproductive and rearing success. Third, analysis involves the delineation of possible reproduction and rearing functions of behaviors. These models can be used in later research to compare with new data. The assumption that what is observed is also adaptive *can* lead to a tautological approach to theory; later independent assessments of such post hoc propositions partially counter this problem.

Fourth, theorists are more concerned with the reproductive and rearing consequences of behavior than with the more immediate causes of that behavior. Although the particular mechanisms which lead from observation of adultery or rape to behavioral response are likely to be quite different, rape and adultery are grouped together because they have similar reproductive consequences.

Fifth, the evolutionary theorist thinks of behavior in terms of complex, purposive behavior. The theorist does not necessarily assume that ducks and bluebirds actually think strategically, but, rather, that they act *as if* they are thinking in this manner. The emphasis on strategic models leads to consideration not only of simple behaviors, but of behaviors that are contingent upon variable occurrences, e.g., sex ratio, or the completion of a rape. Much modeling of animal behavior assumes the capability for acting strategically or the capability for a mechanism that works in this fashion.

Other studies, often laboratory-based, consider changes over time. These investigations utilize species that can be easily handled in controlled settings, and have brief generational spans, so that evolution over many generations can be observed. A selection experiment of open field behavior in mice (DeFries, 1978) is representative of this type of investigation. Open field behavior is a mouse's response to being placed on a brightly illuminated empty plane, and is considered to be genetically based. High levels of this behavior are indicated by exploration of the plane, infrequent behavioral freezing, and low levels of defecation and urination. In this study a heterogeneous group of mice were divided into three lines: (1) selection for high activity, (2) selection for low activity, and (3) no activity selection. Selection refers to the researchers' responses to open field behavior in each generation. In high activity selection, mice that showed high activity were allowed to breed and rear offspring. Their offspring were kept in the high activity line, while lower activity mice were reproductively removed. The opposite preference was shown in the low activity line. After 30 generations, the high activity mice were much more active than the low activity strain, in contrast to the nonsignificant difference between the lines prior to selection. As in the wild, laboratory experiments select for some traits more than others. The same principles of selection apply whether the environment consists of human preferences for open field traits or of physical settings in which open field behaviors vary in adaptability.

While selection experiments demonstrate behavioral evolution, they do not always consider selection parameters that are ecologically relevant to natural settings. Although *natural* selection experiments under controlled circumstances do not seem to be performed very often, they can be designed in workable ways. Consider the effect of food distribution on selection for open field behavior as an example.

Two natural settings would be simulated in the laboratory. In one environment (consistent), food is always placed in one location which is shown to the mice early in life. In the other environment (distributed), food is provisioned in different places over time, so that successful food acquisition involves more exploration. If open field behavior indicates a more general explorative tendency, then predictions of the change in ratio of high/low activity mice in the two locales can be made. Since animals which do not feed effectively will probably be less capable of breeding and rearing, an increase in the high/low activity ratio is likely to be found in future generations in the distributed environment. No significant change, then, would be predicted in the consistent environment, as differences in exploratory tendencies are unlikely to affect success in food getting.

This hypothetical study contrasts in a number of ways with the Barash study. First, data would be collected over time, so that changes in behavior ratios could be observed. Assumptions about whether existing behavior is mostly adaptive or not need not be made. These experiments can serve to assess post hoc analyses made on such assumptions in cross-sectional research. Second, hypotheses are studied within carefully controlled settings in which it is possible to (1) vary only one or two variables that are suspected of affecting reproductive and rearing consequences of the relevant behaviors, and (2) introduce individuals who vary on particular behavior tendencies. The use of multigenerational (longitudinal) data in controlled experimental settings maximizes the rigor with which evolutionary theory, which is genetically based, can be tested.

There have been several recent evolutionary investigations of human behavior, all of which focused on nonindustrial societies and were not longitudinal studies. Several considerations of human descent and wealth transmission systems have yielded a composite model of when wealth distribution is patrilineal rather than matrilineal (Greene, 1978; Hartung, 1976; Kurland, forthcoming). The basic observation is that humans in most societies follow a patrilineal principle of distributing wealth down the generations, i.e., wealth descends from father to son. Evolutionary analysis of this finding involves delineating the reproductive and rearing consequences of wealth inheritance systems. While nonevolutionary explanations of the predominance of patrilineality have focused on the societal benefits of lineage practices, evolutionary explanations focus on activities whose outcomes *may* affect reproductive and rearing success, such as food acquisition, land control and use, or wealth and its investment. Nonevolutionary explanations do not usually draw the connections between these behaviors and reproduction and rearing. Evolutionary treatment of wealth inheritance systems has focused more directly on reproduction and rearing consequences.

Men usually want to transmit wealth to their male rather than female children or their relatives' offspring.[1] If it is assumed that wealth improves the offspring's reproductive and/or rearing success, adaptive strategies of inheritance are likely to be those in which the man benefits the closest relatives he has in the offspring generation. Therefore, it seems likely that a patrilineal descent system will always be preferred over a matrilineal system since the beneficiary is genetically more like the donor in the former systems.

Under what conditions would men distribute wealth matrilineally, to their sisters' male offspring, rather than to their sons? One answer (Greene, 1978; Hartung, 1976; Kurland, forthcoming) lies in variation of paternity certainty, encountered in another form in Barash's research. If the man is fully confident that his wife's offspring are his own, then wealth transmission to wife's sons rather than sister's sons would be more adaptive, i.e., more likely to enhance the reproductive success of individuals who have more genetic similarity to him. But, if paternity certainty is low, it may be more adaptive for a man to give wealth to his sister's sons, since his relatedness to sister's sons can be estimated more reliably and may be higher than that to his wife's children.

If a man is not sure whether his sister is a full or half sister, he can assume that their relatedness is at least $1/4$ and at most $1/2$.[2] Consequently, his relatedness with sister's son is at least $1/8$ and at most $1/4$. The certainty of these coefficients is high since his sister is 100 percent confident of her offspring's maternity. On the other hand, while his wife's son may be his $(1/2)$, they may also have a relatedness no higher than the average among group members, which would be considerably lower than the man's genetic similarity with his half sister's son. Under such conditions, the man who seeks to give wealth to those of the offspring generation who are of higher relatedness to him is better off giving it to sister's rather than wife's son. That matrilineal descent systems are correlated with higher levels of female promiscuity, and thus lower paternity certainty, has been suggested by the investigations of Greene (1978) and Hartung (1976).

Human and animal studies that focus on the common concept of paternity certainty are similar in a number of ways. First, the investigators assume that behavior reflects the effects of genetic or genetic-like influences, but neither researcher specifically evaluates this premise. Second, the observed behaviors are assumed to be the result of a long period of selection which has increased the ratio of more to less adaptive behaviors. Attempts to delineate how such behavior would enhance the reproductive and rearing success of individuals follows from this premise. Third, the model considers strategic, complex, contingent behavior and not stereotyped responses.

As was the case for nonhumans, some of the potential problems found in cross-cultural human data can be alleviated by the use of alternative research strategies. Some studies present hypotheses prior to data consideration, so as to avoid post hoc analysis. Hypotheses are generated by assessment of the selection pressures in various environments, and prediction of which behaviors are more or less adaptive under those conditions. The research then compares these predictions with behavior to see if the predicted patterns are frequently found, e.g., Durham's (1976a) theory of primitive warfare. A more rigorous method, using data from two or more generations, approximates some of the features of selection experiments. Barkow's (1977) study of reproductive success as a function of conformity to dominate values is an example of this technique.

In a study of Hausa society, Barkow (1977) collected data on males' reproductive success and conformity to central societal values. The small and moderate sized correlations found were consistent with the hypothesis that conformity to social "laws" leads to greater reproductive success due to better access to resources.

Barkow did not evaluate the genetic basis of conformity. A lack of concern for this question is typical of much evolutionary research, as illustrated by the other examples presented above. If one assumes that conformity tendencies are either genetically based or function as if they are, it is reasonable to predict that the next generation will have a greater ratio of conformers to nonconformers than did the parent generation. Thus, ratio changes over generations can be inferred. This is the type of data collected in selection experiments, such as on open field behavior in mice (DeFries, 1978).

In contrast to the DeFries study, Barkow's investigation could not control extraneous variables. Ethical and practical limitations prevent the creation of controlled environments and selection standards for humans. Nonetheless, the collection of multigenerational data is an improvement over the more commonly used and less expensive cross-sectional design.

THE LONGITUDINAL (IDEAL) MODEL OF GENETIC EVOLUTIONARY THEORY

The ideal longitudinal model of genetic evolution assumes that behavior is influenced, at least in part, by mechanisms that are either (1) genetic, or (2) work as if they are genetic. The nature of these mechanisms and the evidence for their existence in human social behavior will be considered in a later section.

Assume that at some point in time, t_1, there are environmental conditions, e.g., population density, predators, social dominance systems, and that individuals' responses to these conditions are genetically influenced. At t_1, there are at least two different responses—s_a and s_b. These two responses may have varying consequences for individuals' reproduction and rearing success with respect to both their own offspring and to the offspring of their close relatives. At t_2, at least one generation later, the ratio of s_a/s_b individuals will increase if s_a confers greater reproductive and rearing success upon its bearers concerning their own offspring and/ or the offspring of close relatives. Genetic evolution refers to the changes and continuities in these ratios of alternative responses to environmental conditions.

While the symbol s is used to represent the term *strategy*, the conceptualization of behavior as strategic is more a heuristic device than a claim about motivation. It is not assumed that individuals are consciously engaging in strategic behavior, i.e., behavior which they know will increase reproductive and rearing success, but neither is it claimed that they are not.

Strategic approaches to behavior are common in evolutionary research, as can be seen in the examples on sexual assault in birds and the inheritance of wealth in humans. This conceptualization of behavior resembles similar practices in the rational actor theory. Rather than being a weakness of evolutionary theory (Sahlins, 1976), the use of strategic modeling is a useful device for theory generation. Consider the following. Assume that there is an environment in which lions prey on humans, and are particularly attracted to unprotected human infants. Although social scientists hesitate to think of infant behavior as strategy (Rheingold and Eckerman, 1973), such conceptualization is effective in developing predictions about selection.

Imagine that there are two types of infants at a specific time, t_1 in this environment, and assume that their strategic tendencies are genetically based, or proceed as if they are. One group of infants cries loudly while the other group is silent in response to approaching predators. Also assume that adults try to protect both criers and noncriers. If infants who are mobile are likely to wander away from protective adults, and are approached by predatory lions, it would be expected that in later generations (t_2), there will be a higher ratio of criers to noncriers. The latter's lesser ability to alert adults and engage their assistance in warding off lions would make them more likely to be eaten. Since being eaten at an early age decreases ability to produce offspring and rear them to maturity, noncriers will leave relatively few offspring when compared to criers. In this manner, crying could become a more common trait.

Does this analysis suggest that crying will always become more common in human populations. *No.* One of the most important features of evolutionary predictions is their reference to *specific* environments. In the environment with many predators the ratio of criers to noncriers will probably increase over generations. However, what if there were no predators, or if parents did not let noncriers wander as far as criers? Under such conditions, the severity of selection against noncriers is likely to be reduced.

What might occur if adults did not perceive infant crying as indicative of danger? In this case, both criers and noncriers alike would often be killed. There would be little change in the relative rates of crying to silent infants although both absolute frequencies would decrease. While evolution usually refers to changes in *relative* rates of alternative responses, it might be useful to consider changes in *absolute* frequencies as well. A focus only on relative rates does not distinguish the condition under which adults protect all babies equally well from the condition under which they protect them equally poorly.

The delineation of the environment and its boundaries is a difficult part of evolutionary analysis. The environment is made up of everything other than the particular behavioral responses whose evolution is being considered. Ideally, evolutionary hypotheses should be generated and tested in controlled environments in which the selecting conditions are manipulated, and changes in the frequencies of responses are observed while other parameters are held constant. The most rigorous tests of evolutionary theory should resemble tightly controlled experiments, e.g., DeFries's (1978) study of open field activity. In nonideal conditions, description of the environment is difficult because it has not been constructed by explicit design, and features of the environment may include other evolving behaviors. A component of the environment for one hypothesis may be the focal behavior for another.

Consider the crying example again. One parameter of the environment in which a higher rate of criers to noncriers evolves is adult protection of crying babies but not of endangered infants who do not cry. But, these adult responses may also be evolving. In other words, parents who interpret crying as an indication of danger, and respond protectively, are likely to become more relatively frequent over time.

Given that environments may change rapidly, one could predict that the relative frequency of individuals who are more responsive to variation will increase. Since environments may be changing at a faster pace in modern industrial societies than in other human and animal environments, one might also predict that selective pressure for flexible response is increased under modern conditions. Flexibility, awareness of changing contingencies, and ability to respond to them would be preferentially selected.

Nondirectional predictions of the form "as time proceeds from t_1 to t_2, the ratio of s_a/s_b will change" are trivial. On the other hand, waiting until t_2 to observe the changes that have occurred encourages tautological theorizing in which the existence of behaviors is used to infer adaptation. Triviality and tautology are avoided by the generation of hypotheses based on assessments of the environmental pressures and the nature of behaviors that will be more effective in terms of reproduction and rearing in that setting. While exploratory longitudinal research would help develop more reasonable specific predictions, evolutionary research *can* make predictions about the reproductive and rearing consequences of alternative responses, e.g., Barkow's research strategy in the comparison of the reproductive successes of conforming and nonconforming Hausa men.

Evolutionary theory often labels one response as more "adaptive" than others. Adaptivity refers to the extent to which the consequences of a response facilitate the future existence of a high relative rate of individuals with the same tendency, i.e., reproductive and rearing success. But all behaviors which exist at a particular time are not necessarily highly adaptive, or even more adaptive than alternative responses. Thus, adaptiveness implies existence but existence does not necessarily imply adaptiveness.

EVOLUTIONARY MECHANISMS FOR BEHAVIOR

Evolutionary theory distinguishes two types of mechanisms concerning behavior. *Ultimate mechanisms* are the processes by which a behavior's effects are translated into reproductive and rearing consequences. *Proximate mechanisms* refer to the immediate etiological factors that lead to the behavior. These are the physiological, psychological, and sociological processes which flow from the environmental stimuli to behavioral responses.

Consider the case of incest avoidance, a common behavior in humans and many other animals. Analysis of ultimate mechanisms consists of delineation of how this behavior's reproductive and rearing consequences compare with those of incestuous behavior. Many studies have found that a higher frequency of incestuous than nonincestuous matings produce defective offspring who are then less able to reproduce (Parker, 1976). Since incestuous sexual couplings are more likely to produce fewer reproductively competent offspring, the ratio of incestuous/nonincestuous individuals is likely to decrease.

The question of proximate mechanisms deals with the processes that mediate the flow of events from the stimulus "close consanguinal relative" to the response "sexual avoidance." Parker (1976) has noted that this mechanism may be a general one of the form "as familiarity increases to high levels, arousal decreases." Since close consanguinal relatives are usually characterized by such high levels of familiarity, this "rule" could easily lead to incest avoidance.

This type of analysis suggests that a specific behavior may be one of many effects produced by a more general mechanism. While the evolution of particular behaviors is often the focus of interest in evolutionary theory, general mechanisms are likely to be selected. Behaviors, and their reproductive and rearing consequences, flow from these general mechanisms. One mechanism is selected over an alternative on the basis of the *sums* of their respective reproductive and rearing effects.

The mechanism that leads to incest avoidance—overfamiliarity causes low sexual arousal—also seems to produce other effects. Examples are the avoidance of sexual contact among nonrelated adolescents who were reared together in Israeli kibbutzim (Talmon, 1964), and the lack of sexual interest in prospective spouses who, although nonrelated, were reared in the same traditional Chinese family as brother and sister (Wolf, 1968). It is likely that a similar mechanism leads to boredom following repeated exposure to nonsexual arousal in spouses who have been familiarized with each other in long-term monogamous marriages. The sum of the reproduction and rearing consequences of these outcomes as a group, not just of incest avoidance, determines whether this general mechanism will be selected in favor of alternative mechanisms.

The phenomenon by which one general mechanism has multiple behavioral outcomes, each of which may have different reproduction and rearing consequences, is known as *pleiotropy*. It makes evolutionary analysis more complex than would a one-to-one correspondence of mechanism with behavior. This conceptualization of the nature of selection further stresses the point that it is often foolish to attempt to discover the adaptive value of every observed behavior. For example, an attempt to determine how sexual boredom in long-lasting monogamous marriage might be adaptive would probably be futile. Rather, the various consequences of one mechanism are better considered as a group. In this perspective, it could be noted that, while sexual boredom in monogamous marriage might be maladaptive in that it could interfere with reproduction and rearing, the incest avoidance function of the familiarity—low arousal mechanism has positive consequences that far outweigh the negative effects of marital boredom.

It can be noted that these general mechanisms are not stereotyped responses to stimuli. Rather, they are conceptualized as operating in a strategic, contingent manner. It is not necessarily assumed that individuals are consciously seeking reproductive and rearing fitness, although such conscious motivation could occur. Rather, mechanisms are seen as operating in a flexible way so as to be responsive to environmental contingencies, e.g., the earlier example of how matrilineal and patrilineal inheritance systems are contingent upon female promiscuity.

While evolutionists are interested in proximate mechanisms, research answers which describe these proximate mechanisms usually lead to a search for the ultimate reproductive and rearing consequences. The deepest level of analysis concerns such consequences. Such an emphasis differs considerably from the stress on subjective meaning or *verstehen* that characterizes much social science work. In the search for ultimate mechanisms, evolutionists would view the delineation of the actor's subjective meaning concerning some behavior as an answer that begs the deeper questions. Just as cultural ecologists (Harris, 1974) do not automatically accept an individuals' interpretation of her or his own behavior, neither do evolutionists.

Evolutionary theory focuses on reproductive and rearing consequences of mechanisms and behaviors as the central explanator of changes in ratios of mechanistic alternatives and behaviors. The justification for this approach rests on the existence of genetic or genetic-like bases for behavior. Two such bases are considered here and evidence for their existence is evaluated.

Biochemical Influences

Genetic influence means that biochemicals—DNA—in the organism's cells have an impact on behavior. This influence is effected through the control that DNA has over the coding of protein synthesis, which, through a long chain of processes, affects behavior. When organisms reproduce, DNA is faithfully transmitted to offspring so that progeny share 50 percent of the mother's and 50 percent of the father's DNA composition. Thus, protein synthesis controls are transmitted from parent to offspring to then influence behavior in the progeny as they did in the parent generation. Do such mechanisms in human and nonhumans code for behavior relevant to social interaction and organization?

Biologists usually assume that animal behavior is genetically influenced. Behavior genetics research has yielded considerable support for this assumption. For example, DeFries's (1978) study of open field activity suggests the genetic basis of this trait. Other research has found that breeds of dogs which have been exposed to different selection standards, vary considerably in their responsiveness to human training (Freedman, 1958). But, when evidence is not available for particular behavioral traits, e.g., parent–offspring conflict strategy (Trivers, 1974), or reciprocal altruism (Trivers, 1971), evolutionary theorists are likely to assume that behavior has some genetic basis.

Concerning human social behavior, most social scientists seem to make the opposite assumption in response to ambiguous data. While not denying the genetic basis of animal behavior, most social scientists question its role in human behavior. Several sources of evidence from behavior genetics and social science research are relevant to this issue. First, there are socially relevant behaviors that appear early in life, some even in the neonatal period, e.g., temperament and soothability (Freedman and Freedman, 1969). That such behaviors influence the infant's early social interaction with caregivers has been clearly shown in much recent research (Lewis and Rosenblum, 1974). Although variation in behavior that appears so early in life could be accounted for by differences in prenatal environments, the sooner after birth a behavior appears, the less the potential importance of learning. The finding that blind babies smile in situations similar to those that elicit smiling in sighted babies suggests that social responses such as smiling have some prelearned bases (Freedman, 1964).

There are a number of significant dimensions on which greater genetic similarity among individuals is correlated with greater trait similarity. Monozygotic twins (relatedness = 1) are more similar to each other in their responses to strangers than are same-sex dizygotic twins ($r = 1/2$; Freedman, 1965). Relatedness has been correlated with mental illness, alcoholism, some elements of personality and temperament, and intelligence (McClearn and DeFries, 1973; Stern, 1973).

An alternative explanation of these findings is that they reflect not the influence of genetic similarity, but rather, commonalities in rearing and environment. It has been suggested that identical twins share not only a common heritage but more common environments than do same-sex fraternal twins (Scarr, 1968). Recent investigations (Loehlin and Nichols, 1976) have found that even if identical twins' greater homogeneity in rearing conditions is statistically controlled, monozygotic trait similarities are still greater than those for fraternal twins, suggesting that genetic factors are relevant.

Some researchers have argued that low variance behaviors are more likely to be genetically based (Van den Berghe, 1975). Similarly, others have suggested that the great variation in human behavioral expression indicates the insignificance of genetic influence (Sahlins, 1976). While it is likely that specieswide characteriscs such as capacity for spoken language, or diurnal tendencies, reflect genetic factors,[3] the general use of behavioral variance as an indicator of genetic influence is a crude and inaccurate practice. There is great variation in human intelligence, temperament, personality, sociability, and other traits that appear to have a genetic basis. Just as environmental variation creates different types of behavior, so does genetic variation.

Adaptive Strategies

How does genetic influence apply to human social behaviors that have been the focus of evolutionary research, e.g., wealth inheritance systems, conformity to dominant values, food sharing, or intergroup warfare? Although some researchers may develop theory on the heuristic assumption that such genetic influence exists (Trivers, 1971), there is no direct evidence concerning genetic influence for such specific behaviors. There are two major solutions to this gap in evidence. One is to treat the behavior as if it is produced and transmitted genetically. In this approach, little concern is shown for whether the assumption actually is correct, as is common practice for much evolutionary research on nonhuman subjects as well.

Another solution involves the somewhat different assumption that what is genetically based and selected for in evolution is the *ability* to act as if one is enhancing reproductive and rearing consequences. This model does not claim a specific genetic basis for lineage, or conformity, or altruism, but rather an ability to respond to varying contingencies so as to produce adaptive outcomes. In this manner, the skill that leads to patrilineal wealth transfer under many conditions also leads to matrilineal inheritance when paternity certainty is low. Returning to the example of the adopted child searching for the identity of biological parents, it might be argued that this tendency is not itself genetically programmed, but, rather, flows from the more general capacity to engage in a strategy behavior which will result in reproductive and rearing advantages. Just as rational actor theory postulates that humans behave so as to increase profit, evolutionary theory sometimes assumes that individuals behave so as to enhance reproduction and rearing success.

Does the importance of learning and experiential factors counter the utility of genetic evolutionary theory for human behavior? Several points are relevant to this question. First, genetic evolutionary theory does not deny the importance of nongenetic factors and does not try to explain all behavior. For example, while the ability to solve mazes appears to be a genetically selected trait in mice, success at particular mazes is based on learning the details of those situations. Most humans have a genetically based capacity to acquire language and speak it, but the specifics of the language are based on learning and experience.

In addition, there is evidence that animals are genetically prepared to learn some behaviors easily and contraprepared against others. The genetic basis may not be for the behavior itself, but, rather, for the inclination to easily learn it (Seligman and Hager, 1972). Perhaps easily learned behaviors are more adaptive than difficult to learn alternatives. Possible candidates for this category of easy-to-learn behavior include altruism, sex-role modeling, language acquisition, and self- and group-identity.

There also seems to be a well-tuned interchange between genetic tendencies and individual experience. Infants usually begin to avoid heights by the time they are nine months old. The timing of this avoidance correlates with the extensiveness of the infant's locomotor activities; infants who locomote earlier and more often tend to be more avoidant of depth stimuli (Campos, et al., 1978). These patterns do not deny the significance of genetic factors. Rather, they suggest that genetic mechanisms can be effectively conceptualized in the mold of game theory in that they appear to be contingent upon existing conditions. The genetic basis for depth avoidance appears to function as if "instructing" the infant. "Body, if you are an infant who gets around by yourself, and are likely to be exposed to heights while away from the protective custody of adults, avoid depth cues." The use of game theoretic approaches to evolution is accepted with reference to animals (Smith, 1974; Dawkins, 1976), and reflects a conceptualization of genetic mechanisms that takes into account the experience and condition of the organism along with that of the surrounding environment.

It has been suggested that in humans, a nongenetic mechanism for behavioral influence and intergenerational transmission exists (Durham, 1976b). Behaviors such as warfare, altruistic responses, and kinship systems are considered to be the products of learning. Those which are advantageous to individuals' reproductive and rearing fitness are preferentially retained in human repetoires and thereby increase the proportion of individuals with that response.

Although Durham does not note this point, the proposed mechanism is genetic-like only when special conditions apply; if the acquisition of social behavior is largely based in social learning, such learning and socialization must take place in kin-based settings. If this is not the case, evolutionary predictions that individuals will try to benefit close relatives will not be confirmed. The result is the same whether parents teach their strategies to offspring, or if they transmit it chemically—a mechanism that meets the assumptions of genetic evolutionary theory.

Social science literature on socialization suggests that the kin group is an important place for strategy learning. The stronger the kin bias in socialization, the greater the utility of Durham's evolutionary model. As socialization becomes increasingly influenced by nonkin, e.g., media, schools, and so on, the fit of Durham's mechanism with the premises of genetic evolutionary theory decreases. It may be that the kin bias condition is better met in less technologically advanced societies in which secondary relations, mass culture, and mass media are significant forces in socialization.

The utility of genetic evolutionary theory for human social behavior is increased if genetic and/or Durham's mechanisms exist as the basis for these responses. It may be that social scientists' aversion to genetic mechanisms may stem, at least partly, from the conceptualization of genetic factors as stereotyped, simplistic responses which are not sensitive to learning or experience. This simplistic model of genetic influence is not at all consistent with the way in which evolutionary theorists have conceptualized such mechanisms.

NATURAL SELECTION, ALTRUISM, AND INCLUSIVE FITNESS

Response ratios are modified over time by differences in the reproductive and rearing successes of their bearers though the process of *natural selection*. The term "selection" indicates that some responses are preferred in an environment because they better enable their bearers to reproduce and rear more individuals with the same tendencies. Natural selection has *two* components: individual and kin selection. In *individual selection*, response ratios change as invididuals with more adaptive responses produce and rear to maturity a greater number of offspring than do individuals with less adaptive strategies.

Consider the issue of adoption once again. How could giving up one's offspring, i.e., losing rearing opportunities, be more adaptive than other strategies? It may be that offspring are more likely to be given up for adoption when parents do not have the resources needed to raise their children. Under conditions of limited resources, it is likely that a strategy whereby parents seek other resources, e.g., have some other person rear their children, would be more adaptive than a strategy in which parents attempted to rear them by themselves. It is also common for biological parents to later seek out the children they gave up—perhaps, to see if they have been reared successfully or to offer assistance, which they may now be in a position to provide.

The outcome of individual selection is reflected by *individual fitness* which is measured in units of *adult offspring equivalents*—the number of offspring an individual produces that are reared to reproductive maturity. Evolution of behaviors is indicated by the relative fitnesses of individuals who have alternative tendencies toward the same stimulus. For example, it is likely that in many human environments, crying infants have higher levels of individual fitness than noncriers. Similarly, if alcoholism is genetically based, perhaps it is not selected against because individual fitness differences between alcoholic and nonalcoholic individuals are not particularly large. Individual fitness differences were also demonstrated in Barkow's (1977) investigation of the effect of social conformity on reproductive success. Such differences can be inferred from Barash's work in that male ducks who defend their mate against rapists probably have higher individual fitness than those who do not defend.

That individual fitness is not the only standard for natural selection is suggested by the high frequency of altruistic behaviors that increase the individual fitness of the beneficiary, but decrease the donor's. Altruistic strategies might be selected for if directed at biological relatives, a practice known as *kin altruism*. While such altruism decreases the donor's individual fitness, it benefits the fitness of others who are themselves likely to be altruists since they are biologically similar to the donor. The other part of natural selection is *kin selection* and its outcome is *kin component fitness*. Kin selection refers to the modification of response ratios through effects on the reproductive and rearing success of the individual's biological relatives. Kin altruism is most likely to be selected for when the cost to individual fitness is low compared to the benefit to recipient's fitnesses. In this manner, the ratio of kin altruistic to selfish individuals could increase.

An offspring equivalent refers not only to one's own children, but also to any individual with whom one has a relatedness of 1/2, the coefficient of relatedness that parents have with their offspring. Since siblings are related by 1/2 (if they are full sibs), an individual's relatedness to his sister's children is 1/4 (1/2 for the brother–sister relationship × 1/2 for the mother–child relationship). Two nephews or nieces make up one offspring equivalent and together represent the same probability of genetic similarity to the individual as does one of his offspring. Thus, altruism to kin other than one's offspring could produce a larger total of individuals who have the same altruistic tendency, even if this behavior subtracted from individual fitness.

A pattern of kin altruism is referred to in Chagnon and Bugos's (1979) analysis of an ax fight among Yanomamo men, as indicated by the higher relatedness within than between groups of allies. It may be that giving aid to one's close kin became a common strategy among Yanomamo males because individuals who engaged in altruistic behavior produced more individuals, who also had such tendencies, as opposed to those Yanomamo who either aided only their own offspring or gave aid to any adult regardless of relatedness. Similarly, the adopted child's search for biological parents may be selected because knowledge of the identities of one's biological relatives facilitates more adaptive kin altruism.

The key indicator of natural selection lies in relative inclusive fitnesses of differing behavioral responses. *Inclusive fitness* is the sum of individual and kin component fitnesses. The relative frequencies of individuals with differing responses is affected by both their own production of mature offspring and by the success of their biological relatives.

Altruism toward individuals who are not closely related can be explained by the evolutionary theory of *reciprocal altruism* (Trivers, 1971). Such behavior does not enhance kin component fitness, but may increase the chances that the recipient will later be altruistic to the donor. If the cost of the favor is small compared to the benefit derived from its return, reciprocal altruism could contribute to individual fitness. The alternative strategies of selfishness or restrictive kin altruism could prove to be less beneficial than a strategy that also includes reciprocal altruism.

Food sharing within human hunter-gatherer groups has characteristics of both kin and reciprocal altruism. Individuals are more likely to share food with close relatives than with more distant relatives, but they do share with the latter. What is most interesting in these patterns is that while there is little concern with repayment when the recipient is a close kinsperson, altruism to less related individuals usually carries with it the expectation of balanced reciprocity (S. Feinman, 1979; Sahlins, 1972). Similarly, sociological considerations of the family often note that while the parent–child relation may carry little expectation for reciprocity, the husband–wife relationship demands it. Parent–child pairs are close blood relatives, while husband–wife relatedness is probably not any higher than the average intragroup genetic similarity. The difference in expectations conforms to the difference between effective kin altruism and effective reciprocal altruism.

Adaptive patterns of kin altruism are also contingent on the donor's and recipient's *reproductive and rearing value*, which is each one's current and future ability to produce and rear additional offspring. Altruism to kin, who are incapable of increasing their own individual fitness, cannot benefit the donor's kin compontent fitness. Therefore, kin altruism which is sensitive to variations in the recipient's reproductive and rearing value should be selected over patterns of kin altruism which are not. Similarly, the lower the donor's reproductive and rearing value, the more adaptive it would be to engage in kin altruism, since any further increments to his own individual fitness are unlikely. For the low reproductive and rearing value donor, the cost of kin altruism is very low. It would be expected, then, that kin altruism in which benefit is directed preferentially *toward* high reproductive and rearing valued individuals, and is performed more *by* low valued persons, would evolve.

There is evidence of such selection among humans. In human societies, particularly those under strong ecological pressure, old people are less likely than younger adults or children to be recipients of kin altruism (S. Feinman, 1979; Glascock and S.L. Feinman, 1980). Since the average reproductive and rearing value of old people is lower than that for adults and children, this pattern fits the predicted selection. Old people receive more support in societies with a surplus. The effect of reproductive and rearing value on altruism seems to be contingent on the environmental and economic presures under which individuals live. When there is surplus, the low cost of resource donation does not detract from the donor's individual fitness; in fact, donation of surplus probably does not correspond to the evolutionary definition of altruistic response.

It is interesting to note that even under harsh conditions, old people receive more resources when they are able to perform services for younger people (Glascock and S.L. Feinman, 1980). Under these conditions, donations to old people are not purely kin altruism, but, rather, reciprocal altruism since old people are expected to return the favor in some way. Altruism is contingent upon the recipient's ability to reciprocate when he/she cannot contribute to the donor's kin component fitness because of either a lack of relatedness or, as is the case for old people, because of low reproductive and rearing value.

Altruism is a key behavior in distinguishing evolutionary theory from other functional social science approaches. Cultural ecologists and structural functionalists explain altruism as individual sacrifice for the "good of the group," and view groups, societies, and cultures as the key units of selection. In contrast, evolutionary theory focuses on individuals rather than groups in that adaptive patterns are those that better enhance an individual's inclusive fitness. If groups are composed of closely related individuals, the predictions of individual selection and group selection theories are likely to coincide. But, altruism which benefits the group but does not enhance an individual's inclusive fitness is a behavior for which an evolutionary model cannot be meaningfully constructed. Thus, evolutionary theory would diverge from group selection theories in predictions about altruistic behavior in secondary groups in which kinship ties are weak.

LESS-THAN-IDEAL EVOLUTIONARY MODELS

Hypotheses about individual and kin component fitness should ideally be investigated with data collected over several generations under controlled experimental conditions. Actual studies of human behavior, as well as many evolutionary investigations of nonhuman behavior, are not highly controlled since they are done in natural habitats and collect data at one point in time. This difficulty suggests that alternative models for evolutionary research strategy are needed. The ideal approach needs to be kept in mind when less-than-ideal models of evolutionary theory are presented in this section. A key point to remember is that these models are used only when data needed for the ideal longitudinal approach to evolutionary analysis cannot be obtained because of ethical and/or practical limitations. The two cross-sectional models proposed here differ in the scope conditions under which they can be of optimal use. It is considerably more difficult to rigorously test evolutionary hypotheses with cross-sectional data. But, respect for the conditions under which each of these models is best applied can significantly diminish this difficulty.

Much evolutionary theory, particularly that relating to human behavior, assumes that the observed individuals are descendents of a population that has long lived in an environment which has exerted consistent and strong selection pressure. It is expected that the population of individuals will be highly evolved, i.e., that the ratio of more to less adaptive behavior will be very high. In the *evolved population model*, analysis of data assumes that the observations represent highly adaptive responses, and seeks to determine the mechanisms by which such behaviors conferred higher inclusive fitness than did any alternatives. If alternative strategies are not observed, it is assumed that they existed in previous generations but did not produce and rear sufficient numbers of offspring to be well represented in the present generation. Some investigations do not compare alternative strategies but, rather, concentrate on showing how commonly observed behavior is very adaptive or perhaps even optimally adaptive. This approach is more likely than any other evolutionary research to be troubled by the problems of circularity, for it assumes that what is observed must not only be adaptive but also maximally adaptive. Investigations based on the evolved population model can partially circumvent these problems by generating falsifiable predictions prior to data collection.

Most of the research examples considered thus far fall into this model e.g., Barash's model of duck and bluebird response to mate's sexual behavior, and the various explanations of human inheritance patterns. So, too, do most cross-cultural studies of human societies and cross-species studies that have included humans. Generally, the investigator assumes that what he or she observes is very adaptive and then tries to understand the sources of such adaptivity.

The less frequently used *evolving population model* assumes that the population is either newly arrived in the environment and/or the environment has recently changed. While behavior may have been well adapted to the earlier environment, it is less adaptive under the new conditions. In this model analysis does not seek to understand how observed behaviors are adaptive in that environment. Rather, the evolving population model pictures a lower ratio of more to less adaptive behavior than does the evolved model. It is assumed that over a considerable period of time, the ratio will increase. At that point, an evolved model will be more useful.

Several research approaches may be taken under the conditions of the evolving population model. First, one can point out that certain behaviors are not particularly adaptive. The strategy can be seen in Harlow's analysis of rhesus monkeys' responses to social isolation (Cross and Harlow, 1965; McKinney et al., 1973). These responses are especially interesting from an evolutionary perspective, since decreased sexual interest in females and aberrant sexual behavior in males are observed in socially isolated monkeys. In contrast to Barash's approach to avian adultery and assault, Harlow and his colleagues do not look for adaptiveness in the behaviors of rhesus monkeys once they are released into the social world of other monkeys. An evolving population model underlies this analysis since living in social isolation is not a common feature of rhesus monkey life in either the wild or the laboratory. The assumption of recent change—from social to isolated rearing periods—is well met.

It has been noted that the behavior of laboratory and zoo animals that are newly introduced to these settings from natural habitats is often maladaptive in these new environments. The shift from a socially rich to socially isolated rearing settings consitutes a large change of environment. Under such circumstances, one would initially expect a high ratio of less to more adaptive behavior. If the experimenters did not artificially induce sexual success for individuals who would otherwise have a low level of success there would probably be a decline in less adaptive reproductive and rearing behavior. Assuming that there were some individuals who were better suited to socially isolated rearing, their relative frequency would increase over several generations in such environments. As the ratio of more to less adaptive individuals increased, the applicability of the evolving population model would diminish while that of the evolved population model would rise.

In addition to noting the maladaptive nature of behavior, one can also wonder why such behaviors might have become frequent. Such analysis requires that the frame of reference be the past environment in which the behavior came to have a relatively high frequency, compared to alternative responses, as a result of many generations of long and directed evolution. In other words, an evolved population model must be used with reference to an earlier environment.

Seligman and Hager (1972) have noted animal examples of such analysis in their work on prepared learning. Learning preparedness for particular behaviors has been selected for in the specific environments in which individuals have long resided. When animals are moved to new environments, e.g., from the wild to the laboratory, such prepared responses still exist, but are either of little adaptive use or may even be harmful. Pigeons more easily learn to hop and jump than to peck in order to avoid electric shock, since in the wild the ability to escape from danger is based on the former rather than the latter. Although pigeons rarely escape from danger in the wild by pecking, the laboratory environment often requires such responses. Since laboratory pigeons are the product of selection in the wild, their laboratory behavior can be analyzed using either the evolving model within the context of the laboratory, or the evolved model within the context of the wild.

Under what conditions is each model applicable to human behavior? Some anthropologists (Barkow, 1978; Chagnon and Irons, 1979) have argued that much of the behavior found in modern industrial societies is more adaptive for hunter-gatherer groups. Since humans have existed in industrial environments for 200 years at most, it is to be expected that some modern human behavior will appear to be maladaptive within its current contexts. To understand the adaptiveness of industrial man's behavior, i.e., to apply an evolved population model, such behavior needs to be analyzed with reference to earlier environments.

Others, such as Wilson (1977), have further suggested that genetic evolutionary theory is more applicable to preliterate nonindustrial human societies than to modern ones. Such an assertion is based on the assumption that evolutionary theory is limited to the evolved population model. But, genetic evolutionary theory in ideal longitudinal form is just as applicable to industrial as hunter-gatherer societies. Since humans are only recently arrived in industrial environments after a long period of selective pressure in earlier developed societal types, the ratio of more to less adaptive behaviors with reference to modern environments may be lower than in older societal forms. If this is indeed the case, then human behavior could be analyzed within an evolved population model with reference to Pleistocene environments and within an evolving population model with reference to recent environments.

The evolved population model is commonly used for human as well as nonhuman research. Some problems that can arise in employing this model are considered here. One use of the evolved model which leads to considerable difficulties, is a stress on inclusive fitness *maximizing* behavioral strategic models. Rather than ask how some behavior *compares* to *other* possible responses in that situation, a theorist can compare that behavior to an optimizing inclusive fitness strategy which may not actually exist. While theory construction within the evolved population model is often advanced by the development of predictions that are based on the optimal, it would be a mistake to attempt to use this model for *all* observed behaviors. Attempts to show how all behaviors maximize inclusive fitness not only are inconsistent with the Darwinian stress on change in the relative rates of alternative responses (Quadagno, 1979), but lead to foolish explanations of the adaptive value of behaviors that are clearly maladaptive.

Another problem that sometimes arises with the evolved population model stems from the use of what has been called the *central theorem* of genetic evolutionary theory. This theorem uses the following principle to guide research: actors will behave as if they are attempting to enhance their inclusive fitness. This too is a useful principle for model building, but it can be incorrectly applied. First, the use of this principle can often lead to the specification of optimally enhancing behaviors, resulting in the problems discussed above. Second, this theorem is most appropriate for evolved, not evolving, population models. In an evolving population with a relatively high proportion of less adaptive behaviors, central theorem predictions will have rather low confirmation. The application of this principle becomes increasingly appropriate as the proportion of more adaptive behavior increases, i.e., as the relative frequency of "successful" behaviors and individuals increases. One might say that the central theorem should be reworded to assert that *successful* actors, i.e., actors who show very adaptive behavior, respond as if they were attempting to enhance inclusive fitness. Thus, the use of the central theorem requires careful assessment of whether an evolved population model actually is appropriate for the particular population in its environment.

CONFIRMATION STATUS, DATA, AND NEEDED RESEACH

While there is a great deal of information about animals that is relevant to genetic evolutionary theory, evolutionary data on humans are rare. Acceptance or rejection of the utility of evolutionary theory for social science would definitely be premature at this time. One way to evaluate the fit of this theory with social behavior patterns, though is to use data that have been collected for other purposes. Other than a few studies (Barkow, 1977; Chagnon and Bugos, 1979; Irons, 1979), most evolutionary considerations of nonindustrial human groups have worked with old data and attempted to fit new theory to it (Durham, 1976a; Dyson-Hudson and Alden-Smith, 1978; S. Feinman, 1979; Hartung, 1976). This practice involves a number of problems. First, it usually does not give any measure of the reproductive and rearing success that corresponds to different types of behavior. Second, much data is described with reference to groups rather than individuals. Since evolutionary theory makes predictions based on differences in inclusive fitness among individuals, data on specific individuals is needed. Third, much social science data, for both primitive and industrial man, stress meaning systems, feelings, attitudes, subjective interpretations, and beliefs rather than economic, military, and social status consequences, which are probably more closely linked with inclusive fitness.

New research efforts, designed to acquire data specifically applicable to evolutionary hypotheses, should remedy these problems by collecting data on individual reproductive success and rearing efficacy and by concentrating more on culture core (Steward, 1955) instead of meanings. Such data collection among preliterate humans in rather expensive and time-consuming but can be accomplished (Barkow, 1977; Irons, 1979). Some of the data relevant to evolutionary hypotheses may actually be easier to collect for modern industrial societies since getting data on individual activity, reproduction, rearing, and welfare of offspring is facilitated by society's stress on an individual's importance. Application of research practices of such fields as demography, sexual behavior research, adolescent behavior, and child socialization to the study of human evolution would be a relatively easy step to take.

Where might the reanalysis of old data and the collection of new data begin? First, more attention might be given to human behavior genetics in order to know which responses are most likely to have a genetic basis. For example, there has been a recent interest within psychology and behavioral pediatrics in the variable of temperament, a general state of an individual that is often conceptualized as having dimensions such as activity, excitability, adaptability, liability of emotional reactions, and approach–avoidance tendencies. Some research with infants seems to indicate that temperament differences are found early in life and may have a genetic basis (Carey, 1979; Thomas and Chess, 1977). There have also been some recent attempts to connect the temperament variable with factors of traditional social science interest, e.g., children's success in school (Carey et al., 1977). An analysis of the effects of temperament on ease of being reared as a child, traditional measures of child or adult social success, and rearing and reproductive success as adults would be within the realm of an evolutionary approach. In other words, one might profitably investigate whether selection pressures in modern society are modifying the relative frequencies of different types of temperament.

Second, the extent to which Durham's (1976b) genetic-like mechanism occurs in humans should be investigated more closely. How much do children acquire from relatives compared to other sources of socialization such as media, teachers, and nonrelated peers? This question of "who influences the child" is a major issue and concern in the sociological study of child socialization. Situations with such kin bias in socialization are likely to be profitable targets of evolutionary hypotheses since they would satisfy the requirements for genetic or genetic-like mechanisms.

Third, behaviors that are directly concerned with reproduction and rearing should receive more attention. Some of these behaviors are also of current interest to other social scientists. For example, one behavior which seems to have adverse rearing consequences is child abuse. An evolutionary approach to this subject might ask whether abused children are less likely to survive to maturity and to effectively reproduce and rear offspring. Are infants who show signs of being potentially unfit as adults more likely to be abused? Since patterns of infanticide in some preliterate societies seem to be consistent with such variables, perhaps infanticide and child abuse can be seen within the same conceptual framework. While the conscious motives for each behavior may be rather different, some of the consequences are similar. Perhaps child abuse is an expression of a motivation similar to that for infanticide but modified in form when the social environment forbids infanticide.

Evolutionary theory could be profitably applied to other topics such as voluntary childlessness, the effects of religious ideology on reproduction, the treatment of old people, and the reactions to and treatment of the handicapped. In general, evolutionary theory would probably be better applied to the consideration of micro than macro issues in the social sciences. Although Wilson (1975) has argued for the existence of a "multiplier effect" by which selection of individual characteristics also affects social structure and organization, it must be noted that such higher level effects are one step removed from evolutionary mechanisms. There is no evolutionary selection for group-level characteristics themselves other than as the result of interaction of selection for various individual types. While it is possible to make some predictions about group characteristics that result from selection at the individual level, there seems to be better evidence for predictions made at the individual level.

IS EVOLUTIONARY THEORY USEFUL FOR MODERN SOCIAL SCIENCE

Evolutionary theory certainly *can* be applied to topics that are of substantive relevance to social scientists. Its utility cannot be more definitively considered until further comparisons of theory with data have been made. At the present time, with little empirical confirmation one way or the other, there are a number of points that can be made concerning the probable utility of such theory.

Evolutionary theory's utility for post-Neolithic societies, and particularly for industrial societies, is likely to be just as significant as that for hunter-gatherer groups. If researchers either collect longitudinal data, or use the cross-sectional models that are most appropriate, evolutionary theory can be effectively used for a wide range of human societal types.

Clearly some difficulties involved with the application of evolutionary theory to other animals are increased when dealing with humans. Of greatest significance are the problems generated by the inability to collect data over several generations, and in controlled experimental settings in which the "all other things being equal" condition can be met or at least closely approached. The solution to such problems lies in making more effective and appropriate use of cross-sectional models. An important aspect of the use of such designs is the decision about which type of model to use, since it is clear that the evolved model and the evolving model are each appropriate under different conditions.

The delineation of the scope within which a theory is most useful is an important component of the practice of that theory. Considerable effort has been devoted here to delineating such conditions and considering the nature of human conditions that meet these requirements. All good theories have clearly defined limitations. Expectation states theory in sociology first developed within the scope limitation that groups be task related. Exchange theory and other rational actor theories often assume that action is voluntary, that alternative courses of action are evaluated, and that actors behave as if they are seeking optimum profit. If these conditions are not met, the utility of expectation states or rational actor theories decreases. Similarly, there are conditions under which evolutionary theory performs at its peak, and others under which its application makes little sense.

One important condition for the use of evolutionary theory is that behaviors be based in genetic or genetic-like mechanisms. The theory should not be applied to explain all behavioral variance; this would not be a proper use or fair test of any social theory. Rather, by delineating those behaviors which better approximate the genetic assumption, a kin-learning mechanism, or some other genetic-like mechanism, the parameters within which evolutionary theory most usefully can be applied are defined.

What is most exciting about the application of evolutionary theory to human social behavior is that its perspective differs in significant ways from other social science theories. The stress on individual behavior and the strategies and consequences of such behavior, while found in some other social sciences theories of rational action, further contribute to the body of theory which contrasts with the Durkheimian theories that influence much of social science today. Also, the stress on consequences provides a contrast to the stress on *verstehen* and symbolic interaction found in much research done in the Weberian and Meadian traditions. Evolutionary approaches do not replace the need for a concern with meanings and reality construction. Rather, such a focus has a different place in evolutionary research. A stress on consequences is also found in functional theories as well, but not linked to an emphasis on individual behavior.

What makes evolutionary theory particularly special is its stress on genetic or genetic-like mechanisms, and its subsequent unique emphasis on the reproductive and rearing consequences of behavior. This focus provides not only a different way of looking at reproduction and rearing, but also frames other behaviors within the context of reproduction and rearing. This is the heart of the explanatory device that evolutionary theory provides for human social behavior.

NOTES

1. Although this issue lies beyond the limited scope of the present example, the question of why men prefer to transfer wealth to males rather than to females has been considered in other evolutionary work. Hartung's (1976) theory of wealth inheritance considers this question by placing it within the context of Trivers and Willard's (1973) theory of variation in sex ratio of offspring.

2. These coefficients are probability estimates of relatedness of sibs. With the exception of direct lineal relations, e.g., parent–child, grandparent–grandchild, precise determination of actual relatedness is not possible. Rather, two sibs could be as little related as cousins, or almost as strongly related as identical twins, depending on the actual outcomes of the processes that determine what each child inherits from each parent. The estimate of 1/2 for full siblings and 1/4 for half siblings constitutes the average value for full and half-sib relations. Barash, Holmes, and Greene (1978) have suggested that the distinction of relationships in which actual relatedness rather than estimated relatedness can be known may be significant in social interaction.

3. It can be noted that even near-universal tendencies, such as ability for spoken language, do have exceptions, and such exceptions can be caused by genetic variation from the usual pattern.

REFERENCES

Barash, D.P.
1976 "Male response to apparent female adultery in the mountain bluebird: an evolutionary interpretation." American Naturalist 110:1097–101.
1977a Sociobiology and Behavior. New York: Elsevier.
1977b "Sociobiology of rape in mallards: Responses of the mated male." Science 197:788–9.
Barash, D.P., W.G., Holmes and P.J. Greene
1978 "Exact versus probabilistic coefficients for relationship: Some implications for sociobiology." American Naturalist 112:355–63.
Barkow, J.H.
1977 "Conformity to ethos and reproductive success in two Hausa communities: an empirical evaluation." Ethos 5:409–25.
1978 "Culture and sociobiology." American Anthropologist 80:5–20.
Campos, J.J., S. Hiatt, D. Ramsay, C. Henderson, and M. Svejda
1978 "The emergence of fear on the visual cliff." In M. Lewis & L.A. Rosenblum (eds.), The Development of Affect. New York: Plenum.
Caplan, A.L.
1978 The Sociobiology Debate. New York: Harper & Row.
Carey, W.B.
1979 "The importance of temperament–environment interaction for child health and development." Paper presented at the conference on the uncommon child, Educational Testing Service, Princeton, New Jersey.
Carey, W.B., M. Fox, and S.C. McDevitt
1977 "Temperament as a factor in early school adjustment." Pediatrics. 60 (Suppl.): 621–624.
Chagnon, N.A., and P.E. Bugos, Jr.
1979 "Kin selection and conflict: an analysis of a Yanomamo ax fight." In N.A. Chagnon and W. Irons (eds.), Evolutionary Biology and Human Social Behavior. North Scituate, Mass.: Duxbury Press.
Chagnon, N.A., and W. Irons (eds.)
1979 Evolutionary Biology and Human Social Behavior. North Scituate, Mass.: Duxbury Press.
Cross, H.A., and H.F. Harlow
1965 "Prolonged and progressive effects of partial isolation on the behavior of Macaque monkeys." Journal of Experimental Research in Personality 1:39–49.
Dawkins, R.
1976 The Selfish Gene. New York: Oxford University Press.

DeFries, J.C.
1978 "Genetics of animal and human behavior." Paper presented at the meeting of the American Association for the Advancement of Science, Washington, D.C.

Durham, W.H.
1976a "Resource competition and human agression. Part I: a review of primitive war." Quarterly Review of Biology 51:385–415.
1976b "The adaptive significance of cultural behavior." Human Ecology 2:89–121.

Dyson-Hudson, R., and E. Alden-Smith
1978 "Human territoriality: an ecological assessment." American Anthropologist 80:21–41.

Feinman, S.
1979 "An evolutionary theory of food sharing." Social Science Information 18:695–726.

Freedman, D.G.
1958 "Constitutional and environmental interaction in rearing of four breeds of dogs." Science 127 585–6.
1964 "Smiling in blind infants and the issue of innate vs. acquired." Journal of Child Psychology and Psychiatry 5:171–84.
1965 "Hereditary control of early social behavior." In B.M. Foss (ed.), Determinants of Infant Behavior, Vol. III. London: Methuen.

Freedman, D.G., and N. Freedman
1969 "Behavioral differences between Chinese-American and European-American newborns." Nature 224:1227.

Freedman, D.G., J.A. King, and O. Elliot
1960 "Critical period in the social development of dogs." Science 133:1016–7.

Glascock, A.P., and S.L. Feinman
1980 "A holocultural analysis of old age." Comparative Social Research 3:in press.

Greene, P.J.
1978 "Promiscuity, paternity, and culture." American Ethnologist 5:151–9.

Hamilton, W.D.
1964 "The genetical evolution of social behavior. I & II." Journal of Theoretical Biology 7:1–51.

Harris, M.
1974 Cows, Pigs, Wars, and Witches. New York: Random House.

Hartung, J.
1976 "On natural selection and the inheritance of wealth." Current Anthropology 17:607–22.

Irons, W.
1979 "Emic and reproductive success." In N.A. Chagnon and W. Irons (eds.), Evolutionary Biology and Human Social Behavior. North Scituate, Mass.: Duxbury Press.

Kurland, J.A.
"Matrilines: the primate sisterhood and the human avunculate." In I. DeVore (ed.), Sociobiology and the Social Sciences. Chicago: Aldine.

Lewis, M., and L.A. Rosenblum (eds.)
1974 The Effect of the Infant on Its Caregiver. New York: Wiley.

Loehlin, J.C., and R.C. Nichols
1976 Heredity, Environment, and Personality. Austin: University of Texas Press.

McClearn, G.E., and J.C. DeFries
1973 Introduction to Behavioral Genetics. San Francisco: Freeman.

McKinney, W.T., Jr., S. Suomi and H. Harlow
1973 "Methods and models in primate personality research." In J.C. Westman (ed.), Individual Differences in Children. New York: Wiley.

Mazur, A.
1976 "On Wilson's Sociobiology." American Journal of Sociology 82:697–700.
Merton, R.K.
1968 Social Theory and Social Structure, 3rd ed. New York: Free Press.
Parker, S.
1976 "The precultural basis of the incest taboo: toward a biosocial theory." American Anthropologist 73:285–305.
Peters, R. H.
1976 "Tautology in evolution and ecology." American Naturalist 110:1–12.
Quadagno, J.S.
1979 "Paradigms in evolutionary theory: the sociobiological model of natural selection." American Sociological Review 44:100–9.
Rheingold, H.L., and C.O. Eckerman
1973 "Fear of the stranger: a critical review." In H.W. Reese (ed.), Advances in Child Development and Behavior, Vol. 8. New York: Academic Press.
Ruse, M.
1979 Sociobiology: Sense or Nonsense? Boston: Reidel.
Sahlins, M.D.
1972 "On the sociology of primitive exchange." In M.D. Sahlins (ed.), Stone Age Economics. Chicago: Aldine.
1976 The Use and Abuse of Biology: An Anthropological Critique of Sociobiology. Ann Arbor: University of Michigan Press.
Scarr, S.
1968 "Environmental bias in twin studies." In S.G. Vandenberg (ed.), Progress in Human Behavior Genetics. Baltimore: Johns Hopkins University Press.
Seligman, M.E.P., and J.L. Hager (eds.)
1972 Biological Boundaries of Learning. New York: Appleton-Century-Crofts.
Smith, J. Maynard
1974 "The theory of games and the evolution of animal conflict." Journal of Theoretical Biology 47:209–221.
Stern, C.
1973 Principles of Human Genetics, 3rd. ed. San Francisco: Freeman.
Steward, J.H.
1955 Theory of Culture Change. Urbana: University of Illinois Press.
Talmon, Y.
1964 "Mate selection in collective settlements." American Sociological Review 29:491–508.
Thomas, A., and S. Chess
1977 Temperament and Development. New York: Brunner/Mazel.
Trivers, R.L.
1971 "The evolution of reciprocal altruism." Quarterly Review of Biology 46:35–57.
1974 "Parent–offspring conflict." American Zoologist 14:249–64.
Trivers, R.L., and D.E. Willard
1973 "Natural selection of parental ability to vary the sex ratio of offspring." Science 179:90–2.
van den Berghe, P.L.
1974 "Bringing beasts back in: toward a biosocial theory of agression." American Sociological Review 39:777–88.
1975 Man in Society: A Biosocial View. New York: Elsevier.
van den Berghe, P.L., and D.P. Barash
1977 "Inclusive fitness and human family structure." American Anthropologist 79:809–23.

Wilson, E.O.
  1975 Sociobiology: The New Synthesis. Cambridge, Mass.: Harvard University Press.
  1977 "Biology and the social sciences." Daedalus 106(Fall):127–40.
Wolf, A.P.
  1968 "Adopt a daughter, marry a sister: a Chinese solution to the problem of the incest taboo." American Anthropologist 70:864–74.

THE LOGIC OF SOCIAL FORMATIONS:
TOWARD A SYNTHESIS OF ALTHUSSER, FOUCAULT, OFFE, AND HABERMAS

Sang Jin Han

This paper deals with the logic of social formations on the basis of structural analysis. The logic in question is, however, a theoretical construct. Like the concept of the mode of production, the logic has no direct empirical reference. On the contrary, the logic refers to a set of basic concepts and their relations by which the specific unity of a social formation is explicated.

Analytically, the concept of social formations can be differentiated into diverse instances of formation depending on theoretical strategies. For example, we may say that capital accumulation is as much a part of social

Current Perspectives in Social Theory, volume 1, 1980, pages 161–192.
ISBN: 0-89232-154-7

formation as socialization. Alternatively, we may suggest in line with Althusser (1969:167) that this concept refers to such discrete levels of formation as the economic, the political, the ideological, and the theoretical. Each level or instance of formation is supposed to delineate a specific field of production in society which is unique in terms of its products (e.g., value, power, meaning, subjectivity, and knowledge) and its mode of production. The elementary task confronting us is to specify the logic of production on each field of social formation and the ways in which these field-specific modes of production in society are interrelated or dislocated.

This requires a rigorous structural analysis, and, as in any other inquiry, the choice of basic concepts and strategies determines in a crucial way the knowledge generated from them. Before we get to the main discussion, then, I would like to clarify the strategy that I will use in this paper and reflect on the goal of this analysis in a schematic fashion. This will be followed by a discussion of Althusser's theory of overdetermination and then by a series of critical discussions exploring the reasons why systems theory and linguistics are as important as Marxism for dealing with the logic of social formations.

TOWARD A DISCURSIVE ANALYSIS

We may discuss the regulative principles of social analysis, beginning from Marxism, which has vigorously warned us of the danger of both empiricism and idealism. In particular, Althusser's argument has proved to be highly stimulating in many respects. Being critical of the Hegelian interpretation of Marxism, Althusser has taken care to appreciate the relative autonomy of the superstructural instances of social formation and to renew the question of structural determination and domination. In addition, Althusser's critique of homocentric methods of analysis in social science is as persuasive as his criticism of vulgar materialism. There are thus good reasons to take Althusser's discussion as the point of departure.

The key to Althusser's structural analysis is the concept of overdetermination. Briefly stated, this concept suggests that a contradiction, far from being a simple manifestation of an origin, emerges out of various instances of contradiction as a condensation of them in such a way that structural causes are therein reflected As we shall soon see, this conception is useful. However, the way in which Althusser formulates this concept is not without problems. Three need to be mentioned. First, in dealing with the logic of social formations, Althusser concerns himself primarily with the formation of contradictions, but not with the management of them by the system. It seems necessary to incorporate systems theory more constructively than Althusser suggests to resolve this problem. Second, Althusser's theory of overdetermination, though powerful in many respects, turns out to be limited in exploring the linguistic foundations of social formations, and thus the link between structure and action. A theory of discursive formations is necessary to grasp the interplay between knowledge and social formations in its complexity. Third, Althusser's theory of social formations is far more descriptive than reflexive; thus, the practical intent of theory and its relation to rationality are not properly handled. In view of the fact that knowledge in general, including theoretical knowledge, is itself an element of social formations, a reflexive standpoint must be reinstated in the theory of social formations.

With these considerations I shall leave Althusser's Marxism for what we may call a "discursive analysis" of social formations (for this concept, see Foucault, 1972; Lemert and Gillan, 1977; Han, 1979a). Major theoretical sources for this progression are Jürgen Habermas, Michel Foucault, and Claus Offe. Here the meaning of the term *discursive* must be understood in two different contexts.[1] Placed on the descriptive function of theory, discursive means that, as an effect of reconstruction, the nature-like (*naturwüchsig*) blindness of social formations is transformed into an intelligible object so that it becomes subject to discursive examination. The invisible structure is thereby rendered visible. To attain this effect, however, not only political economy but also distorted communication as a basis of capitalist development must be investigated. In the context in which we discuss the interplay between theory and practice, discursive means that theory, with the knowledge it produces, takes up a specific strategy geared to praxis through discursively attained enlightenment. This strategy is distinguished from both the technical–instrumental and the Marxist–actionist ones. Discursive in this connection means that theory is reflexive of its practical intent and clarifies the conditions for the discursive realization of this intent (Habermas, 1971, 1971a, 1973b).

With regard to Marxism, discursive analysis is aimed at both making materialist analysis more rigorous and explicitly clarifying linguistic foundations of social formations. The latter is as crucial as the former for historical materialism understood undogmatically. Language has turned out to be important, even for Marxism, because all social actions, including revolutionary practice, as constituted within the system of signification (discursive formation for Foucault). With all the stimulating suggestions it offers, Althusser's Marxism has failed, however, to tackle the problem of language in its own right. To go beyond this, it is necessary to bring structuralist semiotics (Foucault) and universal pragmatics (Habermas) into contact with materialism.

The strategy that I shall pursue in this paper is a synthesis of Althusser,

Foucault, Offe, and Habermas concerning the question of the logic of social formations. Neither Marxism nor linguistics alone is sufficient for dealing with this question. Rather, materialist analysis, systems theory, and discursive analysis must be placed within a discursive theory of social formations. Only on this condition can we hope to incorporate diverse and seemingly unrelated inquiries into a coherent framework.

LANGUAGE AND MATERIALISM

The logic of social formations may be better clarified if we can establish the link between structure and action in a more intelligible way than in the past. It is well known that Marxism, for example, has intrinsic difficulty in translating its concept of structures to a theory of social action insofar as it bases itself on materialism. How to relate the law of value to the law of action is highly problematic. This is a serious problem because a social formation cannot be well understood without an adequate reference to social action.

Interestingly enough, it is a theory of language that has offered a clue to the solution of this problem. According to structuralist semiotics and universal pragmatics, social action unfolds within the system of signification and validity. Thus, social action is neither as mechanistic as dogmatic Marxism has implied nor as teleological as interpretive sociology has depicted. Both sociologism and subjectivism are firmly rejected. Instead, social action is understood as constituted within the process of discourse. To put it more broadly, power, things, and subjectivity are viewed not as determined from outside, but as embedded in, discursive formations (Foucault, 1972; Habermas, 1979a). There appears a striking convergence between Foucault and Habermas in that they both attempt to reconstruct the constraints built into communication within the field of discourse, avoiding reductionist explanations.[2] To be sure, the methodological foci of their approaches are drastically different.[3] Nevertheless, they are united by the belief that a discursive formation has its own history and follows its own rules of formation and enunciation. They both think that social action hinges on the formation and the transformation of discourse, and thus is in some way constructed by language. In short, language is viewed as a meta-institution upon which all social formations are based (Habermas, 1970a:287).

Provided the semiotic constraints that this theory grasps can be related to the material constraints that Marxism grasps, it is possible to establish the link between structure and action. But we are presently far away from this. Though we can conceive of this possibility, we have as yet no theory that establishes this. We have only a few guides that seem promising. We start from the premise that social action unfolds within semiological systems and these systems, in which meaning is constituted, are regulated by their own rules of formation and functioning. We can further state that social action can be understood in its meaningfulness *and* determination if we successfully investigate how semiological systems are produced or eliminated in each region of society. An adequate translation of the objective constraints of action to the domain of discourse would be indispensable for this.

Power, for example, has to be located within the system of discourse. Power must be understood as formed in discourse rather than as determined elsewhere and imposed on it.[4] This by no means indicates that the Marxist analysis of power in terms of social classes and the mode of production is invalid. It only suggests that power, as a material existence, can function the way it does only through certain discursive means of selection and exclusion by which it enunciates itself. Viewed in this way, an important task for a theory of social formations is to translate the orthodox conceptual framework of Marxism into a critical theory of discourse.

Generally speaking, the unity of "materialist" analysis envisioned by Marxism is indisputable and, in fact, growing due to the emergence and dispersion of structuralist Marxism. Althusser, Godelier, and Poulantzas, for instance, make important contributions to this in their own ways. What has not yet been clarified is the relation between language and materialism, one of the most delicate and demanding theoretical problems today. Clearly, it is questionable to treat language as a superstructure, i.e., a formation determined by the material conditions of existence. Anthropologically and sociologically, this view creates more problems than it solves. Rather, there are good reasons to treat language as a "material" existence or as a "material" basis of social formations in the sense that it is irreducible to any other and regulated by its own rules of production. This view has been articulated by such structuralist semiologists as Foucault (1972, 1977), Kristeva (1975), Lacan (1977), and Barthes (1967, 1972). Yet it is also quite clear that language cannot be treated as an ideality or as an autonomous development, pure and simple, which is free from the constraints of class society. As Foucault and Habermas have shown, communication remains systematically distorted in class society. Thus, an adequate theoretical framework relating language to materialism is needed for dealing with the logic of social formations.[5]

One of our basic goals is to bring language and materialism as close together as possible to reveal the aspects in which language becomes crucial for material analysis of social formations. By attempting to do so, I claim to achieve no more than an initial interaction between the theory of overdetermination (Althusser) and the theory of discourse (Foucault, Habermas). This interaction is worthy to try for the following reasons.

First, as I already indicated, this enables us to see how the gap between structure and action can be reduced. Second, this reveals that capitalist development is in fact grounded on what Foucault calls discursive formations, and especially what Habermas calls distorted communication. Third, this clarifies the logic of social evolution in an unambiguous way by dealing with the rational basis of evolutionary solutions of system problems. Finally, this helps us articulate the discursive nature of theoretical inquiry. Producing theoretical knowledge involves critique of distorted communication which is, in turn, an element of the transformation of the semiotic basis of domination. With this perspective, theory can be related in a reflexive way to the social formations it investigates.

OVERDETERMINATION

Following the tradition of Marxism, Althusser argues that the logic of social formations lies in contradictions understood as the motor of historical change. Althusser is, however, clearly distinguished from most conventional Marxists in that he addresses himself to contradictions as primarily a theoretical problem rather than as an empirical one. That is to say, Althusser begins by critically examining the theory of contradictions itself. Althusser does so because he thinks that the way in which knowledge is produced is regulated by a specific order which cannot be reduced to either an historical or an empirical one. Thus, Marxist analysis cannot possibly be a representation but is an articulation, which means that it presupposes certain regulative concepts. If these concepts are poorly grounded, fatal consequences would be unavoidable. Althusser thus argues that we must examine the concept of contradictions with care before we employ it for historical research.

Althusser has argued that the concept of contradictions, as a Marxist concept, has been misconstrued in the history of Marxism due to the confusion between Hegel's and Marx's dialectics. Althusser (1969:198–204; 1970:Chap. 9) even contends that whole problems of dogmatic Marxism have their philosophical roots in Hegel's concept of expressive totality according to which history has an inner essence directly expressed in all constitutive elements of the whole. All social formations are then directly subordinated to the hegemonic center. Althusser reasons that if we understand Marx's dialectics simply as a materialist "inversion" of Hegel's speculative dialectics, as alluded to by Marx himself, and as many Marxists have since concluded, then it is difficult to avoid reductionist consequences because here all instances of formation such as politics, socialization, arts, family, and communication are to be seen as direct expressions of economic contradictions conceived of as the essence of all appearances. Althusser has pointed out, however, that the concept of expressive totality cannot provide a reliable basis for Marxist analysis. Althusser (1969:174–175; 1970:187) suggests instead that Marx's works were based on a rejection of this concept and on the introduction of a new concept to which, however, Marx gave no theoretical expression.[6] That is to say, a new concept of dialectics was operative in Marx's theoretical practice but without a theoretical concept for it. For this reason, Althusser claims that Marx's thought has been easily misrepresented by Hegelian Marxism.[7] To break through this, a theory that distinguishes Marx's dialects from Hegel's is necessary. Althusser (1970:186) proposes the concept of *structured totality*, stressing the relative autonomy of social formations and their structural relations. Althusser's thesis is that the Marxist analysis of social formations must be based on the concept of structured totality. To make this thesis stronger, Althusser (1970:187) argues that this concept represents Marx's scientific discovery, i.e., Marx's epistemological break with Hegel's idealism.

Althusser's proposal is consequential. Not only mechanistic determinism but also all brands of homocentric revisions are flatly rejected. Also, contradictions are viewed no longer as an auto-development of an origin, but as a complex problem requiring structural analysis for which Althusser has suggested the following requirements: (1) the concept of subjectivity be treated not as an explanatory resource but as a product situated in the modes of societal reproduction; (2) the concept of social formations be analytically decomposed into such instances of formation as the economic, the political, the ideological, the technical, and the scientific, so that the field-specific logic of production in each instance can be reconstructed with sufficient rigor; (3) an instance of formation be investigated in structural relations with others in such a way that both its relative autonomy and structural determination are grasped; finally, (4) theoretical knowledge be so constructed that the invisible rules of production are thereby transformed into a discursive object. This discursively attained effect of analysis Althusser calls the "knowledge effect."

Developing this concept of structural analysis, Althusser endorses a systems-theoretical premise that social formations are interdependent and interpretative in their modes of producing contradictions. This premise suggests that the more contradictions accumulate in each instance of social formation the greater the degree of interpenetration between them. A few empirical examples are *stagflation* (Altvater, 1973) and *legitimation deficit* (Habermas, 1975:73). Stagflation can be seen as a result of the accelerated interpenetration between economic and political processes in advanced capitalism. A legitimation deficit reflects not only symbolic but the economic contradictions which underly it. This amounts to saying that a contradiction emerges out of a series of contradictions as a concentration of them. To grasp this mechanism fully, the analysis must be structural, and certainly not as simple and mechanistic as in dogmatic Marxism.

The concept of *overdetermination* (Althusser, 1969:206) refers to the processes by which diverse types and tokens of contradictions inside and outside a system merge into certain conjunctures so as to generate a new and concentrated form of contradiction. Overdetermination designates not a linear and mechanistic but a structured mode of determination. Contradictions are overdetermined in the structural sense if: (1) structural causes—"the structure of unevenness in dominance" for Althusser (1969:217)—are so reflected in each instance of contradictions that, although the mode of determination is not immediately visible, the latter finds its expression as structurally circumscribed by the former; (2) this determination takes place in such a way that the specific autonomy of the concerned social formations is fully maintained; and (3) diverse instances of contradictions interact within this structural determination so that, as an effect of this interpenetration, contradictions become ever more complex and sharpened not only in their individual manifestations but also as a whole.

The concept of overdetermination is revealing especially when viewed against the naturelike, politically uncontrolled processes of capitalist development which, as Marxism has well analyzed, are geared to horizontal and vertical unevenness. According to Althusser, all instances of contradiction have their roots in the logic of this capitalist development. The core of this development is, of course, the capitalist economic development of unevenness. This unevenness is, according to Althusser, the condition for the possibility of contradictions.

> So unevenness is internal to a social formation because the structuration in dominance of the complex whole, this structural invariant, *is itself the precondition for the concrete variation of the contradictions* that constitute it, and therefore for their displacements, condensations and mutations, etc., and inversely because this variation is the existence of that invariant (Althusser, 1969; emphases in original).

The concept of overdetermination is then essentially characterized by the "reflection of the conditions of existence of the contradiction within itself," that is, the "reflection of the structure articulated in dominance . . . within each contradiction" (Althusser, 1969:206).

Althusser's theory of overdetermination may be seen as a structuralist reformulation of historical materialism.[8] The simple determinism is clearly rejected with the renewal of materialist determinism in a new framework. According to this reformulation, the dominant role in social formations can be shifted from one field to another (kinships, religion, or the state) but the determinant instance is always the economic mode of production. The relative autonomy of social formations is emphasized here, but "in a specific way of referring back to a system of constraints which determine in the last analysis," that is, economic constraints "which express the conditions of production and reproduction of the material basis of social existence" (Godelier, 1972:xxxviii). Consequently, the structural compatibility and incompatibility of social formations are ultimately determined by the economic mode of production. It follows from this that the evolutionary transformation of society is determined, in the last analysis, by the major transformations that take place in the economic mode of production (Godelier, 1972:ix).

The logic of social formations captured by Althusser's theory of overdetermination is the logic of the accumulation of contradictions. While properly emphasizing the specific unity of each instance of social formations, Althusser grasps contradictions in their complexity against the capitalist context of uneven development. Thus, in Althusser's (1969:216) theoretical framework, contradictions are supposed to grow, through various means and interconnections, to the point of "explosion," i.e., the stage of "unstable global condensation."

It is difficult to prove the empirical validity of this conjecture at the present time. However, the theoretical adequacy of Althusser's framework can be rationally discussed. It can be argued, for example, that in dealing with the logic of social formations we need to be concerned as much with how a system responds to contradictions as with how contradictions grow. To tackle this issue properly, it seems necessary to assimilate systems theory into the theory of overdetermination more fully than we find in Althusser's Marxism. A set of critical discussions will follow in the next pages with respect to the interaction between systems theory and Marxism, on the one hand, and between language and Marxism, on the other.

SYSTEMS THEORY AND STATE INTERVENTIONISM

Althusser's theory of overdetermination, if translated to systems theory, can be a powerful tool for explicating the formation of system problems. The crisis tendencies of advanced capitalism, for example, may be analyzed in the light of this theory. What remains to be demonstrated, though, is how a system, under the pressure of accumulating problems, opens up a new level of social organization; that is, how a structural transformation of society takes place. Obviously enough, this question is as crucial as the formation of contradictions for understanding the logic of social formations.

Systems theory is meaningful in this regard in that it enables us to see the other side of the problem more clearly than Marxism does. This is the steering function of the system vis-à-vis external and internal environments.[9] Two issues deserve special attention. First, if the attempted management of contradictions is itself contradictory, as Marxists (e.g., Altvater, 1973) claim, how and why does it have to be so? Here, it is not meaningful to posit from the outset that the system is implicated in contradictions. Rather, it must be shown, through adequate analysis, why and how a system, in its specific mode of operation, cannot function in any other way than by producing contradictory consequences. For this, the system must be viewed not as a fixed but as a complex and self-expanding system capable of innovations. Second, if system problems accumulate to the extent that they overload the adaptive capacity of the system, as found on the threshold of an evolutionary transition, how does this leap take place? The theory of overdetermination is not very useful in this regard since, as Habermas (1979a:124) notes, it is not possible to "find in the logic of the rise of system problems the logic that the social system will follow if it responds to such an evolutionary challenge." More care must be taken in examining these issues.

The first issue relates to the interplay between contradictions and their management in both synchronic and diachronic aspects within a circumscribed range of variable innovations. By contrast, the second one is concerned with the transformation of what Habermas (1975:7) calls "the organizational principle" of a society by which the range of such variations itself is structurally delineated. Systems theory is useful for considering both issues. With respect to the first, systems theory can show that contradictions can be mitigated, temporarily shifted or displaced, due to interventionist measures. At the same time, systems theory can also reveal that despite, and perhaps because of, this intervention, contradictions may become structurally more complex and intensified (Offe, 1972a; Habermas, 1975). The theory of overdetermination can be further strengthened in this way by using systems theory. Concerning the second issue, systems theory shows that a system facing evolutionary challenges can continue its existence only when it successfully opens up a new possibility of resolving overloaded structural problems. For this, the system-environments boundary must be radically and functionally altered to attain a higher level of system complexity with evolutionary significance (Luhmann, 1970). This argument, though not fully explanatory, leads us in the right direction when we deal with this issue.

One of the best available historical studies in this regard is, perhaps, Klaus Eder's (cited in Habermas, 1979a) study of the emergence of class society.[10] However, in this case, there is no need to apply the concept of overdetermination to explain the formation of system problems that triggered an evolutionary transition. State interventionism in advanced capitalism, however, can be used to support the theory of overdetermination although it is as yet highly ambiguous to explore its possible meaning for an epoch-making evolutionary change. Within this limitation, however, there is no doubt that state interventionism is of decisive importance for clarifying the logic of contemporary social formations, because it is certainly not possible to explain the peculiar features of advanced capitalism without a reference to it (Offe, 1972a, 1972b, 1973, 1975; Habermas, 1975; Altvater, 1973; Poulantzas, 1975; Wright, 1978; O'Connor, 1973; Miliband, 1969). State interventionism signifies a new phase of capitalist development associated with the rapid increase in the function of the political system as the so-called steering agency of the whole system. In this phase, the system problems that once threatened to destroy capitalism are no longer managed through the self-healing function of the market, but by the state which actively engaged in capital accumulation and legitimation of its policies. This innovation can be examined in terms of its contradictory effects as well as the manner in which the system responds to contradictions. Thus, the questions of overdetermination and system innovation can be raised.

To begin with, it is necessary to reject both Marxist reductionism and bourgeois pluralism and to view the state as a relatively autonomous sphere captured by the concept of overdetermination (Poulantzas, 1975; Offe, 1974; O'Connor, 1973). This is a methodological starting point of a discursive analysis of state interventionism. To examine state intervention more carefully, we would have to include in our analysis: (1) the specific modes of the accumulation of system problems; (2) innovative responses of the system to these problems, especially the functional reorganization of the relations between accumulation and the state; (3) the specific modes of operation, especially the rules of selection and exclusion institutionalized in state activities; and (4) the possible evolutionary significance of this new learning process.

Of these, the third issue is crucially related to the possible explanation of such peculiar features of advanced capitalism as the sectoral shift of social conflict. Why has social conflict been transformed from organized labor to the sectors marginal to the system in advanced capitalism? No complete answer to this is as yet available. Much more research seems necessary to explain it with clearer reference to social action than is now possible. Among the attempted explanations to date, however, Offe's (1972a) is most instructive. Visualizing capitalist development as the process of structural exclusion, Offe constructs a model of state intervention to show where the negative consequences of public service fall and why. This model suggests that the state, under the imperative for survival, has attempted to manage the tendencies of crisis in such a way that it gives priority of service to the "concentric" sector of the system because this sector is either functionally most important for the system as a whole (e.g., the monopoly sector) or capable of mobilizing forces whose persistent use would result in fatal consequences (e.g., organized labor). Thus, the management of contradictions by the state has been pursued, according to this model, at the systematic expense of the "peripheral" sectors of the system. This suggests a structural reason why organized labor has been more or less integrated into the dominant rules of the game in advanced capitalism whereas such marginal groups as youth, students, racial and ethnic minorities, criminals, and women have been involved in intensified social conflicts (Offe, 1973; O'Connor, 1973; Baudrillard, 1975).

State intervention, however, can be viewed as contradictory despite its apparent success in managing conflicts in the concentric zone of the system. This view is based on the reasoning that although the state seriously attempts to control crisis tendencies, it can do so only under conditions that, paradoxically, make it difficult for the state to accomplish what it wishes. In other words, what the state can possibly do is not to control the process of capital accumulation from which contradictions are basically derived but to maintain its conditions and to take care of its negative social consequences (e.g., unemployment). As Offe (1975:127–7) puts it, the state finds itself in a position to "manage" accumulation but under such constraints that it must remain "excluded" from and, as a state based on taxation, "dependent" on accumulation. The best thing that the state can do is to help accumulation rather than to rationalize it. There is the question, then, as to whether or not state intervention, whatever its temporal success may be, will create more and more complex and severe contradictions in the long run.[11] Along with this suspicion, remains the question of whether or not, and, if so, how, the conflict zone will move back from the margin to the center of the system.

It is here that the concept of overdetermination can be empirically supported by the example of state interventionism. Most obviously, state economic intervention has turned out to be conducive to a mutated form of contradiction which we call stagflation. Altvater (1973:192) has sharply argued in this regard that "the state produces crises while it manages crises . . . because it never acts as an autonomous subject . . . but is caught in the contradictions of capital." Overdetermination can be seen here in the effects of state intervention which are present in stagflation. We may say that the state overdetermines economic contradictions while it attempts to displace them administratively. The state then becomes more and more caught up in the contradictions of capitalist development. Furthermore, state intervention has also resulted in diffused potentials of protest in society and, to a certain extent, the politicization of domination. Habermas (1975) and Offe (1972b, 1973) have argued that crisis tendencies today emerge as much from the political and ideological domain as from the economic. Overdetermination can be seen here in the fact that these contradictory consequences, themselves conditioned by capitalist development of unevenness, pose a threat to the continuity of capitalism. The stability of the political system, which is in trouble now, is itself an important condition of accumulation.

This discussion shows the importance of the interaction between Marxism and systems theory. This interaction has been deliberately pursued by Claus Offe (1972a,b, 1973, 1974, 1975), among others. In this connection, state interventionism may be seen as an historical problem that necessitates this.[12] With Marxism, we can show where system problems arise. With systems theory, we can examine how the system responds to these problems. But it is with Marxism *and* systems theory that we can properly tackle two new problems: the contradictory effects of state intervention and its evolutionary significance. State interventionism can be viewed as an innovative variation within a capital framework. It is innovative in the sense that the function of the political system—power as a system resource—has been expanded such that, as Offe (1975) demonstrates, accumulation increasingly depends on the conditions of production which not capital, but the state, provides.[13] The state remains within the capitalist framework of variations in the sense that the complementary relationship of the state to accumulation, characteristic of the state since the beginning of the modern era, is still effective. Nevertheless, it is also clear that state interventionism, expressed by welfare policies and regional planning, has initiated a new process of social learning whose evolutionary significance is open to interpretation.

DISCURSIVE FORMATIONS: THE LINK BETWEEN STRUCTURE AND ACTION

The interaction between Marxism and systems theory is a necessary but not a sufficient condition for the clarification of the logic of social formations. As important, or even more important, is an adequate theory of social action of which a social formation is composed. However, Marxism and systems theory have certain difficulties in this respect. For instance, the theory of overdetermination (Althusser) shows how contradictions are formed in their complexity, but does not show clearly how these contradictions are transformed into action, that is, how social actions themselves are constituted in contradictions. Neither a theory of social action nor a theory of subjectivity is well articulated. To a larger extent, the subject is assumed to be the carrier of structurally determined contradictions. Likewise, the link between system and action within systems theory is also surrounded by mounting clouds. Action and subjectivity are here depicted as functional equivalents of the system that can be easily modified or replaced according to the needs of system integration

(Luhmann, 1974). However, it remains highly ambiguous how these needs for imperatives are transformed into social action.

This reveals that the relation between structure and action needs to be considered more carefully than in Marxism and systems theory. Or, to put it in a broader context, the old-fashioned antinomy in sociology between determinism and voluntarism is to be superseded dialectically, so that social action can be explained in its determination and meaningfulness within a consistent theoretical framework. In Marxism and systems theory, however, the concept of structure is so objectively constructed that its relation to action remains abstract. In phenomenology and interpretive sociology, in contrast, the concept of action is so subjectively construed that its structural determination is hidden. Marxism provides a dialectical perspective stressing the interplay between structures and actions, but no theoretical means for translating this perspective to a social-scientific theory of action.[14]

Quite unexpectedly, but not by chance, a clue to the solution of this problem has been found in a theory of language. Saussure (1959), the founder of modern structural linguistics, noted that language is not a representation but an articulation, which means that the world appears within the conceptual (signifying) order produced by language (cf., Culler, 1976). Things, structures, and motives are then not imposed on language from outside as a preestablished origin or synthesis, but are themselves shaped and put in place by language. This suggests that the human world as a whole is constituted within the processes of signification. The implications of this discovery for epistemology and social analysis have been explored further by Foucault, Kristeva, Derrida, Barthes, and Lacan.[15] It has become quite clear from this that signification is a fundamental basis of all social formations and that social action is constituted in, and regulated by, what Eco (1976) calls "sign production." This opens up the possibility of resolving the traditional antinomy between determinism and voluntarism within a theory of language (Lemert, 1979).

The basic premise emerging here is that social action is a signifying practice (Kristeva, 1975; Foucault, 1977; Lacan, 1977). Action is, therefore, never as mechanically determined as vulgar Marxism and sociologism assume. Nor is it as simply based on intention as phenomenology depicts. Rather, social action, as a signifying practice, is made possible within the process of signification and bound to the rules of dispersed language games. This approach, which we call discursive, says that it is no longer meaningful to explain social action in terms of, say, subjective motives, material constraints, and the prerequisites of the system, without seeing these determinants themselves as embedded in and shaped by discursive formations.[16]

The structure of action is thus located at the domain of discourse, not elsewhere. Disclosure here is to be understood as a primitive or, to use Foucault's (1972) concept, "archaeological" concept. That is to say, discourse refers to the primitive process in which what Bourdieu (1971:183) calls "the cultural unconscious" is formed and dispersed in society as if it were natural. Far from being a mere mental image, the unconscious is a specific product of regularized discourse and signification. Discourse in this sense is powerful in delineating the boundary between what is possible and what is impossible, and between what is legitimate and what is illegitimate. Discursive formations in Foucault's sense can, therefore, be understood as a specific mode of production whose product is "meaning," i.e., the system of constraints which regulates social action.[17] This system of constraints is fundamentally of semiotic nature and often invisible.

It is now clear that for discursive analysis the selective and exclusive effects of discursive formations (Foucault, 1977:199) are of fundamental significance for every social formation, both theoretically and practically: theoretically because social action, as the object of analysis, must be grasped within the system of semiotic constraints; practically in the sense that, upon the reconstruction of these constraints, the nature-like obviousness is transformed to an intelligible object, yielding rich practical consequences. For discursive analysis, therefore, the analysis of discourse is indispensable for clarifying the logic of social formations. Foucault (1972:208) thus expects that discursive analysis will make it possible "to articulate, in a less imprecise way than in the past, the analysis of social formation and epistemological description."

Of various intellectual trends in which the idea of discursive analysis is present in some ways,[18] structuralist semiotics and universal pragmatics are distinctive in that they formulate a linguistic model of social formations, though with different methodological foci. Both have developed a systematic argument that have given discourse a prominent place in social formations. To set out this model explicitly, it seems appriorate to distinguish three levels of determination: the objective, the discursive, and the psychic.[19] Each level involves its own mode of structuration—hence the relation between structure and surface, production and products. The objective level designates the mode of structuration which is objectively valid but whose link to social action still remains to be shown. To a larger extent, the Marxist analyses of the mode of production, of social classes, and of capitalist development, and the systems-theoretical accounts of social evolution and system integration remain at this level. The discursive level designates the mode of structuration specific to speech and action. This is the field where knowledge and action are formed, dispersed, and transformed as embedded in the processes of signification. The psychic level designates the mode of structuration of subjectivity, especially that portion of subjectivity which is excluded from public communication and thus remains private.

Of these three levels, the linguistic model of social formations is mostly concerned with the second level of determination, but with the following presuppositions. First, the systems of speech and action are regulated by their own rules of formation and enunciation which can be reconstructed. Second, the objective and the psychic modes of determination are, to a great extent, embedded in discursive formations in the sense that power, which has objective conditions of existence, is formed and exercised through the selective and exclusive effect of discourse. Third, the mode of structuration which is objectively valid (e.g., capitalist uneven development) is itself practically based on determinate systems of discourse (e.g., distorted communication), the rules of which have hitherto escaped analytic attention but can, in principle, be comprehended. Fourth, the psychic mode of exclusion itself is a signifying process and thus can be transformed to an intelligible object through analysis. And, finally, the discursive layer of a society increases in history due to the accumulation of knowledge of the objective, discursive, and psychic modes of determination.

According to this model, power, things, and subjectivity are not determined elsewhere and imposed on discourse, but are embedded in the processes of discourse. This has important repercussions on epistemology and social theory. Discursive analysis takes up this approach to capture the discursive conditions of domination and to translate the objective conditions that Marxism grasps to the domain of discourse. In this sense, discursive analysis presupposes rather than excludes systems theory and Marxism. For discursive analysis, the mode and the relations of production, for example, are viewed as particularly based on the system of "social hegemony" (Gramsci), i.e., determinate discursive articulations in which certain interests are perpetuated (selection) at the systematic expense of others (exclusion). These articulations, as the object of discursive analysis, are far more complex than the ideological formation in Althusser's sense.[20]

Foucault's (1973) analysis of the emergence of the mental institution may be suggested as an exemplar of discursive analysis. Foucault examines this regional instance of social formations as a discursive event that came into existence, not as determined mechanically by any need standing behind discourse, but as articulated through the interconnections of various discursive practices, e.g., scientific, ideological, and political. Foucault does not deny the existence of the economic, political, or symbolic conditions but shows that these conditions were shaped and set in place by a specific articulation which gave rise to clinical discourse. Thus, he uses neither a causal nor a symbolic but a discursive mode of analysis.

Also, this articulation is neither purely scientific nor merely ideological. Rather, sciences and ideologies are interconnected in a determinate way to form a concrete form of articulation. This study, though very limited by itself, nevertheless reveals that the analysis of social formations can be made more rigorous through the analysis of discursive formations.[21]

Discursive analysis is aimed at the practical basis of social formations, i.e., speech and action, postulating that the logic of discursive formations is irreducible to the logic of either capital or system maintenance. No deterministic view of social struggle is adopted here for it is understood that all claimed objective determinants can have their effect only as embedded in determinate discursive articulation within which they themselves are interpreted, politicized, or mitigated. The rise and the decline of social struggle, therefore, cannot be reasonably explained without recourse to discursive formations. The interest in this practical field has recently arisen in Marxism (cf., Poulantzas, 1975; Hindess and Hirst, 1975), but discursive analysis has opened up a fresh approach on the basis of a theory of discourse.

Given the present state of scientific knowledge, a synthesis of Marxism and the theory of discourse is highly desirable, especially with an eye to the link between the objective and the semiotic constraints of action. For example, the sectoral shift of the conflict zone in advanced capitalism, which we examined earlier, may be explained more clearly if we can show how the systems of signification have been so transformed in the concerned sectors of society that this shift must occur. To put it more broadly, the theory of capitalist development may become stronger if the discursive conditions of such structural processes as uneven development and its penetration into everyday life are adequately comprehended. This synthesis seems on the way, especially by those who attempt to deal with both Althusser's Marxism and structuralist semiotics.[22] To pursue this further, however, it is necessary to liberate ourselves from the tendency to reduce discourse to a superstructure. Otherwise, Marxism itself may become ideological in the sense that it fails to appreciate fully the fact that "the system now plays on the economic reference . . . as an alibi against the more serious subversion that threatens it in the symbolic order" (Baudrillard, 1975:139).

In sum, discursive analysis links structures and actions in two ways. First, they are linked in discursive formations in Foucault's archaeological sense. Action is here understood as constituted in, and regulated by, discursive formations. This link is neither abstract nor teleological. Second, discursive analysis links structures and actions in a specifically discursive way by relating the structures which have hitherto remained opaque to reflexive discourse. Discursive formations are here no longer primitive but become "reflexive" in Habermas's sense. Consequently, the primitive link between structures and actions is transformed in such a way that a new latitude of experience and action is created via discourse. It is through discursive formation in Habermas's sense that an emancipatory action is linked to structures. To use the psychoanalytic terms, this is the moment of "transgression" (Kristeva, 1975), "symbolic order" (Lacan, 1968), "self-reflection" (Habermas, 1971), and "resymbolization" (Lorenzer, 1974).

PERIODIZATION AND RATIONALITY

The foregoing discussion shows that to clarify the logic of social formations we must take into account not only the logic of contradictions and of system maintenance but also the logic of discursive formations. The usefulness and the limits of Marxism and systems theory have been explored from this perspective, together with the claim that the link between structure and action can be resolved in the light of a theory of discourse. This discussion reveals that the materialistic framework of determination on which Althusser's model of social formations hinges is restrictive in that it undercuts the complexity of discursive formations. As an alternative, discursive analysis formulates a linguistic model of social formations to show that production and discourse—or, to use Habermas's anthropological distinction, labor and interaction—are two deep structures of society equally fundamental for producing concrete instances of social formations. With this strategy, discursive analysis avoids the latent form of reductionism in Althusser's Marxism and creates a free space for the interaction between language and materialism.

This discursive approach has a number of advantages of which its possible contribution to linking structure and action has been explored. In addition, this approach also shows that the problem of rationality is no less important than the problem of contradictions for clarifying the logic of social formations. This can be shown with regard to the issue of periodization. Thus, in the following pages, I would like to reveal the context in which the problem of rationality becomes important for understanding social evolution and explore the significance of the analysis of discursive formations in this regard.

To begin with, the concept of periodization needs to be clarified in its synchronic and diachronic aspects. As a synchronic concept, periodization may be understood as a "structure-forming" or a "structure-maintaining" process of social formations. Periodization is then characterized by structural unity among social formations. As a diachronic concept, however, periodization may be understood as a "structure-breaking" or a "structure-transforming" process of social formations. Periodization then involves the structural incompatibilities of social formations, and hence an evolutionary transition of a society to a new mode of social organization. Periodization as the process of structuration involves not only mechanical determinations but also functional variations. For example, the feudal or the capitalist mode of production, as a distinctive mode of global structuration, consists of many functionally equivalent variants. Periodization as the process of restructuration, however, is characterized not by the functional variations of the system but by the change in the mode of structuration itself. So distinguished, the synchronic analysis of structuration and the diachronic analysis of restructuration are both necessary for a theory of periodization.

Of these two aspects, special attention should be focused on the diachronic problem of restructuration, not because this is intrinsically more important than the other, but because this still involves many unresolved problems, whereas the synchronic concept of periodization has become much stronger due to the contributions of structuralist Marxism.[23] It is well known that Marx saw the key to social evolution in the dialectics between productive forces and relations. Marx (1970:21) states that "at certain stage of development, the material productive forces of society come into conflict with the existing relations of production." The relation of production then must be revolutionized in order for productive forces to be fully implemented. An era of social revolution thus begins. Based on this formulation, Engels and Kautsky, and recently Balibar and Godelier, have argued that the premise of materialist determinism becomes fully valid during this critical phase of transition. This argument is limited, however, in that it only deals with the problem-generating mechanism in evolution, but not the logic of social evolution itself. The theory of overdetermination is powerful in suggesting where and how contradictions grow, but does not show how evolutionary transformations take place.

Examining this matter carefully, Habermas (1979a:147) sums up the major points Marxism offers as follows:

a. The system problems that cannot be solved without evolutionary innovations arise in the basic domain of a society.

b. Each new mode of production means a new form of social integration which is crystallized around a new institutional core.

c. An endogenous learning mechanism provides for the accumulation of a cognitive potential that can be used for solving crisis-inducing system problems.

d. This knowledge, however, can be implemented to develop the forces of production only when the evolutionary step to a new institutional framework and a new form of social integration has been taken.

What remains to be shown further is, according to Habermas, how this evolutionary step is taken.

The key problem here is not the source of system problems but the logic of their solution with respect to which Marxism and systems theory need to be reconsidered. Marxism explains evolutionary changes in terms of class struggle. Nevertheless, the concept of revolutionary practice still remains rudimentary and lacks adequate theoretical foundations. Marxism contains this concept but doesn't possess the theoretical means for constructing and investigating it. Systems theory, in contrast, explains social evolution in terms of the increase of system complexity. This strategy, though useful, is limited in that it explains neither where system problems arise nor why an innovation must take place the way it does. Systems theory does not explain, for example, why the state in the transition from a kinship society to a class society, and the market economy in the further transition to the modern era, played a decisive role in restructuring the system and in attaining the higher level of complexity. Systems theory has descriptive value but lacks theoretical explanations.

A scrutiny reveals, however, that overloaded system problems can be resolved only when new structures of ratonality are successfully institutionalized, and that these structures of ratonality cannot possibly be determined elsewhere and imposed on social action, but must be formed and tested within determinate processes of discourse in society. It is here that the dialectics between productive forces and relations turns out to be limited in comprehending the issues pertinent to the institutional embodiment of new structures of rationality.[24] To overcome this limit, however, one must properly understand the role which discursive formations play in social evolution, as Habermas (1979a) has shown through a revision of historical materialism. The core of this revision lies in the transformation of the orthodox version of materialist dialectics to the dialectics between production and discourse. The implications of this revision are complex. Habermas (1979a:95, 152) himself insists that this is necessary for historical materialism to improve its analytic rigor and thereby to capture "the universals of social development." Habermas (1979a:152) treats the concept of the mode of production not as "the wrong key to the logic of social development," but as a "key that has not yet been sufficiently filed down." Explicitly introducing the concepts of discursive formation (social learning) and rationality, Habermas thus attempts to illuminate the rational basis of social evolution which Marxism has put aside.

This revision is founded upon "universal pragmatics" which establishes the following principles: (1) The basis of social evolution is anchored in the pragmatic structure of speech. (2) Truth claims and normative claims are both universally built into the structure of every possible speech via statements and intersubjectivity respectively. (3) These two validity claims can be tested discursively, albeit on different conditions.

(4) The possibility of this testing is the ultimate basis of rationality. And (5) two types of rationality, therefore, unfold in the natural history of the species along two types of social learning (cognitive–technical and moral–practical), in which the corresponding validity claims are discursively appropriated within institutional constraints. Bound to discursive formations, rationality is, therefore, historically deterinate and restrictive, but Habermas warns us not to confuse the two types of rationality. For instance, the rationality of social struggle, as a moral–practical learning, cannot be reduced to the rationality of instrumental action. In Habermas's (1979a:120,117) view, the former is measured against "the intersubjectivity of understanding achieved without force" while the latter is weighed against the "heightening of productive forces."

What is crucial for social formations from the perspective of discursive formations is, therefore, how social learning is organized. Class-bound and historically constrained, learning processes produce material effects and are constituted according to their own logic of development. This logic, when comprehended, enables us to see how social learning is at once circumscribed and transformed in evolution. "A learning level means structural conditions of the possibility of cognitive–technical and moral–practical learning processes" (Habermas, 1979b:31). Synchronically, social learning takes place at each developmental level within a structurally circumscribed range of variations. The diachronic problem arises, however, when learning is transformed from one level to another, thereby making a new mode of social organization conceivable.

It can be said from this that the possibility of evolutionary innovations lies in the fact that a new level of social learning is opened up in the transitional society so that a new structure of rationality is discursively formed before institutionalization. Historical examples are the conventional administration of justice on the eve of the emergence of a class society and the contractural organization of labor in capitalist industry during the transition to the modern era (Habermas, 1979a:162; 1979b:38). Decisive for social evolution is the institutionalization of "new levels of learning that have already been achieved in world views and are latently available but not yet incorporated into action and thus remain institutionally inoperative" (Habermas, 1979a:121–122). Which classes initiate this learning and under what condition it is successfully institutionalized depend on many contingent factors. Nevertheless, it is clear that this learning provides the key to social struggle and system innovation.

The thesis that comes out of this is that the logic of social evolution can be adequately clarified only within a theory of discursive formations, but neither by the theory of contradictions nor by systems theory. Especially important is the transformation of the moral–practical learning which is embedded in social struggle and later becomes the "institutional core that determines the dominant form of social integration" (Habermas, 1979a: 154). This allows us to understand social evolution because "only this new form of social integration in which the new learning level . . . is expressed makes possible a further increase of system complexity" (Habermas, 1979b:32). Habermas (1979a:120) thus proclaims that

> the development of these normative structures is the pacemaker of social evolution, for new principles of social organization mean new forms of social integration; and the latter, in turn, first makes it possible to implement available productive forces or to generate new ones, as well as making possible a heightening of social complexity.

Habermas (1979a:117) further claims that "normative structures do not simply follow the path of development of reproductive processes and do not simply respond to the pattern of system problems, but that they have an internal history." This history resides in discursive formations. This claim is close to Foucault's defense of the specific unity of discursive formations.[25] Like Foucault, Habermas thinks that social action, including revolutionary practice, is constituted within the processes of social learning, as embedded in the system of discourse. For both, the discursive system of speech and action is regulated by its own rules of formation. Habermas's claim is, however, much stronger than Foucault's in that is involves a universalist claim absent in Foucault. According to Hagermas, normative structures are not only bound to class interests but also constrained by a developmental logic which is of universal significance. This means that class domination takes place in such a way that it must correspond to the institutionalized level of learning. This constraint is abstract in that it regulates the modes, not the contents, of class domination but, nevertheless, is important. In the modern era, for instance, class domination must be based on postconventional legality rather than on the preconventional or the conventional morality tied to the ruler. Animated by Piaget and Kohlberg, Habermas (1979a:153) thus thematizes social evolution in terms of "developmental-logically reconstructible stages of learning" and the corresponding sequences of normative structures in evolution.

According to Habermas's (1979a) and Eder's (1976) proposal, the pacemaker of the evolution from a kinship society to a class society was the formation of a judicial system which opened up a new level of social learning by permitting the validity of social norms to be tested on the conventional level of learning. The state gained control over kinship systems in this way. Social learning is here transformed from the preconventional to the conventional level of learning. In the modern era, in turn, social learning is further transformed to the postconventional level of learning via bourgeois civil law which establishes the legal-contractural mode of testing independent of the ruler. The system of market economy based on labor contract becomes liberated from the political system of domination in this way. Many functional variations exist at each level of learning; thus the theory of social evolution assumes ''neither unilinearity nor necessity, neither continuity nor irreversibility''(Habermas, 1979a: 140). However, evolution takes place in the sense that normative structures progress from the preconventional through the conventional to the postconventional levels of learning and, once this progression is achieved, regression is impossible.[26] Here we find a novel synthesis of Hegel and structuralism in Piaget's sense).

This discussion shows that the dialectics between production and discourse is more suitable than the orthodox version of materialist dialectics in dealing with how discursive formations, with their own structures of rationality, take part in social evolution. This also reveals that social evolution is characterized not only by the concentration of contradictions but also by the increase of rationality. The latter, of course, involves structural ruptures. That is to say, rationality is restructured within a new framework when social learning is transformed from one level to another. It is from this peculiar dynamic that we can explain the tension between class domination and discursive formation. Class domination can only be smoothly exercised on the basis of distorted communication which, however, becomes ineffective once social learning is transformed so that the present mode of domination is transparent. According to this dialectical view, the level of discursive rationality is heightened in evolution whereas distorted communication becomes structurally intensified simultaneously. The implications of this twofold process of evolution for contemporary social formations are open to interpretation.

A DISCURSIVE PARADIGM OF PRAXIS: CONCLUSION

It has been argued that social struggle, as the practical basis of social formations, and also as a key issue to periodization, can be adequately clarified only within the field of discourse, not because contradictions and system maintenance are less important than this, but because they themselves are embedded in discourse and thus can be translated to discursive formations. It follows from this that to clarify the logic of social formations in a comprehensive manner, it is necessary to develop a synthesis of Marxism, systems theory, and linguistics so that the limits to which each of these theories is bound can be overcome. The proposed synthesis in this paper is a discursive analysis which places contradictions, system maintenance, and discursive formations in a comprehensive theory of social formations. Primarily concerned with the production of discourse, discursive analysis translates Marxism and systems theory to the domain of discourse, radicalizing the concept of language as a practice in order to capture the practical basis of social formations more fully than permitted by Marxism and systems theory.

For a reflexive theory of social formations, however, it is also necessary to investigate the way in which theory itself functions in the social formations that it studies. This theory–practice issue is important because, as Habermas (1976:132) puts it, "the research process instigated by human subjects belongs, through the act of cognition itself, to the objective context which should be apprehended." This dialectical view does not allow a complete detachment of theory from its object but requires theory to inspect its practical function carefully. Thus, I would like to conclude this paper by exploring what discursive analysis may suggest to us in this regard.

Theoretical knowledge can be examined in terms of either its relation to the object that it deals with or the discursive effect that it brings about as a system of discourse. Positivism assumes that the former, namely truth, can be determined independently of the latter. Enlightenment is then nothing more than a pragmatic consequence of scientific discovery, the truth of which is determined objectively. In this view, enlightenment has no methodological significance for redeeming the truth of knowledge.[27]

In the critical types of social science, however, the "knowledge effect" (Althusser) is crucial to the validation of knowledge. This effect basically consists of transforming the nature-like rules of social formations to an intelligible (discursive) object via concepts and theoretical strategies. Althusser, Foucault, Lorenzer, and Habermas all share this view. Mostly taken for granted, and thus invisible, these rules can be rendered visible only after analysis. Thus, it is through this knowledge effect that the discursive conditions for validation are created.[28] That is to say, the seemingly naturalistic but ideological system of discourse is deconstructed through this effect, thereby opening up the possibility of a discursive redemption of knowledge. This means that the process of enlightenment which theory brings about by criticizing distorted communication has methodological significance for the social sciences.

This may be illustrated by Marx's analysis of the capitalist mode of production and Offe's analysis of state interventionism. Obviously these analyses are not primarily concerned with distorted communication itself. Nevertheless, by reconstructing the objectively valid mode of structuration, these analyses render certain systems of discourse problematic in which this mode is deliberately concealed or displaced. Thus, materialist analysis produces the effect of indirectly criticizing distorted communication which discursive analysis can then directly tackle.[29]

It is now clear that theory intervenes into the social formations it investigates, with the knowledge it produces, and that the mode of this intervention is characterized by the critique of distorted communication. This mode is neither immediately political nor merely technical, but rather discursive. This paradigm of discursive praxis stresses the link between knowledge and action through discursively attained enlightenment. Enlightenment is a discursive resource which theory produces, and upon which diffused potentials of struggle are formed. This discursive paradigm of praxis represents the ratonality of overcoming distorted communication, but neither an instrumental nor a bureaucratic rationality. The advocated rationality is practical in nature, as Habermas (1973a, 1979a) has aptly shown. Rationalization in this sense means:

> extirpating those relations of force that are inconspicuously set in the very structure of communication and that prevent conscious settlement of conflicts, and consensual regulation of conflicts, by means of intrapsychic as well as interpersonal communicative barriers (Habermas, 1979a:119–20).

The rationality which is assumed when we speak of contradictions, for example, cannot be simply reduced to the strategic elimination of them, but must properly include the rationality of discursive enlightenment in which individuals and groups freely discuss the concerned matters. By explicitly incorporating the problem of language in the analysis of social formations, discursive analysis captures not only the specific unity of discursive formations but also the specific rationality in discourse, i.e., the rationality which resides in the public spheres of speech and action. Neither Marx nor Weber clearly understood this rationality. Nor do the contemporary theorists of modernization. Consequently, it remains to be shown why and how this rationality becomes structurally deformed in the process of industralization in the cases of developing society. The discursive theory of social formations shows, however, that practical rationality, distinguished from instrumental–strategic rationality, is as important, or even more important, for the comprehensive rationalization of social life.

The key to practical rationality is the discursive testing of social norms, the possibility and the conditions of which Habermas (1973b, 1979a) has shown. Today, this testing, though not institutionalized, takes place in its incipient forms and tends to increase due to many reasons. Offe (1973: 213) shows, for example, that there is an "organizational disjuncture" in the state between the growth-oriented economic policy and the welfare-oriented social policy, in that the former must presuppose the dominant capitalist interests which must be denied by the latter in favor of the universalist claim of the state. In this structural context the class nature of the state becomes unmistakable, especially when the economy enters into recession, because the state must then first take care of accumulation at the cost of public welfare. Diffused potentials of protests thus grow in advanced capitalism, together with the scope of the testing of norms.

Whether or not practical discourse will be as institutionalized as scientific discourse so that the validity of social norms can be as freely discussed as the truth claim is an open question.[30] Though Habermas's (1979a) discussion that the discursive testing of social norms is not only possible but also under way today, especially among the youth, is highly suggestive, many crucial problems are still left for further investigations. In particular, care must be taken to examine: (1) the overloaded system problems which may be resolved by the institutionalization of practical discourse; (2) the innovative variations of the system which may lead to this institutionalization; and (3) the specific modes of transformation in discursive formations through which the discourse-specific conditions for the discursive testing of norms are formed. The evolutionary significance, if any, of state interventionism in advanced capitalism needs to be explored from this perspective.

It is quite clear however, that practical discourse, if institutionalized, will have far-reaching consequences for social evolution because the dominant class interests would then be made subject to the methodically regulated free discourse in which concerned individuals and groups participate. This would be an important step toward the democratization of everyday life, initiating the structural transition from the modern class society to a post-class society. It is here that we can best see the practical intent of discursive analysis in connection with evolution. Discursive social science, as the proposed synthesis of Althusser, Foucault, Offe, and Habermas, not only stresses the analytic rigor of reconstruction but also strives for the rationality of practical discourse blocked by power in a class society. In other words, discursive social science is not merely concerned with purposive rationality as positivism is but also tackles practical rationality, deliberately relating itself to the process of contemporary social evolution. The discursive testing of social norms is here understood as an historical possibility which is suppressed but, nonetheless, can be pursued rationally. For doing so, discursive social science locates an emancipatory interest of knowledge not only in the concept of reconstructive knowledge but also in the concept of discursive testing (for this concept, see Han, 1979a). As we can best see in Habermas (1973a, 1975, 1979a), the discursive paradigm of praxis which emerges from this is radically democratic and distinguished from both positivism and orthodox Marxism.

NOTES

1. Methodologically, the term *discursive* has two interrelated meanings. As related to social analysis, discursive is characterized by the mode of analysis which is neither causal nor hermeneutic but reconstructive. Foucault (1972) articulates the concept of discursive analysis, emphasizing the importance of discourse for social analysis (cf., Lemert and Gillan,

1977). As related to testing, discursive is defined by the mode of testing which is neither merely empirical nor exclusively logical but properly argumentative. Habermas (1973b, 1979a) deals with this issue, exploring the practical significance of this testing. Discursive analysis and testing can be seen as two elements of discursive method which presuppose each other within the program of discursive social science (Han, 1979a,b).

2. A few examples are empiricism, homocentric idealism, dogmatic Marxism, and vulgar sociologism which both Foucault (1970, 1972) and Habermas (1970a, 1970b, 1979a) explicitly criticize.

3. "Signification" is as crucial for structuralist semiotics as "validity" is for universal pragmatics. Foucault's analysis is thus radically historical whereas Habermas's is devotedly universal. Foucault understands discourse as a social practice with selective and exclusive effects whereas Habermas treats it as a reflexive argumentation. Foucault's analysis focuses on the primitive (archaeological) aspect of discursive formation while Habermas's emphasizes its reflexive aspect. The concept of discourse is rigorously descriptive for Foucault, while it is addressed to the theory–practice problem for Habermas.

4. Foucault (1972:74) argues that systems of power are "not determinations which, formed at the level of institutions, or social or economic relations, transcribe themselves by force on the surface of discourse," but they "reside in discourse itself." Foucault (1977:213) thus views the Marxist concept of power as "far too fluid" to show how power, as a practice, is shaped and exercised. Foucault locates power in the exclusive effect of discursive practices materialized in, say, prison, mental institutions, bureaucracy, legal systems, and curriculums. The link between knowledge and power is crucial. For Habermas (1970b, 1979a), power raises a normative validity claim, at least implicitly, whenever it is exercised. This claim, if thematized, can be discursively attacked. Power becomes perpetuated, however, if and to the extent that communication remains distorted, keeping this claim from discursive examination.

5. Foucault (1972:208) states that the analysis of discourse may make it possible "to situate the place of intersection between a general theory of production and a generative analysis of statements." This intersection, however, remains to be established.

6. This suggestion is based on what Althusser (1970) calls a "symptomatic reading" of texts.

7. It must be noted, however, that the rational elements of Hegel's philosophy, especially its emphasis on the theory–practice problem, almost escape Althusser's discussion. As Althusser reconstructs Marx's works against Hegelian Marxism's misunderstanding, it is also possible to reconstruct Hegel's works against Althusser's misunderstanding. This is an intrinsic feature of textual analysis (cf., Bubner, 1974).

8. This revision is as important and as consequential as Habermas's revision of historical materialism (cf., Jäggi, 1976). But the former appears to be more orthodox than the latter in terms of the relationship with Marx.

9. Niklas Luhmann (1970, 1974; see also Habermas and Luhman, 1971) has sharply thematized this issue, radicalizing Parsons's systems theory, in order to clarify the problem of social evolution. Luhmann emphasizes that the system, though affected by contradictions, follows its own logic of steering in evolution.

10. As an important resource on which Habermas's theory of social evolution hinges, this study is basically concerned wtih the transformation of normative structures from the neolithic society to a politically organized class society (for Habermas's use of this study, see Habermas, 1979a:158–164).

11. This suspicion has been theoretically articulated by Altvater (1973) and Müller and Neusüss (1975), among others, basically by tackling state interventionism from the Marxist perspective of political economy. Holloway and Picciotto's (1978) collection reveals this direction well.

12. A basic argument in this regard is that the laws of the economic system in advanced capitalism are not identical with those which Marx analyzed, due to the intervention from the political system. Habermas (1975) and Offe (1972b, 1975) have developed this argument. According to them, the Marxist conceptual framework which assumes the autonomy of a self-reproducing economic system needs to be radically revised.

13. Offe (1975) argues that the state today becomes increasingly "productive" in the sense that its policies are programmed in terms of the estimated productive effects on accumulation.

14. Poulantzas (1975:95) emphasizes "the determination of the practice by the structure and the intervention of the practices in the structure." It is the structure that regulates "a play of possible variations of social forces," but the "effectiveness of the structure on the field of practices is . . . itself limited by the intervention of political practice on the structure." Poulantzas develops this dialectical view, however, within a rather orthodox conceptual system of Marxism.

15. Three points of criticism need to be mentioned here. First, the transcendental concept of structure which still exists in Saussure, Chomsky, and Lévi-Strauss is rejected and replaced by the historical concept of structure stressing heterogeneity and regionality. Derrida's (1976) critique of logocentrism (or phonocentrism) in Saussure and Lévi-Strauss is especially powerful. Second, the concept of language is so radicalized that it is understood neither as a system of formal rules nor as an expression of a preestablished origin but as a social practice in Marx's and Althusser's sense. In other words, language is understood as a specific mode of production no less important than the economic mode which Marxism stresses. Foucault and Kristeva take up this view. Finally, the theory of the subject is constructed as a heterogeneous signifying process or, as Foucault (1977:138) puts it, as "a complex and variable function of discourse." The conjoint movement between semiology and psychoanalysis (Lacan, Kristeva) has made this important contribution (cf., Coward and Ellis, 1977).

16. Foucault (1972:127) states that these determinants "are not imposed from the outside on the elements that [discursive formations] relate together," but "are caught up in the very things that they connect."

17. Foucault (1972:45–6) distinguishes three levels of relations in discourse, the primary, the secondary, and the discursive. It is the last that refers to the specific mode of production of discourse regulated by what Foucault (1972:128) calls the "historical archives" of discourse.

18. Though this idea has been explicitly developed in structuralist semiotics and universal pragmatics, it can also be seen as underlying such diverse intellectual formations as hermeneutics (Gadamer), linguistic sociology (Winch), and ethnomethodology (Sacks).

19. This distinction is mine. However, equivalent distinctions can be found in Habermas, Foucault, and Lorenzer. Habermas (1975) distinguishes outer nature, inner nature, and discourse, proposing that the first two are appropriated by the latter. Habermas (1979a) develops this theme further by distinguishing objectivity, subjectivity, social norms, and language. Foucault (1970, 1972) criticizes empiricism, idealism, and dogmatic Marxism, with the view that both objectivity and subjectivity are embedded in discursive formations. Lorenzer (1974) distinguishes the objective and the subjective modes of structuration, emphasizing the function of language.

20. Neither Marxism nor discursive analysis can be simply reduced to the analysis of ideology. Discursive analysis, however, captures the complexity of discursive formations which Althusser's Marxism undercuts. Althusser's emphasis on the "rupture" between science and ideology also makes it difficult to comprehend the specific mode of "irruption" between them within determinants discursive formations (Lecourt, 1975:211).

21. Foucault (1977:200) systematizes this perspective as follows:

The transformation of a discursive practice is linked to a whole range of usually complex modifications that can occur outside of its domain (in the forms of production, in social relationships, in political institutions), inside it (in its techniques for determining its objects, in the adjustment and refinement of its concepts, in its accumulation of facts), or to the side of it (in other discursive practices). And it is linked to these modifications not as a simple result but as an effect that retains both its proper autonomy and the full range of its precise functions in relation to that which determines it.

22. The basic theme here is the relation between the mode of production and discourse as Coward and Ellis (1977), Hindess (1977), and Hindess and Hirst (1975, 1977) deal with. Baudrillard's (1972, 1975) and Eco's (1976) theory of sign production is also an interesting attempt. From a very different route, Habermas (1979a) reformulates the relation between production and discourse through a revision of historical materialism.

23. Rejecting the historicist concept of evolution, structuralist Marxism has captured periodization not as a unilinear process but as a complex process which yields functionally equivalent variations. For doing so, structuralist Marxism has emphasized the relative autonomy of social formations and their relations, rethinking and relation between determination and domination.

24. Marxism assumes that this dialectics yields "a finite number of structurally analogous stages of development, so that there results a series of modes of production that are to be ordered in a developmental logic" (Habermas, 1979a:139). Marxism thus distinguishes five or six modes of production, treating periodization as developmental sequences of the modes of production. This materialist strategy, though meaningful in many respects, is limited in tackling the specific logic involved in the transformation of the normative structures of society.

25. Habermas (1979a:148) states that "the rules of communicative action . . . follow their own logic." Foucault (1972:139,127) states that the rules of discourse are "irreducible to any other" and has "a history, and a specific history that does not refer it back to the laws of an alien development."

26. There is a parallel between Kohlberg's theory of moral development and Habermas's theory of social evolution. Habermas uses the former for his own ontogenetic explanation of social evolution.

27. This view is based on the correspondence theory of knowledge which is today under severe criticism from many directions (Habermas, 1973b; Foucault, 1972; Hindess, 1977).

28. That is to say, the deconstruction of distorted communication is a methodological condition for testing. Lorenzer (1974:311) is correct, therefore, when he argues that "the transformation of the naturally evolving and thus blind model of society into a [discursive theory] . . . is absurd without defining the critical-hermeneutic process as a methodically regulated, emancipatory discussion."

29. Discursive analysis presupposes materialist analysis but is distinguished from it by its discourse-specific approach to distorted communication (Foucault, 1972:186).

30. Historically speaking, one can say that scientific discourse has been institutionalized at the expense of practical discourse. This has its roots not merely in the economic and political contexts of social development but also in the theoretical paradigm in positivism in which the possibility of a rational validation of normative problems has been systematically denied. Some fundamental steps have been taken, especially by Habermas, to correct this theoretical mistake. Habermas's universal pragmatics thus shows that practical discourse is as conceivable as theoretical discourse, although it still remains to be shown under which historical condition practical discourse can be institutionalized.

REFERENCES

Althusser, Louis
1969   For Marx. New York: Vintage Books.
1970   Reading Capital (with Etienne Balibar). London: NLB.
1971   "Ideology and ideological state apparatuses." Pp. 127–86 in Lenin and Philosophy
       and Other Essays. New York: Monthly Review Press.
Altvater, Elmar
1973   "Zu einigen Problemen des 'Krisenmanagement' in der kapitalistischen
       Gesellschaft." Pp. 170–96 in M. Jänicke (ed.), Herrschaft und Krise.
       Westdeutscher Verlag.
Barthes, Roland
1967   Elements of Semiology. Boston: Beacon.
1972   Mythologies. London: Cape.
Baudrillard, Jean
1972   Pour une critique de l'économie politique du Signe. Paris: Gallimard.
1975   The Mirror of Production. St. Louis: Telos Press.
Bourdieu, Pierre
1971   "Intellectual field and creative project." Pp. 161–88 in M. Young (ed.), Knowledge
       and Control. New York: Macmillan.
Bubner, Rüdiger
1974   Dialektik und Wissenschaft. Frankfurt: Suhrkamp.
Coward, Rosalind, and J. Ellis
1977   Language and Materialism. Boston: Routledge & Kegan Paul.
Culler, Jonathan
1976   Ferdinand Saussure. Hassocks [England]: Harvester Press.
Derrida, Jacques
1976   Of Grammatology. Baltimore: Johns Hopkins University Press.
Eco, Umberto
1976   The Theory of Semiotics. Bloomington: Indiana University Press.
Eder, Klaus
1976   Die Entshehung staatlich organisierter Gesellschaften. Frankfurt: Suhrkamp.
Foucault, Michel
1970   The Order of Things. New York: Pantheon Books.
1972   The Archaeology of Knowledge. New York: Pantheon Press.
1973   The Birth of the Clinic. New York: Pantheon Press.
1977   Language, Counter-Memory, and Practice. Ithaca, N.Y.: Cornell University Press.
Godelier, Maurice
1972   Rationality and Irrationality in Economics. New York: Monthly Review Press.
Habermas, Jürgen
1970a Zur Logik der Sozialwissenschaften. Frankfurt: Suhrkamp.
1970b "Toward a theory of communicative competence." Pp. 115–48 in Hans P. Dreitzel
       (ed.), Recent Socioogy, Vol. 2. New York: Macmillan.
1971   Knowledge and Human Interests. Boston: Beacon Press.
1973a Theory and Practice. Boston: Beacon Press.
1973b "Wahrheitstheorien." Pp. 211–66 in Helmut Fahrenbch (ed.), Wirklichkeit und
       Reflexion. Neske.
1975   Legitimation Crisis. Boston: Beacon Press.
1976   "The analytic theory of science and dialectics." Pp. 131–62 in T.W. Adorno, H.
       Albert, et al., (eds.), The Positivist Dispute in German Sociology. New York:
       Harper & Row.
1979a Communication and the Evolution of Society. Boston: Beacon Press.
1979b "History and evolution." Telos 239:5–44.

Habermas, Jürgen, and Niklas Luhmann
1971 Theorie des Gesellschaft oder Sozialtechnologie? Frankfurt: Suhrkamp.
Han, Sang Jin
1979a Discursive Method and Social Theory. Unpublished Ph.D dissertation, Southern Illinois University.
1979b "Ideology-critique and social science: the use of discursive method." Pp. 292–309 in Scott McNall (ed.), Theoretical Perspectives in Sociology. New York: St. Martin's Press.
Hindess, Barry
1977 Philosopy and Methodology in the Social Sciences. Atlantic Highlands, N.J.: Humanities Press.
Hindess, Barry, and Paul Hirst
1975 Pre-Capitalist Modes of Production. Boston: Routledge & Kegan Paul.
1977 Mode of Production and Social Formation. New York: Macmillan.
Holloway, John, and Sol Picciotto (eds.)
1978 State and Capital. Austin, Texas: University of Texas Press.
Jäggi, Urs
1976 Theoretische Praxis: Probleme eines structurellen Marxismus. Frankfurt: Suhrkamp.
Kristeva, Julia
1975 "The system and the speaking subject." Pp. 47–55 in Thomas A Sebeok (ed.), The Tell-Tale Sign. Lisse, Netherlands: de Irdder Press.
Lacan, Jacques
1968 "The function of language in psychoanalysis," Pp. 3–87 in A. Wilden (ed.), The Language of the Self. Baltimore: Johns Hopkins University Press.
1977 The Four Fundamental Concepts of Psychoanalysis. London: Hogarth Press.
Lecourt, Dominique
1975 Marxism and Epistemology. London: NLB.
Lemert, Charles
1979 "Language, structure, and mesurement: structuralist semiotics and sociology." American Journal of Sociology 84:927–57.
Lemert, Charles, and Garth Gillan
1977 "The new alternative in critical sociology: Foucault's discursive analysis." Cultural Hermeneutics 4:309–20.
Lorenzer, Alfred
1974 Die Wahrheit der psychoanalytischen Erkenntnis. Frankfurt: Suhrkamp.
Luhmann, Niklas
1970 Soziologische Aufklärung. Westdeutscher Verlag.
1974 "Sociology of political systems." Pp. 31–57 in German Political Studies, Vol. 1. Beverly Hills, Calif.: Sage Publns.
Marx, Karl
1967 Capital. New York: International Publs.
1970 A Contribution to the Critique of Political Economy. New York: International Publs.
Miliband, Ralph
1969 The State in Capitalist Society, New York: Basic Books.
Müller, Wolfgang, and Christel Neusüss
1975 "The illusion of state socialism and the contradiction between wage labor and capital." Telos 25:13–90.
O'Connor, James
1973 The Fiscal Crisis of the State. New York: St. Martin's Press.

Offe, Claus
   1972a "Political authority and class structures: an analysis of late capitalist state." International Journal of Sociology 2:73–108.
   1972b Strukturprobleme des kapitalistischen Staates. Frankfurt: Suhrkamp.
   1973   "Krisen des Krisenmanagement." Pp. 197–223 in M. Jänicke (ed.), Herrschaft und Krise. Westdeutscher Verlag.
   1974   "Structural problems of the capitalist state." Pp. 31–57 in German Political Studies, Vol. 1. Beverly Hills, Calif.: Sage Publns.
   1975   "The theory of the capitalist state and the problem of policy formation." Pp. 125–44 in Leon Lindberg, R. Alford, C. Crouch, and C. Offe (eds.), Stress and Contradiction in Modern Capitalism. Lexington, Mass.: Lexington Books.
Parsons, Talcott
   1966   Societies: Evolutionary and Comparative Perspective. Englewood Cliffs, N.J.: Prentice-Hall.
Poulantzas, Nicos
   1975   Political Power and Social Classes. London: NLB.
Saussure, Ferdinand
   1975   Course in General Linguistics. New York: Philosophical Library.
Wright, Eric Olin
   1978   Class, Crisis and the State. London: NLB.

THE PROBLEM OF REIFICATION

David L. Harvey, Elizabeth Safford Harvey,
Lyle G. Warner, and Lawrence Smith

According to common wisdom, theory and research are cross-fertilizing enterprises. An exception to this homily is found in the field of alienation research. This area of inquiry has been colored by an "unhappy consciousness." Theoretical development and empirical application have evolved along mutually exclusive paths. The reason for this is that theory and research have proceeded from opposed assumptions and purposes. Alienation theory, on one hand, has been largely critical in nature. In the twentieth century it has grown out of the crisis of Marxism and its underdeveloped theory of consciousness. The theory of alienated subjectivity has its origins in the first third of this century in the works of such writers as Georg Lukacs (1971), Karl Korsch (1970), and Antonio Gramsci (1971). It has been extended and revised in the works of the Frankfurt School (Jay, 1973) and in the writings of Jean-Paul Sartre (1976). More recently, modern applications and advancements in this tradition have found a voice in the works of such writers as Stanley Aronowitz (1973), Russell

Current Perspectives in Social Theory, volume 1, 1980, pages 193–233.
ISBN: 0-89232-154-7

Jacoby (1975), and Christopher Lasch (1978). From these diverse writers an understanding of the inner contours of alienated consciousness and its ramifications for the reproduction of capitalist social relations has been forged.

Empirical alienation research, on the other hand, has evolved relatively independent of these efforts in theory development and at times in direct opposition to the critical tradition itself (Seeman, 1971). Research has been a predominantly atheoretical exercise in abstracted empiricism (Mills, 1959:50–75). Most empirical studies of subjective alienation have been conducted within the Procrustean confines of a positivist episte-mology and a behaviorist metaphysic. This research, by ignoring critical theory and by attempting to steer a course independent of it, has become a decentered set of propositions and protocols set adrift in a milieu of definitional anomie.

Within the context of this stalemate this essay has two basic goals. First, it will present our observations concerning the dialectical develop-ment of the "idea" of subjective alienation in research over the last two decades. It will argue that the dialectic emerged when the full empirical spectrum of everyday alienation was conceptually truncated in order to exclude its radical, critical, and sociological dimensions from empirical measurement and study. At the same time, this truncated research con-cept was treated by researchers as if it conceptually exhausted the concrete totality of lived alienation.

It will be suggested that this approach is inadequate because it denies the researcher's ability to examine a key element of alienation—its ideological content. Because of this, alienation research in America has exhibited the dialectical irony of noncritical, sociological research being forced to restore many of those same critical presuppositions and struc-tural dimensions. This restoration has been "immanent" in that it has occurred, by and large, within the methodological confines of noncritical alienation research itself.

This essay will trace this dialectical development by delineating its logical unfolding in the works of various American sociologists. In this interpretive reconstruction one must begin with the research model of Melvin Seeman (1959) and then trace its internal revisions up to and including its sublation in the works of Robert Blauner (1964). One can argue that with the Blauner synthesis alienation research has been expanded to include as much critical content as the positivist problematic will allow. Finally, it will be argued that the full restoration of the study of subjective alienation, to be empirically complete, requires that the insights of critical theory, as well as the works of Georg Lukacs on reified consciousness, be integrated into empirical inquiry.

The immanent critique of the first section of this essay ends by sketching the outlines of a critical, sociological theory of alienation. The second section of the essay offers partial confirmation of our theoretical speculations by developing a measure of subjective alienation which is rooted in Lukacs' theory of reified consciousness. Thus, our second goal is to remove the empirical techniques of attitude measurement and scale construction from a strictly positivist context and put them to the service of developing a *critically based measure of subjective alienation*. The development of such a measure based on principles consonant with neo-Marxist ideas concerning alienation can serve two functions. First, it can lend partial credence to the preceding radical critique by showing its practical consequences for developing alternative measures and methods for studying subjective alienation. Second, it may be able to demonstrate that the practice of radical social analysis and the application of empirical research techniques are basically compatible. Having outlined the structure and purposes of this essay let us now examine the dialectics of alienation research.

THE DIALECTICS OF ALIENATION RESEARCH

The Social Context of the Dialectic

In *Reading Capital* (Althusser and Balibar, 1970) Louis Althusser states that a theory should be "read" as much for what it omits as for what it explicitly addresses. That is, every theory has a problematic—a tacit and pretheoretic domain which fixes the limits and contours of that theory. Such a problematic generates the manifest theory and, by indirection, its internal counterforms: its "systematic silences." These dual domains of systematic silences and explicit propositions determine the structure and fate of every theoretical production. In the evolution of a theory these silences constitute the latent seeds of a theory's development and eventual supersession. With some reservations, Althusser's model is a useful framework for the examination of the evolution of subjective alienation in American sociology. The dialectic which shall be discussed in this section can be seen in terms of partial problematics and systematic silences.

However, before tracing this "idealist dialectic," one must grasp the social and ideological context in which that development was shaped. In this paper the Seeman model and the sociological problematic within which it took shape is treated as the ground from which the dialectics of alienation research in America has evolved during the past 25 years (Seeman, 1959). While space does not allow a full discussion of the issue, it is assumed that much of American sociology at mid-century was a centrist ideology, intellectually geared to articulate and facilitate the smooth functioning of a corporate liberal social order. Sociology performed two basic functions. First, it functioned positively to give voice to the highest ideals of a progressive corporate America and to find practical means by which social justice and smooth institutional functioning could be achieved within the technical framework and class structure of monopoly capitalism.

Sociology's second, equally crucial, function was devoted to constructing a set of negating, preempting counterarguments against the worldviews of groups antagonistic to the goals of welfare capitalism. These groups were, primarily, a decimated working-class left and a discredited petty bourgeois right. The successful countering of these "extremes of the right and of the left" required different strategies. The ideology of small capital was dismissed with psychoanalytic calumny and historical distortion. Sociological explanations of the petty bourgeoisie and its resistance were abandoned and replaced with psychological theories of reactive politics. In this case, "status politics" and "paranoid styles" were invoked to dismiss this marginal fraction of capital. By taking a psychoanalytic tack toward the petty bourgeoisie, sociology could articulate an empiricist and centrist political sociology which explained the normal democratic process while also accounting for the existence of the "irrational" social fraction which resisted "democratic values."

The left perspective was not so easily dismissed. The red herring of equating all critical analysis with Soviet orthodoxy was a frequent form of neutralization. In other contexts, the rewriting of populism's history, the discovery of "working-class authoritarianism," and the endless, dreary, misreadings of Marx as an "economic determinist" became temporarily effective forms of neutralization. In most cases, such analyses did not survive the 1960s. More effective by far, however, was the piecemeal cooptation of the radical perspective. In many instances portions of Marxist social analysis were adopted, methodologically stripped of their critical, historical content, reformulated along positivist lines, and incorporated into the umbrella ideology of a "pragmatic" and "eclectic" social theory. The Seeman model would be included within this later strategy and may be seen as epitomizing attempts within sociology to neutralize an alternative worldview.

The Seeman Watershed

Seeman reshaped Marxian alienation into a new set of meanings which were developed in accord with sociology's ideological role. His definition and measure of alienation were psychological, devoid of historically specific structural references, positivistic, and noncritical. The resultant model was a mere shadow of the original dialectical and macrosociological model of subjective alienation employed by Marx.

In the Marxian problematic alienation was a combination of both subjective and objective elements. The study of one moment of alienation already presupposed the other. For Marx the genesis of modern alienation lay in the objective domain of capitalist social relations. Its subjective components were contained in the cognitive models and assumptions which were employed, ideologically, to comprehend and maintain the alienated social mechanisms of the capitalist mode of production. Alienated subjectivity was a special form of intellectual enterprise employed by the bourgeoisie to grasp the workings of the system at the level of empiricist superficiality, without at the same time revealing its essential contradictions and the eventual demise of capital itself. Thus, alienated consciousness was a necessary component of capital's social reproduction.

Marx saw alienation as a historically specific phenomenon. Only under the capitalist mode of production was alienation a necessary component of social existence. Alienation was the existential precondition for entering into objective role performance. The recognition by a person of his or her alienation, while a crucial empirical fact, had little bearing in the Marxian model on ascertaining his or her actual alienation. Wage systems, commodity structures, and class-based production were the crucial determinants of alienation and were all "sociological" in nature. Mere shifts in beliefs and orientations could not alter the objective sociological fact of alienation. Simultaneously, the subjective alienation of a person was expressed in the content of his beliefs and his ideological construction of the world.

When Marx dealt with the subjective side of alienation, he was rarely concerned with the single subject. Instead, his analysis concentrated on the "fetishized" consciousness which typified the dominant intellectual styles of thought under capital's influence (Marx, 1967:71–83). Marx paid only desultory attention to concrete, intrasubjective processes. This is seen clearly in the structure of *Capital*. His critique is shaped by a contrapuntal movement which analyzes, first, the objective and concrete social configurations of capital and then their *theoretically* and *formally* deformed expression in bourgeois political economy. Through such an alternating, pyramiding critique, he exposed both the contradictory practices of capital and the alienated perceptions and postulates which constituted the defective self-understanding of capital.

For Marx alienated subjectivity facilitated the person's adaptation to the alienated social relations of capital. This subjective adaptation was fetishized thought, i.e., consciousness which presents the social reality of alienated roles to the subject as natural and unquestioned "realities." It is the intellectual inversion of reality by which the objective alienation of the capitalist mode of production presents itself to the producer not as a social fact, but as an inevitable, natural, fait accompli. The producer is rendered inert and passive; he watches in contemplative detachment as his products take on the human attributes of "freedom," "self-direction," "autonomy," and "sociation." Alienated subjectivity does not cause personal alarm at such inversions. Rather, it helps the alienated producer to be content with his passive and contemplative role vis-à-vis the humanized active product. It allows him to become more fully integrated into the alienated relations of production.

This was Marx's concept of alienated subjectivity. However, it seldom confronted the phenomenology of individual consciousness. As a result, some have treated this as his systematic silence. Lukacs (1971) and Korsch (1970) began to address this silence in the early part of this century by focusing on the issues of class consciousness and subjectivity. Their concerns became a matter of crucial, practical import when a series of workers' movements collapsed in revolutionary default and gave way to fascism. These movements failed, it was speculated, because the proletariat had failed to act in accordance with its "objective class interests." This generated a crisis within Marxian theory, and comprehension of this failure became one of its central theoretical foci. The goal of Marxist theory was now to create an historically rooted theory of individual consciousness which would dovetail with the solid findings of Marxian political economy.

Seeman's research stood at the juncture of this crisis of Marxian theory and the rising ideological program of the new sociology. Seeman (1959) encountered and dissected these multivoiced, neo-Hegelian variants of Marxian alienation theory. Alienation in capitalist society—historical, dialectically constituted, and sociologically rooted—was Seeman's external object of reference. In his conceptual reconnaissance he encountered Marx and those writers who were either struggling to develop a critical theory of alienated consciousness or who were using Marxian alienation theory to revise earlier sociological perspectives. Seeman drew upon T.W. Adorno's *The Authoritarian Personality* (1950), Karl Mannheim's (1936) technocratic transformation of Georg Lukacs's Hegelianized Marxism, Erich Fromm's (1955) Marxian characterology, David Reisman's (1950) revision of Fromm, and, finally, Robert Merton's Anomie Theory (1949)—referenced by some as a Marxian interrogation of Durkheim. Of the various strands and nuances which Seeman teased out, all, save one, had its origins in this common, if unrecognized intellectual source.

Seeman appropriated these essentially neo-Marxist usages, divorced them from their theoretical context, and cast them into an abstract, atheoretical amalgam. Alienation became the theoretically unweighted sum of five different dimensions: (1) powerlessness, (2) meaninglessness,

(3) anomie, (4) cultural isolation, and (5) self-estrangement. These dimensions were then integrated by translating their meanings into the uniform terminology of social learning theory (Rotter, 1972). The manifold complexity of the original historico-structural conceptualization of alienation was transformed and reduced into an individual expectancy on the part of the subject that his or her fate was determined by agents external to the subject and beyond the subject's control. Alienation had ceased to be a function of the objective contingencies of social structure. Rather, it was a property of a solipsistic space—the intrasubjective expectancies of the research subject. If, on one hand, a person *believed* he or she could not control or understand his or her world, then he or she was alienated. If, on the other hand, the subject *believed* he or she was in control of his or her world, understood it, and could cope with it successfully, then he or she was not alienated.

In Seeman's theory, *powerlessness* was no longer an objective characteristic of a class or status position. It was now reduced to a personal expectancy as to whether the locus of control was internal or external to the actor. *Anomie* ceased to be a function of the objective distribution of instrumental means in a class-based social system. It was now the subjective expectation that illegitimate means were efficacious in obtaining culturally valued ends. *Meaninglessness* was the expectancy that the subject lacked adequate cognitive models by which to predict future environmental outcomes. *Cultural isolation* was the individual expectancy that personal values and commitments were not shared by the subject's immediate, significant others. Finally, *self-estrangement* was defined as an activity which was devoid of intrinsic reward. It was activity whose value for ego was purely instrumental and external to the act itself, while activity performed as an end in itself was not self-estranging. As with the other dimensions, self-estrangement was solely a function of the subject's judgment.

In the early 1960s Seeman's paradigm was dominant in American alienation research. It provided a method which exhibited all of the trappings of logical and observational rigor. Yet, as empirically useful as the model was in generating research material, it could not transcend its theoretical weaknesses. Its definition of alienation remained an internally inarticulate mélange and the theory became the Achilles heel of the entire research tradition.

Silences in the Seeman Model

It must be emphasized that the dialectic of alienation research is not rooted in Seeman's attempt to develop an empirical measure of subjective alienation. Such an index, presented *as one moment* of the manifold phenomenon, could have advanced the critical theory of alienation. The dialectic of alienation research was generated by Seeman's insistence that his subjective expectancy definition and measure could exhaust, within research, the totality of the multidimensional object itself. This dialectic emerged from the conceptual collapsing of the objective components of alienation and their critical manifestations into a narrow psychological construct. The structure of this dialectical process emerged from the conflating of the whole with its part. This movement has been summed up by Theodor W. Adorno in the following brittle passage from *Negative Dialectics* (1973:5):

> The name of dialectics says no more, to begin with, than that objects do not go into their concepts without leaving a remainder, that they come to contradict the traditional norm of adequacy. Contradiction is not what Hegel's absolute idealism was bound to transfigure it into: it is not the essence in a Heraclitian sense. It indicates the untruth of identity, the fact that the concept does not exhaust the thing conceived.

Alienation in Marxist thought consists of more than just subjective expectancies. If Adorno is correct, then any attempt to treat the truncated alienation concept and its concrete social object as being identical was destined to create a countermovement. Such a movement would reveal itself in a series of attempts to internally revise the Seeman model and bring it closer to an actual mapping of its concrete social object. In consequence, the direction which the dialectic was to take lay in the gradual restoration of the previously repressed elements of alienation theory. The original Seeman formulation was expanded and, gradually, sociological components were resurrected within the corpus of the psychological expectancy model itself.

The *form* of the alienation dialectic was shaped by the part–whole tension referred to above. However, the medium in which this dialectic unfolded resided in the empirical problem matter and the contradictions encountered in the actual course of research. This contradictory content manifested itself in five practical and conceptual shortcomings within the Seeman paradigm.

The first of these problems has been alluded to. Seeman's five dimensions were not integrated in a systematic synthesis. No single theory linked them as parts of a unified, conceptual whole. A second problem revolved around his operational definitions. Their content was both too global and too abstract. The content of the powerlessness scale, for example, measured an individual's evaluations of his or her ability to influence the policies of the nation-state. It was too far removed from the immediate behavioral and institutional origins which create an individual's feelings of personal powerlessness. Concomitantly, the scale was too narrow in its institutional references. Unlike the I–E scale, it excluded references to jobs, family life, childrearing, and religious participation.

These possible experiential sources of powerlessness and meaninglessness were ignored in favor of a purely political content.

A third shortcoming was the extreme psychological depiction of alienation. This narrow subjectivity operationally deleted all references to the objective, institutional moment of alienation. Here is a major source of the part–whole tension. Sociological research, by employing such a limited operational definition, constituted an empirical image of subjective alienation shorn of structural references or moorings. The scope of alienation which empirical investigation could encounter was limited: it excluded from possible consideration all interactions between the subject's assessment of his social world and the objective possibilities of that world. Such a radical intrasubjectivity would epistemologically preclude the possibility of discovering the ideological component of subjective alienation because the expectancy paradigm could not include the pivotal class structure of society.

This third problem led to a fourth. The researcher, in ascertaining the subject's alienation, was restricted to using the subject's self-evaluation. Despite potential researcher-based observation to the contrary, the social scientist's ascertainment procedures were restricted to the mere recording of the subject's self-report concerning his alienation. This model allowed for no movement beyond this narrow horizon. The weakness of such a method is revealed in the domain of industrial sociology. By adhering exclusively to subject-based measures, the "nonalienated" worker could not be differentiated from the passive, "happy robot" (Kon, 1967; Horton, 1964), the human relations dupe, or the common garden variety labor scab. Just as orthodox Marxism in the 1930s and 1940s had blanched all elements of "bourgeois subjectivity" from its social theory, now the Seeman model had permitted an equally radical purgation and allowed the pendulum to swing too far in a nominalist and relativistic direction.

These four problems culminated in a fifth. By excluding the ideological components of alienation, which are a part of the day-to-day structure of social life, Seeman overshot the mark. Seeman, seeking to avoid leftist polemics in his operational definition of alienation, had created a definition amenable to the needs of management and its attempts at ideological manipulation. In countering critical Marxism, he needlessly abandoned the examination of the ideological expressions of class-based processes which generate alienation. This omission was then reproduced in the research which followed. As a consequence, subsequent research and measurement only partially mapped the domain of subjective alienation while excluding considerations of objective alienation altogether.

In sum, Seeman took a multifaceted theory of alienation which depicted it as a set of complex dialectical interactions and stripped it of its essential structure and critical content. The Marxian theory with which he began described alienation as class-based, historically specific, sociological in origin, and critical in intent. Following the established protocols of the time, he dismantled and reshaped it. He chose a subsystem of that critical paradigm as his starting point and began his interrogation there. In constructing a psychological version of alienation, a complex theory was collapsed into an abstract approximation of the whole. Instead of creating a measure of subjective alienation, which would either complement the Marxian conception or create a noncritical, *sociological* theory of alienation, Seeman constructed an ultrasubjectivist problematic which totally supplanted the Marxian perspective. It was this replacement of a multi-faceted whole by one of its abstracted parts which now gave rise to the dialectics of alienation research.

Internal Critiques

The first major internal critique of the Seeman position is found in the writings of Browning et al. (1961). They suggested that the five dimensions of alienation were not equal in structure and content, and required a systematic ordering and stratification. This stratification was accomplished when the Browning group attempted to conceptually reorder the five dimensions in a causal chain, beginning with powerlessness and ending with self-estrangement. These five dimensions were now seen as parts of a unified process. *Such a revision provided the five dimensions with an inner sense and determinant ordering.* The five meanings of alienation were arranged in a probabalistic sequence of logical unfolding. They were now moments of a single process which was divided into three phases: the *predisposing stage,* the *cultural disaffection stage,* and the *cultural isolation stage.*

In the predisposing stage of alienation, *powerlessness* was encountered by the subject as the failure to instrumentally manipulate the immediate social environment. This instrumental failure, in turn, could lead to disillusionment with the efficacy of standard cognitive models of understanding which were sanctioned by social authority. When this occurred, instrumental default developed into feelings of *meaninglessness.* If this drift continued unchecked, eventually the normative structure itself would become ensnared in disillusion. When the normative structure came to be regarded negatively, then *anomie* occurred and the next stage of cultural disaffection emerged. Increasingly the person became aware of his or her normative distance from others, and at this stage disaffection gave rise to *cultural isolation.*

Next, Browning and his associates introduced a simple but elegant alteration to the Seeman model. *Self-estrangement* followed on the heels of cultural isolation, but it was qualitatively set off from the other dimensions. It was seen as a purely intrasubjective reaction on the subject's part and was an adaptation to an evolving set of *alienated relationships*. Self-estrangement was not viewed as necessarily pathological, but, rather, as a strategic adaptation to alienated social relations—to social and cultural marginality:

> Here the actor either adapts to the situation by means which cut him off socially, or he is excommunicated from the group. . . . Seeman's problem with the category of self-estrangement is resolved when it is seen as a means of adaptation involving the actor's rejection of cultural goals while he adheres to the instutional means (Browning et al., 1961:780).

This was the crux of the Browning et al. revision. It ordered the elements of the Seeman model logically and in terms of their probability. It also tentatively differentiated between self-estrangement as the purely subjective element of the process and the "relational" genesis of the other four Seeman dimensions.

If the Browning group introduced an "inner" sense of logical coherence into the Seeman model, then the work of Zollschan and Gibeau (1964) may be said to have provided an "outer" or "institutional" sense for the model. They provided the Seeman model with a nascent social form. Using the same tactic as the Browning group, Zollschan and Gibeau constructed a threefold model which divided the Seeman dimensions into: (1) *instrumental alienation* (powerlessness and meaninglessness), (2) *institutional alienation* (anomie and isolation), and (3) *self-estrangement*.

The five dimensions were no longer seen as alienation per se, but, rather, as predisposing conditions of alienation. Alienation for Zollschan and Gibeau was marked by an objective institutional situation in which the presence of conflicting value commitments precluded the exercise of a Weberian-type means–ends rationality. Alienation was now seen in the context of action theory. The five dimensions represented possible blocks to goal achievement and hence *potential sources* of alienation (but not alienation itself). Under the aegis of this action framework, elements of the Seeman model were located in institutional settings. They now functioned to represent institutional and structural possibilities in the generation of alienation. By grouping the predisposing factors as they did, this social action framework allowed differentiation between objective institutional sources of alienation and intrasubjective antecedents of the phenomenon.

These shifts in meaning should not be dismissed lightly. Under Seeman's hand, the dimensions were an inchoate, abstract aggregation. Under the pen of the Browning group and Zollschan and Gibeau, the dimensions of alienation were given an inner logical order and a spatially differentiated articulation. Finally, this spatiotemporal reformulation was given the subject/object structure characteristic of classical social action theory.

The Browning group and Zollschan and Gibeau had reformulated the meaning of alienation by giving it a *new formal structure*. A second line of critical development provided the Seeman model with a *concrete* sociological content. This was accomplished in the short, yet crucially significant, research note of John P. Clark (1959). Clark challenged Seeman's formulation because of its diffuse operational content. Seeman had measured powerlessness, for example, by tapping the person's sense of having power to influence the activities of the nation-state. Clark felt that such a reference point was too diffuse and distant. He believed Seeman's reference point was mediated by too many uncontrolled, intervening variables to be scientifically useful. Clark's solution was simple: one was not alienated from society as a whole, but from concrete, particular roles and role demands. Feelings of alienation had their genesis and locus in concrete role systems. Society was not the proper structural object of alienation research and measures of alienation should reflect this. Further, alienation was not seen as singular and global, but as plural, disjunctive, and role specific. It was possible, from Clark's perspective, to be alienated in one sector of institutional life, while being free from it in another.

With Clark's revisions, alienation research became even more sociologically specific and theoretically diffuse. The Seeman dimensions were now located in a concrete role nexus. Subjective alienation lost its diffuse external referent and was directed toward definite sets of role expectations. Alienation studies were exhorted to examine the *immediate, concrete particularity* of role systems. At the same time, the unified nature of the concept of alienation was lost sight of and in its place one found a plurality of role-specific, possible alienations.

Blauner's Synthesis

Dialectically, Blauner's *Alienation and Freedom* (1964) represents in concrete research application an incremental conjuncture of the various strands of thought discussed thus far. Blauner both synthesized and "realized" the partial critiques of the above writers and combined them in a new sublating structure. This synthesis completed the inner potential of Seeman's model and simultaneously transcended it. Blauner followed a path similar to Clark's injunction. He made the context of alienation research not society, but the factory system and its sociotechnical infrastructure. At the same time, he avoided the tendency in Clark's approach to have analysis dispersed into an infinity of plural alienations—each specific to a concrete collectivity of roles—by allowing the history and evolution of industrial capitalism to unify his four concrete empirical analyses of productive processes.

In dialectical fashion, Blauner retained the shell of Seeman's model and supplied it with a new sociological content. The conceptual content of each dimension assumed an *explicit, objective, sociological form and content* which was wholly independent of its origins. Blauner retained the five dimensions but respecified their content in terms of objective job attributes and technical demands of the work setting. For example, powerlessness was defined in terms of concrete job attributes, i.e., the freedom of the worker to move about on the job, the freedom from repetitive job movements, and the worker's ability to set the pace of work, vary the sequencing of tasks, and use personal discretion on the job. If a job allowed its incumbent to do all of these things, then the worker was *not* powerless and, hence, not alienated. Conversely, if the jobholder was stripped of these prerogatives, he was, be definition, powerless on the job, and hence, alienated at work. Unlike the Seeman conventions, the worker's perception of his or her occupational powerlessness was no longer strictly germane in ascertaining alienation. Blauner's innovation was that he now defined worker alienation by the objective character of work itself. Powerlessness, anomie, isolation, and meaninglessness were treated as attributes of an objective sociotechnical environment.

This is not to say that the subjective moment of alienation was abandoned. It was retained in the form of self-estrangement. However, this was the single index of alienation which still retained an intrasubjective ontology.

The stratification of the alienation dimensions now took on an expanded and more complex structure. Blauner's model of alienation was now divided into three tiers. The first tier was the objective sociotechnical structure of the forces and relations of capitalist production. There were three parameters for this level of alienation: mechanization level, complexity of the technical division of labor, and private property. Together, they determined the shape of industrial organization. These combined to demarcate four historically specific sociotechnical types of production: craft industry, machine tending, assembly-line production, and continuous process forms of production. Each was a unique structural combination of mechanization, division of labor types, and property rights. Each, by dint of that combination, exhibited different potentials for alienation.

The second tier of the Blauner model dealt with the expression of first tier phenomena as they occurred on a particular job in a given sociotechnical setting. At this level, the traits of *objective alienation* (powerlessness, meaninglessness, and isolation) were theoretically linked to technical and interactional aspects of the job.[1]

The third and final tier was that of self-estrangement. The intrapersonal consequences of alienation in work were located at this conceptual level.

It was conceived as a personal reaction to the second mediating level of objective alienation. Self-estrangement, unlike the other three forms of alienation, was never linked to productive structures and the sociotechnical setting directly. It only occurred in a secondary manner, as a "hybrid" response to the objective alienating propensities of the job. The Blauner model is schematically set forth in Table 1.

Blauner's reworking of the dimensional paradigm restored much of the previously repressed Marxian and sociological components of alienation theory. But this model did not take into account the class-based expression of alienation, nor did it yet include critical ideological elements. The dialectical process had not yet been brought full circle, partly because of the failure to distinguish between the *technical* division of labor, which characterizes a mode of production, and the *social* division of labor (Carchedi, 1978). The former refers to the technological distribution of skills in the productive sphere, and the integrating mechanisms of various production stages which are the requisites for the production of use values. The latter term refers to the class domination aspects of production and society. It centers on the political control of production, i.e., the maintenance and reproduction of class boundaries and the extraction of surplus labor from producers in the form of exchange values. In this latter sphere we find the *organizational and sociological essence* of the capitalist mode of production.

An examination of Blauner's alienation analysis reveals that he seldom moves outside the technical division of labor domain in seeking the causes of work alienation. His causal model links alienation and its amelioration to the sociotechnical contours of production, while ignoring almost completely the overarching class context which sets the sociotechnical systems in motion. Alienation is linked to changes in the forces of production, but seldom, if ever, to the capitalist relations of production. Alienation does not appear to be class-mediated for Blauner. Rather, it is created in the man–machine nexus. As a result, he concludes that alienation is not an "inner relation" essential to capital's property relations and that alienation may be technologically ameliorated to a large degree within the class relations of the capitalist mode of production itself. This conclusion is possible only if one analytically downplays the social division of labor and its role in capital's production of alienation.

In mapping the objective antecedents of subjective alienation, Blauner has virtually ignored the social division of labor, i.e., the class structure of industry. He has concentrated almost exclusively on the shaping effects of the technical division of labor in the firm. This becomes apparent in the following discussion in which Blauner (1964:16–17) specifies what he will include under the rubric of powerlessness:

The degree of powerlessness a student imputes to manual workers in industry today depends not only on his sociological and political perspective, but also on the aspects of freedom and control he selects as the most important. There are at least four modes of industrial powerlessness which have preoccupied writers on "the social question." These are (1) the separation from ownership of the means of production and the finished products, (2) the inability to influence general managerial policies, (3) the lack of control over the conditions of employment, and (4) the lack of control over the immediate work process. It is my contention that control over the conditions of employment and control over the immediate work are most salient for manual workers, who are most likely to value control over those matters which affect their immediate jobs and work tasks and least likely to be concerned with the more general and abstract aspects of powerlessness.

The very nature of employment in a large-scale organization means that workers have forfeited their claims on the finished product and that they do not own the factory, machines, or often their own tools. Unlike the absence of control over the immediate work process, "ownership powerlessness" is a constant in modern industry, and employees, therefore, normally do not develop expectations for influence in this area. Today the average worker no more desires to own his machines than modern soldiers their howitzers or government clerks their file cabinets. Automobile and chemical workers, by and large, do not feel deprived because they cannot take home the Corvairs or sulphuric acid they produce.

By ignoring the first two modes of industrial powerlessness in his study Blauner excluded from consideration all class-based sources of shopfloor and worksite alienation. He also surrendered the possibility of including the ideological elements of subjective alienation in his final model. For this reason, his analysis is limited and not theoretically exhaustive.

In our opinion Table 1 suggests an alternative first approximation of a paradigm for the study of alienation in modern productive systems. The arrows represent "causal" relations. It should be noted that the relation between the technical and the social divisions of labor is not reciprocal. We assume that class relations assymetrically shape the types of technical systems employed. That is, we assume that concern for profits and political control of the plant by management are significant determinants of the final organization of work (Margolin, 1974; Stone, 1974).

When examined from this viewpoint, Blauner's work is seen to possess a systematic, self-imposed silence. While correcting many of the simplify-

Table 1. Paradigm for the Study of Alienation in the Firm.

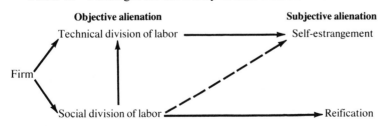

ing assumptions of Seeman's original model, Blauner limited his analysis to an examination of alienation in the immediate, technical spheres of production. As far as his analysis goes, we have little argument with it. However, his theory of alienation systematically deletes and renders mute the causal impact of the evolving class foundations and the ideological expressions of work-role alienation. His formal theory and analysis, although not his general orientation, is silent concerning the mechanics which link work-generated alienation to the class organization of industry.

Class and Objective Alienation

If we were to include the aformentioned class-based expressions of alienation in a research model, then the reconciliation of the divergent trends of research and theory discussed at the beginning of this essay might be accomplished. Beginning where Blauner left off, one needs to expand his model to include class. Given the content of the capitalist relations of production, this would be tantamount to examining the political and ideological components of everyday life which permeate the factory and its larger institutional environs.

One could finally overcome the entire noncritical research tradition by reintroducing the last of the deleted dimensions of the Seeman model: the in situ political and ideological components of alienation. However, this dialectical return would involve more than just a simple additive act by which class components were appended mechanically to the Blauner model. The constituent meanings of the Blauner model would have to be re-read and transformed.

With this recasting, the statement that a certain job content is meaningless, or that the worker is powerless, would be understood not only as a descriptive fact, but also as an historical "judgment" carrying with it a specific social biography. We would now have to consider the concrete historical events which created the alienated content. The social context of technological operations would have to be interrogated as to their ideological, political, and historical content if one were to ascertain the extent to which powerlessness, meaninglessness, and social isolation were class-determined phenomenon.

If this problematic were pursued, questions previously excluded from empiricist alienation research would arise. Alienation research would have to deal with the possibility that alienation was a necessary precondition of managerial hegemony. This line of research is already underway in the radical literature. It suggests that the "technological rationality" of work roles is, in large part, designed to give managers a monopoly of political control over the factory. Margolin (1974) argues that the technological division of labor and knowledge has long obscured a hidden or forgotten agenda designed to maximize managerial dominance. Braverman (1974) gives historical depth to this picture by showing how union-busting was a necessary political prelude and ground-clearing operation for the implementation of Taylorism. An examination of these and other works suggests, first, that worker powerlessness on the job is a way of evading the possibility that work content and factory authority structures will be bilaterally determined. Second, meaninglessness, in Blauner's sense, can be interpreted as an admission that knowledge is power. To deprive the worker of the knowledge of the whole process of production is simultaneously to assure the perpetuation of managerial functional autonomy and political prerogative. Finally, these works suggest that social isolation is not necessarily a social problem for management. While it is a structural impediment to worker integration and communication, it is also a block to the formation of disruptive, informal worker networks which could challenge managerial autonomy. In short, with the interrogation of alienation's critical content, every descriptive element of objective alienation previously delineated by Blauner is revealed to have dysfunctional political ramifications for class control of the firm. Further, critical analysis will show that every element has a history which can often illuminate the latent class content of technical rationality and its division of labor.

In light of the above, the content of work must be seen as being generated at the intersection of two divisions of labor: the technical and the social. Every work task has a dual purpose: it must fabricate a social exchange value and it must reproduce the class and authority structure of society. The technical content and structure of work, from this perspective, would include political components and ideological orientations as necessary descriptive and analytic elements. Control structures, such as unions, grievance and bargaining procedures, the monopoly market position of the firm, government intervention strategies into the market, and the relation of the rank and file to its union, would be included as possible explanatory determinants of objective work alienation. In short, the content of work would no longer be considered a purely technical necessity. Objective work alienation would become a *social relation* produced in the historically specific conditions of class antagonisms which characterize the capitalist social formation.

The introduction of class into the alienation research paradigm would allow another series of extensions, eventually restoring the study of alienation and its objective antecedents to its original societal level. The Marxian concept of class is a natural bridge linking factory and societal forms of social alienation in that it penetrates structural relations at both levels. Work alienation and its genesis would be seen now as an essential part of the larger process of capitalist society—the reproduction of classes and class boundaries. That is, it would be seen to constitute an essential part of the larger reproductive scheme which operates to maintain the class specificity of every institutional setting. Such a process, while located in the production of exchange value, would transcend the finite bounds of a particular firm's operation and spread to embrace the reproduction of the so-called societal "superstructure" itself. In short, *objective work alienation is a prerequisite of the normal reproduction of the social relations of capital as a whole.* In this way, Blauner's specification of alienation studies within the firm can be expanded outward to embrace alienation's origins in the general sociological processes of capitalist reproduction.

Ideology and Reification

Once alienation research has been returned to a sociological context, the content of subjective alienation is altered also. Self-estrangement and subjective alienation are no longer coterminous. Subjective alienation cannot be classified wholly as feelings of degradation, *angst,* or a diffuse sense of unease about work and self. Rather, subjective alienation is a set of subjective orientations which work to reproduce objective alienation each day and with each new generation. It is a set of adaptive ideological orientations and perceptions which intellectually normalize estranged social relations. *Subjective alienation positions the person in a class-delineated ideological space,* and, just as with objective alienation, it is manifested at both productive and societal levels.

At the factory level, subjective alienation is a *perceptual and cognitive style* which reifies the authority structures and decision-making processes in the firm into technologically preordained, natural phenomena. Since subjective alienation must be renewed with each generation of workers, its historical forms have created a continuous ideological parade over the last two centuries (Bendix, 1956), the reifying myths of Taylorism, the Human Relations School, job enlargement plans, and limited worker control movements being but a few of the phases in the struggle to reproduce a passive and subjectively alienated (reified) work force. These programs have been designed to accomplish two tasks: (1) to convince workers that they have a commonality of interest with management (while not going so far as to allow workers to fully manage the enterprise and its profits), and (2) to show that the limits of worker–management equality lay in some inherent inferiority of worker intellect, self-discipline, or moral capacity. Such managerial strategies instill subjective alienation as a normal part of productive activity. They are, in the last analysis, attempts to preempt at the level of the worker's consciousness what management fears might be taken sooner or later through worker action.

Alienated subjectivity occurs at the more global, societal level when the person accepts the self-interested legitimating claims which elites make concerning the democratic structure and the function of institutions while ignoring (or endorsing) the equally potent reality of class division and hegemony maintained by these institutions. Reified consciousness is marked by an orientation which sees the technical division of labor in an institution, but is blind to the institution's more basic and holistic function at the level of the social division of labor. Internally, depending on managerial style, alienated subjectivity either enshrines authority in a set of suprahuman myths or is duped by pseudodemocratic claims. Seldom does it orient itself toward the substrata of day-to-day force and terror which institutional elites use to maintain this cheery vision of social order.

By showing subjective alienation to be primarily an ideological phenomenon and by treating alienation in general as an historically specific characteristic of class-based social formations, we have not only criticized an extant mode of studying alienation, we have also suggested an alternative formulation to the scientific study of subjective alienation. An attempt to implement such a research alternative is the subject of the next section.

THE MEASUREMENT OF REIFICATION

Assumptions of the Research Model

It should be possible now to develop a new measure of subjective alienation which is consistent with the assumptions of the larger, critical theory of alienation which emerged in the closing pages of the last section. It is our intention in the remainder of this paper to report the results of such a project. However, before proceeding with the actual description of the research it will be necessary to discuss our research assumptions. Such a discussion is necessary since our conceptions of society and alienation, not to mention our methodological commitments, radically diverge from past attempts to study the social-psychological moment of alienation. These points of substantive divergence occur in two areas: (1) the status which objective alienation plays in our research model; and (2) the basic anthropological model of man which this study employs in defining the concepts of alienation and reification.

As we suggested earlier, due to the structural locus of alienation, scholarly ascertainment of its existence cannot be limited *necessarily* and *exclusively* to the research subject's feelings and perceptions of the world. That is, while the empirical mapping of these attitudes is a crucial element in the overall study of alienation, it does not exhaust the domain of alienation itself. Rather, the study of subjective alienation presupposes three

postulated conditions: (1) that the researcher possess a coherent definition of alienation; (2) that a concrete research setting have a social
structure which exhibits the character of alienated social relations; and (3)
that the research subject be inextricably integrated into that structure so
that these alienated relations significantly mediate the subject's thoughts,
goals, and actions. If all three of these conditions are met, then the
researcher can judge the subject's objective social milieu and its social
relations as being alienated.

We have dealt with the first of these conditions at some length in the
first half of this essay. The second and third conditions, we feel, have
been ascertained in other studies of American society. It is no longer
necessary merely to posit, a priori, the objective alienation of the subject
when we wish to study subjective alienation. It has been demonstrated in
the cumulative research of two decades. Compelling evidence, arguments, and syntheses have been marshaled by such theoretically diverse
writers on the left as Aronowitz (1973), Baran and Sweezy (1966),
Braverman (1974), Habermas (1975), Mandel (1975), O'Connor (1973),
and Poulantzas (1975). They have amply demonstrated the alienated
structuring of social relations in the capitalist metropoli of the West.
While differing in detail, they have forged a powerful collective portrait in
which alienation is depicted to be both a structural and an interactional
given for every person who draws a wage, is educated into the commodity
perspective, or struggles to maintain a fading margin of profit (for himself
or for another).

Given the validity of these works, the objective moment of alienation
may be treated as a baseline assumption of our present research problem.
By handling objective alienation in this manner our task is simplified:
what remains now to be examined is the subjectivity of alienation at the
level of the empirical subject. That is, we must ascertain the extent to
which men and women actually *perceive* the fact of their objective structural alienation.[2] *The subjective moment of alienation deals with the
phenomenology of the alienated social object, and it is around this issue
that the measurement of reified consciousness finds its proper place. The
research question then becomes: Given the alienated object of social
relations, what form of consciousness is employed to apprehend and
maintain the alienated status quo of social relations?*

The second area of substantive divergence between our model and past
formulations lies in its anthropological presuppositions. We reject the
positivist and behaviorist models of man which depict the individual as
purely reactive. Instead, the social psychological model we used in
formulating our definition of subjective alienation assumes a subject–
object dialectical structure.[3] Here human subjects are freely productive
agents who, in the process of self-realization, construct their social world
through the externalization of their labor, their biographies, and their

"selves" into objects and social relations already at hand in their social environment. A full explication of this model requires the insertion of two other concepts: alienation and reification (Berger and Pullberg, 1965). Alienation refers to the objective loss of the socially produced object. When this process occurs, meaning and meaning-mediated objects, once produced, take on a life of their own. Here, the object comes to dominate its author and gains an autonomy over him or her, to which its creator must now submit. This loss of the object and its subsequent autonomy has its genesis in the historically specific set of productive relations in which the subject is enmeshed.

The process of alienation also has a subjective moment—reification. Thought becomes alienated when it begins to presuppose the *naturalness* of the alienated object's autonomy. This autonomy is interpreted from the reified perspective, not as the expropriated power of an impotent subject, but as an innate property of the object itself.

Lukacs' work on reification is capable of subsuming much of the above phenomenological model, while adding sociological objectivity and historical specificity. For Lukacs the domain of reified thought is not grasped in terms of individual consciousness. Rather, it is the property of an entire epoch's thought; it is a property of "bourgeois thought."

For Lukacs, to talk of class consciousness is to speak of a consciousness which typifies, not a person, but an entire structural fraction of society. Bourgeois thought, in order ideologically to protect its interests and morale, places two contradictory demands on all thought which vies for the status of knowledge in capitalist society: (1) to produce a system of knowledge that allows the full technical development and growth of socially productive activity, and (2) to create a form of instrumental reason which promotes the interests of the dominant class. For Lukacs these two goals of bourgeois consciousness were contradictory and hence "false." (It was in this sense of formal incompatability that reified consciousness was labeled as "false consciousness.") Lukacs argued that given the structural constraints and practical contortions of thought, only a secondary goal was possible for knowledge. While the contradictions of capitalist social relations could not be eliminated, they could be presented as the natural limits of human social existence itself. Hence, the institutions of capitalist society were conceived as having the same obdurate and ahistorical constitution as objects of a physical nature. It is these naturalistic characterizations of society which provide us with the grounding for our operational definitions of alienated subjectivity.

Some Key Definitional Elements of Reification

In this section and in those following we will describe the development and validation of a scale designed to measure subjective alienation. First, we will discuss the "operational content" of our measure of reification. Then, we will present the model and the techniques used to generate and test specific items. Following this, we will discuss the validation of the measurement scale. Finally, we will analyze the factor structure of the scale and further validation attempts.

Six assumptions or reference points Lukacs regarded as crucial to the construction of reality from the standpoint of bourgeois class consciousness were identified as guideposts in the construction of a model or reified consciousness. *These assumptions were not used in a purely deductive process of item generation.* Rather, they provided a broad framework within which specific item content was generated. The reifying assumptions were as follows:

1. *Naturalness of Social Institutions*   This refers to the tendency of individuals to frame explanations of historical and social structural phenomenon within inappropriate "natural science" models. Social relations come to be imbued with a reality and mythical character that give them the appearance of being a "second-nature."

2. *Surrender of Autonomy*   A second presupposition is the willingness of individuals to surrender control of their lives and intellectual productions to the representatives of the institutions of public culture. In this situation, the dialectic of one's own reality construction is arrested and the process is subordinated to the mystical aura of authority which is attributed to "institutional elites."

3. *Natural Limits to Change*   From a reified perspective the limits to social change are perceived as lying not in the need to maintain a given social arrangement—such as a class's hegemony in society—but rather are attributed to transhistorical factors, natural cycles, or preordained institutional destinies.

4. *Individual Interpretation of Structural Phenomena*   In the fourth element, institutional events are explained as though social relations were purely derivative constructions of human motives. This reified model of man and social explanation ignores the systematizing impact of modern modes of production—modes whose essence are the creation and maintenance of social relations which coerce the individual. Pretheoretical examples of this form of reified thought include personalization of bureaucratic behavior, various forms of political paranoia in which complex historical events are given meaning by attributing to them and to their origin personal plots, cabals, scapegoating of "strangers" and "outsiders" to explain catastrophe.

5. *Common Interests*   This presupposition deals with the extent to which a person recognizes structural sources of conflict as they impinge on his or her life in class society.

6. *Inappropriate Sense of Power*   This last point refers to the subject's

perception of his or her own ability to affect the action of those at the center of state and corporate power.

These six dimensions serve as a formal skeletal framework which is used to *bracket* an ideal typical and general formulation of reified consciousness. These parameters of reified consciousness sketch structures of thought and provide boundary criteria of what to look for when perusing the potential universe of concrete attitudes and orientations. As we shall see in the next section, the six dimensions are used to generate two polar, ideal typical *Weltanschauungen. From these two totalizing world views, specific items are generated.*

Item Construction

1. The Model

Within this structural framework inspired by Lukacs, reified and nonreified perspectives were defined as communally produced and logically coherent ideologies. To say that a person possessed a high or low reified intellectual world view was tantamount to locating the person within a specific structural grouping and its totalizing *Weltanschauung,* within a "communication community" (Apel, 1975).

Our conception of communication community encompassed more than Apel's: it sought to include not only intellectuals with their ideational productions, but also persons who consciously lived their lives by precepts which could be designated as high and low reification perspectives. The ideational compositions of both Apel's and our communication communities were, however, formally the same in that the ideal boundaries of each were demarcated by a set of nondemonstrable, metatheoretical "paradigms" and "conventions."

In order to generate items which putatively represented high or low reification it was necessary to locate two communities which Lukacs might specify as possessing a nonreified and a highly reified *Weltanschauung,* respectively. At this point we consciously allowed, for the moment, historically bounded ideology to serve as a *fictive* measure of "truth." The neo-Marxist worldview described by Lukacs was used as an Archimedean point for generating items with low reification content. First, an ideal-typical perspective of neo-Marxist subjectivity was constructed. We inquired as to what views an ideal-typical neo-Marxist *might* hold concerning profit motives, sex roles, family life, or the nature of change.

The selection of a radical worldview was only an approximate first step. If the left, despite its internecine ideological diversity, had developed a common unifying set of epistemological and substantive assumptions, it had not done so in historical isolation. Rather, this viewpoint had been hammered out in a dialogue with the other pure position of capitalist class structure—the bourgeoisie.

High reification items were generated by taking the ideal viewpoint of the commercial petty bourgeoisie. Items were again generated by adopting "the role of the other" on the above listed issues. The commercial petty bourgeoisie was selected as our contrasting ideal type rather than the monopoly capitalist or the soulful corporation for both theoretical and practical reasons. First was the practical fact that small businessmen were more available for interviewing than were members of the corporate and financial establishment. Second, as Marx argued in Vol. III of *Capital*, the actual consciousness of the industrial bourgeoisie of his day was ruled by the self-concepts and meta-theory of *merchant capital* (Marx, 1967:277–337). These market-based metaphysics and archaic explanations of life chances and structural mechanisms in the economy have, since Marx's day, intensified and expanded the viewpoint of merchant capital in both its neoclassical and Keynesian variants.

Even though the objective conditions of the core economy *as a whole* are different from that of the marginal entrepreneur, the social-psychological orientation and self-concept of the core-economy manager is not that different from his small business counterpart. Following Baran and Sweezy, we felt that the actions required of corporate executives in their generation of surplus within the firm weren't that different from the individual strategies employed by cost/price cutting entrepreneurs (Baran and Sweezy, 1966:52–78).

Thus, in its fullest sense, the meaning community toward which we oriented our operational procedures for item generation was the *ideal class communication community* bounded by the radical perspective on one side and the perspective of the classic, commercial petty bourgeoisie on the other.

This study defines the key tenets of reified bourgeois consciousness (discussed in the last section) as though they were what Apel has called "convictions" or "paradigms." They are the tacit taken-for-granted metaphysical assumptions about nature, society, and man which constitute the factual starting points for the practical and discursive model of ideal bourgeois class-based thought. The knowledge produced under these conditions is *noncritical* since inquiry proceeds from assumptions consistent with objective bourgeois consciousness. Such knowledge, it is assumed, replicates in the individual's mind the alienation existent in the objective social order. Given its noncritical assumption (that thought does not produce but only describes reality), reified thought has no choice but to confirm in concept the alienated relations already existing in the social structure.

2. The Method

The six presuppositions developed above were used to delineate the formal boundaries between reified and nonreified styles of subjective perception and social reality construction. Using an ideal-typical strategy approximating that of hermenutics, a series of substantive issues or social challenges was chosen (Palmer, 1969; Burger, 1976:154–67). A radical and a petty bourgeois response or position was generated on each issue. This resulted in a pair of statements for each issue: one representing a radical (low reification) perspective, while the other represented the antithetical viewpoint of the petty bourgeoisie (high reification).

The final form for each attitude item consisted of two polar statements. One statement endorsed a viewpoint which attested to the reification of some social institution or process of public culture as it now operates. A second statement was paired with the first. This statement discussed the same institution or public culture process, but from a viewpoint which saw the institution in a nonreified light. (See Table 2 for these items. The starred items represent "high reification" items.) Subjects were asked to circle the one statement which came closest to expressing their viewpoint on the issue discussed in the paired statements. After having done this, they were then asked to designate the strength of the feelings concerning their choice. That is, they were asked to circle one of four alternatives: "How strongly do you feel about your answer?—'Very Strongly,' 'Strongly,' 'Somewhat Strongly,' 'Not Strongly at all.' " This format was chosen because it allowed the researchers (1) to avoid certain problems of response set and response bias, and (2) to establish an eight-point continuum for each pair of statements by which to rank the subject's response.

These final items, their content and form, were the result of a complex series of validating procedures. The researchers began by composing 136 items (68 paired statements) tapping the reification dimensions. This initial number of 68 paired statements was eventually reduced to 21 after testing for polarity; validation of items by a panel of "expert judges" using the criteria of low and high reification developed in Lukacs's *History and Class Consciousness;* validation in terms of responses by 20 members of the radical left on the West Coast; and checking for scale distribution and discriminatory spread in responses to application of the schedule in interviews in Nevada. As a result of these various validating and winnowing techniques it was concluded that these items constituted a *Reification Scale* which was an internally valid measure of individual, alienated subjectivity. There was still the issue of external validity and to this issue we will now turn.

Criterion Validation of the Reification Scale

Up to this point our validation techniques had concentrated upon a meaning structure wholly circumscribed by Marxist ideology. We had reduced the Lukacs' model of class consciousness to an ideal type of neo-Marxist ideology. While such a procedure produced effective results, the validation attempt was still flawed by the fact that the items' internal validation had taken place solely within the Marxist perspective and had not spanned the total communication community.

As stated above, the Marxist theory of reification developed not in isolation, but as part of a larger set of class-based, social crises. *Marxist theory asserts one pole of the dilemma of experienced reification while its class counterpart holds down the other pole of this idealized dialogue.* To the extent that Marxism is an internal critique of the capitalist mode of social production, we should predict that this nonreified perspective will find its mirror image in the highly reified perspective of the petty bourgeoisie. Given the assumption that the reality of the Marxist perspective is historically lodged in the larger communication community centered around the resolution of class-based contradictions, we would expect our scale to drastically separate the two ideal types of consciousness.

We tested this proposition by comparing the scale score responses of our 20 radicals with those of 16 small businessmen drawn from the Nevada sample.[4] The results are presented in the first two columns of Table 2. Column one of Table 2 reports the standardized discriminate function coefficients. The higher the coefficient, the better is the item's accuracy in correctly classifying individuals as either radical or petty bourgeois. The second column reports the F-ratios for each item's coefficient. This technique was applied to the total reification scale score. The results of this test show that all 36 cases were correctly classified. That is, on the basis of the reification scores alone all 16 petty bourgeoisie were placed in one sector of the discriminate function space while all 20 radicals were isolated in the other sector of that space. On the basis of the reification scores there was no overlapping of groups and hence no misclassification. We may state that the scale performs in a manner in which the theory itself would require.

However, as solid as these findings seem to be, they mean little unless it can be shown that the Reification Scale is relatively unique in its ability to discriminate the ideal poles of this particular communication community. In order to test the discriminate validity of the Reification Scale in distinguishing between these two ideological positions, correlation ratios were computed for the Reification Scale and its subscales (see below for discussion), and Seeman's Powerlessness Scale (Neal and Seeman, 1964), Srole's Anomia Scale (Srole, 1956), Form's Anomie Scale

Table 2. Discriminant Function Coefficients and Factor Loadings for Radical and Petty Bourgeois Criterion Groups and Factor Loadings for Twenty One Items of the Reification Scale for the Nevada Sample.

Reification Items	Standardized Discriminant Function Coefficients	F-Ratio	Rotated Varimax Factor Loadings for Radical and Petty Bourgeois Criterion Groups				Rotated Varimax Factor Loadings for Nevada Sample			
			Factor I	Factor II	Factor III	Factor IV	Factor I	Factor II	Factor III	Factor IV
LEGITIMATION CRISIS FACTOR										
• Don't blame the oil companies for the higher oil prices! The high prices are caused by you and me! we are using more oil products and this drives up prices.	-0.732	48.48	.869	.169	.197	.224	.715	-.069	.065	.089
We are paying these high prices at the gas pump because the big oil firms are getting together and fixing the price of oil.										
• People don't realize that the "huge" oil profits they complain about are being put back into the economy and will create new jobs for young Americans in the future.	1.599	24.89	.840	.152	.377	.062	.677	.031	.127	.039
I'm fed up with this price gouging. The oil firms are stealing money from poor people and putting it in the pockets of the big oil millionaires.										
• If a man loves his country, he will have faith in it and support it even in those times when he knows that it is doing wrong.	0.118	16.77	.733	.347	.080	.074	.164	.359	.138	.011
The truest test of patriotism is actively protesting against the established government when you know it is doing wrong.										
In America, the government has no business, under any circumstance, spying on its citizens.										
• In cases of national security, the government has the right to violate a citizen's constitutional rights and spy on him.	-2.189	61.16	.716	.007	.466	.341	.451	.123	.058	.103
In this country, when a big shot breaks the law, he buys a high-priced lawyer and gets off. When the ordinary guy breaks the same law, he gets nailed hard with a big fine or a stiff prison sentence.										
• Most of the laws that we are asked to obey in society are fair. Those laws apply equally to the rich and poor, black and white - in short, to all Americans.	1.051	29.53	.714	.026	.607	.083	.433	.152	.094	.126
Job rules are usually written so that bosses can sweat as much work out of the worker as possible.										
• Job rules are designed to allow everyone - workers and bosses - to cooperate and do their own job in the easiest way possible.	-0.014	91.20	.629	.118	.303	.609	.146	.081	.060	.565
If I learned anything from Watergate, it is that the big money has been running this country for years. It will take more than electing new officials - we are going to have to change the government itself.										
• We shouldn't over-react and start making a lot of changes because of Watergate. Watergate says nothing about the basic health of our political system - it only means that we have to put up with a few crooked politicians every so often.	-1.956	140.93	.523	.470	.438	.491	.390	.288	.338	.048

219

Table 2. (Continued).

Reification Items	Standardized Discriminant Function Coefficients	F-Ratio	Rotated Varimax Factor Loadings for Radical and Petty Bourgeois Criterion Groups				Rotated Varimax Factor Loadings for Nevada Sample			
			Factor I	Factor II	Factor III	Factor IV	Factor I	Factor II	Factor III	Factor IV
INDIVIDUAL INTERPRETATION OF STRUCTURAL PHENOMENA FACTOR										
* When problems come up in a town, it is because a bunch of outsiders come in and create problems by stirring up things that they really don't understand. / Usually protestors point out real injustices. They don't create the problems the problems are already there before they come to town.	-0.079	10.04	-.126	.102	.238	.869	-.089	.265	.313	-.002
* A lot of social changes fail because a bunch of radicals are trying to make some "far-out" changes that the average American just won't buy. / Many reforms fail in this country because when the reforms start to be effective, the upper class usually blocks them.	1.005	48.96	.625	.063	.208	.657	.108	.261	.126	.139
* Most people who complain about our society are too lazy to work. If they worked steady like the rest of us, they wouldn't have the time to sit and complain. / People who complain about our society aren't always lazy. If we had to work at the dirty jobs that they do, I bet we'd complain plenty.	-0.963	54.21	.538	.224	.204	.600	.062	.322	.032	.234
* In America if a person is poor, it's because he's too lazy to go out and find a good job - the jobs are out there waiting to be filled. / As long as the businessman needs cheap help and can make a man work for slave wages, there will always be poor people in the United States.	1.013	62.49	.413	.423	.449	.472	.172	.070	.311	.410
The basic difference between the rich man and the poor man is that the rich man was probably born into a well-to-do family and had all the advantages, while the poor man didn't. / * The main reason that one man gets rich while the other stays poor is that the rich man has more drive and ambition to work hard and improve himself.	-0.518	314.20	.562	.355	.359	.574	.093	.003	.205	.516
* People don't understand that most of the differences between men and women are rooted in human biology. Men and women are supposed to be different from each other. / There aren't that many inborn differences between men and women. Most of the differences are due to the fact that parents raise boys differently than girls.	-0.545	68.15	.988	.388	.473	.487	.106	.563	-.021	.145
* There is no society on earth where men don't try to compete and make a profit. That type of drive and competition is human nature. / It is more natural for men to cooperate than it is for them to struggle and compete with each other. Of the two, cooperation is the more natural.	-1.691	87.90	.497	.332	.234	.584	-.016	.193	-.077	.213

Table 2. (Continued).

Reification Items	Standardized Discriminant Function Coefficients	F-Ratio	Rotated Varimax Factor Loadings for Radical and Petty-Bourgeois Criterion Groups				Rotated Varimax Factor Loadings for Total Nevada Sample			
			Factor I	Factor II	Factor III	Factor IV	Factor I	Factor II	Factor III	Factor IV
CORE VERSUS PERIPHERY CONFLICT FACTOR										
* The small businessman and the head of the large corporation have the same goal -- higher profits. In most cases, what is good for the corporation will also be good for the small businessman.	-0.725	14.10	.241	.832	-.111	.222	.184	-.093	.589	.229
The corporations are destroying the small businessman. Each year it gets harder for him to make a living while the corporations get fat on higher profits.										
* There is nothing so seriously wrong with this country that we have to rush out and change it right now. Usually most social problems, if left alone, will work themselves out.	-0.992	22.08	.473	.742	.063	.143	.226	.108	.570	.132
We have some social problems that have to be solved right now before serious damage is done. If we ignore the problems they will just get worse -- they won't go away by themselves.										
Most beginning small businesses fail because in a tough competitive system like ours only the very best businesses are intended to survive.										
A lot of small businesses go bust today because the economy and tax system are rigged to favor large businesses. Even before the small businessman opens his doors, he is playing against a stacked deck	0.799	4.61	-.120	.759	.353	.026	.059	.087	.447	.025
BIOLOGICAL EXPLANATION OF FAMILY AND SEX ROLES										
* Marriage is a sacred thing and should not be extended to homosexuals. Allowing homosexuals legally to marry is a very bad idea.	-1.668	23.13	.379	.087	.825	**.105**	-.087	.534	-.273	.167
Homosexuals are humans and need the stability and companionship of marriage as much as anyone else. I favor changing the law so that homosexuals can legally marry.										
* A person cannot really lead a normal and happy life until he has gotten married and started raising a family.	-0.961	26.47	.205	.025	**.787**	**.345**	-.002	-.300	**.027**	**.001**
A person can lead a normal life and in most cases be happier if he never marries.										
* I think women have a "motherly instinct." That's why I get upset when I hear people say that its O.K. for men to raise children while the wife goes out and works.	0.602	38.70	.193	.337	.753	.376	.154	.515	.089	-.144
A woman may not be the best person in the family to raise children. When the man is better at this job, I think he should stay home and raise the children while the wife goes out and earns the living.										
* The military claims that they are experts in war, but generals make mistakes too. Those mistakes often cost people their lives. That's why I'm not so impressed with military experts.	0.499	15.58	.209	.067	.523	.452	.071	.339	.178	.014
The military are trained all of their lives on how to win wars. When a war comes, everybody should stand back and let the generals win the war the best way they see fit.										

(Form, 1975), and the F-Scale (Robinson and Shaver, 1967). Values of correlation ratios refer to the proportion of the total variation in the data which is accounted for by the categories (the independent variable) being used. Thus, the interpretation of the correlation ratio within a PRE format is similar to the r^2 (explained variation) interpretation of the correlation coefficient.

The correlation ratio was used to discover the extent to which the total variation of each of the scale scores could be explained or accounted for when the categories of radical and petty bourgeoisie were used as predictive variables. If a high percentage of variation was accounted for on the Reification Scale and its subscales, and concomitantly little or no variation could be accounted for on the Seeman, Form, and Srole Scales, then this would be further confirmation of the external validity of the Reification Scale. The results are reported in Table 3.

In Table 3 the treatment categories of left-radical and petty bourgeoisie explains 88 percent of the variation in the overall reification scores. This compares favorably with 27 percent for Seeman, 12 percent for Srole, and 11 percent for Form's Anomie measure. Furthermore, as predicted, the Reification subscales have more of their variation explained by the dual category than do the Seeman, Srole, and Form measures. The F-Scale, on the other hand, has 63 percent of the variation of its scores explained by the radical/petty bourgeoisie dichotomy. This was expected, however, since a reading of Adorno's theoretical writings in *The Authoritarian Personality* shows him framing the problem of authoritarianism in terms strikingly similar to Lukacs's basic paradigm (Adorno et al., 1950:617–

Table 3. Correlation Ratios and Point Bi-Serial R Conversion for Radicals versus Petty Bourgeoisie on Reification Scale, Factor Sub-Scales, Seeman Powerlessness, Srole Anomia, Form Anomie and F-Scale.

Scale	Correlation Ratio	Point Bi-Serial R
Seeman's Powerlessness	.2673	.517
Srole's Anomia	.1235	.351
Form's Anomie	.1111	.333
F-Scale	.6316	.795
Reification Scale	.8833	.940
Legitimation Factor	.7310	.855
Core/Periphery Factor	.3794	.616
Biological Explanation of Sex Roles Factor	.5678	.754
Individual Interpretation Factor	.4943	.703

22). The basic difference between Lukacs and Adorno, though, is in the psychoanalytic operational transformation given the ideas by Adorno.

In sum, the discriminate function analysis and the correlation ratios reported in Table 3 suggest that the Reification Scale uniquely taps parameters which structure the dialogue between radical and petty bourgeoisie in their specific ideal class communication community. As a confirmation of the discriminate validity of the Reification Scale, the scores of the Seeman, Srole, and Form Scales performed less well in this task and context. The magnitudes of the correlation ratios for the F-Scale, on the other hand, served as a convergent validity check.

The Factor Structure of the Reification Scale

The preceding section noted that the radical perspective is, in part, internal to the process which creates the intellectual milieu of contemporary capitalist society. Its position cannot be articulated, nor its origins understood, unless it is located vis-à-vis another, antithetical ideological position. The radical position, to the extent that it is conceptualized as internal to the system (a product of the system), cannot claim an Archimedean critique for its ideological positions. Rather, it has the status of a Weberian ideal-typical model and merely represents one pole of the total antinomical dialogue. At this level of abstraction the radical ideological position can only exist correlative to its petty bourgeois antithesis. *The unity of these two positions demarcates the contemporary parameters which ideologically structure modern bourgeois culture, its conflicts, and its contradictions.*

Given this relational conception of ideological content, it is appropriate to treat the radical ideological model and its petty bourgeois counterpart as polar opposites within a larger unity. Further, it is posited that a comparison of the responses of these polar types would provide a picture of the structure underlying the item content of the Reification Scale. That is, an examination of these responses to the reification items would yield something approximating a "pure structure" of reification, a structure not clouded by confounding parameters. To this purpose an orthogonally rotated Principle Axis Factor Analysis of the Reification Scale was completed. The results are reported in the second section of Table 2.

This analysis produced four factors which, when combined, accounted for 80.5 percent of the variance in radical and petty bourgeois responses. The first factor accounted for 58.40 percent of item response variance. This factor consisted of seven items which dealt with whether or not the respondent felt that social processes in America were governed by universalistic and democratic norms. These seven items were in turn classified into three thematic groups. The first two items dealt with perceptions as to whether the present oil cartel was subject to universalistic demands of the market and working for the common good. A second set of items (items 5 and 6 in Table 2) dealt with whether or not the respondent believed that regulatory rules and laws in general were universally applied and designed to neutrally facilitate the social welfare of all. The final group of items dealt with the subject's willingness to surrender control of democratic decision making and have faith that political discretion would be exercised in a legitimate direction. These last three items referred to the issues of mass loyalty and the political system's ability to transform that mass loyalty into sovereignly executed administrative decisions. (We have labeled this factor the *Legitimation Crisis Factor* cf., Habermas, 1975; O'Connor, 1973). In terms of this first factor, to the extent that a respondent endorses the statements which are starred in Table 2, we have a social-psychological approximation of a subject's endorsement of the legitimacy of the state's accumulation activities and its modern role. To the extent that a subject endorses the nonstarred statements, we have a social-psychological measure of nonconfidence in the state's discursive claims to universalistically legitimated activity—in other words a legitimacy crisis.

The second factor refers to the conflict of interest between small businessmen and their monopoly counterparts. It accounts for 8.6 percent of item variance and is named the *Core Versus Periphery Factor*. This factor has as its basic referent the extent to which the respondent sees the crisis of the small businessman as a problem located in the social structure of productive relations.

The third factor explains 7.9 percent of total item variation and bears the title *Biological Explanation of Family and Sex Roles*. This factor is almost a literal translation of Lukacs' assertion that reified consciousness tends to explain the content and structure of social relations as though they were objects of nature. This factor contrasts two differing interpretive models of family and sex-role relations.

The last factor is labeled the *Individual Interpretation Factor* and accounts for 5.6 percent of the variation in item responses. Most of these items deal with "accounts" which people give of perplexing social predicaments (Scott and Lyman, 1968). Reified accounts blame the victim of a problem ridden situation by attributing the problem's cause to an action or moral imperfection of the victim. The starred items in Table 2 are statements representing this reified perspective.

The third section of Table 2 reports the results of a factor analysis which was performed on the Nevada sample. In this analysis we attempted to find out if the structures which shaped the responses were similar to those which underlay the responses of the criterion groups. The results were similar. The Nevada data was forced to a similar four-factor solution and rotation. The amount of explained variance for all factors, as expected, were much lower (40.7 percent). At the same time, however, the same factor structure seemed to emerge. The Legitimation Crisis Factor was still the central factor accounting for 17.5 percent of the item variance. On all factors individual loadings were lower than those found for the criterion groups. The second and third factors were extracted in reverse order in the Nevada analysis. The Family and Sex Role Factor (9.5 percent of the explained variance) and the Core/Periphery factor (7.2 percent), while retaining their item content, had for all practical purposes been reversed. The last factor suffered most in the translation from one group to the other.

In sum, we may state that the factor analysis of the Reification Scale provides additional support for its basic validity. The strongest finding and the least expected was the emergence of the Legitimation Crisis Factor. Its emergence not only allows the scale to be multiply rooted in a later tradition of Marxian social analysis, it also allows that connection to be extended from the scale to a relatively recent attempt at analyzing subjective alienation within a political economy context. Finally, the factors extracted from the criterion group analysis and the Nevada population factor analysis are similar enough to suggest that these elements may also be structuring the scale responses of the general population.

Predictive Validity

Thus far we have employed various techniques of reliability and validity testing in order to fix and locate the Reification Scale vis-à-vis the Lukacs' model and similar intellectual formulations. In large part these attempts have been of an internal validating nature. They have tried to show an internal consistency between the constructs of reification as expressed in one variety of critical Marxism, and the specific items used to measure the abstract and limited moment of reification as expressed in social-psychological terms. The factor analytic findings were, in large part, of an internally validating nature since the major connection was made with the works of Habermas—a critical theorist. In this section we will attempt to further establish the validity of the scale by employing the technique of predictive validity. To this end we will test certain hypotheses concerning the predicted relations between the Reification Scale and measures of Powerlessness, Anomie, Anomia, and Authorianism.

Multiple Connections with Other Scales

The predictive validity used in the cross-validation of the Reification Scale concerns a series of hypotheses concerning the covariation of that scale with other scales. Working with responses from just the Nevada sample (N = 232), the following four hypotheses were framed and tested:

1. There will be an inverse relation between the respondent's scores on the Reification Scale and the respondent's scores on Seeman's Powerlessness Scale.

2. There will be an inverse relation between the respondent's Reification Score and his score on the Srole Anomia Scale.

3. There will be an inverse relation between the respondent's Reification Score and his score on the Form Anomie Scale.

4. There will be a direct relationship between the respondent's Reification Score and his score on the F-Scale.

The first hypothesis concerned the relation between the Reification Scale and Seeman's Powerlessness Scale. The seven paired-items version of Seeman's Powerlessness Scale was used in the present study (Neal and Seeman, 1964). It was hypothesized that a person scoring high on the Reification Scale would score low in feelings of powerlessness. The full line of our argument has been developed elsewhere (Harvey et al., 1976). Its basic logic, however, is as follows: the reification process elevates (in the person's consciousness) objective class and power relationships to the level of natural phenomena. If reification is a successful process, the person will accept his or her objective, role-based powerlessness as a matter-of-fact condition of life. Not only will the person not feel a lack of internal control over his social environment; in most cases it should not be a major problem in his life at all. Thus, we would predict the two scales to be negatively correlated. Table 4 shows a correlation coefficient between the two scales of $-.169$. What is crucial for our findings is that the direction of the correlation confirm our first predictive validity hypothesis. The magnitude of the correlation leaves something to be desired. Even though significant at the .01 level, that significance may be largely an artifact of the large sample size.

The second and third hypotheses will be treated together since both the Srole and Form Scales measure an aspect of Durkheimian anomie. The Srole Scale is a measure of psychological adjustment and measures the degree of cynicism which a person brings to perceptions about the social world. The original nine-item version of the Srole Anomia Scale was used in this study (Srole, 1956). The Form Scale is less interested in the psychological moment of anomie. Rather, it seeks to tap the subject's phenomenological perception and evaluation concerning institutional anomie. The writers used a five-item version of the scale which Form had shown to scale unidimensionally on a sample of American auto workers (Form, 1975).

Following the basic argument of Peter Berger (1967) we posited that life is least anomic when individuals perceive their constructed meanings as having transhuman and extrasocial origins. Low Anomie is pegged to high reification. Conversely, when meaning systems are at their most trans-

Table 4. Correlation Coefficients for Reification Scale and Sub-Scales and Various Criterion Scales (N=232)

	Reification Scale	Seeman Powerlessness Scale	F-Scale	Srole Anomia Scale	Form Anomie Scale	Legitimation Scale	Core/Periphery Scale	Biological Sex Role Sub-Scale	Individual Interpretation Sub-Scale
Reification Scale	x	−.169*	.363	−.170	−.252	.800	.575	.587	.765
Seeman Powerlessness Scale		x	.137	.286	.338	−.220	−.088	.027	−.129
F-Scale			x	.258	.060	.187	−.008	.472	.343
Srole Anomia Scale				x	.519	−.176	−.261	.062	−.114
Form Anomie Scale					x	−.230	−.260	−.020	−.180
Legitimation Sub-Scale						x	.362	.236	.397
Core/Periphery Sub-Scale							x	.129	.304
Biological Sex Role Sub-Scale								x	.380
Individual Interpretation Sub-Scale									x

*r = .1676 is significant at the .01 level

parent, and expose their origins in human will and not in divine precept, man's freedom to construct his world is at a maximum. Reification is at its nadir. At the same time, however, systemic and personal anomie, according to this model, are at their highest. Berger posits a balance and trade-off between the inversely related qualities of alienation and anomie.

Following this logic we should predict a negative correlation between the Reification Scale and these measures of anomie. These expectations are born out in Table 4. The correlation coefficient between the Reification Scale and the Srole measure is −.170, while the Reification Scale and Form's Anomie Scale show a correlation of −.252. Again, the magnitudes of the correlations are "significant;" as before, the direction of the correlation supports our hypotheses.

Finally, we have argued in this paper that *The Authoritarian Personality* shares a common ground with Lukacs's conceptualization and that high reification would be related to high authoritarianism. To test this thesis the shortened 12-item scale developed by Berkowitz was administered to the Nevada sample (Robinson and Shafer, 1969). This line of thought is supported by a positive correlation coefficient of .363 which was computed for the reification scale and the F-Scale. This finding is one of convergent validity and supports the fourth and final hypothesis.

Summary

In this section we have tested various hypotheses in order to establish the validity of the measuring instrument developed in this study. Drawing from sociological theory which had been developed externally to the reification model, a set of predictions were made concerning the relation between reification scores on the one hand and the Srole, Form, Seeman and F-Scale measures on the other. All of the hypotheses were confirmed as far as the predicted direction of the correlation coefficient—although in many cases the magnitudes were low. This final form of validation further cross-references the content of the scale and adds further support to the validity claims of the Reification Scale.

SUMMARY AND CONCLUSION

The essence of dialectics is process and the tracing of that process. This paper has provided a descriptive reading of such an unfolding as it has occurred in the field of alienation research. It has also suggested a direction in which future research might develop. There is little to add by way of conclusion.

We began this essay by critiquing the Seeman model and its general problematic. As is befitting of a dialectical analysis, the presentation was structured so as to underscore the continuous and progressive movement by which abstract, psychologically framed ideas of alienation were replaced by more complex sociological conceptions. Also in conformity with dialectics, the earlier model gave away gradually to its antithesis—a theory of alienation which was historical and critical in nature.

From this expanded theoretical conception of alienation we developed an alternative content for the measurement of subjective alienation. The final goal of this essay was to show the efficacy of our earlier theoretical speculations by applying them to a practical research problem. In presenting the Reification Scale, we were able to return to the starting point of our critical inquiry and present a measure of subjective alienation which contained within itself the sublated elements of the preceding critique. The Reification Scale represented a measure which was developed from a neo-Marxist theory and was ostensibly free of the limitations which had marked earlier efforts to study alienation empirically.

Before concluding this essay, we would like to comment on one more issue: where does such an instrument as the Reification Scale fit into the overall structure of critical research and inquiry? We have tried to underscore in this essay the uses to which we believe such techniques can be put in developing a critical theory of modern social formations. Within the Marxist problematic, our efforts have been directed toward developing an approach to studying what Sartre might call the "ideological mediation" of social existence (Sartre, 1968:35–85). We have developed an approach to the study of the ideological structures which mediates the individual's project and the larger sociohistorical formations of the capitalist mode of production.

Our efforts have been developed within a dialectical methodology and, we feel, are compatible with that specific approach to the study of social life. The scale's basic purpose is to measure "what is" as it pertains to the ideological commitments of the concrete individual. Its constructions and subsequent findings *complement* critical social analysis in that dialectical analysis always proceeds in its inquiry from a negation of "what is." It is from this empirical stratum of "Being" that the essences and appearances of social existence are distilled and comprehended. Such empirical instruments and procedures as we have presented here can be extremely useful in establishing the precise nature of social structures and ideational states and hence can give dialectical analysis a firmer ground from which to proceed. Empirical technique, once stripped of its positivist presuppositions, can become a valuable tool for radical social analysis.

Finally, our effort has been ameliorative and reconciliatory in intent. We have refused to abandon research techniques which may still supply us with invaluable insights. At the same time, we have refused to continue in a research tradition in which sociological theory has seldom played the central role which it deserves. In the process of this "double refusal" we have tried to shape an alternative route for studying subjective alienation.

We have tried to rethink sociology's treatment of alienation. However, we cannot claim that we have been substantively exhaustive in our treatment. We can only claim a promising beginning at best. While we have rooted the Reification Scale as best we can in a firm theoretical explication, we have not been able to comment on the application of our ideas in a concrete research setting.[5] Theoretically, our work is self-admittedly partial and has been limited by the problem at hand. Nonetheless, given these shortcomings, we have presented an interpretive critique and suggestion for redirecting empirical research in alienation. In its very presentation, debate and exchange are invited. The intent of our work has been dialectical: if its purpose is to be realized it should provoke in its very statement a rethinking and amending of alienation theory and research.

ACKNOWLEDGMENTS

We would like to acknowledge the contributions of three people, Karl Kreplin, Michael Reed, and Warren d'Azevedo to this paper. They have been particularly central to our intellectual development over the last three years. We are also indebted to Stanley Aronowitz, Berch Berberoglu, Andrew Feenberg, and Joachim Israel for their critical comments and kind encouragement. Finally, Dr. Young Koh deserves special thanks for his unstinting assistance and concern on details of how to manipulate computers without becoming their captive.

NOTES

1. We shall drop the concept of anomie as alienation from our discussion. This is done for several reasons. First, it plays a minor role in Blauner's overall argument and its inclusion in our discussions would be superfluous. Second, as we have shown elsewhere (Harvey et al., 1976), Seeman's inclusion of anomie as a form of alienation results from a confused misreading of Merton. Finally, Berger (1967) and Berger and Pullberg (1965) have convincingly argued that alienation and anomie are diametrically opposite phenomena and cannot be conceptually equated.

2. The prior research problematic which we have critiqued does not even recognize this problem nor our solution to it. Prior research confounded the objective and subjective moments of alienation in formulating its problem and in designing its measure.

3. We have adopted the purely nominal convention of using the term reification to refer exclusively to the role which subjective and individual processes of consiousness play in the dialectical production of capitalist social relations while reserving the term alienation to designate the objective social relations within which such subjective construction of reality takes place. To our mind, this is merely a useful terminological convention in that the usage violates neither the sense nor the spirit of the concepts as employed within the works of Marx and Lukacs. The distinction itself follows the convention of Berger and Pullberg (1965). It allows us to conceptually differentiate between the subjective construction of social relations, on the one hand, and the objective, socially necessary product of those

alienated productive relations on the other. In adopting such a convention we hope to gain in conceptual rigor what is lost in faithfulness to Lukacs' original formulation. We are grateful to Andrew Feenberg and Joachim Israel for helping us clarify our thought on this point.

4. The 21 items of the scale were subjected to a discriminate analysis. This form of multivariate analysis works with "known groups" and allows the researcher to determine the efficacy of each item as well as the total scale score to unequivocally partition two or more groups. Discriminate function analysis is a technique which provides the researcher with a way to judge the distinctiveness of known groups as delineated by empirical responses to attitudinal statements.

5. Research results showing a strong relation between various aspects of work satisfaction and reification scores are now in the process of being written up in an article tentatively entitled "Work Satisfaction and Reification: A Re-test of the Generalization Hypothesis."

REFERENCES

Adorno, Theodor W., Else Frenkel-Brunswick, Daniel J. Levinson, and R. Nevitt Sanford
1950   The Authoritarian Personality. New York: Harper & Row.
Adorno, Theodor W.
1973   Negative Dialectics. New York: Seabury Press.
Adorno, Theodor W., et al.
1976   The Positivist Dispute in German Sociology. New York: Harper Torch Books.
Althusser, Louis, and Etienne Balibar
1970   Reading Capital. New York: Pantheon Books.
Apel, Karl-Otto
1975   "The problem of philosophical grounding in light of a transcendental pragmatic of language." Man and World 8(3):239–75.
Aronowitz, Stanley
1973   False Promises: The Shaping of American Working Class Consciousness. New York: McGraw-Hill.
Baran, Paul, and Paul Sweezy
1966   Monopoly Capital: An Essay on the American Economic and Social Order. New York: Monthly Review Press.
Bendix, Reinhard
1963   Work and Authority in Industry. New York: Harper & Row.
Berger, Peter
1967   The Sacred Canopy: Elements of a Sociological Theory of Religion. Garden City, N.Y.: Doubleday.
Berger, Peter, and Thomas Luckman
1966   The Social Construction of Reality: A Treatise in the Sociology of Knowledge. Garden City, N.Y.: Doubleday.
Berger, Peter, and Stanley Pullberg
1965   "Reification and the sociological critique of consciousness." History and Theory 4:196–211.
Blauner, Robert
1964   Alienation and Freedom: The Factory Worker and His Industry. Chicago: University of Chicago Press.
Braverman, Harry
1974   Labor and Monopoly Capital: The Degradation of Work in the Twentieth Century. New York: Monthly Review Press.
Browning, Charles J., Malcom F. Farmer, H. David Kirk, and G. Duncan Mitchell
1961   "On the meaning of alienation." American Sociological Review 26(5):780–1.

Burger, Thomas
   1976   Max Weber's Theory of Concept Formation: History, Laws and Ideal Types.
          Durham, N.C.: Duke University Press.
Carchedi, Gugielmo
   1978   On The Economic Identification of Classes. London: Routledge & Kegan Paul.
Clark, John P.
   1959   "Measuring alienation within a social system." American Sociological Review
          24:849–52.
Form, William
   1975   "The social construction of anomie," American Journal of Sociology 80(5):1165–
          91.
Fromm, Erich
   1955   The Sane Society. New York: Holt, Rinehart and Winston.
Gramsci, Antonio
   1971   Selections from the Prison Notebooks of Antonio Gramsci. New York: Interna-
          tional Publ.
Habermas, Jürgen
   1975   Legitimation Crisis. Boston: Beacon Press.
Harvey, David L., Lyle G. Warner, Larry Smith, and Ann Safford Harvey
   1976   "A critical analysis of Seeman's concept of alienation." Paper presented at the
          annual meetings of the Pacific Sociological Association (mimeo).
Hauser, Arnold
   1972   "Propaganda, art, and ideology." Pp. 128–51 in Istvan Mészáros (ed.), Aspects of
          History and Class Consciousness. New York: Herder & Herder.
Horton, John
   1964   "The dehumanization of anomie and alienation: a problem in the ideology of
          sociology." British Journal of Sociology 15(4).
Jacoby, Russell
   1975   Social Amnesia: A Critique of Contemporary Psychology from Adler to Laing.
          Boston: Beacon Press.
Jay, Martin
   1973   The Dialectical Imagination: A History of the Frankfurt School and the Institute
          for Social Research, 1923–1950. Boston: Little Brown.
Kon, Igor
   1967   "The concept of alienation in modern sociology." Social Research 34(3):507–28.
Korsch, Karl
   1970   Marxism and Philosophy. New York: Monthly Review Press.
Lasch, Christopher
   1978   The Culture of Narcissism: American Life in an Age of Diminishing Expectations.
          New York: Norton.
Lukacs, Georg
   1971   History and Class Consciousness: Studies in Marxist Dialectics. Cambridge, Mass.:
          M.I.T. Press.
Mandel, Ernest
   1975   Late Capitalism. London: NLB.
Mannheim, Karl
   1936   Ideology and Utopia: An Introduction to the Sociology of Knowledge. New York:
          Harcourt Brace Jovanovich (Harvest Book ed.).
Marcuse, Herbert
   1955   Eros and Civilization: A Philosophical Inquiry into Freud. New York: Vintage
          Books.

Margolin, Stephen A.
1974   "What do bosses do?: the origins and functions of hierarchy in capitalist produc-
       tion." The Review of Radical Political Economy 16(2):60–112.
Marx, Karl
1967   Capital, Vols. I–III. New York: International Publ.
Merton, Robert K.
1949   Social Theory and Social Structure: Toward a Codification of Theory and
       Research. New York: Free Press.
Mills, C. Wright
1959   The Sociological Imagination. New York: Oxford University Press.
Neal, Arthur, and Melvin Seeman
1964   "Organization and powerlessness: a test of the mediation hypothesis." American
       Sociological Review 29:216–25.
O'Connor, James
1973   The Fiscal Crisis of the State. New York: St. Martin's Press.
Palmer, Richard E.
1969   Hermeneutics: Interpretation Theory in Schleiermacher, Dilthey, Heidegger, and
       Gadamer. Evanston, Ill.: Northwestern University Press.
Poulantzas, Nicos
1975   Classes in Contemporary Capitalism. London: NLB.
Riesman, David
1950   The Lonely Crowd. New Haven, Conn.: Yale University Press.
Robinson, J.P. and P.R. Shaver
1969   Measures of Social Psychological Attitudes. Ann Arbor, Michigan: Institute for
       Social Research.
Rotter, Julian
1972   "Generalized expectancies for internal vs. external control of reinforcement." Pp.
       260–295 in Julian B. Rotter, June E. Chance, and E. Jerry Phares (eds.), Applica-
       tions of a Social Learning Theory of Personality. New York: Holt, Rinehart and
       Winston.
Sartre, Jean-Paul
1968   Search for a Method. New York: Random House.
1976   Critique of Dialectical Reason: Theory of Practical Ensembles. London: New Left
       Books.
Scott, Marvin, and Stanford Lyman
1968   "Accounts." American Sociological Review 33(1).
Seeman, Melvin
1959   "On the meaning of alienation." American Sociological Review 24:783–91.
1971   "The urban alienations: some dubious theses from Marx to Marcuse." Journal of
       Personality and Social Psychology 19:135–43.
Srole, Leo
1956   "Social integration and certain corrolaries." American Sociological Review
       21:709–16.
Stone, Kathleen
1974   "The origins of job structures in the steel industry." The Review of Radical
       Political Economy 6(2):113–73.
Zollschan, George K., and Phillip Gibeau
1964   "Concerning alienation: a system of categories for the exploration of rational and
       irrational behavior." Pp. 152–74 in George Zollschan and Walter Hirsch (eds.),
       Explorations in Social Change. Boston: Houghton Mifflin.

POLITICAL ECONOMY, IMPERIALISM, AND THE PROBLEM OF WORLD SYSTEM THEORY

Gary N. Howe and Alan M. Sica

Since 1974 much of American sociology has been involved in elaborating a new discourse, whose central concept is the "world system." Viewed as radical (Marxist) by many of its proponents, world system theory (WST) claims to be a totally new paradigm. Springing in part from the bankruptcy of traditional "modernization" theory—with its treatment of developing nations as independent, autonomous units of analysis, and its emphasis upon cultural variables in social transformation—WST presents, by contrast, the ultimate totalizing vision. Changes throughout the world are linked into a genuinely grand system, principally via economics. All national economies are presented as linked, and these linkages assume a hierarchic scheme of domination among three inequitable statuses: core, semiperpiphery, and periphery. Domination expresses itself in exploitation, with the industrialized core sucking "surplus" from the

Current Perspectives in Social Theory, volume 1, 1980, pages 235–286.
Copyright © 1980 by JAI Press Inc.
All rights of reproduction in any form reserved.
ISBN: 0-89232-154-7

periphery, and maintaining its economies in complementary rather than competitive relations.

This orientation to "underdevelopment," international exploitation, and domination would seem to indicate that American sociology had at last arrived at a rapprochment with classical Marxism, that of the "Old" Marx. Not only does it appear that American sociology moved left in this area of research, but also that it formed a bond with contemporary non-American currents in social and economic theory. At first glance, world system theory seems to be part of an international intellectual development, joining with Latin American dependency theory, the African school of analysts of neocolonialism, and classical European critics of imperialism. This crossing of international boundaries is paralleled by a crossing of disciplinary boundaries. In Wallerstein's *The Modern World System* a program is suggested which, if followed, would lead sociology into history, while simultaneously reorganizing historiography around a single all-embracing system. Claiming inspiration from Braudel (1973), Wallerstein puts the whole world, synchronically and diachronically, in sociology's new net of global systematization. World system analysis promises to become a totalizing science of a total system—an historical, Marxist science which might destroy the fragmented, ahistorical, and ideological illusions of bourgeois social science. If the deed were to be anything like the promise, American sociology is threatened with destruction from within.

In fact, the threat is counterfeit. The "school" which has emerged from the initial collective effervescence is neither Marxist, nor systematic, nor effectively historical. This is clearest in the empiricist wing of world system research, for in striving to encompass the world of "facts," it gains a "world" but loses the system in all but the most positivistically informed senses. The situation is less clear regarding Wallerstein's followers, whose commitment to histories and an avowed "Marxist" politics (see their organ, *Review*) would appear to constitute a radical development. It can be argued, however, that this "appearance" is just that, since their methods do not stray very far from traditional analysis used by American social science.

The development of American WST does not represent the elaboration of a preconstituted theory of Marxist inspiration. We will argue that so-called radical critiques of the world system have gone through at least three different stages. These stages did not involve the unfolding of the potentiality of an invariant *original position*, but involved fundamental changes in the *problematics* of the successive theories-in-dominance in the radical camp. The first stage, represented by the early Marxist theories of the world system, was essentially concerned with the internationalization of commodity production and the homogenization of relations within that system. And the tools of its analysis were provided by the Marxist theory of capital and surplus value. The second stage, represented by dependency theory, was oriented to inequality and exploitation among nations. In some ways reflecting the development of Marxist theory from the end of the second decade of the twentieth century, the basic theory mobilized was a theory of the *political,* involving a return to a form of mercantilist economics. The third stage, that of current world system theory in the United States, is oriented to an empirically new phenomenon. This is not the exploitation of nation by nation, but the emergence of a global economy apparently ruled by an impersonal structure of law-bound economic relations. It should be noted, however, that while we may say that world system theory reacts to a new phenomenon, it is not necessarily aware of it, at least insofar as it does not recognize that this organization is a relatively new empirical fact. Theoretically, American world system theory rejects the theory of political domination implicit in ''empirical'' analyses of international relations, a position expressive, perhaps, of an intuition that the world system is no longer dominated by a single hegemonic power. On the other hand, WST does not return to a Marxist theory of *economic* relations.

MARXIST POLITICAL ECONOMY AND THE WORLD SYSTEM

At this point it is worth reviewing a very basic element of the Marxist theory of the economy, i.e., the economy does not exist as a thing-in-itself. Economic categories are nothing more than social relations which men enter into in the reproduction of existence. The economy is nothing more than the ensemble of social practices, with different modes of production (i.e., different ensembles of practices) necessarily producing different economic concepts and theories. There is no single economy or economic theory; least of all does there exist an economy standing apart from and dominating social relations (the economy itself being a structured set of social practices and *nothing more*). Consequently, Marx's theory of the necessary development of the international system is expressive of the social contradictions of capitalism and the long- and short-term consequences of these contradictions for national units and the system as a whole. For reasons which we shall discuss at a later point in this paper, dependency theorists displaced the socialized character of the economy from the constitution of economic concepts to social regulation of the economy—by the state. In this case, the political structure comes to represent the dominance of society over the economy, but this reunification at the empirical level is conditional upon differentiation at the conceptual level. While arguing for the political nature of the economy, dependency theory breaks from Marx in the implicit affirmation of the conceptual autonomy of economics, with social influence being exerted *over* the economy rather than entering into its very constitution.

We may recommence with the question of the theory of American WST. We have noted that it is split, at least superficially, into historicist and empiricist schools, but behind this we can detect a certain unity. As we have noted, WST rejects the theory of political determination advanced by the dependency theorists while appropriating elements of their terminolgoy. Both wings of world system theory reject the social basis of the economy—the minimal outpost of which is precisely the neomercentilism of dependency theory. The historicists' formalistic use of economic theory, constituting the economy as an eternal essence and system of decontextualized concepts, and the empiricists' resort to empirical correlations are part of a single theoretical moment involving the denial of a dominant social logic in the world system. Empiricism denies *any* necessary systematic logic, and seeks its truth in the less than chanceful covariation of supposedly independent variables. The historicist wing locates the logic of the system in a universalized and hypostatized "economy." In neither development does a determinate *social* structure form the starting point of inquiry. Marxist political economy is definitively abandoned, and even the politics of dependency theory must be left behind in this theoretical development.

We shall argue that the apparent continuity of radical concern with the world economic system obscures a series of ruptures in the organization of discourse in terms of both questions asked and theories mobilized. We shall also argue that modern American WST represents the very antithesis of Marxist analysis. To be sure, references can be made to Marx's allusions to the impact of the core upon the periphery, and to the early critique of imperialism, which might appear to indicate the existence of a practico-theoretical strand running from Marx to WST. However, such a vision overestimates the amount of theoretical groundwork already accomplished for a general theory of the world system; ignores the fact that the various periods of this "tradition" have been marked by quite different theoretical and practical problematics; and generally renders unproblematic the question of the meaning of current WST. As a prolegomenon to addressing the last issue we must turn to the history of radical thought on the international economy before it became a legitimate branch of American sociology.

Marx's comments on the international system did not systematically address the mechanism of international exploitation, nor did he suggest that its development necessarily involved consequences detrimental to the periphery in the long term. Indeed, for the purposes of dissecting capitalist production, he explicitly ignored the existence of nations and international differences. "In order to free the general analysis of all irrelevant subsidiary circumstances, we must treat the commercial world as one nation, and assume that capitalist production is everywhere established and has possessed itself of every branch of industry" (Marx, 1967a: 581 n.). This is not to say that he ignored the international system. On the contrary (and as Wallerstein later repeated), he saw the development of the international trade system as one of the major factors in the early development of European capitalism, due to expanding markets and merchant profits (Marx 1967a:750; 1967b:323–37). According to Marx, the relationship between the world market and capitalist development reached a new stage with the development of industry. Here restrictive monopolistic commerce was pushed aside, vastly expanding the penetration of core industrial products into peripheral areas to absorb the material surpluses of capitalist industry. This thrust for markets changed the social organization of the extra-European areas, and, for example, destroyed the stability of the age-old Indian village community (Marx and Engels, 1959:35–41), compelling all nations "on the pain of extinction, to adopt the bourgeois mode of production" (Marx and Engels, 1976:488). This process ruined the native cotton textile industry of India (Marx and Engels, 1959:35–41), comment upon which might be taken as indicative of Marx's subscription to the view that core expansion is destructive of possibilities of industrial expansion in the periphery. Yet Marx did not feel that capitalist penetration into India would *necessarily* be detrimental in the long run. He refers to the necessity of British capital to transform India into a "productive country" as the best way to serve British interests. In particular he held that the introduction of the railways would become the "forerunner of modern industry" (Marx and Engels, 1959:81–87). This is hardly a picture of necessary "underdevelopment" of the periphery.

What might be constructed as an adumbration of dependency theory is encountered in *The Communist Manifesto*: "[j]ust as it [the bourgeoise] has made the country dependent on the towns, so it has made barbarian and semi-barbarian countries dependent on the civilised ones, nations of peasants on nations of bourgeois, the East on the West" (Marx and Engels, 1976:488). However, this statement must be read in context. It is clear from other parts of the *Manifesto,* as in the later article "The Future Results of the British Rule in India," that dependence for Marx does not refer to a system of international domination and exploitation. He is concerned instead with the spread of capitalist manufacturing as it destroys local and national independence and autarchy: "In place of the old local and national seclusion and self-sufficiency, we have intercourse in every direction, universal interdependency of nations" (Marx and Engels, 1976: 488). For Marx, this was hardly a negative aspect of capitalist development. On the contrary, exactly this process "rescued a considerable part of the population from the idiocy of rural life" (Marx and Engels, 1976: 488), and has created "conditions of a new world in the same way as geological revolutions have created the surface of the earth" (Marx and Engels, 1959:87).

Scrutiny of Marx's comments on colonialism and the global economy does not support the thesis that in Marx's *work* a theory of exploitation among nations (necessarily associated with capitalist development) can be found. British exploitation of Ireland, Dutch exploitation of Java (Marx and Engels, 1976:313–5), and profit remittances from India (Marx and Engels, 1976:307) are noted but these do not constitute a theory of international capitalist exploitation. In fact British exploitation of Ireland long antedated the development of capitalism, and both the Indian and Javanese cases refer more to primitive accumulation than to the regular mode of capitalization in a developed commodity system. This remarkable indifference to inter*national* exploitation (which was later to become the core of "left" critiques of international capitalism), as opposed to the internationalization of the commodity system, cannot be attributed to a theoretical lapse on Marx's part, nor, we believe, to lack of time to work out an appropriate theory. The lacuna is necessarily inscribed in the theory of capital itself. For Marx the collapse of mercantilism led precisely to the development of a true commodity system relatively free from political determination. This development of industrial capital marked a definitive departure from a feudal mode of appropriation founded directly upon political power. In the epoch of free trade the basis of surplus value was capital's relation to labor rather than to state power, which implies that capital freed itself from national identities in order to flow to areas with the most advantageous conditions for surplus extraction—irrespective of geopolitics. If Marx remained silent on the issue of international exploitation, it was because there was no room for the question within his analysis of capital as an economic "phenomenon." The dominant antagonism in the theory was not among nations, but between labor and capital without regard to its "citizenship." This international (or, better, "a-national") character of capital (as a social relation rather than an eternal economic "thing in itself") came to be ignored (for political reasons) in later theories of the international system, with the most lamentable consequences.

MARXISM AND THE THEORY OF IMPERIALISM

If Marx cannot be invoked as the distant father of the various schools of international exploitation which flourished after World War II, perhaps the forefathers are among those who wrote on the international system in the first two decades of the twentieth century, who took the empirical phenomenon of European imperialism and turned it into a theoretical problem. The emergence to prominence of the term *imperialism* in Marxist and social democratic thought appeared to locate definitively the international system of exploitation at the center of leftist analysis. However, to create retrospectively a "tradition" on this basis would be to confound the continuity of a problematic with the continuity of a term within it. Examining the historical context is informative. Even superficial perusal of Lenin, Hobson, and Trotsky shows that the theory of imperialism in the period did not revolve around the exploitation of the periphery, and, a fortiori, was *not* about the underdevelopment of the periphery. The dominant focus was upon relations among core states rather than between core and periphery, and the immediate problem was that of military conflict on a global scale. This focus necessitated a theory of core involvement in the periphery, but it was essentially concerned with contradictions and tensions in the core itself. Given the location of theoretical production in Europe, and the practical engagement of socialist theoreticians in the European class struggle, the periphery was not studied in itself, but as the expression of contradictions within the core and as the immediate site of conflicts among core states. While there was some elaboration of the effects of imperialism upon the periphery, the effects charted were quite different from those identified by post-World War II theorists, since they were not seen as necessarily deepening international disparities in wealth and types of production. Rather, the economic factors creating imperialism as a political system of unequal power and domination were portrayed as conducive to a relative *homogenization* of economic development throughout the world system—a legacy of Marx's attitude. It is necessary, then, to distinguish between imperialism as *political* domination and later usages connoting *economic* domination and exploitation. In relation to the latter, it is further necessary to distinguish between the dramatic short-term gains of speculative finance capital and the long-term effects of core capital seeking secure havens for investment outside the core itself.

Early twentieth-century theorists saw imperialism as a response to internal crises of the industrial capitalist economies. Two major, but not mutually exclusive, explanations were developed to account for the rapid expansion of imperialism between 1870 and 1910: the underconsumptionist thesis and the surplus capital thesis—both of which claimed inspiration from Marx's analysis of capital. All major theorists agreed that the need to export industrial commodities was an aspect of the imperialist thrust, but it fell to Luxemburg to base her theory exclusively on this ground (Luxemburg, 1972). Hobson claimed that the rationale of imperialism could be undermined by expanding the consumption of the core proletariat (Hobson, 1938). Luxemburg, however, saw the crisis of under-consumption as a necessary aspect of capitalist development, and imperialism as a necessary (if only temporary) solution to the problem. Luxemburg's thesis was the following: In order for surplus to be realized in the money form, surplus value (commodities) must be sold in *pre-capitalist* areas; these are to be found in some areas of advanced countries, but their major locus is in the periphery.

Luxemburg, at the very least, deviated from orthodox Marxist theory (as Bukharin, 1972, was at pains to demonstrate), but even within the strict terms of her theory, there is no conceptualization of international exploitation. At face value the theory describes a flow of surplus from periphery to core. The point is, however, that surplus flowing from periphery to core in money form was *produced* at the core. The periphery is not a sphere of exploitation, but merely the site where commodities are exchanged for money. To the extent that goods exchange at their value in the periphery, there is no exploitation here—as long as the core's relations with it are purely commercial. The notation of exploitation through trade requires the additional postulate of monopolistic mercantilism, a stage of capitalism which Marx had argued was definitely transcended by industrial capitalism.

While all theorists saw the extension of exports as an element in the economic base of imperialism, the predominant theoretical line emphasized the role of export capital, an empirical fact which clearly distinguished the imperialist stage of the world system from the prior, almost purely commercial, organization. Starting with J.A. Hobson in 1905, the crisis of industrial capitalism producing imperialism was identified not as a surplus of commodities, but as a capital surplus. Imperialism as a political system corresponded to the export of capital from the core to the periphery (e.g., Lenin, 1975:58). Though differences emerged between the expositions of Hobson, Lenin, and Trotsky, there was substantial agreement that the development of trusts and cartels in Europe and the United States (to regulate crises of overproduction) restricted domestic outlets for the investment of surplus value extracted from the core proletariat. Put simply, cartelization assured relatively high levels of surplus, but at the same time restricted the competitive expansion of the industrial base which might absorb that surplus in further core investment (Lenin, 1975:59). Lenin emphasized that the imperative of the cartel, i.e., to control all phases of production, impelled it to invest in the periphery to secure and monopolize sources of raw material, while Hobson, treating capital more as an international abstraction and less tied to the interests of this or that nation or cartel, emphasized simply the necessity to seek abroad for any profitable investment site. Nonetheless, there was substantial agreement that imperialism was essentially a struggle over spheres of investment, and that this export of capital expressed the increasing concentration of capital (in the sense of an increasingly monopolistic structure of industrial organization) in the core. The focus of concern was eminently Europocentric. It involved analyzing the crisis of the core and its effects on core politics and economics. From the point of view of the proletariat, it involved the effects of imperialism on core investment and consumption and, above all, the possible involvement of the working classes in international conflicts over controlling areas of new investment (Lenin, 1975:92).

Again, the discussion of effects upon the periphery was relatively underdeveloped—beyond the recognition already expressed by Marx that capitalist expansion required transformation of social relations at the periphery. In fact, given the material condition of most peripheral areas at the time, it could hardly be expected that the debate would revolve around the development or underdevelopment of peripheral capitalist economies, the most striking phenomenon being that of the transition from precapitalist to capitalist organization. Lenin did comment upon "unequal development" in the world economy, but this notion did not refer to inequalities between core and periphery, nor a fortiori to such inequalities as expressions of international flows of capital and commodities. The term *unequal development* actually referred to imperialist core nations, and the probability of imperialist wars redistributing imperial possessions according to shifts in the relative power of core states (Lenin, 1975:58, 92). The expression "associated and unequal development" may have been introduced by Lenin's work, but it did not have the connotation of international core-periphery exploitation which it was to gain in dependency theory. This does not mean that Lenin did not see imperalist relations as exploitative. In his comments on Britain Lenin gave the opinion that it was becoming a *rentier* nation, enjoying a mounting income from abroad which allowed sections of the proletariat to be "bought off," to be mobilized to support the imperialist interests of the British bourgeoisie (Lenin, 1975:13–14). It should be noted, however, that such income was derived from investments broad, and that while such investments certainly generated "unearned" income for the British, they also contributed to the development of the periphery, actually closing the gap between core and peripheral areas. In the 1920 preface to German and French editions of *Imperialism, the Highest Stage of Capitalism*, Lenin referred to "a handful . . . of exceptionally rich and powrful states which plunder the whole world simply by 'clipping coupons'" (Lenin, 1975:3), as in a similar vein he described "the financial strangulation of the overwhelming majority of the population of the world by a handful of 'advanced' countries" (Lenin, 1975:11). By 1920 Lenin clearly was passing from economic theory to political practice, seeking not a scientific understanding of the world system but political allies in the struggle against imperialist powers. In 1916, however, quite a different note had been sounded, in which the *economic* logic of the theory of imperialism led to somewhat different conclusions about the periphery (Lenin, 1975:61):

> The export of capital influences and greatly accelerates the development of capitalism in those countries to which it is exported. While, therefore, the export of capital may tend to a certain extent to arrest development in the capital-exporting countries, it can only do so by expanding and deepening the further development of capitalism throughout the world.

Elsewhere Lenin refers to the "process of levelling the world, of levelling the economic and living conditions in different countires" (Lenin, 1975: 76).

Precisely the same point was made by Trotsky (1970:19), who is worth quoting at length on this point:

> In contrast to the economic systems which preceded it, capitalism inherently and constantly aims at economic expansion, at the penetration of new territories, the surmounting of economic differences, the conversion of self-sufficient provincial and national economies into a system of financial interrelationships. Thereby it brings about their rapprochement and equalizes the economic and cultural levels of the most progressive and the most backward countries. Without this main process, it would be impossible to conceive of the relative leveling out, first, of Europe with Great Britain, and then, of America with Europe; the industrialization of the colonies, the diminishing gap between India and Great Britain.

The implication is that explanations rooted in Marxist economics saw a tendency toward homogenization of international conditions. The flow of dividends from periphery to core was not denied, but it was clear that such a transfer could take place only on the basis of increasing the productive powers of the periphery itself such as to *reduce* international differentiation.

Between 1916 and 1920 Lenin had moved from scientific economics to political opportunism. This prefigured the discourse on "Imperialism" whose object was less to reveal the dynamics of international capitalism than to patch together ad hoc political alliances, whose maintenance required the theoretical suppression of basic structured conflicts among *classes* in favor of conflict among *nations*. According to Arrighi (1978:20), it is this theoretical transition that created the astonishing disarray on the left after World War II. This transformation was intimately connected to the change in the social and geographic location of theorizing about "imperialism" from the core to the periphery, and from the organized working class to a Third World intelligentsia whose objectives were not revolution but "development."

Before discussing this transformation it would be useful to emphasize some salient dimensions of the classic theory of the international economy: once established by force, the system of production and exchange is dominated by an ''economic'' logic; this logic, however, expresses the unique structure of the capitalist mode of production as a *social* organization; and the tendencies of the economy at any given time are expressive of the stage of development of inter- and intraclass conflict. In relation to the latter point, it was keenly appreciated that merchant capital organized the system in a manner quite different from that adopted by industrial capital (e.g., Lenin, 1975:77). Equally, the development of imperialism within the bosom of industrial capitalism was expressive of crisis tendencies rooted in that particular system rather than in tendencies of economies-in-general. At no point was materialist analysis carried over into an economism which ignored the social organization of economic relations. And rarely was the state presented as anything other than an institution captured by interests which were material and antagonistic. Even in the case of the supposedly more social-democratic Hobson, the action of the state in the imperialist thrust represented a decisive affront to working-class economic and political interests (Hobson, 1938:46–51), being nothing more than means for the realization of surplus value by the capitalists at the expense of the working class.

FROM EMPIRE TO INTERNATIONAL DEPENDENCY

As Owen and Sutcliffe observed (1972:320–1), critiques of imperialism after World War II were characterized by a decisive swing toward analyzing its impact upon peripheral economies. This movement, in part, expressed declining interest in the crises of the advanced economies associated with the eclipse of revolutionary movements in Europe. Much more important, however, were political changes in the world system, particularly the collapse of imperialism as a political system with the wholesale achievement of political independence by ex-European colonies. The Bandung conference of 1955 signaled the socioeconomic emergence of the Third World. It also highlighted a new intellectual problem, that of ''development.'' Having acquired political independence, the new nations confronted their *own* economic problem, i.e., ''underdevelopment.'' The term imperialism at this point came to represent not specific political relations between core and periphery, but the world capitalist system as a whole and the alleged exploitation of the Third World within it. Taking a line quite opposed to the new American school of ''modernization,'' Third World theorists suggested that the advanced world *caused* their underdevelopment, that the international system operated to the benefit of the advanced industrial regions and to the detriment of periphery, in spite of the latter's liberation from political bonds of submission (for the classic statement of this position see Frank, 1972a).

One of the most fecund sites for the new critique of the world system was Latin America, where discussion within ECLA on the problems of development in the region burgeoned into an identifiable "theory" of international exploitation in the 1950s, 1960s and 1970s. "Dependency theory" insisted that Latin American development could be understood only in terms of the structure of the world system of production, and, specifically, that the industrial underdevelopment of Latin America was due to two factors: (1) difficulties of domestic industrialization in the face of international competition and attempts by advanced industrial capital to stop or control such development, and (2) export of surplus from Latin America diminishing the domestic capital supply available for industrial development (for a review of significant literature, see Chilcote, 1974). Two elements of this theory were particularly noticeable. First, that the dominant contradiction in the world economy appeared between nations or national capitals; hence *American* capital exploited Brazil and struggled to preserve its industrial hegemony. Second, that development was defined as industrializaton, and that difficulties experienced in passing from agricultural exports to domestic industry constituted *ipso facto* evidence of international exploitation. In short, the influence of core over periphery produced increasing polarization of the world system in terms of the distribution of wealth and industry.

Remarkably, these ideas lacked any developed explanation of why concentration in agricultural production should necessarily be disadvantageous. Neither Marxist nor bourgeois economics explained why nations exchanging agricultural for industrial products should suffer in the process (in fact, Emmanuel, 1972, specifically rejects any explanation of international exploition based upon the nature of products exchanged). The theoretical lapse, however, was explicable in terms of dependency theory's implicit politics. Latin America existed, politically independent, for more than 130 years before dependency theory was created. During this time, it had exported raw materials to Europe and the United States, yet no widely disseminated critique of this relation arose. The reason for this curious silence is clear: the ruling class was engaged in primary exporting, from which it drew handsome rewards. The rise of dependency theory, emphasizing the "facts" that agriculture made for poverty and that foreign capital's only interest was in exporting surplus, was not contingent upon a radically new understanding of the international economy (notwithstanding the claim of direct descent from Lenin and Trotsky—see Cardoso, 1973), but upon the rise of the industrial bourgeoisie during international disruption between 1930 and 1945. The economic and political interests of this class were embodied in dependency theory: the definition of development in terms of industrialization argued for massive support of the industrial sector; stigmatization of foreign capital as a mere exporter of surplus meant rigorous control of foreign manufacturing investment, designed to maximize the market share of the national bourgeoisie; and identification of the dominant system of exploitation as international allowed the national bourgeoisie to place itself at the head of "nationalist" movements in which internal class contradictions had no place. *In a certain sense dependency theory's real basis was not the organization of the international economy, but the struggle between classes and class fractions within the periphery itself.* This is not to deny that the conjunctural "problems" facing Latin America were real. There were real balance of payments crises and outflows of capital. But the particular way in which these problems were defined—the necessity of industry and the common interest of the nation in fighting external "oppressors"—was very much influenced by the composition of the ruling interests in the period.

The revised theory of imperialism disarticulated the critique of imperialism from the critique of capitalism in general (and national capital in particular). *The vision of a world system dominated by abstract capital, whose major conflict was with labor, was replaced by a view emphasizing the fragmentation of capital into national units and their mutual conflict over industrial development.* While claiming continuity with earlier critiques of imperialism, dependency theory decisively changed the terms of the argument. Engaged in a politico-theoretical practice in which links were being (temporarily) forged between the "masses" and the peripheral industrial bourgeoisie (see, for example, the nationalist-populist-developmentalist nexus in Latin American politics in the 1950s and 1960s), depenency theorists displaced the level of polemic from the abstract realm of capital and value in a commodity system to the more concrete and empirical realm of "nations," "agriculture," "industry,' and "international relations." While maintaining a standardized terminology, the underlying historic materialist theory (which would not support the political position) was abandoned: in face of the pressing interest of the national industrial bourgeoisie in controlling surplus value, the Leninist/Trotskyist/Marxist thesis that international capital would develop the periphery was largely forgotten. Also forgotten was the dialectical thesis that relations within a system changed with the class-in-dominance, and consequently that the relations of the mercantilist past could not shape present understandings. Finally, the development of the economic system was not seen as guided by social forces and contradictions within the mode of production. In a technicist turn the economy became the realm of formal, neutral economics, with social influence being externalized in a state which represented not *classes* but *nations*. With the development of dependency theory debate about the international economy was situated in a quite new theoretical terrain. While ostensibly presenting a program to "humanize" the economy, dependency theory emphasized the latter's essentially extrasocial constitution (outside of the realm of direct class relations). Furthermore, the immediate interest in industrialization and the "common" interest of the nation radically diverted attention from the real politico-economic constitution of the system (class conflict and surplus value) to conjunctural phenomena (populism and industry) mystifying its problematic. A form of political and economic empiricism and opportunism led dependency theory away from classical Marxist analysis, a process which was to end in the metropolitan areas with the total disarticulation of the "theory of imperialism" from the theory of capital.

DEPENDENCY THEORY IN THE CORE

Two elements of dependency theory were particularly important in the United States, establishing two lines of research which proceeded more or less independently in the 1970s. First, dependency theory placed current "problems" in a long-term historical context. The underdevelopment of Latin America was attributed to its articulation into the international system dating from the early sixteenth century, to the benefit of the European metropoli and to the disadvantage of their Latin American satellites. This theme was taken up and generalized by Wallerstein, who applied the model to the international system as a whole, addressing not only the causes of "underdevelopment" but, also, of increasing concern in the core itself, the origins of capitalism (or the transition from feudalism to capitalism) in Western Europe.

However, while dependency theory certainly insisted upon "history," it did not resolve the question of what "history" is. The discovery and exploitation of the New World opened a new historical epoch which might be designated "capitalist," yet the question remained whether this epoch was homogeneous in its internal organization and mode of exploitation. Frank (1971) emphasized continuity in monopolistic forms of satellite exploitation, forms which were certainly characteristic of early trading relations between metropoli and satellites. Wallerstein later suggested a different organization more compatible with classical theories of international trade. While WST and dependency theory clearly diverged at this point, an element of continuity remained, i.e., "history" (however defined) remained homogeneous, with transformations referring more to the system's geographical extension than to its internal organization. In spite of claims to Marxist inspiration, both dependency theory and WST were markedly undialectical in their construction of the new "history."

The second significant element of dependency theory was indirectly linked to the first, and also found itself fully expressed in one branch of WST in the United States. As noted, dependency theory fractured the early unity and coherence of Marxist theories of imperialism by emphasizing the theoretical significance of such "empirical" units as the nation and concrete forces of production (e.g., industry). From the point of view of a theory of capital-in-general both sets of phenomena were irrelevant. No theorist of capital expected capital or capitalists to be essentially nationalistic (cf. Luxemburg, 1977), nor was the form of productive activity seen as directly significant to the question of surplus value. That is to say, there was no coherent theoretical indication of the *necessity* of the relation between national politics and industrialization (as, indeed, there could not be). In a certain sense, therefore, dependency theory cleared the ground for the emergence of an empiricist epistemology, its significant concepts were raised in the falsely concrete level of empirical phenomena, and the disarticulation of the latter from a rigorous general theory gave the analyses of the dependency theorists an essentially probablistic character. The unity-in-development of a given mode of production was not intrinsic, but a programmatic goal unified only by state policy. The question of the international economy acquired a *pragmatic* complexion in which theory/policy was oriented to what would "work" within the immediate conjuncture rather than to an elucidation of the general structural principles of the system. It is, of course, precisely as an endeavor pursuing the common features of conjunctures rather than the structural features of generic systems that American sociological empiricism might be defined, and therein lies the connection between dependency theory and American social science—a common empirico-pragmatism and the appropriation (as real) of the superficial categories of capitalist relations. Somewhat curiously, the historicist and empiricist wings of American WST met. Substantively separated by their respective inclinations to diachrony and synchrony, and epistemologically separated by their respective emphases upon causation and correlation, there existed an essential similarity already heralded in the development of dependency theory. We suggest, however, that the "refinement" and development of the distinctions between dependency theory and the classic theory in the American sociology of the world system cannot be attributed to the pressing logic of the immediate *practical* situation. If the basic ideas of Marx, Lenin, and Trotsky were excluded from dependency theory because they were politically inconvenient, they were absent from world system theory because of an underlying epistemology and ontology which *necessarily* displaced the classical concepts irrespective of the avowed politico-ethical intent of their perpetrators.

FROM DEPENDENCY TO WORLD SYSTEM THEORY

In 1974 Wallerstein published the *Modern World System,* which received astonishingly broad acclaim in a profession usually torpid regarding historical analysis. Its appeal was immediate: purporting to analyze the emergence of a world capitalist system, it raised dependency theories (especially those of Frank and Cardoso) from their more or less parochial stature and allowed them to encompass the whole globe, while totalizing and radicalizing history within a politico-economic analysis "useful to those groups which represent the interests of the larger and more oppressed parts of the world's population" (Wallerstein, 1974:10). Unlike dependency theories and critiques of contemporary imperalism, this early representative of world system theory had a potentially wide basis of support. Though avowedly dealing with international exploitation, it avoided being stigmatized for criticizing *American* imperialism by focusing upon the "long sixteenth century"; while dealing with the development of capitalism, it sidestepped the natural indictment of the bourgeoisie by dwelling upon the force of the *system* and its laws. Dependency theory had acquired prominence in Latin America because of its direct implications for national political practice, and the prime example of world system "theorizing" achieved equal prominence in the United States precisely because it had no obviously divisive political implications. That, at least, could not have been said of dependency theory in the United States.

The ultimate meaning of Wallerstein's contribution is not yet known. He has announced that *The Modern World System* is the first volume of a four-part series encompassing the history of the world system from the long sixteenth century to the present. He has yet to present an analysis of the contemporary world system such as would fulfill his promise of being useful to the world's oppressed. At face value Wallerstein's magnum opus would seem only historically interesting (the subject being situated four centuries in the past), and in those terms it is difficult to explain its great popularity. It is clear, however, that his analysis of the long sixteenth century is meant to do much more than illuminate the past. It is also the key to the present. Wallerstein aims to identify the laws of the world system at its inception, and with these to systematize events of the present. This assumed systemic continuity is defended thus: "social reality is emphemeral. It exists in the present and disappears as it moves into the past. The past can only be told as it truly is, not was" (Wallerstein, 1974:9). Here we encounter the laudable recognition that the historian labors under the prejudices of his time, but rather than noting the error of projecting the present upon the past, Wallerstein seems to feel that the historian cannot escape this, and proceeds as if the present really *was* in the past. The attraction of this book, then, is that it reveals the "laws of the present" within a conception of history compatible with American sociology's positivist epistemology (e.g., the emphasis upon "law"), and uses "system" in a way that decisively tears the analysis of the world capitalist system from Marxist political economy. To be sure, the "decisive" concept of exploitation is not absent from Wallerstein's discourse, but it occurs rather like bad weather—as the product of an objective system outside of human controlling interest.

Wallerstein's initial proposition is that during the sixteenth century, the modern world capitalist system was formed. In this period an international division of labor emerged in which the periphery developed export agriculture and the core (particularly northwest Europe) inclined toward industry. This division of labor was not, however, the only stimulus given by the international system to the development of industry at the core, for it allegedly generated a flow of "surplus" from periphery to core facilitating rapid accumulation of capital (Wallerstein, 1974:100). Precondition for this included the emergence of nation-states in the core and the use of state power to support capitalist expansion and exploitation of the periphery, a development which according to Wallerstein could not occur in the ancient empires. The periphery was at a double disadvantage: not only was agriculture a more precarious basis for the expansion of wealth, but insult was added to injury by core appropriation of its smaller surplus— themes which we have already encountered in dependency theory.

That the early global trade system required an international division of labor is beyond dispute. At issue, however, is the nature of the forces creating it and the form of accumulation dominant within it, for if the early world system responded to "laws" of a capitalist global economy, we might expect its current (and future) version to exhibit similar structure, but in exaggerated form. Two arguments can be drawn from the text on the exploitative character of the world system leading to unequal distributions of income and industry, the economic activity which Wallerstein sees as the real basis of the expansion of affluence (Wallerstein, 1974: 350). He first argues that mercantile profits invested in the core were drawn from the periphery (e.g., Wallerstein, 1974:121). His second line of argument alleges that peripheral products were "cheap" and facilitated accumulation at the core (Wallerstein, 1974:219, 302). It is certainly true that great profits were made in international trade in peripheral products, *but* it is far from certain that these profits can be considered "surplus" drawn from the periphery. Wallerstein's position must be predicated upon the assumption of free trade. Where goods exchange at their value, the source of profits/surplus value must be the exploitation of the worker (Marx, 1967a:146–176), in this case the peripheral worker. However, free trade was not characteristic of the long sixteenth century. On the contrary, it was the age of mercantilism, to which Wallerstein pays little attention—presumably because his vision is shaped by his self-confessed inability to theorize beyond the structure of contemporary capitalism. The essence of mercantilism is monopolistic trade in which commodities do *not* exchange at their value (Barrat-Brown, 1974). In such a structure a significant part of merchant profits came not from direct exploitation of peripheral producers, but from exploiting core consumers by selling peripheral commodities far above their value. In short, the magnitude of merchant profits does not prove that such a surplus was generated at the periphery. In fact, it is possible to conceive of a situation in which merchant profits involved no exploitation of the periphery at all, but represented only the redistribution of core wealth (which may also have been the true impact of the importation of bullion into the European economy).

As for the "cheapness" of goods produced at the periphery, two alternative theses might be spun out of Wallerstein's text. The first would suggest that this cheapness contributed directly to core accumulation insofar as it represented a hidden transfer of value from periphery to core. If this refers to the price of commodities, then it would be equally accurate to claim that India exploited Great Britain in the nineteenth century by buying its cheap cotton goods. Using Emmanuel's *Unequal Exchange* it is possible to give some meaning to Wallerstein's notion of "cheap" by affirming that peripheral goods embodied more abstract labor than core goods of an equivalent price. However, Wallerstein does not demonstrate that this was actually the case. Furthermore, there is absolutely no reason to believe that peripheral status per se (agricultural exporting in the world economy) must necessarily produce cheap commodities, this being determined by the levels of class struggle and technology in the periphery. A second thesis is possible which does not involve exploitation of the periphery, i.e., that importing subsistence commodities at prices lower than they could be produced at the core (which does not mean that peripheral exports were cheap in Emmanuel's sense) lowered the cost of reproducing labor in the core, and consequently contributed to the rate of core capital accumulation. In the long sixteenth century, however, the role of peripheral products in provisioning the core labor force was minimal. Until the end of the seventeenth century Europe was a net *exporter* of basic agricultural staples to the periphery (Frank, 198:51). Contrary to Wallerstein's conviction (1974:41–2), the substance of the international system was very much trade in preciosities (i.e., luxury consumer goods) with no major impact upon subsistence costs of core workers. It may be true that the real costs of reproducing the European labor force declined in the Great Inflations caused by the massive inflow of bullion from America, but the basis of this achievement was the reduction of levels of consumption rather than importation of cheap peripheral products. In fact, it is difficult to see how the periphery could play such a role until the restrictions imposed by merchant monopoly had been overthrown.

Wallerstein's failure to exhibit any consistent understanding of the basic concepts of Marxist political economy is consistent throughout his fragmented discussion of "surplus," a term which in his work is not unambiguously equated with surplus *value*. In his repudiation of the thesis that the international expansion of the long sixteenth century was based upon trade in preciosities, Wallerstein demonstrates a curious inclination to apply standards of maximization of *use values* to an economy which is organized around *exchange values*. Furthermore, his treatment of the early capitalist mode of exploitation, without any reference to the question of the hegemonic class fraction in the period, signifies a curious disarticulation of economic relations from social relations, just as the "silence" about exchange value ignores the specific social representation of commodities in capitalist society. These quiet "subtractions" from Marxist analysis are but the negative side of a thesis which is most clearly revealed in Wallerstein's discussion of the development of the international division of labor, where the latent mechanicism of his hidden theorizing manifests itself in a socially decontextualized "economic" analysis. For Wallerstein its emergence is explicable via the law of comparative costs (1974:98): conditions in the core and periphery at the inception of the world system gave them each "advantages" in the production of industrial and agricultural commodities, respectively. The initial industrial advantage of the core could only grow with advancing production technology, leading to an ever more profound industrial concentration in the core. On the basis of initial differences in costs, the system necessarily developed a rigid division of labor which apparently reflects the logic of international capitalism. This explanation has the advantage of neoclassical clarity, and the disadvantage of being incorrect. The Ricardian analysis of the division of labor (upon which Wallerstein bases his argument) assumed free trade and the imperative to maximize overall levels of production. Again, this was not the situation at the inception of the international division of labor, as Smith so vehemently pointed out (Smith, 1937:360). *Mercantilism was the basis of the emergent system, providing the conjunctural politico-economic basis for what Wallerstein ex post facto poses as a general economic necessity or law.*

Whatever the advantages of peripheral agricultural production, the system which emerged reflected the coalition of mechant and royal interests at the heart of mercantilism (Knapp, 1973). Industry and other transformational forces at the periphery did not disappear because of the difficulty of competing with core products in the free market, but because of political decree. The periphery was not *allowed* to industrialize by the political fiat of core power. Hence Brazil, the major world producer of sugar, did not produce cane rum since the Portuguese forbade it in order to protect their domestic industry. Two sets of interests were at work in the fabrication of this system. On the one hand, international merchants were dependent upon maximizing the international division of labor. Without this there could be no trade, and without trade there could be no profits for the merchant or tax revenue for the prince. On the other hand, princes in the emergent core nation-states had an interest in supporting domestic industry regardless of comparative costs. In this way exports of bullion to satisfy growing demand for industrial products could be minimized, and the logistic base for warfare could be maximized. Far from illustrating the laws of free trade, the world system at that point reflected a conjuncture of class and political forces constructing international economic relations in their own interests on the basis of force. As such the early structure of the capitalist world economy could not be taken in any way as indicative of the subsequent form of the system under the domination of quite different interests—as Marx, at least, was well aware by emphasizing the profound significance of the transition from the hegemony of merchant capital to that of industrial capital.

In the early period of the international system, the law of comparative cost could not assume decisive significance for it had to await the triumph of industrial capital. Yet its relevance, as stated, seems restricted even in the later period. The accumulation of improvements in core industrial technique of production would seem to have constituted a stable basis for consolidation of its industrial monopoly—at least in Wallerstein's view. But what Wallerstein seems to have forgotten is that the "law of comparative costs" extends to more than the technical factors of production in determining industrial location. More specifically, it includes the cost of labor. Within a capitalist system industrial location is clearly determined by the particular character of the ends of industrial production, which is *not* the most efficient form of production considered in terms of physical factor mixes, but the maximization of surplus value. In this case, it is clear that industrial location must be related to (inter alia) the differential development of class struggle (as Wallerstein's [1974:81, 107] own comments on the decline of Italian textiles would clearly suggest). This factor was not of great relevance for the mercantilist period, when "relative costs" were far from the most significant factors in the location of production and routes of trade, but comparative cost may have been a significant factor in location at later stages of development of the system, and Wallerstein may have been quite right in giving it analytical prominence, though it was anachronistic for the period that he discussed. That comparative cost cannot be discussed merely in terms of techniques of production, but does in fact reflect class relations, is obscured in Wallerstein's usage in which location seems to be governed by the iron laws of the accumulation of technique rather than the to and fro of the human struggle over the accumulation of capital. In placing such heavy emphasis upon economic laws in a form of misconceived neo-Smithianism (Brenner, 1977), Wallerstein fails to grasp the world system as a human product, as an accomplishment of classes in a series of more or less separate struggles within the context of shifting power, changing modes of accumulations, and reorganization of the geographical distribution of productive activity. His inability to step from the naturalistic concept of surplus to the social relation of surplus value in the analysis of international "exploitation" is tellingly paralleled by his refusal to depart from the abstract notion of economic forces to the class struggle.

This understanding of the system as "law-bound" is not restricted to the international distribution of agriculture and industry, but penetrates into the consideration of the very relations of production themselves. The importance of slavery in the periphery as opposed to that of free labor in the core is not posed in terms of different class interests and powers, but as a technical matter. Hence slavery predominated in the periphery because of the special aptness of peripheral agriculture techniques for slave labor (Wallerstein, 1974:87)—a stunning perspective given the fact that peripheral export of raw materials expanded substantially in the latter part of the nineteenth century under a regime of free labor. The point hardly needs belaboring: while ostensibly presenting a radical, even "Marxist" analysis of the world system, Wallerstein's picture is devoid of the transformative motor of capitalist development—class conflict. *While preserving the history of an economy he mobilizes an "economics" which can have no history because of its abstraction from the social categories of production and exchange.* Posing as historical and Marxist, the study is, in fact, neither. Marx emphasized that the overthrow of merchant capital decisively changed the complexion of the international system, while early twentieth-century critics of imperialism believed that changes in the class structure of the core were contributing to concomitant changes in the international distribution of capital and industry.

Wallerstein, on the other hand, seems to suggest a history of a system whose future is inscribed in its conception. Without the notion of differential organization of surplus appropriation according to variations in the dominant class, and without the dialectics of accumulation and investment opportunities inscribed in the early theories of imperialism, Wallerstein's world system seems to involve merely expansion without transformation, a progressive unfolding of "tendencies" implicit in its origins. Fleeing from any possible imputation of idealism, Wallerstein throws himself into an equally untenable materialism: untenable not because of the attempt to offer an "economic" explanation, but because Wallerstein's economy has no subjects. We see here not interaction between classes possessing material interests of a definite kind, but a hypostatized subject (the economy) changing the real organization of man according to its own laws.

WORLD SYSTEM THEORY: ONE STEP FORWARD, TWO STEPS BACK

If our characterization of Wallerstein's social ontology is correct, the resounding "silences" in relation to class conflict (as *constitutive* of the system rather than as a "factor" within it) and modes of surplus appropriation are not simple omissions or oversights, but reveal the *real* existence of the historical wing of world systems theory. In spite of the radical trimmings (and truly astonishing level of involvement in questions of empiricist historiography) its vision is no stranger to American sociology. It is a mechanical systematics pervaded by an absolute insensitivity to dialectics—not only at the logical level, but also in the absolute failure to realize that men make history, and that in doing so they make and transform both themselves and the society around them. If history meets normal sociology in WST, the honors clearly go to sociology, which, once again, demonstrates that in its contacts with other disciplines (e.g., history and Marxism) it is able to subtract from the other without adding to itself. The meaning of the sociologization of history is rather clearly revealed in Wallerstein's practice. The *effects* of the historically specific mercantilist structure (international division of labor and mercantile accumulation) are explained in terms of economic "laws" (of comparative advantage and unequal exchange), which could not possibly have been the *causes* of the effects by virtue of the conjunctural absence of the social condition for their operation. These conjuncturally unreal causes (and "their" effects) are then posed as timeless necessities by virtue of the universality of the laws (within an undifferentiated "capitalist" history), so that an alleged drain of surplus from periphery to core and concentration of industry in the latter can be represented as "natural" tendencies of the capitalist world system—in direct contradiction to the most developed Marxist theory and even the misguided politics of dependency theory, which for all its neglect of class forces was at least willing to recognize that history is made by human groups (e.g., nations), and not by "laws." In this case the theoretical suppression of mercantilism, which allegedly emerged as a "full-scale policy" only "from about 1650," i.e., conveniently after Wallerstein's period (see Wallerstein, 1974:309), is of more than historical interest and concern, for it strikes to the very heart of Wallerstein's New Science, whose search for Law in the classic positivist mold involves not the celebration of history (either as discipline or dialectical process) but its denial. And this denial is not a choice but a necessity: the very existence (once-upon-a-time) of mercantilism proves that "capitalism" may be organized in different ways according to changes in the relative power of classes and class fractions, i.e., it indicates that class struggle might affect not only the distribution of wealth, but also the very structure of the system. Law could only be affirmed (in its universality and domination of matter) by negating mercantilism. It might be justly affirmed that the most peculiar omission of mercantilism indicates not that Wallerstein is a bad historian, but that he is a most dutiful sociologist.

For all its radical rhetoric, therefore, WST (or at least this historical wing) represents the ultimate integration of the reality of the global system into sociological theory. This is not immediately apparent, for, after all, is not the world systems vision and critique directed at traditional sociological theories of modernization and development? This is most certainly so, but unlike Frank's classic statement (Frank, 1972a) the thrust of Wallerstein's work would lead us not *out* of sociology but into a different area; specifically, away from the implicit voluntarism of traditional modernization theory to the reified, transhistorical determinisms of systems theory. And while Wallerstein is at pains to note that this is a *capitalist* world system, he nowhere introduces concepts expressive of the particular social relations and means of capital accumulation characteristic of a capitalist economy. On the contrary, he mobilizes a form of classical and neoclassical economics which, according to its self-understanding, can be applied to *any* "economy," or, alternatively, might be understood as being applicable to no economy at all by virtue of its role as a purely ideological misrepresentation of capitalist relations of production and distribution. In either case Wallerstein loses: if he accepts the validity of the claims of bourgeois economics his insistence upon the capitalist nature of the world system is totally irrelevant, for all economies are organized identically; if the capitalist nature of this system is important, bourgeois economics is irrelevant for practical analysis. We have here an apparent contradiction which is resolved in practice by the abolition of one of the poles of the opposition. The reality of Wallerstein's perspective, his true object, is not the capitalist world system, but the *modern* world system; the contrast is not between capitalist and precapitalist global systems but, as his first chapter clearly tells us, between world systems politically organized and world systems economically organized.

The significance of this chapter is, in fact, crucial to the real meaning of Wallerstein's text, for it reveals that Wallerstein's problematic is quite disconnected from both the classical schools of imperialism and dependency theory. Wallerstein sows the seeds of confusion himself in referring to the capitalist nature of the system and to international exploitation, including the promise to help the peoples of the Third World improve their situation. However, the issue is clouded by his failure to explicitly introduce concepts to handle these issues, and by the development of a history which in many ways unfolds before us without the help of either of these two factors. This "cloudiness" is a function of the coexistence of *two* problematics pointing in quite different "directions." The surface problematic organizes the rhetoric of the argument, and this precisely corresponds to the issue of capitalism and international exploitation; the "deeper" problematic gives the text its structure and does not run parallel to that of the surface. The essential point is that this deeper organizing problematic is *exactly* Adam Smith's problematic: the concern is with the differential organization of "political" economies and "economic" economies, and the probable effects (in terms of division of labor/structural differentiation and "wealth") of the organization of the economy on "economic" principles. The question is not one of "capitalism" at all, but of "market" society—or, better, of market economy, for the market is represented as a thing-in-itself. It is noteworthy that insofar as these "eternal" principles of the "economic" are considered in their social aspect (by Smith), society enters not as that which organizes the economic, but as that which is organized by it. Essentially, the same is true of Wallerstein, where the "surface" text of class conflict is constantly falsified by the deeper text of the economy as the cause rather than the result of social relations. The difference between Smith and Wallerstein is that Smith's work is still programmatic even in the eighteenth century, which indicates that in Smith's eyes the international economy at that point had *not* been organized on "economic" lines (cf. Tribe, 1978:88), whereas Wallerstein's purports to describe what actually has transpired.

If Smith's denial involves the negation of a political system on the decline in a pre- or proscriptive fashion, Wallerstein's denial involves the negation of the real organizational features of the dominant system in a descriptive fashion. Both thinkers are ideological, but Smith's ideology was of the transcendence of the present, whereas Wallerstein's is part of the grim science in which all that exists is necessary, in which the eminently social phenomenon of the economy is assimilated without apology into nature.

It is clear, then, that the debate around the world system has suffered successive displacements in terms of those who conduct it, the terms in which it is conducted, and the constitution of the subject itself. The first, European phase of the debate saw the "underdevelopment" of the periphery as conjunctural, and in the process of being swept away by changing class relations in both core and periphery. The second phase, that of dependency theory, preserved the terminology of its predecessor, but actually analysed the situation in terms of national units and industrialization rather than classes and the conditions for the maximization of surplus value. The historical wing of world system theory (at least as exemplified in Wallerstein's modern world system) marks the further displacement of the international queston from peripheral politics to the universities of the core. If dependency theory's emphasis upon nations had undermined the dialectics of the original Marxist analysis by virtue of a relative inattention to class relations in the global economy, WST discarded the dialectic for positivist laws of an economy-above-society. Classes are displaced by "factors of production" which lack even the self-determination granted by dependency theory to its illusory actors, the nations. Wallerstein's critique of the international division of labor and exploitation appeared Marxist by virtue of its subjects, but the exposition practically denied all principal Marxist contributions to a formal theoretical understanding of the world system. The impact of Wallerstein's magnum opus was not to "Marx-ize" American sociology, but to Americanize/sociologize the Old Marx in much the same way that the "Young" Marx had been treated in the late 1960s and 1970s.

To this point we have dealt largely with Wallerstein as representative of American WST, but, as was earlier pointed out, there exist two branches of American WST. The second, empiricist wing constitutes the world system within an episteme different from Wallerstein's, while maintaining an equal distance—ontologically and epistemologically—from the classic theory of imperialism from which both wings of the American enterprise are so eager to claim descent. Analysis of this "distance" in Wallerstein's work involved the reconstruction of the implicit text, a hidden theory giving the lie to the apearance of the text itself. Passing on to the empiricist wing of WST involves a change in critical method and discourse. The question does not involve contradictions between implicit and explicit theories, for there is no implicit theory, but only a method. It is a method which necessarily constitutes theories-as-resources in exactly the same way as it constitutes the world, i.e., as an agglomeration of elements/factors without necessary or logical relations. If Wallerstein's questionable practices seem a form of counterfeiting, representing silver as gold, those of the empiricist wing assume the form of alchemy, but in a typically inverted bourgeois form—involving the transformation of gold into base elements rather than vice versa.

THE QUANTIFICATION OF DEPENDENCY THEORY

A striking feature of many articles recently published by American sociologists, which speak in the language of "world system," is their distinct lack of a politics, of a political position. They either have none (in bold contrast to the theories upon which they have grafted empirical commentary), or theirs is too amorphous to register as politically informed.

For some researchers tied to "value freedom," this is a virtue, even a professional necessity. The "liberationese" which typically saturates theories of dependency and imperialism spawned in the Third World is taboo in American sociological journals, or so one assumes from representative articles. But one suspects more is at work here. Not only have these researchers bowed to the discipline's narrative norms by excluding rhetoric and politics from their "findings," but at the same time have made it impossible for themselves to construct—let alone be directed by—a truly political economic understanding (hence, theory) of global events or trends. This phenomenon becomes comic when empiricists, in their ritual "theoretical overviews," cite the litany of idea men (Frank, Emmanuel, Amin, and others), as if to claim kinship with this polemical strain of writing, yet then report a type of research which these very progenitors find contemptible. This peculiarity of world system study in the United States has produced a schizoid literature, on one hand "proving" repeatedly that dependent economies remain so due mainly to world structure, yet on the other using methodologies and data which are thoroughly repugnant, on epistemological and political grounds, to the originators of these expropriated, Americanized ideas. This development in U.S. dependency research has created a gulf between the original conceptualizaton of how the world system functions, quasi-Marxist in design, and the apparently *simpatico* results of quantifiers bent on scientific demonstration. Not only has a mature politics been dropped from the program, but in using methods and data of certain types, Americans and their likeminded colleagues, perhaps inadvertently, have *tamed* a new theoretical impulse. This is precisely consistent with the cultural imperialism of the past. We shall see how this current bastardization of Third World ideas has taken place, and what significance it holds for future work on global political economics.

Conventional American sociology was introduced several years ago to dependency, or world system theory (WST) via Chase-Dunn's article in the *American Sociological Review* (Chase-Dunn, 1975); or rather introduced to its quantification. (Portes [1973] had already deflated modernization theory, but he did not quantify his critique as did Chase-Dunn.) Without for the time being considering Chase-Dunn's procedure, it is worth noting that he involved a body of literature which had been in print for many years, but had not surfaced in the *American Sociological Review* as an explicit antidote to modernization studies. In place of the warhorses of that tradition (Rostow and others), Chase-Dunn cited Amin, Baran, Barratt-Brown, Dos Santos, Emmanuel, Frank, Galtung, Girvan, Johnson, Lenin, Marx, Pinto, Prebisch, Sunkel, and, of course, Wallerstein. Some of the conventional students of the Third World (Bendix, Eisenstadt, Myrdal, etc.) appear in the article only as foils to dependency positions. The alternative list constitutes a good portion of the litany referred to above.

It is undeniably fortunate that Chase-Dunn rejected modernization dogma and constructed a research design which could respond to a few of the theoretical claims put forth by dependency theory. It is fortunate because modernization theory and its empirical fruits were clearly used up either as science or ideology. But the "litanization" of everyone from Amin to Wallerstein has created problems for subsequent researchers which jeopardize Chase-Dunn's original contribution. As he himself surely realizes, there is great theoretical and political distance, even enmity, among many of the quasi-Marxists whom he groups bibliographically; in fact, as much disagreement between some of them individually as between all of them collectively and the heinous modernization sect ("Los Chicago School"). Within the individual writings of Amin, Cordoso, Frank, Emmanuel, Palloix, Sunkel, Pinto, and others, are theoretical and empirical worlds which students of development and dependency minimize or abrogate at their risk. This is the first difficulty one encounters in American dependency empiricism, if it may be so termed, and it has continued to crop up in virtually all later works which are constructed similarly to Chase-Dunn's.

Research papers that have recently added to this American stream include Bornschier et al. (1978), Delacroix (1977), Delacroix and Ragin (1978), Rubinson (1976, 1977a,b, 1978), Snyder and Kick (1979), and Steiber (1979). All these papers appeared in major sociological journals, and all but two in the *American Sociological Review (ASR)* or the *American Journal of Sociology (AJS)*. Dependency studies with advanced quantification have obviously found the mainstream. Not only that, they have already begun inspiring a critical literature, specifically Bach (1977), Irwin (1977), the response by Rubinson (1977b), and Goldfrank (1979). Chase-Dunn continues to contribute (1978) and, with his colleague Rubinson, has branched out into the perilous world of theorizing *sans* numbers (1977). Because Chase-Dunn and Rubinson have between them produced nearly half the important literature to date, it is their work which will be examined more closely in the following pages. It seems quite fair to treat their corpus of world system research as representative of what it means to practice American dependency empiricism. As we shall see, their kinship with Third World researchers and theorists is frequently more apparent than real.

What we have to say is not original for the most part. That is, Bach (1977) attacked Rubinson for lack of historicity and violation of major research premises underlying the Wallerstein/*Annales* perspective. Irwin (1977) provided a technical critique of Rubinson's statistical procedures, and questioned many of Rubinson's interpretations of findings. (Rubinson's response to both critics will be examined momentarily.) Frank, Amin, and Cordoso have been particularly outspoken over the years in chastising cross-sectional aggregative empiricism for all the reasons one would expect from the Marxist flank.

Our enterprise, then, does not aim for originality, nor does it attempt to annihilate the Chase-Dunn/Rubinson research program on one set of grounds or another. What we intend is at once simpler (and less given to internecine polemics), but at the same time more difficult to handle conclusively, for our questions are these: Can a sociologist interested in the Third World (*sic*) learn very much about how these countries fare in the world system from American dependency empiricism? And correlatively, if so, where does this leave the classical dependency literature; if not, how can American work be improved? And, to resuscitate the classical Marxist debate on imperialism, can this new variant of research illuminate the mechanics of the global economy as a unitary phenomenon beyond what we already know?

Interrogation of these few essays may begin by deferring to Lewis Coser, whose ASA presidential address was published in the same issue of the *ASR* with Chase-Dunn's opening salvo. Coser (1975) ventilated his objections to path analysis and ethnomethodology as reified methods, which through convenience of application on one hand, clique idolatry on the other, had, so he believed, seduced their respective partisans into what might be called "substantive lethargy." Coser objected to means supplanting ends among his American colleagues, the apotheosis of method and the trivialization of research which inevitably follow. Coser worried over "the new generation of sociologists" trained "not to bother with problems about which data are hard to come by," encouraged instead to use ready-made data. This would result in "piling up of useless information" or "in a kind of tunnel vision in which some problems are explored exhaustively while others are not even perceived" due to the production of "young sociologists with superior research skills but with a trained incapacity to think in theoretically innovative ways" (1975:693). He continues:

> Careers, especially those of people with modest ambitions, can be more easily advanced through quantity rather than quality of publication. This leads to an emphasis on methodological rigor, not on theoretical substance. One way to publish rapidly is to apply 'the same procedure, task, or piece of equipment over and over, introducing new variables or slight modification of old variables, and thereby generate a host of studies rather quickly" (J.E. McGrath and I. Altman, 1966:87). The formulation of theories, moreover, is time consuming, and may not lend itself easily to publication in journals increasingly geared to publishing empirical research, and to reject "soft" theoretical papers. There exist, then, a number of factors in our present systems of training and of rewards that exercise pressures on incoming generations of sociologists to refine their methods at the expense of developing innovative lines.

We do not mean to saddle Chase-Dunn, Rubinson, or others in their train with the full weight of Coser's sentiments. But his sense for present deficiencies of method, theory, and scope in social research applies in part to the studies at hand. A crucial disjuncture—between the principal elements of dependency theory and their empirical specification by Americans—may have less to do with the target of Coser's wrath than with the intrinsic limitations of methods chosen *in good faith*. But a disjuncture exists nonetheless and requires examination, which heretofore it has not received. Let us pursue the nature of this disjuncture.

One might be leery of deducing a researcher's epistemological values and inclinations—his philosophy of research—from examples of published work. But Rubinson saves us from this dilemma by admitting, in his rebuttal to Bach and Irwin, that he subscribes to the ultra-scientific notion of sociological praxis, which holds (among other things) that methods are transferable from subject to subject so long as appropriate variables and their interrelationship can be specified.

> Both Bach and Irwin assert that using a regression technique assumes that nations must develop along a set path. . . . But all a regression analysis does is to describe the relationship between [*sic*] variables, in this case by minimizing the sum of the squares of the errors. The variables that are included in the model and the interpretation of the process relating the variables are derived from the substantive theory of the researcher. They are not contained within the statistical method of minimization (Rubinson, 1977b:818).

It is perfectly obvious that a researcher married to these (conventional) beliefs will approach his work in a particular way. Without rehearsing the myriad statistical limits of multiple regression, memorized and forgotten by graduate students, it should be emphasized that users of regression must be hunting for data of a particular type which arranges itself—or so they believe—in the "real world" in certain ways. It so happens that the kind of data freely expelled daily from the World Bank and the United Nations fits these requirements beautifully, unless one asks for details about their collection. (A gentlemen's agreement prevails among those who do aggregative research not to harass each other over the extraordinarily low quality of the comparative data they must use.)

We do not mean to pillory Chase-Dunn or Rubinson simply for their choice of "tools." Their conformity in this regard with many who believe themselves to be the avant-garde in sociology is nearly perfect. Their only deviance is in selecting a research area which until recently has been monopolized by qualitatively spirited Marxists, not American regressionists. Our objection is more pragmatic and fundamental than Bach's (concerning the false assumption of linear development for all nations; 1977: 812–3), and not so technically involved as Irwin's (worried about the limits of cross-sectional technique; 1977:815–7). Even if Rubinson's retort is in places coy or simply ingenous (e.g., "Historical data is [*sic*] merely older than contemporary data"; 1977:819), it could be allowed that he defended himself ably enough, that he protected his type of sociology competently; but even so, this is not sufficient. Bach accuses Rubinson of "de-dialecticizing" structural change in the world system through his methodology, a claim which Rubinson does not rebut. (It is impossible, of course, for regression to consider dialectics at all.) But even this objection pales beside another at a far more fundamental level. Chase-Dunn and Rubinson have not, we would argue, studied dependency theory as such, or, if they have, such study does not inform their research. They have instead latched onto several catchwords (core, periphery, unequal exchange, etc.), easily understood and operationalized at a pretheoretical level, put to use standard, low-quality data sets for international economic conditions, then applied their universally adaptable method. Our point, then, is that even if all of their published work to date were flawless *on its own terms,* the prior and perhaps preeminent question remains unaddressed (thus unanswered): What exact theoretical relation do their regression coefficients bear to socioeconomic understanding of conditions in the Third World?

On a more technical plane, is it enough to go along with Rubinson's heuristics and allow exports and imports as percentage of GDP to "stand for" or "measure" economic dependency in the external market (1976: 654)? We are not contesting Rubinson's *model,* which asserts that external pressures on a national economy will have impact upon internal distribution of income, or as he puts it, "the fact of having to import or export puts the state and its economic actors in a position of less power and control in the world economy" (1976:654). (But what is a "state"? how does it function in the global economy? what different types are there and what do they do? and what of Japan, which by Rubinson's logic would be very weak internationally?) Rubinson conforms to standard sociological practice by proclaiming that "the results show strong support for the hypothesis." Specifically, as imports and/or exports make up more and more of a GDP, the share of national income accruing to the lower quintiles of the population lessens, with the top one-fifth getting more in relative, not absolute, terms (cf. 1976:648). His "strong support" rests in coefficients of .307 and .253 (1976:655).

What, then, is "strength" in a statistical finding? For sociologists imitating physicists, it is anything over either the .05 or .10 levels of "significance." There are those who argue that when using aggregate data and large samples, any coefficient under .5 is suspect. But what, from the sociologist's point of view—the sort interested in the quality of life in developing countries—can be concluded from Rubinson's coefficients

(Gini index figures)? To be precise, if one puts data from 47 countries (ranging in nature from Dahomey to the United States) into a formula, *overall*, and including a dozen of the world's richest countries, there is "a positive relationship" of .307 between exports as percentage of GDP and national income inequality, and .253 between imports and inequality. What one is to make of this beyond the studied confines of mainstream sociological technique we are at a loss to say. Is it good to know that Rubinson, working as carefully and scrupulously as he could, has given us these "hard" statistics (ignoring once again the softness of the data)? Is it important to know that between about 1950 and 1970 (according to Paukert, Rubinson's data source), in a nonrandom sample of 47 nations (minus socialist states), given the limitations of interpreting regression coefficients, that certain relationships could be determined among several circumscribed "measures" of dependency and income distribution among quintiles of households? If it is better to know *anything* than to know nothing, then we owe Rubinson thanks. But the problem persists, and will be treated below, that American dependency empiricism of this type is, in Weberian, Marxian, and Parsonian terms, theoretically primitive and underdeveloped at best, atheoretical at worst. And correcting this malady will not take place by "refining our techniques" of "improving our data." As Rubinson rightly said in rebuttal to his critics, hypothesizing variable relationships is the proper function of theory alone.

What makes both Rubinson's and Chase-Dunn's first articles perplexing is that both display considerable awareness of earlier dependency theorizing. In fact, Rubinson commits exactly half his article to reviewing arguments and literature in admirable breadth. His statistical study seems almost an afterthought, though this surely could not be the case given his epistemology. As he writes, "But if one's interest is in theory, then one should study relationships among variables; and the fact of uniqueness is irrelevant for that purpose" (1977:819). He goes further along this hyperempiricist tangent by explaining that "the logic of comparison" cares not whether variables are related in "time" (time-series), "space" (cross-sectional analysis), or both (panel study); thus it is "the same" to compare Chile between 1934 and 1944 as it is to compare any dozen nations, using like variables, at one instant. He maintains that "from the logic of empirical research, both comparisons are equally valid, since both types of comparisons are comparing instances of the replication of a process,"[1] which is "the only thing that matters" for research of his type (1977:819–20).

It comes as a shock that this sort of ahistorical, acultural, atheoretical, apolitical, asociological casuistry is put forward by the same man who wrote an "excellent theoretical and historical discussion of the mechanisms of control and the relations to the dominant mode of production in the world-system" (Bach, 1977:812). Much the same could be said for Chase-Dunn. It is as if precise knowledge of the world system is carefully absorbed, then jettisoned, belittled, even distorted to suit the needs of methodological technique. Perhaps the key word which explains this dilemma is "logic" as used by Rubinson above. It is entirely possible, even simple, for empiricists to propose and measure variable relationships born out of exercises in nothing but "the logic of comparison" or "emprical research." Shoe size and income can indeed be correlated. But since dependency theory and research have produced so rich a literature, some of which (like Amin's) overflowing with testable propositions, one can only wonder why American dependency empiricism contents itself with such slim substance. What, after all, does one have left when the world economy is "conceptualized" free of historical relationships ("older data"?), as a function of three poorly measured items whose *actual* interrelation surely varies with country and time, and which are therefore mythically grouped to fit the needs of computation and fleshless logic? To return to an earlier page, what one has left is a "tamed theoretical impulse." Is it fair to conclude that American dependency empiricism is worthless for students of Latin American, African, European, or our own Wallersteinian researchers who have written so much and often so well on the socioeconomic meaning of dependency and peripheralization? I think not.

Much said thus far *contra* empiricist fetishism and reductionism could be aimed at a substantial portion of dependency theorizing. There is indeed some ironic homology between the grand inferences made from small coefficients and, on the other side, mighty "world-historical" generalizations and accusations made to spring from the labor theory of value generously applied. For the nonpartisan naif who would like to ascertain how the world system works, another approach, perhaps a synthetic one, would seem promising. And here, oddly enough, we return for the moment to Chase-Dunn and Rubinson.[2]

THE THEORETICAL REDUCTION OF WORLD SYSTEM THEORY

Chase-Dunn and Rubinson in their earliest *ASR* papers left themselves open to attack on various grounds, but since then they have published six more articles which draw on similar data and employ roughly the same "logic of comparison," in which to perfect their work. We turn to some of these now to examine texts in which theorizing is carried out for its own sake, relatively unobstructed by the complication of data. These are perhaps more important finally than the others, since here is offered an interpretation of the world system which might become the conventional American version of dependency theory.

We view with some alarm such a core–periphery theory minus political economy and history, in some ways worse that the modernization dogma it supposedly replaces. It might be remarked that by neutralizing or masking, even if inadvertently, the important rhetorical, as well as political economic component of dependency thinking, the two writers have participated in what Marcuse identified as "the affirmative character of culture," and what some of his followers have since labeled "artificial negativity," a notion which means exatly what it says.

For purposes of comparison a brief reminder of their first conceptual work is useful. Chase-Dunn (1975) thought that he could test the dependency approach by correlating "investment dependence" and "debt dependence" with development (using panel regression). Before getting to the "important part" of the essay, he reviews, in this order, the discursive theories of Myrdal, Marx, Lenin, Baran, Frank, Emmanuel, Baumgartner, Amin, Dos Santos, Ehrensaft, Singer, Hirschman, Prebisch, Griffin and Enos, Beckford, Johnson, Wallerstein, Galtung, Hayter, Sunkel, Viner, Pearson, Schelling, Chenery and Strout, Ricardo, Samuelson, Eisenstadt, Bendix, Parsons, Moore, and others in slightly more than four pages. This careful hermeneutic yields a "summary of propositions" cast in terms of "predictions" putatively made by dependency "theory," as opposed to "theorists." (Reification has already set in.) These propositions, obviously designed for testing and consequently connected remotely with "the dependency literature reviewed above" (1975:725), actually describe "mechanisms" of dependency, development, and income inequality via investments and debt, all phrased in terms of "negative" or "positive" impacts. (One might recall Bach's objection to "de-dialecticizing" inherent in this type of model.) With a judicious caveat ("a comparative test . . . enables us to estimate whether aggregate effects are positive or negative, but does not differentiate between all the mechanisms hypothesized above. Any estimated aggregate effect may be the resultant of the simultaneous operation of different mechanisms" [1975:726]), Chase-Dunn reports his findings.

We have rehearsed this to make one important point: a related series of ruptures, stunning in dimension, obtains between (1) the dependency literature itself, (2) Chase-Dunn's synoptic litanization of that literature, (3) his operationalization of the original notions into sets of bipolar relationships, and (4) his actual "measurement" of the latter schematization. It is fair to interject: is this not the currently accepted format for quantitative social research? Yes, but nowhere do the inadequacies of empiricism in this style show themselves so clearly as in "cross-national studies." For instance, Arghiri Emannuel's world reputation rests upon the notion of "unequal exchange," which he publicized in the early 1970s. His theory is complex, highly technical in places, couched resolutely in the language and thought of Marx's labor theory of value—which he restructures radically—and requires considerable acumen to penetrate even minimally well (see Pilling, 1973). Chase-Dunn "handles" this writer in a small superficial paragraph and, strange to say, for no apparent reason vis-à-vis his research as it actually unfolds. Nowhere else do Emmanuel's ideas, even in stripped form, reappear. Again and again Chase-Dunn feels obliged to compress major intellectual achievements into bite-sized chunks, e.g., Samir Amin's two-volume landmark shrinks to six lines (1975:722).

Rubinson's first statement (1976) is more involved than Chase-Dunn's speculatively but less so technically. As already noted, the first half of the article sketches in schematic form a multitude of ideas concerning state power, the evolution of the world system class relationships, and so on. After first disposing of Lenski's views on stratification, since they do not fit the world system model as well as one which highlights intrastate production systems, Rubinson briefly restates the cardinal points from a Wallerstein essay bearing on world economy structure. In fact he continues to list and discuss many ideas about state strength, internal inequality, the history of peripheralization, and so on, with blinding speed. If form bears any relation to content in anything so traditionally lifeless as a sociology journal article, then it might occasion some shock to consider Rubinson's penchant for lists of stages, ideas, propositions, and the like. In order of appearance, his model makes "two assumptions"; Lenski locates "four causes" for historical change in inequality; Wallerstein's model wins support from "two types" of evidence; the discussion then falls into "three parts"; Wallerstein's model has "three features"; the world geographic division of labor has "two consequences"; state dominance in world markets can be achieved in "three major ways"; political control over worldwide production is important for "three reasons"; "three mechanisms of control" affect the world economy; income distribution is affected by state differences in "three interrelated ways"; and so on (1976:638–43).

We have progressed scarcely five pages from Lenski's demise. Rubinson's listing forms a neat symmetry of compositional logic with Chase-Dunn's staccato citation of germane works. But Rubinson's approach to analysis is more dangerous than Chase-Dunn's, for the latter is probably a planting of foliage in the interest of substantive legitimacy. For theorizing as such, Rubinson's practice of "boiling down" entire monographs into two, three, or four notions is treacherous. It may well fit the demands of empiricism, but the practice guarantees vacuity or inaccuracy. For instance, in discussing "power and control in the world economy" (1976: 641–3) (a vital component of his perception of how the global system functions), Rubinson claims that "strong states are effective mechanisms for protecting econmic actors from the risks and uncertainties generated by the world market" (1976:642). He goes on to "document" this claim, which on its face seems reasonable enough, by citing Frank's signature piece, the essay on the development of underdevelopment. His next of three "reasons" for the importance of political power in the market system is that "states are effective mechanisms for securing privileged access to resources and markets (1976:642), and his source for this insight is Hobsbawm's (1968) primer on English economic history from 1750 to 1967. It is typical of Rubinson to advance a proposition, write a paragraph in explanation, then cite a book or article at the end. Almost never does he give a specific page number, which seems a breach of elementary scholarship, for at times he is citing long books inclusive of great detail which, if taken holistically, are much less concrete and unequivocal in supporting Rubinson's point than the naive reader would imagine. Let us look for a moment at both Rubinson's substantive contentions in this regard, and his documentation.

Frank published the essay in question in 1966. Rubinson used an abridged version (1972), and the material which he seems to count on appears between pages 9 and 13. Is it surprising to learn that Rubinson not only fails to note that Frank's entire essay is a series of historically produced "hypotheses" and in no way a definitive revelation of fact, but that he also misconstrues the hypotheses presented? Rubinson is tied to Polanyi's theory of the "free market," a dependence he probably inherited from Wallerstein, whose work is likewise constructed around this fiction (as discussed above). By contrast, Frank is a Marxist analyst. Rubinson gives no sign that he honors the distinction between the theory of competitive advantage and the ideal of free trade on one hand, the global circulation of capital on the other. These sets of ideas constitute diametric views of how the global economy functions, or fails to function. One cannot embrace both simultaneously, except in the world of schematic, syncretistic research reports. Frank's point is *not*, as Rubinson claims, that "when the demand for these materials declined [those produced in Latin America], the capital and organization which exploited these resources were withdrawn," thus demonstrating the importance of "strong states" which could halt this outflow of capital. Rather, Frank (1972:11–2) shows that:

> When the metropolis recovers from its crisis and reestablishes the trade and investment ties which fully reincorporate the satellites into the system, or when the metropolis expands to incorporate previously isolated regions in the world-system, the previous development and industrialization of these regions is choked off or channelled into new directions which are not self-perpetuating and promising. This happened after each of the five crises cited above.

There is a difference between "demand declining" and development being "choked off" or rechannelled, and it epitomizes a central aspect of the Marxian reaction to bourgeois economics. In a neutral, emotionless "system," demands can indeed sometimes "dry up," or appear to, if one looks no further than the surface of phenomena. But in Frank's vision of imperialist domination in Latin America, in the world system of metropoles and satellites, there is no place for neutrality. Instead there are highly orchestrated programs for the engineering of dependency, formulated between the bourgeoisie of core states and the comprador elites in Latin America, with the initiative and final say resting in the former, of course. Now, as explained earlier in this essay, Frank's insistence upon the nation-state as the locus of theorizing and research (which is true of most dependency studies), and the injection of voluntarism in large doses into his Marxist economics, both distance Frank considerably from Marx and his more orthodox followers. (For them, of course, capital circulation and accumulation follow "laws," not predominantly the choices of diabolic bourgeoisie; and the nation-state is not the locus of history, but rather the entire capitalist system taken together.) Rubinson's conceptual distance from Frank in this regard is well illustrated in a nearby passage in which he writes (1972:641):

> Different areas of the world, and the states within those areas, tend to specialize in different economic roles (suppliers of raw materials versus suppliers of manufactured goods, for example) and, consequently, occupy different positions in the overall system.

"Tend to specialize"? It is inconceivable that a student of Frank's essay could have written this passage. Rubinson's expression of differences in state strength suffers from the same weaknesses inherent in any purely "logical" surmise, and easily lends itself to parody:

> Different ethnic groups in the U.S. (e.g., Blacks), and the laborers within them, tend to specialize in different economic roles (janitors versus Senators, for instance) and, consequently, occupy different positions in the overall system.

Just as any empiricist can dream up "interesting" potential relationships among variables and subject them to correlations, so too can any world system theorist, without too much concern for history and its contemporary resultants, fabricate such "hypotheses" as this. (There are other problems in Rubinson's reliance upon Frank's early essay. In an autobiographical account [1978:11–23], Frank explicitly notes what students of his work have known for nearly ten years, that he has altered his position drastically since 1966, adding subtleties and clarifications, many of which were already available in *Lumpenbourgeoisie, Lupendevelopment* [1972]. Rubinson contented himself, however, with the earliest, most rudimentary expression of Frank's ideas.)

So far as the Hobsbawm reference goes, it is difficult indeed to decide what documentation Rubinson had in mind. Perhaps no one represents excellent British Marxist historiography to Americans better than Hobsbawm, and his books are usually dense. This one is no exception. In it he gives two chapters specifically to the interplay of the British government and the intra- and international economy. But what is most interesting about his treatment is that he, first of all, tempers the common contention that Britain's national economy actually dominated world manufacturing trade in the nineteenth century (Hobsbawm, 1968:110, 190), and secondly, points out that in fact the role of the government was intentionally curbed for most of the period between the industrial revolution and modern times, so that laissez-faire was more than a political economic slogan. Were one looking for support from the British case—beset as it is with idiosyncrasies—then the preceeding volume of the set to which Hobsbawm contributed, the book by Christopher Hill (1967), woud serve far better, for in it the mercantilist program is dissected. And yet even this strategy might force the issue. As Hill notes, quoting Tawney, "Before 1640 mercantilism had been a policy imposed by the goverment on business interests; after it, it became, to an increasing degree, a policy imposed by business interests on the government" (Hill, 1967:6). (This is another reminder of the cogency in Bach's demand that a dialectical, nonstatic conceptualization of history be employed.) But in any case, even if Rubinson was not thinking of the mercantile state at all, if his only point was that some states have in the past enjoyed remarkable success at affecting markets, he certainly could have supplied a source other than Hobsbawm's entire treatise, which, being so enthusiastically dialectical in construction, could hardly be counted upon to provide hard-edged "proof."

DEPENDENCY EMPIRICISM AS THEORY

The past few pages have been an exercise in tracing sources and in trying to understand empiricism's link to historical fact and speculation. Perhaps it is needless to say that the examples of Emmanuel, Frank, and Hobsbawm were drawn virtually at random from the two articles in question; further tracing would, I believe, produce similar results. The only citations in which one can have full confidence are those in which the researchers are acknowledging technical difficulties, and are toeing the line scrupulously so as to avoid the charge of faulty procedure (a charge still brought, almost inevitably it seems). But when theory per se, or its close relative in dependency research, history, is relied upon to give the entire research project its general direction, it is usually the case that tremendous condensation—and therefore distortion—takes place. And by the time one has moved from the level of Wallerstein, Marx, or

Emmanuel to aggregate data on 47 nations, the original impetus to research is a dim memory. These observations about problems in current research are hardly unique to Chase-Dunn and Rubinson, of course. But their apparent self-confidence as researchers of the world system, along with what is perhaps serious unawareness of problems just discussed, singles them out for critique since they have established in the last few years a new trend which, as noted above, might well "choke off" the spirit and substance of world system study as previously envisioned. Though they might disagree, this new trend seems to be as utterly apolitical in its tone and results, and therefore inferior from inception to alternative approaches.

But we still have to consider their most recent work, far less indebted to empiricism of the type analyzed above. Five subsequent publications are of interest. Bornschier, Chase-Dunn, and Rubinson (1978) is a survey of research on foreign investment, and aside from a useful summary of 16 articles, the empirical portion offers nothing new in terms of basic approaches to the question. But a new circumspection has entered their orbit, perhaps introduced by Bornschier, since they feel called upon to note for the first time (1978:679):

> These highly aggregated studies, however, can take us only so far in understanding these processes. Three types of studies more micro-sociological in nature are needed. First, dependency situations are not homogeneous, and there are considerable differences in the dynamics of situations such as export enclaves, national export economies, and dependency industrialization. . . . Second, studies of individual countries and of the effects of foreign investment disaggregated by composition are necessary to clarify the specific mechanisms by which these processes operate. Third, direct studies of the operations of multinational corporations and of their relationships with the state are necessary. There has already been considerable research in these three areas, and an important task is to integrate the many disparate findings into a theoretically organized scheme.
>
> Finally, we note that the empirical relationships we have found occurred during a specific period, from 1950 to 1970. It is possible that these relationships are conditional on features of the world economy at that time.

Coming at the end of an article which fails to do any of these things, one might fairly wonder how the remarks are to be taken, if they are anything other than a sop to potential critics. But this does signal a change in perspective, an enriching of what before bore the marks of sterile enumeration. Yet there is still something askew, as we shall see shortly.

In 1977 Rubinson also published a study on government revenue, growth, and dependency which does not advance beyond the *ASR* article theoretically or methodologically, except for his borrowing, from Chase-Dunn, panel regression over simple regression. In a symposium volume (Kaplan, 1978), both writers contributed articles. Rubinson's is uncharacteristically free of statistics, and assays the entrance into the world system of Germany and the United States during the nineteenth century. The paper is interesting for its reliance on conventional historical treatments of both nations and for its occasional lapse into the conceptual style of "elite-theory" studies of the 1960s, in spite of the world system jargon. Yet it does not propose any key alterations to previously enunciated theory. Chase-Dunn's paper, by contrast, is a formal model of core competition, and is an advance of sorts. But the most interesting statement of all was published in 1978 (though bearing a 1977 imprint), an article in a Marxist journal coauthored by the pair. It is by far the most detailed lay-out yet provided of the Chase-Dunn and Rubinson theory of world system. Naturally, it demands attention.

To this point the suggestion is lodged that Chase-Dunn and Rubinson practice "reductionism," which in their writings takes various forms. First they reduce empirical (actual) life in dependent states to a handfull of "measures" for ease of sociological comprehension. Then these measures (though probably contrived as a function of available data) are reduced to whatever loosely collected statistics are provided by various agencies. Reduction continues since these data are then poured into the supreme minimizer of all differences, the regression technique. And lastly, statements of probable empirical relations are proposed on the basis of coefficients, which themselves bear slight substantial affinity with socio-political-economic conditions. Yet prior to all this is a form of theoretical reductionism which is more bothersome. We have come to expect from certain empiricist social science the sort of hyperminimizing tendency given full expression in these two men's quantitative work. It is, as already noted, the standard form of presentation, the acceptable "level of discourse." But we are more interested in questioning their willingness to use well-established theories of political economy in a way which diverges diametrically from their currently accepted meaning (not to speak of their "original" properties). The work now under discussion (Chase-Dunn and Rubinson, 1977) offers an opportunity to document their borrowing from Wallerstein, Poulantzas, Marx, Mandel, and others with an eye to theoretical precision.

The goal of their article is to offer a noncausal (descriptive) schema of structures in the world system, with commentary upon each component of the schema, made up thus:

I. Structural constants
   a. Core periphery division of labor
   b. State system
   c. Capitalist commodity production
II. Structural cycles at the system level
   a. Core–periphery control structures

    b. Distribution of power among core-states (multi- and unicentric)
    c. Expansion and contraction of production: long waves
III. Upward trends in the system
    a. Accumulation of capital
    b. Number of states in the system
    c. Expansion of the system to new territories and populations

The motors which propel all these are

Mechanisms of Core–periphery reproduction
a. Power-block formaton
b. State formation
c. Unequal exchange
d. Class struggle

Not all portions receive equal elaboration within the text, nor are all equally important to their "description." It is impractical to consider each of these categories in turn, but some will be examined momentarily.

Chase-Dunn and Rubinson, if judged by their footnotes, are firmly lodged on the left theoretically—even given their remarkably static, undialectical schema. This would suggest that either they agree with Marxist epistemology in its original form (which among other things claims that the "merely" observable is not synonymous with the "real"), *or* they subscribe to a contemporary variant. Their citations would suggest Poulantzas (hence, Althusser) and the structuralist perspective as a leading possibility, plus, of course, Wallerstein's view. But what do Marx and Poulantzas themselves have to say about "data" and their use to "science"?

The *German Ideology* and the *Grundrisse* can be understood as Marx's attempt to distinguish appearance from reality, phenomena from essences, what seems to be from what actually (theoretically) is. The former is a destruction of seemingly avant-garde social thought; the latter work attacks "vulgar" economics on every front. In both cases Marx follows this dictum: "It seems to be correct to begin with the real and the concrete, with the real precondition. . . . However, on closer examination this proves false" (1973:100). And in a related passage, "These imaginary expressions ["the value of labor"] are categories for the phenomenal forms of essential relations. That in their appearance things often represent themselves in inverted form is pretty well known in every science except Political Economy" (1967a:537). And finally, in a famous section:

> It should not astonish us, then, that vulgar economy feels particularly at home in the estranged outward appearances of economic relations in which these *prima facie* absurd and perfect contradictions appear and that these relations seem the more self-evident the more their internal relationships are concealed from it, although they

are understandable to the popular mind. But all science would be superfluous if the outward appearances and the essence of things directly coincided (1967b:817).

It is in the world of "estranged outward appearances" that most sociological empiricism operates, quite by intention of course, and in this Chase-Dunn and Rubinson are no exception. As one travels with them through their nine descriptive elements, it is clear that their "theory" of global economics does not penetrate beneath that level of economic relations at which journalists, "the popular mind," and their fellow positivists work. This in itself would not occasion comment *except* that the authors persist in identifying their theory—for that is what it is, despite their protestations to the contrary—with those of Wallerstein, Mandel, and others listed above. They seem to believe they can eviscerate the Marxist legacy of its "essentials," while continuing adherence to positivist epistemology, which is roughly like fitting Mills's approach to power into Parsons's in order to "save" functionalism. And what adds to the unfortunate condition of their attempt is that they have not seized on the "essentials" of Marxist theory at all, but rather on its jargon, undialectically presented.

There are dozens of other "contradictions" between the two authors' notion of theorizing and that employed by Marx, Lenin, Bukharin, Luxemburg, Gramsci, and others of that tradition vis-à-vis the global economy (whose ideas were sketched above). But we shall skip cataloging these divergences and move instead to the latest Marxist work on the world system and the place of the nation-state within it. In an important footnote Chase-Dunn and Rubinson identify Poulantzas as the source for their crucial notion of "power-block" (1977:467n.). This note is filled with inaccuracies. First of all, the term is "power bloc," not "block," for as any dictionary will attest, the former is a political concept, the latter something which stands in the way of something else. Poulantzas (1973: 229ff.) correctly uses "bloc." The note claims tha Poulantzas is "following Gramsci" in this phrase. This too is incorrect. Gramsci used "bloc" in connection with the following: ideological; intellectual; rural intellectual; entire social; intellectual–moral; reactionary; national; urban; rural; Northern industrialist and rural farmer; right-wing; united; homogeneous social; dominant social; historical; and new, homegeneous, political-economic historical bloc (Gramsci, 1971:60, 72, 74, 76, 94, *passim*). He did not use a term like "power bloc," which is apparently Poulantzas's invention, precisely because its generality and lack of historicity violate Marxist method as Gramsci saw it. (Poulantzas does not claim, incidentally, that "power bloc" is Gramsci's term, quite to the contrary: "The concept of hegemony is also used in another sense, which is not actually pointed out by Gramsci. The capitalist state and the specific characteristics of the class struggle . . . *make it possible* for a 'power bloc' . . . to function" [Poulantzas, 1973:141. Emphasis in original]).

The authors' substantive characterization of Poulantzas's idea is done in less than a score of words; the original delineation required 17 pages and is incomprehensible unless one knows Althusser's theory of Marxist "science," plus Gramsci's "hegemony" as grossly "ahistoricized" and transmogrified by the demands of structuralist epistemology. In short, Chase-Dunn and Rubinson have once again chosen to adorn their prose with a concept from the Marxist canon in such a way that it becomes indistinguishable from mainstream bourgeois usage. The difference between their "power block" and the "interest groups" of 1950s power research is small indeed. But what separates Poulantzas's "power bloc" from American research of that flavor is an entire French debate on the faults not only of Anglo-American empiricism, but of the "historicism" of the early Marx, Weber, Gramsci, Lukacs, Korsch, and everyone else preceding Lévi-Strauss and his search for the "absent cause" within structures. What we have in this is a debate as fundamental to the future shape of Marxism as Weber's ideal-type has been to American sociology, positively and negatively.

While it is true that Chase-Dunn and Rubinson are under no obligation to alert their readers to this debate and its results, they are obliged to write as if they were themselves aware of it—having decided to rely upon Poulantzas—and this they have not done. As a consequence, and as one would imagine, the four motors which supposedly "reproduce" core–periphery relations—power-block formation, state formation, unequal exchange, and class struggle, all clearly Marxist in origin—are inexorably bowdlerized, misstated, and misapplied to the nine essential non-Marxist "constants," "cycles," and "trends" which make up their schema. Their use of terms central to current Marxist analysis—articulation, variable and constant capital, hegemony, class struggle, unequal exchange, and so on—is frequently suspect in its looseness or downright inaccuracy. In fact their own "sponsor" Poulantzas can be easily turned against their version of how theory ought to be handled (Poulantzas, 1973:145–146):

> This conception of typology [Weber's] as a schematization of reality and ultimately as a generalization and an abstraction is dependent on an empiricist conception of knowledge which cannot recognize the proper autonomy of theory. It implies that a pre-ordained harmony between the "abstract" and the "real" is postulated: typological abstraction is seen as an asymptotic adequation of the concrete reality from which it is drawn. But in the Marxist problematic in this theory, we are attempting rather to produce the concept of a regional instance of a mode of production, not by an abstraction from the concrete real phenomena of a social formation, but by the process of theoretical construction of the concept of this mode of production and of the articulation of the instances which specify it. The science of models or schemas leads to notions which cannot give an account of the specific object of a particular science: in fact this object cannot be schematized concrete reality, but only a theoretically constructed concept.

A stronger repudiation of quasi-Weberian categorizing and the limitless, purely logical construction of typologies which goes with it, could hardly be written.

In addition to deviations, distortions, and omissions from Marx, Gramsci, Poulantzas, Emmanuel, and Frank (noted earlier), there remains the question of Wallerstein's work itself, for the Chase-Dunn and Rubinson article is "based on the work of Immanuel Wallerstein" (1977: 453). The summary of Wallerstein's four seminal publications occupies four pages and as such is neither good nor bad, simply slight. Yet the leap from the précis to an extension of his work, at the level of "descriptive schema" of "structural elements," includes acceptance of the "Wallersteinian heresy," i.e., his rejection of Marx's definition of capitalism. Specifically, Wallerstein believes that Marx erred in restricting the capitalist mode of production exclusively to wage labor. His "heresy" includes serfdom and slavery as potentially part of the capitalist mode of production and also "asserts that it is the *articulation* of relatively less coerced labor in the core with relatively more coerced labor in the periphery that is constitutive of capitalist production relations" (Chase-Dunn and Rubinson, 1977:461n.). This is accomplished through "juridicial forms of labor control" (not to be confused with Poulantzas's "juridico-political instances"), resulting in "multitiered systems of exploitation." When Laclau attacked Frank on related grounds (Laclau, 1971), Wallerstein felt called upon to defend Frank's (and his own) version of Marxism by using the ancient dodge "Without diverting ourselves into a long *excursus* on Marxian exegetics, let me say simply that I think Laclau is right in terms of the letter of Marx's arguments but not in terms of its spirit" (Wallerstein, 1974:126). Again homology reigns as Chase-Dunn and Rubinson fend off the stunning attack upon Frank and Wallerstein's "Marxism" mounted by Brenner (1977), who coined the phrase "Neo-Smithian Marxism," a reference to Wallerstein's conventional understanding of "markets" and the key role their conceptualization plays in his sixteenth-century "division of labor." Their "repudiation" of Brenner can be found on page 473, note 32. In it they reveal the novel idea that the periphery serves "the political function" of allowing "the accumulation process [at the core] to adapt to its own contradictions."

The key, then, to the two authors' entire schema is in the phrase "seeking to distort the market," which is semi-Wallersteinian, non-Marxist, and in accord with conventional economic expression. For them the goal of "power blocks" is to capture the state's "resources" and further their own economic interests, nationally and internationally. In what follows, a great many "tendencies" are recited, several, in fact, which are already familiar to readers of earlier essays. At one point we are reminded that "Different areas of the world . . . tend to specialize in different economic roles'' (Chase-Dunn and Rubinson, 1977:456), an idea dealt with above; in another section a memorable statement from Rubinson (1976) is recycled concerning ''strong states,'' and the fallacious example of Latin America where ''the demand for . . . materials declined,'' and capital was therefore ''withdrawn'' (1977:469), a version of history which Frank, for one, would not support. All sorts of fake binary relations obtain: ''the type of alliances and the nature of power-block formation in the core are possible because of the creation of the complementary and opposite type of power-block formation in the periphery'' (1977:471). Presumably Lévi-Strauss would be cheered to learn this, but artful symmetry has more to do with this assertion than historical fact. Pseudodialectics are also in evidence: ''this explains why the political structure of the core is more 'pluralistic': there is a far greater range of economic interests, all of which make political demands on the state. The periphery is less 'pluralistic' for exactly the opposite reasons'' (1977:471). Then there are clear inaccuracies: ''where the interests in a state are composed primarily of manufacturing and commerce, those economic actors put great demands on the state to create an aggressive foreign policy'' (1977:470). Throughout the paper facile historical and national examples are given, in weak imitation of Barrington Moore's comparative style. Usually we hear of the United States, Britain, Brazil, China, Russia, or Holland. But if their axiom, quoted above, is true across the board, how does one explain contemporary Japan, Germany, Britain, Italy, or Sweden, in which an ''aggressive foreign policy'' is an artifact of 40 years ago, if then? There are remarks of similar character, particularly regarding the nature of ''strong'' (core) versus ''weak'' (peripheral or semiperipheral) states. Strong states ''can erect barriers to prevent external control of production'' and ''can regulate the flow of capital and profit to ensure that the gains of production are not withdrawn from the country'' (1977:469). Not only is this flatly wrong when one considers the international mobility of capital (foreseen even by Marx), both through multinationals and through independent speculators, but it betrays a central flaw in their approach, one which could be largely remedied had they taken Marx more seriously. The whole point of Marx's labors, of course, was to prove that capitalism is not about capitalists, or states, or companies, or laborers, or types of products a nation markets. Marx's analysis concerned itself with these only *after* tracing the ''laws'' of accumulation and circulation. Chase-Dunn and Rubinson's ''strong states,'' busily ''securing privileged access to resources and markets,'' ''stimulating a diversification of production,'' ''organizing economic actors to work in concert,'' etc. (and their ''weak states'' doing ''precisely the opposite'' things) are all pre-Marxian in conception. There is no theory of the global economy in these pages, nor of a world system, if one cares to differentiate between the two. There is no ''labor theory of value," nor a surrogate; there is no idea like "modes of production," nor a substitute; there are no "laws" of capital (nor anything else, merely "tendencies" which as often as not do not work). Without these, one is reduced to bourgeois charting of "events" in time, to classical empiricist inductionism. And from that sort of activity—when one must use history as one's foremost data—even "tendencies" tend not to arise unambiguously, not of their own accord.

PROGRAMMATICS AND PROBLEMATICS

Space does not allow the full articulation of an alternative perspective here. However, we can outline the general characteristics of the theorizing needed to restore some level of sophistication to the analysis of the world system. We emphasize the "theorizing" required because, as we have attempted to show, the problems of dependency theory and American WST are wrapped up in a complex series of theoretical displacements involving undefended changes in what a theory about the world system "looks" like, its units of analysis, and the nature of its "laws." One possible line of development is that represented by Samir Amin. As has been explained elsewhere (Sica, 1978), Amin's project for over 20 years has revolved around understanding the global economy, historically and today, from a revised Marxist perspective (though not à la Althusser). Though not unflawed, it is a powerful version of how it all works, and has recently profited form mutual critique by Frank, Emmanuel, and other important Third World writers. If one permits these authors, and Amin especially, their portion of "liberationese" and can see past it into the ideas themselves, plus the richest imaginable documentation, an understanding of the world economy becomes more than an exercise in positivistic logic, in "model-building" free either from the demands of theorizing or from history carefully considered. In these writers we approximate the subject/object of global political economic analysis which disappears in positivist and empiricist analyses. Amin represents the reintegration of Marxism into dependency theory and the problematic of the periphery.

There still remains the fundamental question of the extent to which contemporary Marxism is adequate to the task of analyzing the world system. We suggest that it is not, that the analytical framework present in the classic theory of imperialism was not developed to the point at which we can simply turn back and resume where we were so unfortunately interrupted. Marxism itself did not remain stagnant while theorists of the world system put more and more distance between their concepts and the real categories of capitalist existence. Marxism, too, developed in much the same direction—toward a theory dominated by the pragmatics of immediate politics, toward a theory of the political dominated by what would work in the short term rather than by an elaboration of the mode of production-specific relation between polity and economy. Such a Marxism is not an adequate basis for a conceptual restructuring of the world system. What is required is a respecification of the dynamics of a global capitalist economy put in terms of the logic of capital itself, rather than in those of nations, states, local "interests," and use values. One such structuralist definition of the global economy has been presented in embryonic form by Palloix (1975). Equally important for a mode of analysis in which class conflict is the dynamic factor is a structural definition of class and class fractions, in terms of the real complexity of the productive process and the interests involved in it (e.g., Rey, 1973), as well as of the particular relation between state and social class in a capitalist economy (e.g., Poulantzas, 1973, 1975). Western Marxism is going through an agonizing period of reappraisal of the theoretical developments (or degeneration) of the last half century, changes primarily involving a relapse into theory which somehow begins and ends with practice, and never seems to raise its head beyond the immediate appearance of things as revealed in practical "problems." It is in response to this change that the work of Louis Althusser should be understood (particularly 1970a, 1970b, 1971), *not* as a form of "obscurantism," but as its precise opposite. Althusser represents the attempt to restore to Marxism the level of *theoretical* clarity and explicitness found in *Capital*. This involves a new definition of mode of production, regional theories of state, ideology, etc., and the explication of the relation between "regions" within particular modes of production.

All this appears rather distant from the question of the world system, but, in fact, this pronounced structuralist turn (especially in French Marxism) is critical to the elaboration of the dynamics of the world system. If we are to transcend the alienated rigidities of positivism, we must have a specific theory of the capitalist mode of production, implicit in which is a definition of what does or does not constitute a mode of production (cf. Hindess and Hirst, 1977). Equally, if we are to emphasize the dominance of capital-in-general (see Rosdolsky, 1977:41–50), we must have a precise formal definition of capital *and* a clarification of the unique relations between economy and political and ideological spheres in the capitalist mode of production.

In short, any theory of the world economy must stand at the confluence of two currents. One is that which defines the capitalist mode of production as a theoretical object, in terms of what it *is*, the structures and relations unique to itself. The other is that which is oriented to what capitalism *does* to specific groups in particular places (e.g., the periphery). Both currents are necessary for the articulation of a theory of the world system, and it is necessary to emphasize that a revolutionary attitude to the doing is not the exclusive indicator of rigorous Marxist analysis. To quote Althusser (1971:68, author's emphasis): "*Marxism is not a (new) philosophy of praxis, but a (new) practice of philosophy.*" We are not suggesting that any theory of the world system must (on pain of error) be free from value commitments, but merely that politics—being the art of the possible—must be informed by a theory of limits which itself does not derive from political experience and interest (the problems involved in such being clearly demonstrated in the case of dependency theory). Given the poverty of Marxist political economic theorizing in the last 50 years (cf. Anderson, 1976), it may well be that the most fruitful field for investment is in theory rather than tactics, and that the starting point for any analysis of the world system is not the theory of imperialism but the theory of the nature of the capitalist mode of production itself. At the risk of stating the obvious, the starting point of any theory of a historical conjuncture is the theory of the mode of production dominant within it—in order to understand the capitalist world system we must understand what capitalism *is*.

In most theories of the world system we find the "nature of capitalism" derived from observation of the conjuncture, rather than an understanding of the conjuncture derived from the theory of the capitalist mode of production—*the point being that until a viable definition of the capitalist mode of production is produced, world system theory will not see through conjunctures to the basic laws of transformation of the system, but will merely reflect conjunctures and their "mysterious" changes—engendering a crisis in so-called "theory" every time the superficial topography of the system changes*. Such a situation is not a recipe for the intervention of a theoreticized politics in crises, but for the intervention of crises in politicized theory. Somewhat paradoxically, the greater the involvement of theory with practice the weaker the theory and the less efficacious the practice. Rather than the disengaged and engaged positions being antagonistic, the former is critical for the effectiveness of the latter. Yet it is precisely that former attitude which has been absent from world system studies since Lenin took his trip from Switzerland to the Finland Station, sealing the fatal union of political economy with the pragmatics of power.

NOTES

1. Rubinson would have to explicate "process" to see the irrelevance of this dogma to *social* as opposed to physical or mathematical occurrence.

2. Since our prime goal for the present is to illuminate the lack of substantive connection between two streams of world system thought which, one would think, ought to share a great deal, we will not take on the considerable task of criticizing Chase-Dunn's and Rubinson's research internally. (So far, with small exception, our critique has been external, of course.) Bach and Irwin have ably begun this task, but perhaps we might note several prob-

lems which could be pursued given enough space. First and most scientifically damaging is the condition of data one is virtually forced to use in cross-national studies, something mentioned above. There are economists and political scientists who have carried out international studies of this kind long before it became fashionable to mainstream sociology, and some have become so disenchanted with the accuracy of official statistics, particularly those originating in Third World bureaucracies, that they have dispensed with them and now try to collect their own. The alternative, of course, is to pursue case studies or to use revised historical figures which might have more validity, having escaped political economic pressures of the day. But for contemporary sociologists without a private army of researchers in dependent nations, there is no getting around these poor data, crucial to regression technique. It is also known that the best data are usually associated with banking figures and are put together by European or American institutions. Among the poorest are the more properly sociological data for peripheral nations, those regarding literacy, nutrition, education, housing, and so on, many of which are known to be inflated or otherwise misreported. There is the other obvious difficulty that "development" may "increase" as reported by a given naton simply because as they modernize, they have at their disposal steadily improving agencies for data gathering; thus "development" between, say, 1950 and 1965 may *seem* far greater in certain African countries (where research bureaucracies were being set up in affiliation with the UN) than during the last decade—even considering one recession worldwide. But where real change begins and data-gathering artifacts end remains to be determined. Other data problems, of validity, autocorrelation, and so on, have not been uniformly addressed by American dependency empiricism.

Secondly, there is the problem of finding data which can be converted into a variable (we use this imagery intentionally), which can in turn be justifiably interpreted as a strong "measure" of dependency or autonomy. The fact is that data precede theorizing, that their availability often determines the shape of a model. It is one thing to acknowledge the apparent validity of Baran's and Frank's contention that underdevelopment is an achievement of the core perpetrated upon the periphery; it is another to find data which "prove" this historically generated proposition via regression. This is obviously what Chase-Dunn and Rubinson have been after, to turn history and theory into "science." But their victory, we argue, has been Pyrrhic since dependency has been watered down drastically to fit their computational needs. Thus finding or assembling suitable data for research of this type, particularly as it moves from the exclusively economic to the sociological, is a continuing dilemma.

Another internal problem concerns generalizing from coefficients to the world system at large. For scientists of a certain type this is not problematic since *any* solidly derived finding is better than speculation or "impressionistic" observation. But the distance, it seems to us, between current political economic and social conditions in the periphery, taken together as a "social fact," and the often ambiguous or mildly informative findings of regression analysis (see, e.g., Delacroix's anomalous report on exports [1977], which appears to contradict dependency thinking) are separated by a gulf which must be closed if the latter is to serve any but scholastic purpose.

It should also be pointed out, along Bach's lines, that even with a panel design, true historicity has not yet been confronted by empiricist treatments of the world system. It is one thing to lag a variable or two over the last 25 years (before that it is not usually possible, good data not being available), and another to understand how, for instance, Argentina's internal development has been tied so rigorously to U.S. metal-mining interests for 50 years. Rubinson terms the latter "doing history," the former "doing the theory of development" (1977:819), but surely this lapse is attributable to the demands of polemics. If this were true, Weber was not a social theorist—nor Marx, nor Mills. This view is acceptable to some enthusiasts of "theory construction," but given Rubinson's willingness to handle concepts and substance which cannot be subsumed within single variables, certainly he does not belong to that group. In the same vein, just as Menger and Schmoller never resolved the *Methodenstreit* a century ago, it is equally unlikely that a "definitive" position can be found reconciling ideographic with nomothetic knowledge today. But if "history" (those past forces which shape today's opportunities) be reduced on one hand to mere "uniqueness" or idiosyncrasy, on the other to variable configurations, any hope of discovering the evolving mechanisms of the global economy is lost.

Finally, there is the perennial drawback of regression studies which has nothing to do with the skill which goes into doing them. No matter how many caveats are posted along the way, it is most difficult to avoid visualizing independent as well as dependent variable(s) in the equations as enjoying some appreciable form of empirical relatedness. Chase-Dunn's first paper (1975) for instance, uses GNP/capita, kilowatt hours consumed, percentage of non-agricultural male laborers, domestic capital formation, and mining specialization of the national economy. Give or take a few variables, this is a typical modus operandi in dependency empiricism. As the mind roves over his report, without constant vigilance, the natural tendency is to accept "for the sake of argument" that these variables are "theoretically" linked or bear some mutual, necessary relation in actuality. This is the burden of the model. But what if the model is completely wrong? Again, a gentleman's agreement applies such that this initial challenge to the entire research enterprise is seldom, if ever, lodged. It should be understood that this is not an extension of those familiar arguments about linearity or its lack in the phenomena which one's data supposedly represent. It is possible to secure "significant" findings correlating several variables, later to discover that confounding influences (like historically fashioned social structure) created this spuriousness. And since the world economy, even when one considers a single nation within it, involves hundreds of actual variables, and because dependency empiricism never handles more than a half dozen of undetermined signficance in one equation or set of equations, is not the likelihood of this problem pellucid? Add to that the ease with which researchers hint of causality when reporting correlations, and the weakness of this research regimen becomes more manifest yet.

Perhaps the major difficulty has to do with "scope assumptions" and the fit between theory, method, and substance, but discussion of this will occur later.

REFERENCES

Althusser, Louis
1970a For Marx. New York: Vintage.
1970b Reading Capital. London: NLB.
1971 Lenin and Philosophy. London: NLB.
Amin, Samir
1974 Accumulation on a World Scale: A Critique of the Theory of Development. New York: Monthly Review Press.
1976 Unequal Development: An Essay on the Social Formations of Peripheral Capitalism. New York: Monthly Review Press.
1977 Imperialism and Unequal Development. New York: Monthly Review Press.
Arrighi, Giovanni
1978 The Geometry of Imperialism. London: NLB.
Bach, Robert L.
1977 "Methods of analysis in the study of the world-economy. (Comment on Rubinson, ASR, August, 1976.)" American Sociological Review 42(5):811–4.
Barrat-Brown, Michael
1974 The Economics of Imperialism. Harmondsworth: Penguin.

Bornschier, Volker, Christopher Chase-Dunn, and Richard Rubinson
 1978 "Cross-national evidence of the effects of foreign investment and aid on economic growth and inequality: a survey of findings and a re-analysis." American Journal of Sociology 84(3):651–83.
Braudel, Fernand
 1973 The Mediterranean and the Mediterranean World in the Age of Philip II, 2 vols. New York: Harper & Row.
Brenner, Robert
 1977 "The origins of capitalist development: a critique of neo-Smithian Marxism." New Left Review 104(July–Aug.):25–92.
Bukharin, Nikolai
 1972 "Imperialism and the accumulation of capital." Pp. 150–270 in Rosa Luxemburg and Nikolai Bukharin, Imperialism and the Accumulation of Capital. London: Allen Lane—The Penguin Press.
Cardoso, Fernando H.
 1973 "Notas sobre estado e dependencia." Sao Paulo, Brazil: CEBRAP (Caderno II).
Chase-Dunn, Christopher
 1975 "The effects of international economic dependency on development and inequality: a cross-national study." American Sociological Review 40(6):720–38.
 1978 "Core-periphery relations: the effects of core competition." Pp. 159–76 in Barbara Kaplan, (ed.), Social Change in the Capitalist World Economy. Beverly Hills, Calif.: Sage Publs.
Chase-Dunn, Christopher, and Richard Rubinson
 1977 "Toward a structural perspective on the world-system." Politics & Society 7(4): 453–76.
Chilcote, Ronald H.
 1974 "Dependency: a critical synthesis of the literature." Latin American Perspectives 1(Spring):4–29.
Coser, Lewis
 1975 "Presidential address: two methods in search of a substance." American Sociological Review 40(6):691–700.
Delacroix, Jacques
 1977 "The export of raw materials and economic growth: a cross-national study." American Sociological Review 42(5):795–808.
Delacroix, Jacques, and Charles Ragin
 1978 "Modernizing institutions, mobilization, and Third World development: a cross-national study." American Journal of Sociology 84:1(July):123–150.
Emmanuel,Arghiri
 1972 Unequal Exchange. New York: Monthly Review Press.
Frank, André G.
 1971 Capitalism and Underdevelopment in Latin America. Harmondsworth: Penguin.
 1972a "The development of underdevelopment." Pp. 3–17 in James D. Cockcroft, André Gunder Frank, and Dale L. Johnson (eds.), Dependence and Underdevelopment: Latin America's Political Economy. New York: Anchor Books.
 1972b Lumpenbourgeoisie: Lumpendevelopment (Dependence. Class, and Politics in Latin America). New York: Monthly Review Press.
 1978 World Accumulation, 1492–1789. New York: Monthly Review Press.
Goldfrank, Walter L.
 1979 "Dialectical analysis and closed systems: class societies or world economy." American Sociological Review 44(1):172–4.
Gramsci, Antonio
 1971 Selections from the Prison Notebooks. New York: International Publs.

Hill, Christopher
  1967 Reformation to Industrial Revolution: The Making of Modern English Society,
        Vol. 1:1530–1780. New York: Pantheon.
Hindess, Barry, and Paul Q. Hirst
  1977 Pre-capitalist Modes of Production. London: Routledge & Kegan Paul.
Hobsbawm, E.J.
  1968 Industry and Empire: The Making of Modern English Society, Vol. 2: 1750 to the
        Present Day. New York: Pantheon.
Hobson, J.A.
  1938 Imperialism: A Study. London: Allen & Unwin.
Irwin, Patrick H.
  1977 "Cross-sectionalism, mismatching theory and model. (Comment on Rubinson,
        ASR, August, 1976.)" American Sociological Review 42(5):814–7.
Knapp, J.A.
  1973 "Economics or political economy?" Lloyd's Bank Review 107:19–43.
Laclau, Ernesto
  1971 "Feudalism and capitalism in Latin America." New Left Review 67(May–June):9–
        38. [Reprinted as pp. 15–50 in Laclau's Politics and Ideology in Marxist Theory.
        London: NLB, 1977.]
Lenin, Vladimir I.
  1975 Imperialism, the Highest State of Capitalism. Moscow: Progress Publ.
Luxemburg, Rosa
  1972 "The accumulation of capital: an anti-critique." Pp. 47–150 in Rosa Luxemburg
        and Nikolai Bukharin, Imperialism and the Accumulation of Capital. London:
        Allen Lane—The Penguin Press.
  1977 The Industrial Development of Poland. New York: Campaigner Publs.
Marx, Karl
  1967a Capital, Vol. 1. New York: International Publs.
  1967b Capital. Vol. 3. New York: International Publs.
  1973 Grundrisse. Harmondsworth: Penguin.
Marx, Karl, and Frederick Engels
  1959 On Colonialism. Moscow: Progress Publs.
  1976 Collected Works, Vol. 6. London: Lawrence & Wishart.
Owen, Robert, and Bob Sutcliffe (eds.)
  1972 Studies in the Theory of Imperialism. London: Longman.
Palloix, Christian
  1975 L'internationalisation du capital. Paris: Maspero.
Pilling, Geoffrey
  1973 "Imperialism, trade and 'unequal exchange': the work of Aghiri [sic] Emmanuel."
        Economy and Society 2(2):64–85.
Portes, Alejandro
  1973 "Modernity and development: a critique." Studies in Comparative International
        Development 8(3):247–79.
  1976 "On the sociology of national development: theories and issues." American
        Journal of Sociology 82(1):55–85.
Poulantzas, Nicos
  1973 Political Power and Social Classes. London: NLB.
  1975 Classes in Contemporary Capitalism. London: NLB.
Rey, Pierre-Philippe
  1973 Les alliances de classes. Paris: Maspero.
Rosdolsky, Roman
  1977 The Making of Marx's "Capital." London: Pluto Press.

Rubinson, Richard
  1976   "The world economy and the distribution of income within states: a cross-national study." American Sociological Review 41(4):638–59.
  1977a "Dependence, government revenue, and economic growth, 1955–1970: a cross-national analysis." Studies in Comparative International Development 12(2):3–28.
  1977b "Reply to Bach and Irwin." American Sociological Review 42(5):817–21.
  1978   "Political transformation in Germany and the United States." Pp. 39–73 in Barbara Kaplan, (ed.), Social Change in the Capitalist World Economy, Beverly Hills, Calif.: Sage Publns.
Sica, Alan
  1978   "Review essay: dependency in the world economy." American Journal of Sociology 84(3):28–39.
Smith, Adam
  [1776] The Wealth of Nations. New York: Modern Library.
  1937
Snyder, David, and Edward L. Kick
  1979   "Structural position in the world system and economic growth, 1955–1970: a multiple network analysis of transnational interactions." American Journal of Sociology 84(5):1096–126.
Steiber, Steven R.
  1979   "The world system and world trade: an empirical exploration of conceptual conflicts." Sociological Quarterly 20(1):23–36.
Tribe, Keith
  1978   Land, Labour and Economic Discourse. London: Routledge & Kegan Paul.
Trotsky, Leon
  1970   The Third International after Lenin. New York: Pathfinder Press.
Wallerstein, Immanuel
  1974   The Modern World-System. New York: Academic Press.

ON THE REIFICATION OF
SOCIAL STRUCTURE

Douglas W. Maynard and Thomas P. Wilson

To reify a social structure is to treat it as an object that is analytically independent of the actions by which it is produced.[1] Here we are concerned with such a conception of social structure, not only as a fundamental presupposition of the mainstream of contemporary sociological theory, but also as a feature of everyday life in bureaucratic industrial society.

The question of the reification of social structure was raised over a century ago in Karl Marx's discussion of alienation, abstraction, and the fetishism of commodities. Since then, however, it has ceased to be a significant substantive problem within any of the major streams of American sociological thought.[2] Instead, it has come to be treated as an essentially philosophical issue in debates between methodological individualists and holists, and in this guise it arises occasionally in polemical exchanges between schools taking different a priori attitudes toward the reality of social structure, such as behaviorism, structural functionalism,

Current Perspectives in Social Theory, volume 1, 1980, pages 287–322.
Copyright © 1980 by JAI Press Inc.
All rights of reproduction in any form reserved.
ISBN: 0-89232-154-7

and structuralism. There is, then, good reason to examine the question of the reification of social structure anew, particularly since the broad framework that, in its social system, conflict theoretic, and symbolic interactionist forms, has dominated sociology since World War II shows increasing signs of disintegration, and the behaviorist and structuralist alternatives are untenable.[3]

In addressing the problem of reification we wish to reestablish the status it has in Marx's writing as a substantive empirical matter. That is to say, for Marx the conception of social structures as things standing in autonomous causal relationships to one another and to things at other levels is a product of particular historical circumstances rather than an essential a priori presupposition underlying social theory or a matter for methodological debate between rival schools of social thought. The issue, then, is not whether social structures are properly thought of as constituting a realm of independent facts sui generis. Rather, the problem involves two related questions. First, under what circumstances can such a conception arise and be viable within society? Second, by what processes is the notion of the autonomy of social structure produced and sustained? Marx concerned himself with the question, arguing in effect that the reification of social structure is codeterminate with particular relations of material production, namely those that provide for the creation and exploitation of surplus value. However, whatever the merits of Marx's analysis on that point, the second question has been neglected, particularly with regard to how reification is located in direct interaction between particular concrete individuals. The latter issue, nevertheless, is a critical one, for it is central to the thesis that history is produced by the activity of real people. Neglect of this crucial point has helped foster the dogmatism of orthodox Marxism as well as the tendency for most sociologists to see Marx as essentially a ''conflict theorist,'' and generally an obsolete one at that.[4]

Our task in this paper is theoretical and consists of four main parts. First, in order to see the problem in its broad context, we must discuss briefly the way the issue of reification has been disposed of in the mainstream of sociological theory, focusing particular attention on Durkheim, Weber, and the synthesis of what has been taken to be their thought in conventional sociological theory. Second, we need to specify more precisely how our approach is informed by Marx's work. Particularly, we are concerned neither with Marx's substantive analysis of nineteenth-century bourgeois capitalism and subsequent elaborations and extensions by others, nor with current debates within Marxism. Instead, what concern us are certain basic methodological presuppositions that fundamentally separate Marx's work from more conventional positions in the behavioral and social sciences, for it is these that provide for the possibility of viewing the reification of social structure as an historically contingent matter. Third, we shall propose that empirical investigation of the process by which reification of social structures occurs in direct social interaction requires an ethnomethodological framework. Finally, we discuss briefly some of the critical issues raised by these ideas.[5]

SOCIAL STRUCTURE IN CONVENTIONAL SOCIOLOGICAL THEORY

The reigning conception in contemporary American sociology is that of society as consisting of systematically, though not necessarily harmoniously, interrelated parts exhibiting regularities, describable, at least in principle, in terms of universal laws. Whether "equilibrium," "conflict," or "interaction" is the guiding metaphor, the notion of society as a system, the structure and dynamics of which can be described in terms of general universal propositions, is fundamental to virtually all sociology and certainly to the pursuit of sociology in the image of natural science. Complementary to this is the concept of an actor, generally described in terms borrowed in varying proportions from psychoanalytic, symbolic interactionist, behaviorist, and utilitarian traditions. Actors are seen as linked to the social system through socialization into particular roles and a culture of symbols with shared meanings, as well as through the sanctioned expectations associated with the statuses they occupy in the social structure. The internalized dispositions and institutionalized expectations thus lead actors to define situations and react to them in patterned ways. From the point of view of understanding the behavior of an individual or an aggregate of similarly situated persons, social structure provides the given conditions necessary for social-psychological explanations. And, from a sociological perspective, the individual actor is theoretically relevant as the locus of a set of roles in the social structure, a carrier of a particular socialization history, and the physical vehicle through which social action actually occurs.[6]

This basic conceptual framework, often expressed in superficially differing terminology and frequently elaborated in incompatible ways, has its origin in a synthesis of ideas drawn from Durkheim and Weber in the context of the peculiar Anglo-American mixture of individualism, voluntarism, and scientism. The two Continental progenitors of the modern sociological tradition, however, had views concerning the reality of social structure quite different both from each other and from what has emerged as the dominant position in sociology.

Durkheim was heir to the holist tradition in French social thought, represented after the French Revolution by such otherwise diverse thinkers as the conservative Catholics Bonald and Maistre and the positivists St. Simon and Comte (Lukes, 1973; Hayek, 1952; Macruse, 1960). For Durkheim (1901), the question of the nature of social reality is settled a priori by his tendency to treat social facts as a domain of causal reality sui generis that cannot be identified with or reduced to the observed patterns of interaction among actual people. In this view, social structure is a reality underlying social phenomena, and observable patterns such as suicide rates or legal codes merely reflect the social facts lying behind them. Moreover, for Durkheim the concept of the individual is a thoroughly social construct: even egoistic individualism, which he saw as symptomatic of the pathology of contemporary society, derives from society itself through the emergence of the "cult of the individual" (1902:172) as one aspect of the moral counterpart of the organic division of labor, on the one hand, and the inadequate development of the constraining aspect of that same morality, on the other. The consequence of this position, clearly, is that social structure, construed as the structure of social facts, is the logically prior reality. From this point of view, if anything is an hypostatized abstraction, it is the concept of the individual, particularly as this notion figures as the foundation for classical political economy and subsequent liberal social thought.

In contrast, Weber's position was a thoroughgoing methodological individualism (Weber, 1920; Burger, 1976). In his view, social structures are essentially fictions, ideal types constructed by the researcher to facilitate a specific investigation. Consequently, it is meaningless to treat such ideal objects as things that can stand in causal relations to one another or to actually existing concrete things. Causality, instead, lies at the level of the individual, and the "cause" of any historical structure must be sought in the myriad causal chains extending back from each of its concrete individual components. Likewise, the "effects" of such a structure consists of the innumerable chains of consequences leading forward from each of those components. For Weber, as for Durkheim, then, the question of the reality of social structure is settled a priori by the basic presuppositions of his methodological framework, though, of course, it is settled in exactly the opposite way: for Weber, any talk of social structure that fails to recognize its ideal-typical status is reification.

In the synthesis of ideas from Durkheim and Weber in contemporary sociology their opposed views on the reality of social structure are resolved in the doctrine of emergent systems.[7] Durkheim's tendency to see social facts as lying behind social phenomena and only reflected in observable events is supplanted by the conception of social structure as in fact consisting of the actual interactions of concrete individuals. However, Weber's thoroughgoing reductionism is softened, for his view of social structures as fictions is abandoned in favor of their treatment as real systems obeying emergent laws not deducible from laws describing the behavior of individuals. In the dominant framework of contemporary sociology, then, the issue of the reality of social structures is resolved by according equal ontological status to individuals and social systems, and the resulting question of the relations between them is dealt with through the concepts of role and socialization or the equivalents. In this view there is a two-way causal process: individuals are affected by social structure, through socialization and sanctions, but there is a residual element of individual uniqueness and effect on action that cannot be explained in social terms; and equally, individual actions do affect the directions of social change, but only within constraints allowed by the natural laws that ultimately govern social processes. The problem of reification, then, disappears in the mainstream of contemporary sociology, surviving only in attenuated, marginal, and distorted form through occasional allusions to latent functions, self-fulfilling prophecies, and W. I. Thomas's dictum that if people define a situation as real, it is real in its consequences. But the concepts of status, role, reference group, social structure, and culture, in terms of which latent functions and self-fulfilling prophecies are analyzed, are not themselves viewed as subject, say, to Thomas's theorem (see Merton, 1976:175–177). Thus, in conventional sociology, the status of social structure as an analytically independent domain of lawful regularity is secured by the a priori presuppositions of the emergent system doctrine.[8]

Reification, then, cannot be addressed as an empirical sociological matter within the confines of the classical distinction between individual and society in Western social thought. To treat it as an historically contingent occurrence in Marx's fashion requires transcending this distinction in a stronger sense than conceding the analytical independence of individual and social structure and seeking to connect the two categories through such notions as role and socialization. For such an alternative, we find it useful to turn to Marx's work, particularly his attitude toward the relation of the individual to society and the related but more fundamental division between subject and object, between mind and body.

REIFICATION AS HISTORICALLY CONTINGENT

Marx, it is often said, "transcended" this or that pernicious "dualism" by means of "the dialectic." What this means, however, depends entirely on how the term "dialectic" is understood. Unfortunately, it appears that many interpreters of Marx tend, quite unwittingly, to construe the notion within the context of their own methodological assumptions without noticing that Marx's approach represents a major departure from those presuppositions. The result is that interpreters in talking about "the dialectic" often adopt Marxist phraseology but actually employ the term in a sense quite incompatible with Marx's usage.[9] Consequently, it is essential that we sketch briefly how we understand these matters.

The background of Marx's thought was the philosophical tradition of Kant and Fichte and the Romantic protest against the Industrial Revolution. His immediate early intellectual milieu was the ferment in Germany during the 1830s and 1840s arising from the confluence of Hegelian philosophy, St. Simonian and socialist ideas imported from France, and British political economy. Here, however, we are not concerned with what Marx adopted from these sources, such as the terminology of "bourgeoisie" and "proletariat," the concept of class conflict, the idea of the priority of the productive process over property, distress over the conditions of factory workers under capitalism, and the like. It is as trivial as it is correct to note Marx's indebtedness to others in these respects (cf., Halévy, 1955; Hayek, 1952) for what is important is what Marx made of these matters in his own analysis of nineteenth-century capitalism. Our concern, in particular, is the framework of presuppositions that Marx employed in his analysis of capitalism, for there, we claim, lies his truly fundamental and revolutionary departure from the mainstream of Western thought.

Reflexive Determination

For present purposes, the point to note about Hegel is in his idealist view that objects in the external world are projections of consciousness, and hence that "alienation" consists in experiencing the world of external objects as existing independently of consciousness. Transcending "alienation" in Hegelian terms, then, means reestablishing the connection between apparently independently existing objects and their origins in consciousness. Though Marx began with a thorough study of Hegel, he specifically rejects Hegel's identification of objectification with alienation and argues for an objectively existing external world (1844:109–17). However, just as Marx rejects idealism, so he also avoids the other two familiar attitudes toward the classical Western division between subject and object. On the one hand, despite all the talk about "materialism" in his work, he does not accept the materialist position that treats consciousness as an epiphenomenal function of the physical world (Marx, 1845:Thesis I; Marx and Engels, 1846:164–5). Nor, on the other hand, does he adopt the more common dualist attitude, which treats subject and object as equally real and independent things that must somehow be connected in order to resolve the resulting mind–body problem (cf., Ollman, 1971:Chaps. I, II). Rather, Marx abandons the subject–object dichotomy altogether in what he calls "consistent naturalism" (1844:115). He does indeed retain these categories, but the relation between them is of a totally different kind: it is one of mutual *reflexive determination*.

Let us illustrate the idea first with a perceptual metaphor. Consider the well-known face/goblet illusion: seen one way the picture is of two faces in silhouette with a white space between them; seen another way, it is of a white goblet against a black background. Either way, each part of the contour separating the white and black areas is what it is only in the context of the others parts and the whole. Thus, for instance, one portion is a nose only in the context of another portion that is a chin, and vice versa; moreover, these can be a nose and a chin only in the context of the face as a whole; but, finally, a face can be seen at all only because of the presence of a nose and chin, and vice versa. Clearly, we have here a form of determination between nose, chin, and face, but equally clearly it is neither causal in an empirical sense nor a conceptual or logical connection between ideas, for there are no independent things or ideas between which such relations of temporal, causal, or logical priority can obtain. Rather, each part of the whole is what it is only in the context of the whole and the other parts, and the whole itself is what it is only in the context of the parts. It is this that we mean by "reflexive determination."[10] We have chosen an ambiguous figure for this illustration to emphasize the crucial role of the reflexive interdependence between parts and whole in determining what the parts are and what the whole is. However, while it is especially evident in ambiguous displays of this sort, the mutual reflexive determination of parts and whole should not be thought of as a peculiarity of such figures: rather, it is fundamental to all pattern recognition.[11]

We emphasize that this example is a metaphor in order to underscore the point that we are not proposing some sort of notion that "it's all in how you look at it." Notice, for instance, that the face/goblet drawing cannot reasonably be seen as anything one wants, for example, as displaying a system of partial differential equations or a picture of a sailboat with birds circling around it. To treat the example literally rather than metaphorically we must expand the whole to include not only the drawing but also the person perceiving it and his or her actions in relation to it. The crux of this move is to recognize that the perceiver and his or her actions are reflexively codetermined with the features of the perceived object in exactly the same way as the nose and chin were in the metaphorical example. The elements of the whole, then, consist not only of the objects being perceived but also the observer and his or her actions, all of which are reflexively interrelated.[12]

We understand the term "dialectical" in Marx's usage to be essentially equivalent to "reflexive." Thus, the reflexive relation between action toward and knowledge of objects to which we have just alluded is the notion of *praxis* that figures so importantly in Marx's thought. Similarly, we construe the word "determine" in a reflexive sense rather than in causal terms. Likewise, the relation of subject to object and the relation of individual to society must also be construed reflexively if we are not to read into Marx some form of idealism, materialism, or dualism entirely foreign to his work.[13]

Finally, within this framework, the pivotal concepts of abstraction and reification receive natural interpretations that we hold are congruent with the way these notions figure in Marx's work. To *abstract* is to extract an object or relation between objects from the reflexive content within which it is embedded and, on the basis of some specified features, treat it as a member of a category in a fashion indistinguishable from other objects similarly detached from their reflexive contexts. Thus, left behind in the process of abstraction are the reflexive connections through which the object or relation has those features that allow it to be categorized in a particular way in the first place. However, abstraction is not reification, for while abstraction neglects the reflexive embeddedness of objects or relations, it does not deny that embeddedness in principle. But when reality comes to take on the appearance of consisting of abstracted objects and abstracted relations between them, their reflexive embeddedness is denied effective factual status, and it is proper to speak of *reification*. Here it should be noted that what is "factual" and "real" is that which the participants in the actual situation treat as the warranted bases for inference and action.[14]

The Reification of Social Structure

Observe that, from the point of view developed here, structures of social relations are reflexively connected with the individuals and interactions comprising them: the interactions of individuals have the meaning and content they do in the context of the social structure of which they are a part, and equally the social structure has the character it does only because the individuals and interactions comprising it are of the sort they are. This, of course, does not deny an historical process. Each generation is born into a social world not of its own making and creates under those conditions the circumstances for the next generation. Indeed, people awaken each day to face circumstances generated in the past and act within those constraints to produce the circumstances they will confront on the morrow. However, to confuse this historical process with the reflexive connection between individual and society is to trivialize the latter by rendering it equivalent to the concept of a causal system with lagged or unlagged feedback loops. The point instead is that social reality cannot, without major distortion, be divided into analytically independent domains of individual actions and social structures standing in unilateral or bilateral causal relations to one another. Thus, while social structure is most certainly real, its reality is not what conventional social theories assume.

The reification of social structure occurs, then, when social objects, such as social categories, organizations, norms, rules, and so on, are systematically abstracted from their reflexive contexts and accorded the status of things that are not merely real but are analytically independent of individual action. The paradigmatic example of such reification in Marx is the fetishism of commodities, in which actual relations between persons take on the appearance of relations between things. As a consequence, according to Marx, commodity production involves a number of contradictory elements. Concrete labor becomes abstract, and the activity of individuals transforms into labor which is "social in its character" (Marx, 1887:58–59), in the sense that qualitatively different forms of labor become abstracted and compared to each other quantitatively in terms of the amount of time expended. To the producers of commodities, "their own social action takes the form of action of objects, which rule the producers instead of being ruled by them" (Marx, 1887:75). Other examples of reification include the complex of nineteenth-century notions of the individual and his rights, capital, the market, property, and so on, which Marx criticizes the classical political economists for taking over without recognizing that they were historically situated abstractions rather than universally valid categories. Still another instance is the present-day set of concepts deriving from the notions of status and role which sociologists have adopted uncritically, not recognizing that, as Coleman (1970) and Smith (1974a) have observed, the idea of separating person from role is a social invention, and indeed one of recent origin since the medieval period.

Reification, then, is fundamentally a phenomenon occurring within society itself at a particular time and place. From this perspective, it is not an essential a priori presupposition of social theory; moreover, it is not an inevitable feature of stable social organization; nor, finally, is reification usefully thought of simply as a basic epistemological error to be avoided. Rather it is a characteristic of society and its parts that originates within society itself. As such, reification must be seen as reflexively codeterminate with other features of society.

THE PRODUCTION OF REIFIED SOCIAL STRUCTURE

We have said that the problem of reification was initially raised by Marx, but that the question of the process by which the reification of social structure is produced in actual interaction within society has been neglected.[15] The problem is a critical one, since unless it is dealt with the concept of reification must remain murky and insubstantial. Without presuming to offer a definitive account of the matter, we turn now to some suggestions as to directions in which further research, particularly of an empirical sort, might be profitable. Our central proposal on this score is that an ethnomethodological approach is the proper framework for the study of how reification is produced in actual social interaction.

The Ethnomethodological Framework

In the present discussion, two things are crucial about ethnomethodology. First, by a route quite different from and completely independent of Marx's work, ethnomethodology has established itself on essentially reflexive methodological foundations. Second, from its inception, ethnomethodology has been concerned with how the factual status of accounts of the social world is accomplished in interaction between people on particular occasions. Ethnomethodology, then, provides a uniquely suitable framework for studying the production of reification.

With regard to the methodological foundations of ethnomethodology, it is perhaps necessary to clear the air at once by noting that, while Garfinkel and Cicourel were well acquainted with the work of Schütz and phenomenologists such as Gurwitsch, ethnomethodology as we conceive it cannot be classified as a phenomenological sociology. The point has been made elsewhere by Zimmerman (1976; 1978), and we simply take it for granted here. Of greater importance in the present context are the implications of certain leading ideas in ethnomethodology. Throughout the work of Garfinkel and his students, one finds a pervasive concern for what are called "indexicality" and "reflexivity." In an early statement, Garfinkel (1967:78) discusses these ideas in describing the documentary method of interpretation, which consists of treating an actual appearance as "the document of," as "pointing to," as "standing on behalf of" a presupposed underlying pattern. Not only is the underlying pattern derived from its documentary evidences, but the individual documentary evidences, in their turn, are interpreted on the basis of what is known about the underlying pattern. Each is used to elaborate the other. The point can be made another way in terms of indexicality, that is, the dependence of an account on its context of use for its meaning. Since, on this view, every account is indexical, the particulars making up the context for a given account are themselves specifiable only in terms of their contexts, part of which consist of the original account. Thus, the basic presuppositions of ethnomethodology are reflexive (see Wilson and Zimmerman, 1980), and consequently, in adopting an ethnomethodological framework to understand reification as construed in terms derived from Marx, we do not run the risk of attempting to mix incompatible methodological presuppositions.[16]

From this follows a derivative but no less important point of convergence between Marx's presuppositions and an ethnomethodological approach. In contrast with conventional sociological viewpoints, both treat the apparently stable and concretely existing features of society as the accomplishment of ongoing practical activity by actual living people.[17] Moreover, they both assume that the categories in terms of which social organization is described do not have their origins in a scientific conceptual scheme defined independently of any particular social context but rather are ideas founded in formulations produced and maintained within that society itself. Thus, for Marx, notions such as commodity, capital, private property, division of labor, and the like cannot be treated as givens or as universally valid categories, as in classical political economy. Rather, as Lukacs (1923:179) observes, the premise of Marx's approach to understanding society "is that *things should be shown to be aspects of processes.*" Thus, the categories of economic thought should be seen as reflexively codetermined with the relationships of real individuals, their activity, and the material conditions under which they live (see Marx and Engels, 1846:150). Similarly, for ethnomethodology, such notions as norm, status, role, and so on, are not simply theoretical constructs devised by social scientists, but are aspects of processes within society that are developed and used by members of society in conducting their everyday affairs and cannot be detached from the practical activities that achieve ordinary features of interaction. Ethnomethodology, then, avoids analytic categories whose status in a conceptual scheme, theory, or account hides "the society 'in back of' the various situated appearances constituent of everyday, located scenes" (Zimmerman and Pollner, 1970:99). If commodities, capital, and the division of labor are treated as aspects of processes and not as givens in Marx's view, so roles, statuses, common understandings, and social categories are treated as aspects of processes and not as explanatory resources for the ethnomethodologist.

There are, however, differences in application of this principle. Sociological analysis deals with the institutional structure and dynamics of society. For example, Marx took it for granted that the social world confronting people as a seemingly independent object is in fact produced by them, and he proceeded to analyze private property and capital in terms of their reflexive codeterminations with each other and with actual human labor in an historically specific mode of production. In contrast, ethnomethodology has concerned itself not with analyzing institutional structure and dynamics, but rather with the processes through which, on any given occasion of interaction, members of society generate and sustain the features of that local setting. Those features include, among other things, its historical continuity, its structure of rules and the relationships of activities to those rules, and the ascribed or achieved status of its participants (Zimmerman and Pollner, 1970:94), and, we add, the reified character in modern society of these categories of social structure. It is evident, however, that this difference in research programs does not turn on a fundamental difference in underlying conceptions of the social actor or the nature of social reality, for in both cases the members of society are agents in the active sense of the word, creating the arrangements that characterize the society and which confront the individual as its organized features. Our concern now is to suggest how these two levels of analysis might be linked.

Empirical Illustrations

We are concerned with how abstracted social relations and reified social structures are simultaneously confronted as facticities, or realities, which seem to impinge externally on direct human interaction and yet are the outcome of members' practices for making them observable. Empirical analysis of face-to-face relations within an ethnomethodological framework provides a way of understanding and locating the means whereby components of social structure which permeate face-to-face interaction are members' accomplishments. These components do not reflect some supposed coercive and automatic character of an independently existing organization logic of society but rather are produced and reproduced in direct, everyday encounters through various members' practices.

In examining the following illustrations we shall employ a number of concepts from conversational analysis, but we must emphasize that our purpose here is to illustrate what we mean by the production of abstraction and reification in interaction, not to provide the range of data and detailed analyses appropriate to an empirical study. Moreover, we shall make a number of assertions about the data that depend on more detailed analyses than can be presented here. However, since our purpose is illustrative rather than demonstrative, these limitations are not crucial so long as they are clearly understood. Thus, in line with the theoretical nature of this paper, we here propose a direction for further research rather than carry out the program itself.

Abstraction

In this section, we examine an actual conversation with two interrelated purposes. The first is to show that abstracted relationships are in part a matter of conversational sequencing, that is, the outcome of members' step-by-step employment of conversational procedures. The point we will make is that conversationalists are not engaged in employing specific mechanisms of talk because their relations are, in the first place, abstracted. Rather, members accomplish such characteristic relationships through various conversational procedures.[18] The second purpose of this section is to argue that although abstracted relations involve the conversational activity of categorizing persons, such relations are a feature of the *way* a category is used in a conversational segment and not an automatic outcome of its employment. That is to say, abstraction is not a fixed characteristic of a category but rather is contingent on the way it is used on a particular occasion.

Some preliminary definitions are in order. We draw on Sacks' (1972a,b) notion of a membership categorization device, which contains a collection of categories that may be applied to the members of a given population. For example, a prominent device is "occupation," where the categories applied to various members include "student," "teacher," "mechanic," "stockbroker," and so on. A related idea is what Sacks (1972b) terms "category-bound activities": specific activities which are supposedly done by members of given categories. Thus, taking classes is an activity bound to the category "college student," while selling bonds is an activity bound to the category "stockbroker."[19]

Next, we observe that while a category may be used in explicit categorization to assert that a person belongs to a particular category, it can also be used to warrant the relevance of what is being said in some turn in a conversation. Thus, in the simplest case, the fact that in a given situation a person can be categorized as a college student can be used to warrant talk about what classes he or she is taking. We shall say that the use of a membership category is in the *abstract mode* if it is used to warrant talk consisting of further categorizations or of matters such as category-bound activities that are impersonal in the sense that they can be seen as relevant to any person to whom the category can be applied.[20] Note that this accords with our earlier definition of abstraction, since such use of a category systematically ignores the reflexive contexts to which the person and his or her actions are connected. In contrast, we shall say that the category is used in the *concrete mode* if it is used to warrant talk consisting of descriptions or matters pertaining uniquely to the person and context in question.

Consider now the following fragment, occurring at the beginning of a conversation between two students at X University.[21] It illustrates the use of a membership category and a category-bound activity.

1. George: 'R you takin' Sosh or what. Or
2. Laura: Ye:ah. (.) Sosh two

George's question, in line 1, employs a candidate person description[22] formulated as an activity bound to the category "student at X University." In line 2, Laura acknowledges that the candidate description is correct ("yeah") and adds a component "Sosh two" that further specifies what she is taking. While the category "student at X University" is not explicit in the conversation, we propose that it figures crucially in the participants' production and understanding of the two utterances.[23] Note, further, that this implicit use of "student at X University" is abstract rather than concrete, since the talk it is used to warrant is in terms of a category-bound activity.

Next, we look at a segment from the same conversation that will exemplify the production of abstraction as a step-by-step process and the fact that abstraction and concreteness depend on the way a category is used on a given occasion.

```
 1. George:   There's discuss:ion: an:: short- .h there's ya know written
 2.           an' oral exams frequently. Er- once in a while at least.
 3. Laura:    Yeah, I'd like to take uh- ┌something like┐ HISt'ry of
              philosophy                 └             ┘
 4. George:                               └.hhh-hh-hh-hh┘
 5. Laura:    'r something where you don' afta do any of that kind- I
              don't thINK
 6.           that way, I'm not that logical. I never go step by step.
 7.                            (1.2)
 8. Laura:    "N I just- I'm REally an irRAtional person sometimes. So
 9.                            (1.4)
10. George:   Where do you li:ve in Eye Vee? or
11. Laura:    Yeah I live in uh- at the Tropicana
12. George:   A:h
13. Laura:    Good ole' Trop
14. George:   'Dja try to get into the dorms or
```

In the first turn (lines 1–2), George completes a brief description of a philosophy course. Laura, in line 3, gives an acknowledgment, "Yeah," and continues an account of the kind of course she would like to take (line 3). Thus Laura's turn begins with a description of herself in terms of an activity ("I'd like to take something like history of philosophy") again bound to the category "student at X University." Following that, she provides a characterization of the course ("'r something where you don' afta do any of that kind-" in line 5), but cuts that utterance off and issues a series of self-assessments, "I don't think that way," "I'm not that logical," "I never go step by step" (lines 5–6) not bound to category membership in the way the prior utterance is. Thus, the category-bound activity (taking a class) is utilized to warrant the particularized self-assessments, and hence according to our definition the category "student at X University" is used concretely here.

After line 6, however, which is a transition relevance place at which George can appropriately initiate a turn (Sacks, et al., 1974), there is a large silence. In line 8, Laura provides an additional self-assessment ("I'm really an irrational person sometimes") followed by "so," and then there is another silence, again at a transition relevance place, at which George elects not to talk. The effect of both of these silences (lines 7 and 9) is to bring the topic to a close and thereby prepare the way for the introduction of a new topic (see Maynard, forthcoming, for a more detailed analysis). At line 10, George asks a question ("Where do you live in Eye Vee?"), the relevance of which is provided not by Laura's immediately preceding self-description but again by her membership in the category "student at X University." Laura's reply (line 11), "Yeah I live in uh- at the Tropicana," is a reference to a locally well-known apartment house in Eye Vee, a community bordering on X University. In line 12, George acknowledges Laura's reply, and in line 13, Laura produces an assessment of the apartment, "Good ole Trop." Then, in line 14, George asks another question employing a category-bound activity as a candidate description of Laura. In both questions (lines 10 and 14), then, George pursues talk on matters relevant to any person in the category "student at X University." That is, George is using the category *abstractly.* And further, through a series of maneuvers, including George's declining to take the turn at points that would grant sequential implicativeness[24] to Laura's concrete talk, and through invoking questions and answers that perpetuate the abstract use of the category "student at X University," the participants engage in the procedural accomplishment of an abstracted relationship.

In sum, the use of a particular membership category can be abstract or concrete on a given occasion, depending on how it figures in the actual talk. How it is employed and treated on a turn-by-turn basis has consequences for the accountable nature of the participants' relationship as it is constructed and displayed through their interaction. However, as we have already noted, abstraction is not identical with reification, and we turn now to the way abstract use of categories can become locked in so that the enforceable reality in a situation comes to consist of abstracted categories and abstracted relations between them.

The Production of Reification

Consider the following change in a courtroom. The interaction is between a judge, a public defender (P.D.), and a district attorney (D.A.) regarding a defendent who had earlier pled guilty to second degree burglary; the defendent was also present but did not speak. The question now before the court is that of sentencing.[25]

1. P.D.:   Your Honor, we request immidiate sentencing and
2.   waive the probation report.
3. Judge: What's his record:
4. P.D.:   He has a prior drunk and a GTA [Grand Theft Auto].
5.   Nothing serious. This is just a shoplifting case.
6.   He did enter the K-Mart with the intent to steal.
7.   But really all we have here is a petty theft.

```
 8. Judge:   What do the people have?
 9. D.A.:    Nothing either way.
10. Judge:   Any objections to immediate sentencing?
11. D.A.:    No.
12. Judge:   How long has he been in?
13. P.D.:    Eighty-three days.
14. Judge:   I make this a misdemeanor by P.C. article 17 and
15.          sentence you to ninety days in County Jail, with
16.          credit for time served.
```

We begin with some general observations and then turn to the question of reification.

General structure.   Note that the segment begins with a request by the P.D. (lines 1–2) and ends with a response by the Judge to the request (lines 14–16). The exchange as a whole is an instance of a common type of conversational structure, a request–response pair (Schegloff, 1972: 76–77). The basic structure of such a pair is <request, response>, where the slot immediately following the request is to be filled by a response, and absence of a response at that point would be noticeable and call for repair, such as repetition of the request. However, this basic structure can be transformed into the more complex form <request, insertion sequence, response>, in which the insertion sequence is seen neither as a response to the request nor as occasion for noting the absence of a response (Schegloff, 1972:78,109–10). Rather, an insertion sequence displays an orientation to the initial request by eliciting formulations relevant to providing the response.[26] In the present example, then, lines (3–13) comprise an insertion sequence.

There are two important points to note here about an insertion sequence. First, in any given turn, the speaker is accountable for displaying understanding of the preceding utterance.[27] Second, in each turn in the insertion sequence the speaker is accountable for displaying an orientation to what is required to construct the response, since it is this orientation that allows the talk in the insertion sequence to be seen as neither the response itself nor a noticeable absence of response. In any given turn in the insertion sequence the speaker is heard as displaying both an orientation to the initial request and projected response and an understanding of the prior talk as similarly oriented.

Consider the P.D.'s rejoinder in lines 4–7 to the Judge's question, "What's his record." The first utterance by the P.D., "He has a prior drunk and a GTA" (line 4), could by itself be heard as an answer to the question insofar as the question itself is heard as oriented to the request for sentencing and the defendant's prior record is understood as bearing on provision of a response to that request. In addition, however, the P.D. expands this initial statement by systematic topical development procedures. The topical structure of the P.D.'s reply as a whole can be outlined as follows:

a. Person description, consisting of a list of prior offenses ("He has a prior drunk and a GTA")

b. Assessment ("Nothing serious")

c. Refocus ("This is really just a shoplifting case")

d. Acknowledgement of culpability ("He did enter the K-Mart with intent to steal")

e. Minimization of the offense ("But really all we have here is a petty theft").

The first of these, *a*, constitutes a possible direct answer to the Judge's question. However, it is followed by an assessment, *b*, which is a prototypical terminator of a line of talk (Pomeranz, 1975:40), and then by a refocusing, *c*, that shifts the referent from the defendant and his prior record to the case now under consideration. Consequently, the refocusing is an orderly event prepared for by the preceding terminating assessment, *b*. Moreover, this shift is done by describing the present offense as "just a shoplifting case," which implies dissent from the original felony charge, which is made explicit in *d*, and *e* by a general procedure for doing disagreements in conversation (Pomeranz, 1975): provision of an agreement, *d*, followed by a contrasting component, *e*, conjoined to the agreement by a transition marker ("but really"). The P.D. produces a formulation of the offense in a sequential manner that, viewed in terms of its internal structure, is topically procedural. However, there is also a further point to note. This turn by the P.D. is located within the insertion sequence and, as part of that sequence, is oriented to the initial request for sentencing. Observe, for example, that it is in the context of sentencing that the characterization "This is really just a shoplifting case," *c*, can be heard as a disagreement with the original burglary charge, for, from some other point of view, "shoplifting" and "burglary" might be heard as equivalent: they are both crimes, and, indeed, both are nonviolent property crimes. But in the context of sentencing the difference between the two is relevant, one being a misdemeanor and the other a felony. The status of *c* as an implicit disagreement and the relevance of the subsequent explicit disagreement procedure in *d* and *e* depend on the initial request for sentencing and thereby display an orientation to that context. In sum, the P.D.'s reply to the Judge's question in line 3 is constructed using systematic procedures of topical development, where the fitting of one utterance to the next throughout this turn (lines 4–7) depends on the larger insertion sequence context.

We see, then, that the question–answer pair in lines 3 and 4–7 displays an orientation to the initial request for sentencing. Moreover, each further question–answer pair in the insertion sequence (lines 8–13) exhibits a similar orientation. And finally, in lines 14–16 the Judge displays this orientation in providing response to the P.D.'s original request by in fact pronouncing sentence.

Reification.   The crucial point for our purposes is that it is through the abstract use of categories that each turn in the sentencing exchange is constructed and displays a dual orientation to both the prior utterance and the request for sentencing. The P.D.'s turn in lines 4–7 employs a series of classifications that are relevant to anyone without regard to the particular circumstances of his or her offense. "Shoplifting," "prior drunk," "GTA," "intent to steal," "petty theft," are all categories deriving from the penal code and the subculture of the courtroom (Rosett and Cressey, 1976:81–94). And each of the series of questions and answers following the P.D.'s turn (lines 8–13) and the Judge's sentencing further maintain the abstract use of categories.

In this exchange, then, the eminently concrete and social character of the individual's offense, why it was done and how it should be treated, takes on the character of relationships between legal categories that could apply to various individuals regardless of their particular circumstances. The defendent is a man with a "prior drunk" and "GTA." He did enter with "intent to steal" but it was just a "petty theft," which offense is made into "a misdemeanor by P.C. article 17." In other words, who the defendant is, what he did, and what will happen to him appear as character and action attatched to categories rather than to concrete persons and situations. The individual thus is a derivative of the categories, and what is treated as real consists of what is formulated in terms of these categories. This, we propose, is the reification as it is produced in social interaction.

Summary.   The primary conversational mechanism in the last illustration is a request–response pair with an insertion sequence. While this mechanism can be and is employed in a wide variety of contexts, it is not the only one through which the structure of interaction is built. There are, for example, question–answer pairs, various ways of formulating place and time, mechanisms for assuring the orderly exchange of turns, procedures for repairing failures in understanding, and so on. A central feature of all of these mechanisms, however, is that their correct and competent use requires the speaker in a given turn to display understanding of what has been said up until then in relation to the actual context in which the interaction is taking place.[28] The crucial question with respect to reification, then, is the manner in which categories and impersonal talk figure in this process of understanding: to the extent that categories are used in the abstract mode to the exclusion of their concrete use, so that the projects and purposes of the interaction are completed in terms of categories used abstractly, we can say that the effective reality, the basis for warranted inference and action, is a reified one consisting precisely of abstracted categories and abstracted relations between them.

Implications

In the foregoing examples, the abstract use of categories might be attributed to idiosyncratic characteristics of the persons and situations, and certainly this seems plausible for the first two excerpts. However, though we do not have the data to demonstrate the point, we suggest that what we have analyzed as the production of reification in the courtroom example is capable of being seen by the participants and other members as warranted grounds for inferring that the sentencing on this occasion was done "objectively" and "impartially," without intrusion of favoritism or prejudice, and in conformity with the law. Such matters are, of course, a concern for members, taking the form of issues such as "due process," "rights of the accused," "protection for society," "reversible error," and the like, that could appropriately be raised on subsequent occasions. Note further the peculiarly powerful nature of the process in this example: the defendant's record, which in part determines the out-come of the present case, is characterized in terms of precisely the same sort of categories used throughout this interactional episode, but that record itself is the product of the same kind of interaction we have just examined (cf., Smith, 1974b). Thus, if this person has further encounters with the criminal justice system, the concrete particulars of his present offense will not appear in the record but rather only the legal categories employed in the current interaction. We propose, then, that it is through the fact that particular situations of interaction constitute retrospective and prospective contexts for one another that social categories come to be reified, not accidentally in isolated situations, but systematically across situations within the context of the criminal justice process.[29]

We must emphasize that this reflexive connection between concrete occasions of interaction making up the criminal justice process and between these occasions and the institution itself is not metaphorical or metaphysical, but rather concrete and empirical. For, it is clear that in the episode we have examined coherent organization of interaction on that occasion depends on the orientation of the participants to both what is implied by previous actions, as in references to the defendant's record, and what the present action implies for the future, in this case, the matter of sentencing. More generally, we propose that competent participation in any such interaction requires this kind of orientation to context, but equally the character of the context to which the participants are oriented is itself produced in these same interactions. Thus, we argue, reification is not some preexisting quality of the criminal justice system that is somehow imposed externally on particular occasions. Rather, the systematic reification of categories is produced in concrete interaction, which in turn reproduces the institutional context.

Note further that while some of the categories employed in the courtroom illustration apply to matters occurring outside the context of the criminal justice system, such as the present offense, others pertain to the personnel and activities within the institution itself, such as sentencing. Thus, the social structure of the criminal justice system is not only reifying, in the sense that it systematically produces reification across the concrete situations comprising it; in addition, it is self-reified to the extent that the categories pertaining to its own personnel and activities are among those that are systematically reified. The peculiar feature of a self-reified social structure is that it produces a systematically abstracted account of its own structure and functioning, and it is perhaps in this sense that the term "reified" is most appropriately used in a Marxian context.[30]

In a more speculative vein, we can connect these ideas with Weber's discussion of rationalization and bureaucracy by suggesting that formal rationality in Weber's sense (1922:220,298–9) requires the use of categories in the abstract mode. Thus, to the extent that the effective reality in an institution is constituted by formally rational discourse, the activities of that institution are reified. This suggests in turn that pervasive reification in an institutional setting cannot be construed as a scheme by those in dominant or administrative positions to hide some allegedly "real" state of affairs from others.[31] Rather, as Smith (forthcoming) has noted, particular categories and their use in the abstract mode embody and define the basic interests and practical concerns of decision makers and administrators. This, in turn, raises the intriguing possibility that it is those in positions of power and influence within such institutions who are, more than any other group, prone to mistake accounts in terms of abstract categories for the realities they purport to describe.

In conclusion, we note that social structure can be reified not only by the members of society in the processes of their day-to-day interaction but also in the discourse of social scientists. Thus, to the extent that social scientists treat social categories, norms, and the like as existing independently of the particular contexts in which they are produced, their conceptual schemes and theories deal not with society but with reified abstractions. When such abstractions are derived from abstractions reified within society itself, social theory mirrors the ideological pre-occupations of society (cf., Smith, 1974a). And when reified abstractions, formulated, for example, as sociological concepts such as status, role, and so on, are applied to a society in which such notions are not native, the result is, we hold, thoroughgoing distortion of life as it is actually lived by the people in question. In either case, social science loses its grasp on social reality and defaults on its promise of providing a rational empirical understanding of how a particular society is organized and functions.

CRITICAL ISSUES

We have ignored until now several issues that might call our enterprise into question. Some of these have been dealt with elsewhere (Wilson, 1971; Zimmerman, 1976, 1978), but here we must take up three matters that are directly relevant.

The first of these is raised by Giddens, among others, who argues that, while ethnomethodology is correct in viewing the production of society as a skilled accomplishment of its members, it neglects the fact that "if men make society, they do not do so merely under conditions of their own choosing" (1976:102,126). In a similar vein Smith (1975:367) has remarked that, in seeking to study the everyday world as a phenomenon, ethnomethodology cuts that world off "from the ways it is in fact embedded in a socially organized context larger than may be directly known" from within the particular setting; that is, she argues, there are aspects of any given situation that do not emerge out of a logic intrinsic to that setting (Smith, 1975:370). And related misgivings have been expressed by others (e.g., Chua, 1977). We have here the obverse of the criticism we directed earlier at Marxian thought, namely, its neglect of how social structure is produced and reproduced in direct interaction, with a resulting tendency to reify social structure in spite of the avowed commitment to demystify. It is important, then, to attempt some clarification of the issues.

In fact most ethnomethodological research is ahistorical but it is so by virtue of its explicit concern for how the features of particular settings are produced by members' activities within the setting itself. Obviously, when the focus of investigation is the analysis of the way accounts are produced, one must suspend temporarily concern for other matters, in particular for the "adequacy, value, importance, necessity, practicality, success, or consequentiality" of those accounts (Garfinkel and Sacks, 1970:345). But this is not an ethnomethodological "principle," much less an epistemological, ontological, or metaphysical commitment; instead, it is merely a "procedural policy" (Garfinkel and Sacks, 1970:345) that directs attention to the specific phenomena of interest to ethnomethodology per se. Clearly, this policy of "ethnomethodological indifference" does not justify the claim sometimes heard that ethnomethodology denies the possibility of analyzing historically situated social structures. Rather, it merely states that such analysis is not the task of ethnomethodology as such.[32]

Unfortunately, however, the issue has been confused considerably by the way ethnomethodological criticisms of conventional sociology have been formulated. The usual statement of the ethnomethodological critique is that the features of a given setting cannot be generalized across settings since the apparent trans-situational character of those features depends on the situated activity of members. And this indeed does appear to deny the possibility of a coherent analysis of trans-situational social structures. This familiar version of the ethnomethodological critique is misleading and must be revised: the point is that one cannot extract the feature of particular settings from the reflexive contexts in which they are embedded and treat them without reference to their social context, for to do so is to engage in precisely that sort of abstraction that results in reification (cf., Wilson and Zimmerman, 1980). Thus, the ethnomethodological objection to conventional sociology is not that it concerns itself with large-scale social structures, but rather that, in pursuit of the natural science model, it ignores the fact that the features of such social structures are produced in actual interaction between real people and cannot be analyzed as though they existed independently of the activities that produce them. But, to recognize that the features of a setting are produced by the activities of the members of that setting is not to deny that these features are at the same time aspects of institutional and historical processes. And, conversely, institutional and historical processes must be seen as aspects of situated activity of real people if they are not to be reified as independently existing social "forces" or "structures." The relationship between "micro" and "marco" social phenomena is, as we have attempted to illustrate, a reflexive one.

The second issue is a corollary of the first and can be dealt with more briefly. If, it is sometimes argued, features of occasions constitute a reflexive context, it makes no sense to attempt to count or otherwise quantify them. Hence, the conclusion is drawn that survey, economic, census, and other quantitative data have no legitimate place in the study of social phenomena. However, this claim overlooks the distinction between the use of quantitative data in any fashion and the specific presuppositions underlying some particular mode of interpreting quantitative data. There is in fact nothing to prevent interpreting quantitative data as reflexively interdependent with the interpretation of information from other sources, such as documents, direct observation, interviews with informants, and so on. This, of course, means that the results of statistical analyses, no matter how sophisticated, cannot be treated literally and as standing independent of other data (Wilson, 1970), but such a conception of quantitative sociological data in any event would involve an untenable reification of social structure. There are, then, no grounds for rejecting the use in sociological analyses of quantitative data per se. Rather, the appropriate objection is to abstracting such data from the reflexive contexts in which they are embedded and treating them as having the same sort of analytically independent status that is accorded descriptions in the natural sciences.

The third issue is the question of how, using the approach we have proposed, one could establish general trans-historical propositions about social structure. For, if even quantitative sociological data must be interpreted reflexively rather than literally, the very logical possibility of such universal generalizations disappears. Thus, a fatal weakness in the whole approach appears to be that its results, however fascinating or illuminating of the particular, remain tied to the particular. In short, sociology would become a purely ideographic discipline, not the nomothetic science it should be.

This objection, though, takes for granted an unexamined assumption that we expressly reject, namely that there can be a genuine nomothetic sociology modeled on the natural sciences. To be sure, the vision of a scientific sociology has fascinated sociologists from August Comte (1822) to Peter Blau (1980), and there is much talk about science in sociological methods' textbooks and theoretical treatises. However, the actual achievements of sociology in the way of establishing conceptually precise nontrivial general propositions about social structure that hold true across cultural and historical contexts are meagre or nonexistent, despite recurring claims to the contrary. Thus, the conception of sociology as a nomothetic science is at best an ideal that remains unrealized despite the efforts of generations of sociologists. One can, then, without flying in the face of the facts, hold that the ideal itself is unrealizable and inappropriate, and that its pursuit leads to a distorted picture of the nature of social phenomena. So long as the scientific status of sociology remains merely an assumption, rejection of that assumption cannot be criticized simply on the grounds that it denies the assumption.

In addition to this formal consideration there is a more important substantive point: the nomothetic–ideographic distinction is too crude to be useful here. Within a given historical social structure, there are of course apparent regularities (across situations or individuals located in distinctive places within the structure) that seem to operate independently of particular human intentions. These regularities, which consist of patterns of actions meaningful to the members of society that transcend particular persons and situations and may in fact be unknown to members, are the stuff of substantive sociology (Wilson, 1970).[33] Typically they are described by propositions of covariation, frequently multivariate, that have a lawlike form. However, the crucial point is that the categories and propositions in terms of which such substantive regularities are described cannot be abstracted and applied to all social structures, irrespective of time or place. Rather, the relevance of the concepts is itself an aspect of the society in question, codetermined with other aspects. Hence sociological concepts must be treated as historically situated (cf., Wilson and Zimmerman, 1980), and the lawlike character of propositions describing such regularities is codeterminate with meaningful activities in society that cannot be formulated in the propositions themselves. The implication of this is not that sociologists should not seek to discover regular patterns in social phenomena; instead it is that sociological explanation does not stop with the formulation of general-seeming propositions. One must proceed from this point to provide an empirically grounded analysis as to why these particular propositions hold at this particular time in a particular society. Failure to carry out this last analysis is to substitute reified images for an understanding of how society works.

CONCLUSION

Methodological questions have been particularly important to our argument. The classical dualisms in Western thought have pervaded much of sociological theorizing through a unilateral or bilateral causal conception of the relation between the individual and society. Even approaches that ostensibly draw on Marx tend to perpetuate a parallel treatment of two analytically independent domains, individual and society, which we argue must be understood instead as reflexively connected. This is important for understanding reification, that is, removing some concrete phenomenon from the reflexive connections in which it is embedded and in which its realization is attained and treating it in its removed state as if that were its real existence. Commodities are reifications to the extent that they appear to have an existence apart from the concrete labor which produces them, to the extent that they appear as qualitatively equivalent in terms of their exchange value, to the extent, in short, that they are removed from the totality of working relationships involved in their manufacture, distribution, exchange, and consumption. The same can be said for such standard sociological concepts as status, role, and culture. Reification, then, is not, as Berger and Luckmann (1966:90) would have it, simply a matter of bestowing ontological independence on institutions or structures or roles. Rather, it is treating social forms as not merely as real but as separable from the reflexive contexts wherein they are produced by, and are aspects of, acting, creating individuals—their interrelations and their actions.

Reification is apparent not only in the way social scientists theorize about social structure, and in the ways members of society themselves employ notions of how economy and society work, but indeed also in face-to-face interaction. It is an outcome of specific interactional procedures that accomplish, in the kinds of conversational accounts that are collaboratively made to happen, the removal of individuals from their biographical contexts of interaction and activity and the transformation of those individuals and their activities into derivatives of the categories employed in such conversational accounts.

In closing we wish to stress three major points. First, in speaking of the conventional sociological conception of social structure as "reified" we are not suggesting that social structure is not real, but rather that the nature of its reality and relation to human action is fundamentally different from what is usually taken for granted. Second, this in turn calls for a different conception of the nature of social science than has dominated the imagination of the field since Comte. Rather than seeking to emulate the natural sciences in the search for universal, transhistorical concepts and laws, the task of sociology is the analysis of specific social structures and how they work within the context of their historical development. This, we hold, is a rational empirical enterprise, even though it cannot be pursued on the model of the natural sciences. Instead, the evidence concerning particular historical social structures must be interpreted contextually, so that each fact, rather than being what it is in isolation, gets its essential meaning from its reflexive connections with other facts, whether these be the result of the most searching and circumspect historical analyses of documents or the most sophisticated applications of modern quantitative techniques. Further, lawlike regularities, instead of being the end of explanation must themselves be explained in relation to underlying institutional arrangements in the particular society. Third, though we have drawn heavily on ideas from Marx and ethnomethodology, what we regard as important is not loyalty to the original texts but rather understanding social life. The question is not, what is the Marxian or ethnomethodological "position" on some question, but, instead, what is the nature of the social world and how does it work?

ACKNOWLEDGMENTS

Revised version of a paper presented at the 1977 Annual Meeting of the American Sociological Association. Thanks go to Richard P. Appelbaum and Don H. Zimmerman for helpful comments. The sequence of the authors' names reflects an alphabetical ordering rather than a division of labor. This research was supported in part by the Social Process Research Institute, University of California, Santa Barbara.

NOTES

1. On analytical independence, see Parsons (1937:31–34).

2. The work of Berger and Pullberg (1966) and Berger and Luckmann (1966) seems to be an exception. However, when their argument is examined in detail, this appearance dissolves (see n. 9, below). Israel (1971) provides a more satisfactory account but neglects the central issue of this paper, namely, the production of reification in social interaction. Reification, of course, has been a central concern in British and European sociology. However, our purpose here is not to review this literature, but to propose a distinctive approach informed by an ethnomethodological perspective.

3. See Brewer (1974) for a massive review of empirical evidence concerning operant conditioning, and Glucksmann (1974) and Appelbaum (1979) on structuralism. Glucksmann's critique of structuralism is far more conclusive than she appears to recognize in her final remarks. Note that Glucksmann construes "structuralism" broadly, so as to include, e.g., Althusser (1969). For an interpretation of structuralism that excludes Althusser, see Pettit (1975).

4. We follow Giddens (1971:185,fn.2) in using the term *Marxian* to refer to ideas we attribute directly to Marx; we use *Marxist* (and *Marxism*) for interpretations and elaborations by professed followers of Marx.

5. The argument in this paper raises an extraordinarily wide range of issues that cannot be ignored. We ask readers to bear with what may seem like unnecessary elaboration of matters that they may take for granted but which may be unfamiliar or problematic to others.

6. It is important to reemphasize that this framework is indifferent to whether equilibrium, conflict, or interaction is the fundamental concern. For example, Chambliss and Seidman (1971) and Collins (1975), avowed conflict theorists, explicitly employ this set of fundamental notions. Note further Turner's argument (1974:103) that Dahrendorf, another self-identified conflict theorist, employs essentially this same framework. Contemporary symbolic interactionism, in contrast with the earlier Chicago school, also invokes this conceptual scheme, particularly when large-scale social structures are considered. See Wilson (1970) for a brief discussion of some of the issues.

7. The critical documents are Parsons (1937), Radcliffe-Brown (1937), and Merton (1949).

8. It must be noted, of course, that holist and individualist assumptions have not altogether vanished from contemporary social thought. The former, for example, appear in the structuralisms of Lévi-Strauss and Althusser, and the latter are evident in views such as Skinner's and Homan's as well as in much of contemporary economic theory.

9. Berger, Pullberg, and Luckmann's efforts are instructive in this regard. In seeking to reconstruct the sociology of knowledge in a manner critical of structural functionalism, they ask how Weber's meaningful actions can become Durkheim's social facts, and to answer the query they propose to employ notions drawn from Marx. Their foundations, however, are primarily phenomenological rather than Marxian, and they commit themselves to both a neo-Kantian methodological individualism and the assumption that the structure of consciousness can be analyzed independently of cultural and historical circumstances, which is fundamental to a phenomenological approach. As a consequence, they have no way of getting outside the consciousness of the isolated individual except by invoking the independent existence of society (e.g., Berger and Luckmann, 1966:57–8). One result is that "the dialectic" in practice comes to mean internalization of culture by individuals through socialization, and individuals then acting in those terms to create the circumstances under which the next generation is socialized. Another is that their exposition is internally inconsistent. For instance, the role given to society in the socialization process seems incompatible with the methodological individualism presupposed in their commitment to Schutz's framework. But what is most important here is that their abstract description of the notion of dialectical relations sounds very Marxian, while their actual use of the term renders it simply

as an obscure way of talking about reciprocal causal process. In the end, when Berger, Pullberg, and Luckmann's *actual explanatory apparatus* is considered, their theory reduces a fairly standard version of structural functionalism couched in exotic terminology, and both their criticisms of structural functionalism and their invocations of Marxian terminology seem oddly incongruent with what they actually do.

10. See Wilson and Zimmerman (1980). This concept is discussed as a "gestalt contexture" by Gurwitsch (1974), and Gurwitsch's approach is developed further in application to phenomenological sociology by Wieder (1975). However, we avoid this terminology in order not to commit ourselves to the Husserlian phenomenological presuppositions of their work.

11. The literature on pattern recognition in psychology and artificial intelligence is vast. The relevant point is that work in these areas depends on restricting applications so that the reflexive aspects of the problem can be dealt with by the theorist or programmer rather than the theory or the program. For example, see ARPA SUR Steering Committee (1977), Winograd (1972a,b), and Newall and Simon (1972); Raphael (1976) provides an easily accessible overview. In these reports absorption of reflexivity by the programmer is evident though ignored by the various authors. Dreyfus (1972) and Weizenbaum (1976) offer useful critiques of the field, Weizenbaum's being better informed. An exuberant account of the artificial intelligence field is given by Simon (1977) who, however, ignores the questions that have been raised. In psychology, recent work appears to be dominated almost totally by the computer model (e.g., Estes, 1975). Contextual phenomena are, of course, well known in the psychological literature (e.g., Neisser, 1968; Lindsay and Norman, 1972); it is their significance that has been overlooked.

12. It might be thought that a fundamental, context-free descriptive vocabulary could be borrowed from the natural sciences, but this is not so. For, in the natural sciences, the world is viewed in abstraction from the particular practical motives and concerns of people and interpreted solely within a scientific conceptual framework in which purposes, myths, and values have no proper place. This approach is historically a very peculiar one that can be sustained only under quite special circumstances and which is not tenable in everyday life (cf., Garfinkel, 1967:Chap. 8). The importance of a scientific community in establishing and maintaining the framework within such scientific description has its meaning is, of course, by now a commonplace. What is of particular note, however, is that the observer in the natural sciences is not concerned with whatever meanings, if any, planets may give to their motions, but rather need only understand the meaning of discourse within the relevant scientific community. In contrast, the phenomena of interest to the sociologist cannot be defined or identified without explicit or implicit reference to meanings held by the persons whose actions are being studied (for a critique of behaviorism on this score, see Powers, 1973, especially pp. 351–352; see also Wilson, 1970).

13. It should be emphasized again that the word "materialism" appearing in Marx's work must be seen in polemical contrast to Hegelian idealism and does not reflect commitment to materialism in the usual philosophical sense. Failure to recognize this fact is evident in orthodox Marxism and underlies the doctrine known as "dialectical materialsm." A contemporary idealist interpretation of Marx can be found in "structuralist" Marxism (e.g., Althusser, 1969; cf., Appelbaum, 1979), in which the leading idea seems to be derived from Marx's directive that appearances must be penetrated to find the essence, but the notions of "dialectic," "appearance," and "essence" are interpreted by structuralists in what amount to Aristotelian terms. In the present view, in contrast, Marx's formula is not a commitment to Aristotelian metaphysics but rather directs attention to the fact that what appears to be an independently existing thing must be located within its reflexive context to be properly understood. A drift toward idealism can also be noted in Ollman's attempt (1971:Chap. 3, ff.) to interpret Marx in terms of a philosophy of internal relations, which holds that all properties and relations of a thing are essential to its being, again in an Aristotelian sense; when this is combined with the usual view that necessary properties are knowable a priori to a suffi-

ciently large mind, the result is an idealist metaphysics (for an effective challenge of this identification of the necessary with the a priori, see Kripke, 1972). Our understanding of Marx coincides perhaps most closely with Appelbaum's (1978), Avineri's (1968), and the first two chapters in Ollman (1971).

14. The closely related concept of alienation can also be defined in these terms: once the reflexive connections between abstracted objects are suppressed from view by reification, each reified object is *alienated* from the others. This definition is considerably more general than Marx's, but in the situations Marx was concerned with, it is equivalent.

15. There has, of course, been a traditional concern in sociology with the rationalization and bureaucratization of human life and activity, and the supercession of formal, impersonal relations over more traditional, informal, and personal relations. In an early analysis, Tönnies (1887) distinguished between *Gemeinschaft* and *Gesellschaft* as orientations in social relations. Weber (1922) later contrasted formal with substantive rationality in bureaucratic and legal settings, Mannheim (1929) discussed a similar opposition between functional and substantive rationality, and Merton (1968), among other contemporaries, has noted the difference in terms of primary versus secondary relations. Some sociologists argue that the problem in present-day society is attaining the proper balance between formal and substantive rationality (Merton, 1968:258–259), or in maintaining a formalized structure which performs functions that would be impossible through less formalized relationships (Bendix, 1949:87–88). However, others have expressed concern over an inevitable and ubiquitous progression of impersonal relations, a tendency for social relations in all spheres to move toward the *Gesellschaft* or formally rational pole rather than the *Gemeinschaft* or substantively rational one (Weber, 1909; Holland, 1974:201).

From the Marxian perspective we are given the picture of a society wherein commodities and commodity relations have come to dominate every aspect of life. As the concretely different labor embodied in products is abstracted by relating those products on the basis of the labor time involved in their making, so such relations among things have attained a dominance over actual human relations. Lukacs, who examined extensively how the production process emerges as the a priori of human existence, emphasizes repeatedly that commodity fetishism "stamps its imprint on the whole consciousness of man" (1923:100). Lukacs not only looked to Marx but to Weber as well, for he also probed the role of bureaucracy in amplifying the "formalized, standardized treatment" of affairs such that there is an "increasing remoteness from the material and qualitative" aspects of human relations (1923:99).

However, while much discussion has centered around the problem of formalization of social relations, apparently insofar as it is considered to be a feature of direct interaction, it is viewed as influencing, impinging on, or distorting that interaction. Even Lukacs (1923:100), for example, speaks of human relations being increasingly "subjected to" this process. But, as Marx stated, the given relation of individuals to nature and one another is at each historical stage simultaneously a condition and expression of their labor (Marx and Engels, 1846:164–165). Our purpose is to inquire into how reification is an expression of members' interactive work.

16. This, of course, takes for granted the interpretation of Marx's work sketched above. The genealogy of ideas in fact begins in ethnomethodology (see Wilson and Zimmerman, 1980), and retrospectively it was seen that Marx's work could be made sense of by construing his position to be a reflexive one, which then provided the basis for applying the technical apparatus of ethnomethodology to the problem of reification.

17. It is sometimes suggested that the Chicago tradition growing out of American pragmatism via Dewey and Mead embodies a similar conception of social structures. While one may be able to construe the Chicago tradition this way, one must also recognize its explicit pragmatist philosophical foundations, which involve, among other things, the assumption that the methods characteristic of the natural sciences are the highest development of

humankind's effort to know the world, and that this approach should supplant all others. The parallel here with St. Simon and Comte is evident, though the equally important divergence on the score of methodological individualism as opposed to holism should also be noted. In this sense, pragmatism stands squarely within the individualistic voluntarist tradition of Anglo-American scientism. In contrast, in the view advanced here, the approach to knowledge characteristic of the natural sciences is a very specialized one (see n. 12, above). This issue has been muddled on the one hand by Marx's own confusion concerning the epistemological status of the natural sciences, and on the other hand by vulgar interpretations of the orthodox Marxist understanding of praxis, which procede by severing the notion from its reflexive foundations. Thus, in support of a pragmatist interpretation of Marx, one might cite the famous Afterword to the second German edition of *Das Kapital* and a supposed convergence between a denatured idea of praxis and a pragmatist theory of knowledge, but this, in our opinion, does serious violence to the corpus of Marx's thought. It should be noted that Marx's confusion is understandable, since the issues involved did not begin to become clear until the middle of this century when the centrality of Brentano's earlier distinction between extensional and intensional expressions began to be appreciated widely (see Quine, 1951, 1960; Pap, 1958; Putnam, 1962; see also Suppe, 1977, for an overview of recent debates in the philosophy of science).

18. The argument has been made elsewhere regarding the accomplishment of intimacy (Sacks, 1970; Jefferson, 1975) and acquaintedness and anonymity (Zimmerman and Maynard, 1979).

19. The categories associated with a membership categorization device are what are generally referred to as "social categories" in the sociological literature, where we may regard Sacks's formulation (1972a,b) as an important explication of this often loosely used term. While we cannot enter into detail here, it is important to note that the notions of category and category-bound activity are defined in terms of the way members of society employ them in formulating descriptions, e.g., the various user's, hearer's, and viewer's maxims that Sacks (1972a,b) proposes. Our usage, it should be noted, explicitly extends Sacks's formulation to allow, for instance, for an activity being bound to a category if it is seen as being done in response to a preceding event, but we cannot take the space here to develop these extensions explicitly. It should also be emphasized that the notions of social category and category-bound activity do not coincide with the conventional sociological concepts of status and role as developed following Linton, Parsons, and Merton. For example, one of the things babies do is cry, and this activity is bound to the category "baby," but one would hardly want to say that there are sanctioned role expectations requiring babies to cry on specified occasions. Similarly, one of the things students do is be late to classes, but we would call such behavior deviance rather than performance of the student role in the conventional sense. Finally, we observe that the term "role" sometimes is employed in the sense of "social category" as used here, but we shall avoid such usage.

20. The term "abstract mode" is adapted from Smith (in press). However, at some points where she uses the term "abstract," we would use "reified."

21. This is a segment of talk between two previously unacquainted students who had been told to "relax and get to know one another" in a laboratory decorated as a conference room while their conversation was, with their knowledge, audio- and video-recorded. It goes without saying that the laboratory setting influenced and furnished much of the content of the talk that occurred. However, our concern is not with what was said but rather with how it was said. We are indebted to Candace West for the transcripts from which the excerpts in the subsection are drawn. In line 1, the "h" in parentheses indicates a laughter syllable. In line 2, the ":" indicates prolongation of the preceding syllable, and in line 3 "(.)" indicates a very brief pause.

22. On person descriptions, see Maynard (1979).

23. It will be noticed that we are relying here on the reader's as well as our own ability to

understand written English as a resource for the analysis. At first, this might seem to pose a methodological problem, but we should note two points. First, conventional sociological analysis, even of the most quantitative sort, depends for its data on interviewers, coders, and observers understanding what the subjects or respondents did and said, and hence is subject to exactly the same considerations on this score (see Zimmerman, 1979; Wilson, 1970). Second, to be taken seriously, any proposed alternative reading of the transcript must be one that demonstrably provides for the turn-by-turn display of understanding by the participants themselves (Moerman and Sacks, 1971; Schefloff and Sacks, 1973:290, 296 *et passim*; Sacks, Schegloff, and Jefferson, 1974:728–729). This is a very strong requirement that serves to distinguish unconstrained speculative interpretations from genuine ambiguities notable by the speakers. It is, of course, important to emphasize that we are not dealing here with imputations by the analyst of motives or purposes that might give rise to the observed conversation, but rather with the structure of the conversation itself by which the participants pursue whatever purposes they may in fact have.

24. By "sequential implicativeness" of an utterance is meant that in its particular context it projects certain matters and actions as following appropriately (Schegloff and Sacks, 1973; Sacks, et al., 1974). Note that when a previous utterance is used to warrant current talk, the current talk fits within the sequentially implicative context projected by the previous utterance.

25. The transcript is taken from Mather (1973:199–200).

26. We ignore here the possibility of side sequences (Jefferson, 1972), consideration of which would complicate the discussion but not alter the conclusions important for our purposes.

27. See Moerman and Sacks (1971), Schegloff and Sacks (1973), and Sacks, et al. (1974:728). This condition in its simple form is suspended at topic changes (Maynard, forthcoming) and in pretopical sequences (Zimmerman and Maynard, 1979). In the case of an insertion sequence, topical organization is provided for by the initial request that projects a forthcoming response.

28. Technically, this characteristic of conversational structures is known as "context sensitivity." In addition, these mechanisms are also said to be "context free" in the sense that they are available for employment by participants across innumerable particular situations and occasions (Sacks, et al., 1974:699). This approach contrasts sharply with that adopted by Mchoul (1978), which, in effect, proposes that basic conversational mechanisms vary with institutional settings. Instead, we propose that the basic conversational mechanisms are the same across institutional contexts and that the context is observable in a given situation through the context-sensitive use of these mechanisms.

29. It should be emphasized that not all interaction in the criminal justice system, nor even all interaction within the courtroom, is conducted in terms of categories used in the abstract mode. For example, in plea bargaining, the concrete use of categories is very frequent, for in such interactions the task is to determine which of the available categories will be applied to the case at hand (see Maynard, 1979). We suggest that the concrete use of categories will be frequent in just those organizational situations in which it is necessary to locate individuals and events in their "proper" categories; however, on subsequent occasions in which categories are reified, such interactions will not be treated as "real" or as having official standing, but instead the resulting categorizations are what will be taken as the reality.

30. There is a terminological problem here in that we have defined the term "reified" to refer to a certain way of using categories in direct interaction. This, as we noted earlier, can occur because of an adventitious concatenation of circumstances or it can occur as the systematic result of the context in which the interaction is reflexively embedded. In the former case, one might speak of "episodic" reification, and in the latter, of "systemic"

reification. Further, the term "reification" by itself appears to be used in the social science literature predominantly in the sense of systemic reification within a social structure of the categories of that social structure itself, that is, systemic self-reification. We do not seek to legislate terminology here, but it is important to note the nature of the phenomena that can be involved in the various uses of the term "reification."

31. It is perhaps important to recall here that power is a phenomenon of social organization and cannot be exercised by dominant persons or groups unless institutions and organizations function in expected and anticipatable ways. Thus, "power" and "domination" are not things that can be invoked as explanatory or causal factors analytically independent of the processes of social organization with which we are concerned in this paper.

32. Contrary to the impressions of many of its critics, ethnomethodology has never claimed to be a complete sociological framework. Thus, the appropriate question is not, what does ethnomethodology have to say about power or conflict, but what would an ethnomethodologically informed analysis of power or conflict look like? In addition to the general answer proposed here and in Wilson and Zimmerman (1980), see efforts to deal with particular cases, as in Molotch and Lester (1974), Zimmerman and West (1975), and Smith (1974b, forthcoming).

33. It should be emphasized that the conversational mechanisms discussed earlier are not of the same order as the regularities of interest here, but rather are the means by which the latter are produced. Thus, the possibility arises that conversational mechanisms may be trans-situational but the socially meaningful content produced using these mechanisms is not. See Wilson and Zimmerman (1980) for further discussion.

REFERENCES

Appelbaum, Richard P.
  1978   "Marx's theory of the declining rate of profit." *American Sociological Review* 43:67–80.
  1979   "Born-again functionalism? a reconsideration of Althusser's structuralism." *Insurgent Sociologist* 9:18–33.
ARPA SUR Steering Committee
  1977   "Speech understanding systems." SIGART Newsletter 6(Apr.):4–8.
Althusser, Louis
  1969   For Marx. London: Penguin.
Avineri, Shlomo
  1968   The Social and Political Thought of Karl Marx. New York: Cambridge University Press.
Bendix, Reinhard
  1949   Higher Civil Servants in American Society. Boulder: University of Colorado Press.
Berger, Peter, and Thomas Luckmann
  1966   The Social Construction of Reality. Garden City, Doubleday.
Berger, Peter, and Stanley Pullberg
  1965   "Reification and the sociological critique of consciousness." History and Theory 4:196–211.
Blau, Peter M.
  1980   "Elements of sociological theorizing." Humboldt Journal of Social Relations 7:103–122.
Brewer, William F.
  1974   "There is no convincing evidence for operant or classical conditioning in adult humans." Pp. 1–42 in Walter B. Weimer and David S. Palermo (eds.), Cognition and the Symbolic Process. Hillsdale, N.J.: Erlbaum Associates.

Burger, Thomas
   1976   Max Weber's Theory of Concept Formation. Durham, N.C.: Duke University
          Press.
Chambliss, William J., and Robert B. Seidman
   1971   Law, Order, and Power. Reading, Mass.: Addison-Wesley.
Chua, Beng-Huat
   1977   "Delineating a Marxist interest in ethnomethodology." The American Sociologist
          12:24–32.
Coleman, James S.
   1970   "Social inventions." Social Forces 49 (Dec.):163–73.
Collins, Randall
   1975   Conflict Sociology. New York: Academic Press.
Comte, August
   [1822] "Plan of the scientific operations necessary for reorganizing society." Pp. 9–67 in
   1975   Gertrude Lenzer (ed.), August Comte and Positivism. New York: Harper
          Torchbooks.
Dreyfus, Hubert L.
   1972   What Computers Can't Do. New York: Harper & Row.
Durkheim, Emile
   [1901] The Rules of the Sociological Method. New York: Free Press.
   1938
   [1902] The Division of Labor in Society. New York: Free Press.
   1933
Estes, William K.
   1975   Handbook of Learning and Cognitive Processes. Hillsdale, N.J.: Erlbaum
          Associates.
Garfinkel, Harold
   1967   Studies in Ethnomethodology. Englewood Cliffs, N.J.: Prentice-Hall.
Garfinkel, Harold, and Harvey Sacks
   1970   "On Formal Structures of Practical Actions." Pp. 338–66 in John C. McKinney
          and Edward A. Tiryakian (eds.), Theoretical Sociology: Perspectives and
          Development. New York: Appleton-Century-Crofts.
Giddens, Anthony
   1971   Capitalism and Modern Social Theory. New York: Cambridge University Press.
   1976   New Rules of the Sociological Method. New York: Basic Books.
Glucksmann, Miriam
   1974   Structuralist Analysis in Contemporary Social Thought. Boston: Routledge &
          Kegan Paul.
Gurwitsch, Aron
   1964   The Field of Consciousness. Pittsburgh: Duquesne University Press.
Halévy, Elie
   1955   The Growth of Philosophic Radicalism. Boston: Beacon Press.
Hayek, F.A.
   1952   The Counter-Revolution of Science. Glencoe, Ill.: Free Press.
Holland, John B.
   1974   "Contrasting types of group relationships." Pp. 197–201 in Edgar A. Schuler, et
          al. (eds.), Readings in Sociology. New York: Crowell.
Israel, Joachim
   1971   Alienation: From Marx to Modern Sociology, A Macrosociological Analysis.
          Boston: Allyn and Bocon.

Jefferson, Gail
　　1972　"Side sequences." Pp. 294–337 in David Sudnow (ed.), Studies in Social Interaction. New York: Free Press.
　　1975　Unpublished lectures. Department of Sociology, University of California, Santa Barbara.
Kripke, Saul
　　1972　"Naming and necessity." Pp. 253–55 in Gilbert Harmon and Donald Davidson (eds.), Semantics of Natural Language. Dordrecht, Netherlands: Reidel.
Lindsay, Peter H., and Donald A. Norman
　　1972　Human Information Processing. New York: Academic Press.
Lukacs, Georg
　[1923]　History and Class Consciousness. Cambridge, Mass.: M.I.T. Press.
　　1971
Lukes, S.
　　1973　Emile Eurkheim: His life and Work. An Historical Study. Baltimore: Penguin.
Mannheim, Karl
　[1929]　Man and Society in an Age of Reconstruction. Boston: Routledge & Kegan Paul.
　　1940
Marcuse, Herbert
　　1960　Reason and Revolution. Boston: Beacon Press.
Marx, Karl
　[1844]　"Economic and Philosophic Manuscripts of 1844." Pp. 66–125 in Robert C. Tucker
　1978a　(ed.), The Marx-Engels Reader, 2nd ed. New York: Norton
　[1845]　"Theses on Feuerbach." Pp. 143–5 in Robert C. Tucker (ed.), The Marx–Engels
　1978b　Reader, 2nd ed. New York: Norton.
　[1887]　Capital, Vol. I. New York: International Publ.
　　1967
Marx, Karl, and Frederick Engels
　[1846]　The German Ideology, Part I. Pp. 147–200 in Robert C. Tucker (ed.), The Marx–
　　1978　Engels Reader, 2nd ed. New York: Norton.
Mather, Lynn M.
　　1973　"Some determinants of the method of case disposition: decision-making by public defenders in Los Angeles." Law and Society (Winter):187–217.
Maynard, Douglas
　　1975　"The initiation of topic in conversation." Unpublished Master's thesis, University of California, Santa Barbara.
　　1979　"People processing: plea bargaining in municipal court." Unpublished Ph.D. dissertation, University of California, Santa Barbara.
　Forth　"Placement of topic changes in conversation." Semiotica.
　coming
Mchoul, Alexander
　　1978　"The organization of turns at formal talk in the classroom." Language and Society 7:183–213.
Merton, Robert K.
　　1949　Social Theory and Social Structure. New York: Free Press.
　　1968　Social Theory and Social Structure, enlarged ed. New York: Free Press.
　　1976　"Social knowledge and public policy." Pp. 156–79. In Sociological Ambivalence and Other Essays, New York: Free Press.
Moerman, Michael, and Harvey Sacks
　　1971　"On 'understanding' in the analysis of natural conversation." Presented at the American Anthropological Association Annual Meeting. New York.

Molotch, Harvey, and Marilyn Lester
1974 "News as purposive behavior: on the strategic use of routine events, accidents, and scandals." American Sociological Review 39:101–112.
Neisser, Ulric
1966 Cognitive Psychology. New York: Appleton-Century-Crofts.
Newall, Allen, and Herbert A. Simon
1972 Human Problem Solving. Englewood Cliffs, N.J.: Prentice-Hall.
Ollman, Bertell
[1971] Alienation: Marx's Concept of Man in Capitalist Society, 2nd ed. New York:
1976 Cambridge University Press.
Pap, Arthur
1958 "Disposition concepts and extensional logic." Minnesota Studies in the Philosophy of Science 2:196–224.
Parsons, Talcott
1937 The Structure of Social Action. New York: McGraw-Hill.
Pettit, Philip
1975 The Concept of Structuralism: A Critical Analysis. Berkeley: University of California Press.
Pomeranz, Anita
1975 Second Assessments: A Study of Some Features of Agreements/Disagreements. Unpublished Ph.D. dissertation, University of California, Irvine.
Powers, William T.
1973 "Feedback: beyond behaviorism." Science 179(26 Jan.):351–6.
Putnam, Hillary
1962 "What theories are not." Pp. 240–51 in Ernest Nagel, Patrick Suppes, and Alfred Tarski (eds.), Logic, Methodology, and Philosophy of Science: Proceedings of the 1960 International Congress. Stanford, Calif.: Stanford University Press.
Quine, W.V.
1951 "Two dogmas of empiricism." Philosophical Review 60:20–43.
1960 Word and Object. Cambridge, Mass.: M.I.T. Press
Radcliffe-Brown, A.R.
[1937] A Natural Science of Society. Glencoe, Ill.: Free Press.
1957
Raphael, Bertram
1976 The Thinking Computer. San Francisco: Freeman.
Rosett, Arthur, and Donald R. Cressey
1976 Justice by Consent: Plea Bargains in the American Courthouse. Philadelphia: Lippincott.
Sacks, Harvey
1963 "Sociological description." Berkeley Journal of Sociology 8:1–16.
1970 Unpublished lecture transcription. University of California, Irvine (Feb. 6).
1972a "An initial investigation of the usability of conversational data for sociology." Pp. 31–75 in D. Sudnow (ed.), Studies in Social Interaction. New York: Free Press.
1972b "On the analyzability of stories by children." Pp. 325–45 in John J. Gumperz and Dell Hymes (eds.), Directions in Sociolinguistics: The Ethnography of Communication. New York: Holt, Rinehart and Winston.
Sacks, Harvey, Emanuel Schegloff, and Gail Jefferson
1974 "A simplest systematics for the organization of turn-taking for conversation." Language 50:696–735.
Schegloff, Emanuel
1972 "Notes on a conversational practice: formulating place." Pp. 75–119 in David Sudnow (ed.), Studies in Social Interaction. New York: Free Press.

Schegloff, Emanuel, and Harvey Sacks
1973 "Opening up closings." Semiotica 8:289–327.
Simon, Herbert A.
1977 "What computers mean for man and society." Science 195(18 Mar.):1186–91.
Smith, Dorothy E.
1974a "The ideological practice of sociology." Catalyst 8:32–54.
1974b "The social construction of documentary reality." Sociological Inquiry 44(4):257–68.
1975 "What it might mean to do a Canadian sociology: The everyday world as problematic." Canadian Journal of Sociology 1(3):363–76.
Forth "A sociology for women." In Julia Sherman and Evelyn Beck (eds.), The Prism of
coming Sex: Essays in the Sociology of Knowledge. Madison: University of Wisconsin
        Press.
Suppe, Frederick
1977 The Structure of Scientific Theories, 2nd ed. Urbana: University of Illinois Press.
Tönnies, Ferdinand
[1887] Community and Society. [Orig. German Title: Gemeinschaft und Gesellschaft.]
1963 New York: Harper & Row.
Turner, Jonathan
1974 The Structure of Sociological Theory. Homewood, Ill.: Dorsey.
Weber, Max
[1909] "Max Weber on bureaucratization." Pp. 125–31 in J.P. Mayer, Max Weber and
1944 German Politics. London: Faber & Faber.
[1920] Letter to Robert Liefmann (9 Mar.). Quoted on p. 44, fn 2, of W. Mommsen, "Max
1965 Weber's Political Sociology and His Philosophy of World History." International
        Social Science Journal 17:23–45.
[1922] Wirtschaft und Gesellschaft. Tr. in part by Hans Gerth and C. W. Mills (eds.), From
1946 Max Weber: Essays in Sociology. New York: Oxford University Press.
Weizenbaum, Joseph
1976 Computer Power and Human Reason: From Judgment to Calculation. San
        Francisco: Freeman.
Wieder, D. Lawrence
1975 "An approach to phenomenological sociology." Presented to the 1975 Ethno-
        methodology Colloquium, Santa Barbara, Calif.
Wilson, Thomas P.
1970 "Conceptions of interaction and forms of sociological explanation." American
        Sociological Review 35(Aug.):697–710.
1971 "The regress problem and the problem of evidence in ethnomethodology."
        Presented at the Annual Meeting of the American Sociological Association,
        Denver.
Wilson, Thomas P., and Don H. Zimmerman
1980 "Ethnomethodology, sociology, and theory." Humboldt Journal Relations.
        7:52–58.
Winograd, Terry
1972a Understanding Natural Language. New York: Academic Press.
1972b "A procedural model of language understanding." Pp. 152–86 in Robert C. Shank
        and Kennedy Mark Colby (eds.), Computer Models of Thought and Language. San
        Francisco: Freeman.
Zimmerman, Don H.
1976 "A reply to Professor Coser." The American Sociologist 11 (Feb.):4–11.
1978 "Ethnomethodology." The American Sociologist 13:6–15.

1979 "Ethnomethodology and symbolic interaction: some reflections on naturalistic inquiry." Presented to the Society for the Study of Symbolic Interaction, Boston.

Zimmerman, Don H., and Douglas W. Maynard
1979 "Pretopical sequences in talk between strangers." Presented at the Annual Meeting of the American Sociological Association, Boston.

Zimmerman, Don H., and Melvin Pollner
1970 "The everyday world as phenomenon." Pp. 80–103 in Jack D. Douglas (ed.), Understanding Everyday Life. Chicago: Aldine.

Zimmerman, Don H., and Candace West
1975 "Sex roles, interruptions, and silence." Pp. 105–29 in B. Thorne and N. Nehley (eds.), Language and Sex: Difference and Dominance. Rowley, Mass.: Newbury House.

JÜRGEN HABERMAS'S RECONSTRUCTION OF CRITICAL THEORY

John Sewart

In his essay "Between Philosophy and Science: Marxism As Critique," Jürgen Habermas put forth the idea that a critical theory of society must somehow be located between philosophy and science. That is, critique should be both empirical and scientific without being completely subsumed under the prescriptions of empirical-analytic science.[1] As Habermas (1973:79) expresses it, a critical social theory must "not relinquish that methodological rigor which is the irreversible achievement of modern science." At the same time, critical theory must preserve its philosophical and practical moments oriented toward an emancipatory sociopolitical practice. This is the meaning of critical theory's concern that it be an "empirical philosophy of history with a practical intent."

Following the lead of the earlier work of Adorno, Horkheimer, and Marcuse, a central component in Habermas's overall program for a criti-

Current Perspectives in Social Theory, volume 1, 1980, pages 323–356.
Copyright © 1980 by JAI Press Inc.
ISBN: 0-89232-154-7

cal theory of society is the critique of positivism.[2] What makes Habermas's work outstanding and an advance beyond the earlier work of his Frankfurt School colleagues is his careful synthesis of several divergent intellectual traditions, while simultaneously breaking with and transcending the limitations of those traditions. His synthesis—of Marxism, hermeneutics, systems theory, structural functionalism, and the pragmatic theory of language and linguistic philosophy—represents a shift away from earlier formulations of critical theory (e.g., Adorno's "negative dialectics"). The type of thinking Habermas embraces is, instead, a "positive dialectics" (Heller, 1978), or what has been characterized as an "offensive critical theory." "Critique" still remains central to his vision of an emancipatory social science, but the position from which he criticizes, and the alternative position for which he argues, is elaborated much more clearly and in much greater specificity than the original members of the Frankfurt School (Adorno, Horkheimer, Marcuse). This accounts, in part, for the disappearance of attitudes of despair in Habermas's extensive oeuvre. This positive attitude also accounts for the appreciation and critical appropriation of opposing arguments which are *not* ignored or dismissed in an *aprioristic* fashion. Instead, Habermas recognizes that an adequate and comprehensive theory of society must be sensitive to and engage opposing arguments—a necessary step if critical theorizing is to achieve the fullest understanding of human needs and suffering, and further the process of rational enlightenment.

THE FRANKFURT SCHOOL AND THE CRITIQUE OF POSITIVISM

The leitmotif of the work of the Frankfurt School as a whole can be characterized as a critique of positivism. It is against positivism that the requirements a critical theory of society should meet are delineated. In speaking of positivism and the positivistic attitude, I am aware that the term no longer has any standard usage[3] nor does it refer to a clearly defined theoretical school of thought. Indeed, the term has become an epithet, usually employed in polemical attacks. Those who use the term today certainly do not have in mind the scientific history and method of Comte, J. S. Mills's system of logic, or the logical positivism of the Vienna Circle. Despite this inconsistency in the general usage of positivism, the legacy of logical positivism persists in a number of significant schools of thought in all of the social sciences and humanities.[4] Before beginning discussion of the Frankfurt School and Popper (whose critique of the positivist program was significant for Habermas's development), I will provide a brief overview of positivism as a *philosophy* and positivism in *sociology*.[5]

As a *philosophy,* positivism implies two main positions. One is that what qualifies as "knowledge" must be connected to a reality which is observable by all. This is the rule of phenomenalism—the idea that only that which is immediately perceptible can provide the basis for legitimate scientific knowledge. Second, is the notion that value judgment and normative statements are void of any empirically based propositions. That is, statements of value are not grounded in a sensorily apprehended reality and hence are without an experiential foundation and incapable of being tested for validity. In other words, normative and evaluative propositions have no relation to an observable reality and hence do not count as legitimate scientific knowledge.

Applied to sociology, the positivist attitude asserts that only those categories and techniques used in the natural sciences can be adopted if we wish to create a natural science of society. According to this naturalistic approach, the methodological procedures and analytic techniques of the established sciences of nature (e.g., physics, chemistry) must be adopted by the social scientist. This means that the "subjective" and "meaningful" dimensions of human and social action do not require any special treatment in order to grasp their meaning and significance. In short, the intersubjective constitution of the meaning of social action is identical to an object in the natural world.

Another key aspect of the postivist attitude in the social sciences is that a science of society must aim at the construction of laws and generalizations of social conduct which are of the same logical status as those of the natural sciences. Any agenda for social inquiry which fails to construct these lawlike generalizations is clearly outside the domain of science. Lastly, the positivistic attitude maintains that the knowledge which is produced through social scientific inquiry is purely instrumental in character. There are no logically implied consequences of social research; it is neutral and value-free with respect to normative and ethical positions.

The influence upon the social sciences of the positivist enthronement of the deductive model cannot be underestimated.[6] The general features of the deductive model—that the standard of scientific reason must assume the form of logical explanation—are part of a philosophical tradition that extends throughout history, from J. S. Mill to Galileo to Aristotle. I cannot attempt here to explore the numerous versions of the deductive model that have been espoused over the centuries.[7]

May Brodbeck, a philosopher concerned with the philosophical basis of social inquiry, has outlined the deductive model (1968:363):

> This model holds . . . that to explain an individual fact we deduce it from one or more other such statements in conjunction with one or more generalizations or laws. A law, in turn, may be explained by deducing it from other laws. Prediction, upon the model, has the same logical form as explanation. In predicting something as yet unknown, one deductively infers it from particular *facts and laws already*

known . . . . It follows that if anything can be explained deductively by a set of premises after it has occurred, it could in principle have been predicted from these premises before the event. Nor does it make any difference whether the premises are statistical or deterministic. If they are deterministic, we may predict an individual event; if they are statistical, only statements about classes of events may be either explained or predicted. Virtually all those who accept the deductive model hold that it applies not only to physical but also to human phenomena, whether individual or social, whether in past or in the present.

According to this model, the touchstone of social scientific inquiry is the search for laws and lawlike generalizations; without these explanation and prediction (i.e., science) are impossible. Another way of stating this model is as follows: we (as scientists) begin with the statement describing X (explanandum) and relate it to a series of affairs Y (as initial conditions) and Z (general laws). That is, any claim that Y causes X (Y as a necessary and/or sufficient condition) is to say that whenever Y occurs X will occur, or vice versa (Hempel, 1965).

Brodbeck does recognize—unlike many contemporary social scientists—that the deductive model is a sort of ideal-typical representation of scientific explanation, especially with regard to the social sciences. The deductive model is seen as a philosophical and methodological thesis, rather than as an empirical description (Brodbeck, 1968:340*ff*.). Nevertheless, the deductive model is still held up as the ideal toward which social scientists *ought* to be striving and the standard by which social inquiry should be judged.

The fact that the deductive model is incompatible with the actual practice of both the natural and social sciences presents no problem to positivists. They point out that to demonstrate the gap between actual social scientific practice and the methodological prescriptions of positivism in no way substantiates a claim of logical inadequacy (Hempel, 1965). Moreover, that generalizations in social science do not take the form of universal laws but, instead, are statistical uniformities, creates no problem for the positivist. This is due to the immaturity of social scientific research tools for the purpose of developing lawlike generalizations. As soon as social science does away with ambiguous and opaque concepts and develops precise conceptual schemes, it is argued, the formulation of lawlike generalizations can begin. (See, e.g., Nagel, 1961; Merton, 1968; Zetterberg, 1965; Blalock, 1969; Smelser, 1968, 1969; Parsons, 1950.) All we have to do is wait for a Newton or Einstein to arrive on the scene.[8] However, utilizing Habermas's work, I will attempt to show that this yearning for a social scientific Newton is fundamentally misguided. As Giddens (1976:13) has remarked, "those who still wait for a Newton are not only waiting for a train that won't arrive, they're in the wrong station altogether."

The underlying theme of the work of Adorno, Horkheimer, and Marcuse is the contestation of the natural scientific method transferred into the realm of the social sciences. Their alternative model of social inquiry does not stop at the production of empirical knowledge about the social world. Rather, their conceptualization of knowledge is ultimately based upon an image of human action in which the Kantian idea of reason or practical wisdom is central. This image of human action is linked with an image and ideal of society based upon the reasonable conduct of life, in the course of which human agents construct their social world. As such, the Frankfurters draw upon the classical Greek conception of knowledge as continuous with ethics and the living of the good and just life (cf., Arendt, 1959; Bernstein, 1971). This ideal of knowledge is not limited to the discovery and construction of logically integrated systems of quantitative, lawlike statements about the physical world. Because of the practical import of knowledge (the cultivation of virtuous character in individuals so that they may lead a good and just life), and the character of its subject matter (the continuously changing realities of social life as such), the classical conception of reason was incapable of achieving the status of a "rigorous empirical science of nature." As Thomas McCarthy (1978a:2) expresses it:

> Because it had to take account of the contingent and variable, it had to rest content with establishing rules of a "more or less" and "in most cases" character. The capacity thereby cultivated, and the keystone of the virtuous character, was *phronesis,* a prudent understanding of variable situations with a view to what was to be done.

In a number of articles and reviews published during the late 1930s in the Frankfurt School's journal *Zeitschrift für Sozialforschung,* Horkheimer and Marcuse developed a full-scale attack on the positivist orientation to social inquiry.[9] The Frankfurters rejected the positivist claims for the unity of scientific method, the reduction of scientific discourse to methodological issues, the political claims made by the scientific community, the equation of scientifically produced knowledge with substantive reason, and the exclusion of the knowing subject from the production of knowledge.

In Horkheimer's 1937 essays "Traditional and Critical Theory" and "The Latest Attack on Metaphysics," we find the clearest distinction developed between critical and traditional (positivist) theory. Horkheimer (1972:244) begins by summarizing his notion of traditional theory.

> Theory in the traditional sense established by Descartes and everywhere practiced in the pursuit of the specialized sciences organizes experience in the light of questions which arise out of life in present-day society. The resultant network of disciplines contains information in a form which makes it useful in any particular circumstance for

the greatest number of possible purposes. The social genesis of problems, the real situations in which science is put to use, and the purposes which it is made to serve are all regarded by science as external to itself.

Horkheimer (1972:244) contrasts this way of knowing with a critical theory of society based on Marx's critique of political economy.

> [Critical theory] has for its object men as producers of their historical way of life in its totality. The real situations which are the starting point of science are not regarded simply as data to be verified and to be predicted according to the laws of probability. Every datum depends not on nature alone but also on the power man has over it. Objects, the kind of perception, the questions asked, and the meaning of the answers all bear witness to human activity and the degree of man's power.

Carrying the critique of traditional science over into a critique of bourgeois society, Horkheimer argues that the treatment of the object of inquiry as distinct from its subject is essentially allied to a system of technical rationality which forms a block to rational political practice. Because of the attempt to find a methodology common to both the natural and social sciences, there is a strong tendency for positive science to treat history as a natural process governed by natural laws rather than a human process capable of being influenced by human activity.[10] The positivist's ontological restrictions confine the activity of science to that which is, i.e., the facts. Knowledge of social reality is merely neutral information which can be integrated into the existing institutional arrangements of society. In short, the Frankfurters' claim against positivism is that it is inherently conservative in that it is incapable of challenging the existing system *qua* science. Instead, positivism lends support to the exisiting system via its separation of facts and values; consigning the latter (as *senseless*) to the arbitrary and subjective realm of personal preference. Social science becomes an activity far removed from the sphere of practical or moral action except in terms of assessing the adequacy of means toward *given* ends and the unintended consequences of a particular value position. Such an epistemological position, according to a contemporary critical theorist,

> [s]upplies the social engineers of the industrial system with the legitimation of measures in accordance with the dominant value system, which is withdrawn from any effective public discussion: this means—in accordance with the stabilization of the existing social power structure (Wellmer, 1971:21).

For the critical theorist the touchstone of positivistic reason is "knowledge in the form of a mathematically formulated universal science deducible from the smallest possible number of axioms, a system which assures the calculation of the probable occurrence of all events. Society, too, is to be explained in this way" (Horkheimer, 1972:138). The consequence of this approach is that only that which is immediately derivable from sensory experience can count as legitimate knowledge. Accordingly, the role of the subject of knowledge drops out of the scope of a positivistically oriented theory of social inquiry. The mediation of sensory experience and the sociohistorical processes influencing the selection, interpretation, and evaluation of the given factual data are incapable of being thematized within the positivist framework. Horkheimer (1947:82ff.) points out that facts and concepts "cannot be accepted as the measure of truth if the ideal of truth that it serves in itself presupposes social processes that thinking cannot escape as ultimates . . . [T]he task of critical reflection is not merely to understand the various facts in historical development . . . but also to see through the notion of fact itself, in its development and therefore in its relativity." Horkheimer (1972:208) goes on to note that positivism completely eliminates reflection on the subject of knowledge such that "the genesis of particular objective facts, the practical application of the conceptual systems by which it groups the facts, and the role of such systems in action, are all taken to be external to the theoretical thinking itself."

KARL POPPER AND CRITICAL RATIONALISM

In the preceeding section we saw how the critical theory of the early members of the Frankfurt School rejected the major elements of a positivist methodology of social inquiry. In taking the subject matter of the social disciplines as constituted by objective facts, the positivist program worked with three major assumptions: (1) the unity of the scientific method; (2) the logical separation between knowledge/theory and its application or use in the social world; and (3) the minimization of the role of the subject (i.e., theorist) in the theoretical process. As was indicated, the Frankfurters repudiated all of these claims. However, as will be shown, these are the same claims made against positivism by Karl Popper—one of the major antagonists to critical theory and Marxism. What, then, distinguishes critical theory from the Popperian critical rationalist logic of the social sciences and the Popperian social technology? Through a consideration of Karl Popper's macrotheoretical program for the "proper study" of social phenomena, I will be able to throw some much needed light on the exact nature of a critical theory of society, thereby taking us beyond bland programmatic statements about "critique," "dialectical thinking," "grasping social relations in their totality," and so on. In so doing, we are led to a consideration of the weaknesses in the first formulation of critical theory and, most importantly, to a confrontation with the work of Habermas and his program for a reconstruction of critical theory which is at once empirical, interpretative, *and* critical.

Popper has consistently rejected the claims of the positivists' about the precision, reliability, certainty, and validity of knowledge. According to Popper, knowledge is not reducible to the canons of deductive logic, the logic of mathematics and taxonomy. Scientific knowledge is not merely a process of deductively deriving the laws of the natural and social world; nor is there completely reliable knowledge. Popper (1968, 1969) proposes to replace the model of apodictic (i.e., certain) knowledge employed by the positivist with the theory of "fallibilism." For Popper (1972:81), scientific activity is "the method of bold conjectures and ingenious and severe attempts to refute them." Human knowledge is not certain information—we advance conjectures the truth of which can never be deductively arrived at; only the falsity of a knowledge claim can be deduced.

Popper is thus in agreement with those thinkers (including the Frankfurt School) who have recognized the hidden ontology and aprioristic claims of positivism. Like Hume, Popper argues that "singular statements" cannot justify universal ones. That is, the singular statements "A_1 is B" and "A_2 is B" and . . . "A_n is B," does not enable us to logically deduce the universal claim that "All A are B." According to Popper (1968:425):

> Universal laws transcend experience, if only because they are universal and thus transcend any finite number of their observable instances; and singular statements transcend experience because the universal terms which normally occur in them entail dispositions to behave in a law-like manner, so that they entail universal laws (of some lower order of universality, as a rule).

In rejecting the claims of positivism to have achieved apodictic empirical knowledge, Popper avoids any relapse into subjectivism. Popper's approach to this problem is to show how we can increase our knowledge about the world despite the fact that there is no possibility of attaining certain knowledge. Claims to knowledge are justified not merely by their ability to elicit feelings of personal satisfaction on the part of the individual theorist (1972:39–44,60–4). The practice of science must be a public and open process. Knowledge consists of hypotheses which have not been falsified (i.e., not proven) in spite of the scientific community's active attempt to falsify such claims through severe tests. Popper issues methodological injunctions prescribing that we (as the community of scientists) continually attempt to refine and improve (thereby eliminating errors) claims to knowledge through critical intellectual and experimental scrutiny.

Popper's critical rationalism stands in line with the critical theorists' rejection of the objectivistic illusion of traditional theory. Like the critical theorists' rejection of absolute premises of any kind, Popper recognizes that scientific procedures are human products. He realizes that there is no Archimedian point of knowledge; indeed, it is not fruitful to search for one. Instead, Popper embraces the tradition that upholds the categorical imperative of thought; the necessity to reject all dogma and authority, and to think independently on one's own—constantly thematizing one's basic presuppositions. For Popper (1962: Vol. II, 230–40), like the Frank-furters, the adherence to the scientific enterprise and reason necessarily involves a moral decision and a way of life. An additional element in Popper's critique of the positivist account of knowledge deals with the role of the subject in the acquisition of knowledge.

Popper argues that the positivist position presupposes a subject of knowledge in that consciousness is required for sense certainty, i.e., there has to be a subject who perceives immediately given facts. In his essay, "The Bucket and the Searchlight: Two Theories of Knowledge," Popper points out that the observations *made* by the subject are not merely passive reflections on an external nature. All hypotheses and knowledge claims contain "basic observation statements" about a given phenomenon taking place on a specific spatiotemporal plane. However, these observation statements are actively constituted by the subject of knowledge.

> In science it is *observation* rather than perception, which plays the decisive part. But observation is a process in which we play an intensely *active* part. An observation is a perception but one which is planned and prepared. We do not "have" an observation (as we may "have" a sense experience) but we "make" an observation . . . . An observation is always preceded by a particular interest, a question, or a problem—in short, by something theoretical (Popper, 1972:342).

Rather than minimizing or eliminating the inescapable subjectivity of any knowledge claims, Popper argues that data are conditioned by a plethora of historical, cultural, biological and subjective factors (1972:345).

Popper's position on the active role of the subject in the generation of knowledge, as noted, rejects a naive subjectivism. The involvement of the subject is not fatal. He wants to make explicit the active moment of the subject in the process of scientific inquiry. In other words, he demands—like the critical theorists—that we recognize subjectivity as an integral moment and thus be self-reflexive in our activities.[11] Moreover, in a manner similar to Kuhn, Popper stresses the importance of historical tradition in the scientific process:

> Science never starts from scratch; it can never be described as free from assump-tions; for at every instant it presupposes a horizon of expectations—yesterday's horizon of expectations, as it were. Today's science is built upon yesterday's science (and so it is the result of yesterday's searchlight); and yesterday's science, in turn, is based on the science of the day before. And the oldest scientific theories are built on pre-scientific myths, and these, in their turn, on still older expectations. (Popper, 1972:346–7; quoted in McCarthy, 1978a:46).

Popper is traditionally viewed as an exponent of the unity of the scientific method, i.e., the techniques and procedures successfully developed in the study of natural phenomena are directly transferrable to the study of social phenomena. However, there is a significant amount of evidence in Popper's own work to suggest that Popper's metatheoretical program for the social sciences does not uphold the thesis of a unity of general explanatory schemes for *all* disciplines—social and natural.

In The *Poverty of Historicism* Popper (1957:136) makes the proposal that "the task of social theory is to construct and to analyze our sociological models carefully in descriptive or nominalist terms, that is to say, *in terms of individuals,* of their attitudes, expectations, relations, etc." Accordingly, a central concern of social theory becomes the understanding of social phenomena as active human creations, *not* as the products of physical laws. Human action, according to Popper, has an emergent quality which cannot be reduced to a purely causal logic:

> Now I want to make it clear . . . that there may be no reduction [of human action to physical laws] possible; life is an *emergent* property (1972:292).

> If we act through being influenced by the grasp of an abstract relationship, we initiate physical causal chains which have no *physical* causal antecedents. We are then "first movers," or creators of a physical "causal chain" (1969:298).

In other words, human action does not have the same ontological status as events in the world of nature. Because of this distinction between the "dead" and "passive" character of events in the physical realm, and the active and autonomous creation of the social world by human agents, the logic of understanding of social phenomena is not of the same kind as the nomological laws of the natural sciences (see Popper 1969:124ff.).

Following from this distinction, Popper argues (1962: Vol. II, 265) that in order to explain social phenomena the social disciplines require an understanding of the general logic of the situation:

> As a matter of fact, most historical explanation makes tacit use, not so much of trivial sociological and psychological laws, but of what I have called . . . the *logic of the situation;* that is to say, besides the initial conditions describing personal interests, aims, and other situational factors, such as the information available to the person concerned, it tacitly assumes, as a kind of first approximation, the trivial general law that sane persons as a rule act more or less rationally.

The theory of situational logic thus requires that we situate action in an understanding of the tradition and institutions within which a given social action takes place; in this way we can see the point of action.

Despite Popper's "official" thesis that there exists but one general explanatory schema for all the sciences (human natural), we can see that his views on the subject matter of the social disciplines as requiring a situational logic contradict the unity of method thesis. Although his views on the specificity of social inquiry are not particularly well developed,[12] we can see that his reflections on the nature of social inquiry transcend the positivist program for social research. (This insight also indicates another point of agreement between critical theory and the critical rationalism of Popper.)

Popper (in agreement with critical theory) makes the inherent *practical* relationship between a theoretical position and its use in the world. The practical side of an objective science of society is the creation of a system of domination and oppressive social relations (Wellmer 1971:69). If history is portrayed as an automatic process without the active self-emancipation of human subjects, with human subjects instead passively emancipated by history, then the very basis for emancipation is undercut. This is the underlying source of Popper's rejection of the possibility of absolute certainty in knowledge. It is also the point of his constant battle with all forms of dogmatism and unreflective thought and his stress on the necessity of remaining critical of all knowledge claims—which must be relentlessly scrutinized. The possibility of an open community of scientists and critical rationalism itself rests upon the condition of an open, pluralistic society. It is only through the establishment of the open society that the rational individual will ever develop—that is, the possibility of individuals, as members of society, standing together in rational communication and coming to a decision about the practical questions involved in the making of society.

Popper's critique of the positivists' presuppositions is a significant step in the right direction.[13] His discussion of the constitutive role of mediations between the subject and object such that knowledge is not reducible to mere observation and experience is squarely in line with critical theory's understanding of the quasi-transcendental conditions of knowledge. However, Popper fails to take the critical step toward extending his logic of inquiry to the structure of the constitution of knowledge itself. Instead he retreats to an objectivistic notion of truth. In his papers written at the end of the 1960s—"Epistemology Without a Knowing Subject" and "On the Theory of Objective Mind"—Popper attempts to ground his correspondence theory of truth in a Platonic-like realm which he calls the "third-world." He makes a distinction between three different worlds:

> In this pluralistic philosophy the world consists of at least three ontologically distinct sub-worlds; or, as I shall say, there are three worlds: the first is the physical world or the world of physical states; the second is the mental world or the world of mental states; and the third is the world of intelligibles, or of *ideas in objective sense;* it is the world of possible object of thought: the world of theories in themselves, and their logical relations; of arguments in themselves; and of problem situations in themselves.

One of the fundamental problems of this pluralistic philosophy concerns the relationship between these three "worlds." The three worlds are so related that the first two can interact, and that the last two can interact. Thus the second world, the world of subjective or personal experiences, interacts with each of the other two worlds. The first world and the third world cannot interact, save through the intervention of the second world, the world of subjective or personal experiences (1972:154–5).

This "third world" is composed of objective ideas, thoughts, and theories. Popper relies on this eternal dimension to guarantee the objectivity of knowledge. As Thomas McCarthy (1978a:48) has perceptively noted, his relapse into an objectivistic ontology of the factual (i.e., real facts) as eternal and immutable

permits Popper to maintain the independence of facts and to argue for an objectivistic conception of theories as striving to approximate an adequate conception of an independent reality. This effectively short-circuits the transcendental turn implied by his own thesis that facts are constituted only within frames of reference or horizons of expectations. *Given* the independence of facts, Popper can avoid pursuing the consequences of his view that basic observational statements are established by convention . . . . The surprising and inconsistent, retention of an objectivistic notion of facts is at the root of Popper's failure to complete his transcendental turn.

Popper's objectivism also leads him into a voluntaristic frame of reference when the questions of the foundation and goals of science itself are addressed. Popper tries to base his commitment to critical rationalism on the "objective" methodological processes of error elimination and conjecture and refutation. Although Popper takes every step possible to install a series of controls on the subject which will provide "objective" and compelling reasons to choose between theories, it is still not possible to justify or rationally opt for critical rationalism itself. The attempt to guarantee the objectivity of knowledge claims through the critical *method* still rests, for Popper, upon an irrational and subjective base. Popper (1968:53–4) sees the only legitimate commitment to science as a trust in the unified method of critical argumentation. But how are we to argue for methodological rules? Popper (1968:55) argues that my "only reason for proposing any criterion of demarcation [between science and metaphysics] is that it is fruitful." In other words, one should be scientific because it is fruitful for science. If scientists accept the Popperian definition of science, then science will progress more rapidly than otherwise. The question—which is of central importance to critical theory—of why we want scientific knowledge, demands no answer. Science becomes an end in itself. The task of epistemology is to invent methodological rules which promote the growth of knowledge: "the central problem of epistemology has always been and still is the problem of the growth of knowledge. . . . Epistemology, or the logic of scientific discovery, should be identified with the theory of scientific method" (Popper, 1968:15,49).

In short, Popper limits rationality and reason to the paradigm of critical argumentation—as the comparison with objective facts. Reason is thus reduced to and equated with the logic of a deductive scientific methodology.

As I have attempted to argue, Popper's reflections on the logic of inquiry allow us to consider a rejection of the positivist program for social science. However, in spite of his emphasis on tradition, convention, and frames of reference, Popper's critical attitude subverts itself in his "epistemology without a knowing subject" and his ephemeral "third world" of objective facts. In so doing, Popper falls victim to the "disease" of scientism, viz., "science's belief in itself: the conviction that we can no longer understand science as one form of possible knowledge, but rather must identify knowledge with science" (Habermas 1971:4). Concerned only with constructing a pure methodology, a positivistically based science unreflectively slips over the questions of the cognitive interests of social inquiry, its constitutive features, and the place of knowledge in human life:

> Once epistemology has been flattened out to methodology, it loses sight of the constitution of the objects of possible experience; in the same way, a formal science dissociated from transcendental reflection becomes blind to the genesis of rules for the combination of symbols. In Kantian terms, both ignore the synthetic achievements of the knowing subject. The positivistic attitude conceals the problems of world constitution. The *meaning* of knowledge itself becomes irrational—in the name of rigorous knowledge (Habermas, 1971:68–69).

Jürgen Habermas has provided the most systematic and thoughtful approach toward understanding and resolving the issues involved in the relation of thought to the everyday practice of life and, more specifically, the epistemological and methodological nature of an adequate and comprehensive critical social theory.

HABERMAS'S RECONSTRUCTION OF CRITICAL THEORY

Habermas's efforts to articulate the normative and epistemological foundations of critical theory have been at the heart of his work since his earliest publications. The most significant feature of critical theory is the relation of theory to practice, i.e., how the categories, presuppositions, and grammar of critical theory are constructed with the intent of realizing the good life. In Habermas's words (1973:2), critical theory

> encompasses a dual relationship between theory and praxis. On the one hand, it investigates the constitutive historical complex of the constellation of self-interests, to which the theory still belongs across and beyond its acts of insight. On the other

hand, it studies the historical interconnections of action, in which the theory, as action-oriented, can intervene. In the one case, we have a social praxis, which, a societal synthesis, makes insight possible; in the other case, a political praxis which consciously aims at overthrowing the existing system of institutions.

It is this dual relationship of theory to practice which is *the* distinguishing characteristic of critical theory. My aim is to explore Habermas's contribution to the illumination of the issues surrounding the relation of critical social theory to social practice and the nature of social inquiry in general.

The dilemma of specifying the ground or Archimedian point for the critique of existing society derives, in part, from the failure of history to conform to the Frankfurters' expectations. In the earliest conceptualizations of critical theory the historical possibility of a socialist reorganization provided the base from which critical theory justified itself. That is to say, the struggle by oppressed classes to reorganize society along rational lines constituted the source of validation. Grounding the possibility of critique in concrete historical factors—which failed to materialize—the original members of the Frankfurt School were left without any self-justification. In face of this historical roadblock to the practical realization of critical theory, the Frankfurters fell back upon an extreme pessimism (Horkheimer), an ontological version of critique based on a biological "need" for liberation (Marcuse), or a conception of critique and the possibility of a rational society defined only in negative terms (Adorno). Habermas also argues that the Marxian critique of political economy no longer suffices, on its own, as a logical justification. He rejects all of these formulations for ignoring the crucial problem facing critical theory, viz., the need to establish the ground of the critical standpoint. At this point, I will turn to a consideration of Habermas's efforts to flesh out the bond between cognition and critique.

Habermas's earliest conceptualization of critical theory as an empirical philosophy of history with a practical intent is developed in a still untranslated review article "Literaturbericht zur Philosophischen Diskussion um Marx und den Marxismus."[15] In this piece Habermas takes a position very similar to that of his mentors, i.e., critical reason must be historical and engaged in the realization of practical ends. Critical theory is thus demarcated from traditional theory by virtue of its practical intent. The basic concepts and presuppositions of critical theory reflect an interest in the overcoming of domination insofar as it (critical theory) addresses a potentially society-transforming historical agent, i.e., critical theory serves as a vehicle for the enlightenment and emancipation of human beings through the provision of an analysis of the conditions of and the possibility for change (especially of overcoming alienated labor).

> The critique of ideology and the doctrine of revolution combine to form a single piece, or better, a single circle, in which each reciprocally provides the presuppositions of the other. . . . The doctrine of revolution is for critique the doctrine of categories. What is can be grapsed only with an eye to what is possible. An historical theory of what exists, if it is to be appropriate to its object, must be a theory of its transformation. (Habermas, quoted in McCarthy, 1978b:4.)

This classical formulation of the nature of critique is not without its problems. The major problem is the epistemological basis and adequacy of critical theory's conceptualization of reality. The problem of the Archimedian point of knowledge is an especially delicate issue in light of critical theory's claim that reason is practically engaged and historically constituted.

In his earlier writings Habermas's position is close to that of the earlier members of the Frankfurt School. He argues that the empirical validity of critical theory's analysis is to be checked (not verified) by the insights of empirical social science. The critical/practical intent is realized through its demonstration of the irrationality of the status quo. The critical theorist thus utilizes the insights derived from empirical analytic science and then critically interprets its findings. Social science (like classical political economy in Marx's work) stands in an *external* relation to the critical project.[16] The critical theorist uses the (uncritical) findings of empirical social research in order to play them off against "normative" concepts which transcend their given form. In this manner, critical theory claims to be capable of demonstrating the partiality and lacunae in the findings of empirical social research. However, the techniques and presuppositions of empirical social research are left intact and regarded by Habermas as "independent . . . in the framework of a philosophical critique that is related to practice" (Habermas, quoted in McCarthy 1978b:6). In short, the findings of empirical social research are interpreted as a mere approximation of a social reality in need of a radical transformation (cf., Adorno 1976:1–67).

Habermas later abandons this formulation of critical theory—where empirical social research stands in an external relation to critique. Habermas's line of reasoning is as follows: all knowledge of the social world is possible only from a pragmatically oriented point of view. That is, social theory has an intersubjective core. The critical theorist is an inextricable part of the social reality he/she wishes to critically understand the concepts and categories devised to understand that world, and the evaluation of the findings of that analysis—all of these aspects are an integral part of and derive from the social world under investigation. The recognition of this hermeneutic/interpretative dimension of critical social inquiry is central to Habermas's reformulation of a critical theory which is neither a claim to a First or Pure Philosophy, nor a form of positivistic inquiry claiming insight into the realm of objective facts. This hermeneutic turn also provides the basis for the self-conscious and self-reflexive understanding which critical theory must have if it is to make transparent the manner in which its theoretical framework is linked to an emancipatory social practice. Accordingly, it is necessary to take a closer look at Habermas's critical appropriation of the hermeneutic/ interpretative tradition in order to fully grasp his project for the reconstruction of the basic concepts and presuppositions of critical theory.

A major thread in Habermas's discussion of the logic of critical social inquiry deals with the consideration of the intersubjective meaning that is constitutive of social life.[17] Habermas's program for a reconstruction theory of society, in contrast to positivism's, thematizes the interpretative tradition of social inquiry which holds that the social sciences must explain social phenomena through an understanding of the "situational logic of action," i.e., social reality is constructed of and based upon the categories of experiences in the possession of acting human agents. Accordingly, a critical social theory cannot be limited to the observation of objective and material events. Instead, an adequate theory requires hermeneutic understanding—as the reconstruction of the contexts of social action by individual actors and the concepts and categories necessary to establish analytic communication between the theorist and the actions of those whom he/she studies (Habermas, 1976:139).[18]

For Habermas, the conceptualizations, standards and rules employed by the theorist emerge from the concrete context of which the theorist is a part and which he/she wishes to understand. The point at issue is the recognition that the process of understanding social reality (qua theorist) necessarily involves a process of self-understanding. It is impossible for the theorist to throw off his/her own horizon of preunderstanding and approach the subject matter at hand as a tabula rasa (cf., Ricoeur, 1971; Gadamer, 1975).[19]

Habermas's interest in the interpretative tradition is more than a purely methodological one. The research-guiding and research-motivating interests of this tradition center on the problem of human emancipation. It is concerned with the problems of increasing the understanding which social actors have of their sociohistorical situation, of themselves and, ultimately, with illuminating the existence of hypostatized and reified social forces which may impinge upon autonomous action. Ideally, this approach is designed to further the achievement of mutual understanding between individuals and thus the very condition for action in society. To this extent the contribution of the interpretative tradition lies in its relevance for sociopolitical practice.

This reading of the potential emancipatory contribution of the interpretative approach is one not always shared or made explicit by those who operate within the interpretative framework. Although Habermas embraces the hermeneutic turn as a distinct advance over the positivistic separation of subject and object, he is just as quick to point out the inadequacies of a purely interpretative approach. Such an approach would be adequate if human action was totally transparent. Simple hermeneutic understanding has no way of checking the extent to which the existing structure of social interaction is decisively affected by coercive sociohistorical influences.

The thrust of Habermas's critique of the phenomenological perspective is that the analysis of social structures, traditions, norms, values, etc., drops out of the conceptual armory available to the social theorist. Although the phenomenological perspective is a necessary counter to positivistic social inquiry which studies regularities and causal relations, it is just as one-sided in its own methodological prescriptions. A fully adequate interpretation of social action, according to Habermas, must also illuminate the causal determinants of social action and the significance of objective structures upon intersubjective understanding.[20]

> The rules of interpretation [for transforming social norms into individual motives] are not part of the invariant life-equipment of individuals or groups. They constantly change with the structure of the life-world, sometimes in unnoticeable, continuous shifts, sometimes in a disconnected and revolutionary manner. . . . They are not ultimates, but products of social processes that have to be understood. Apparently the empirical conditions under which transcendental rules take shape and determine the constitutive order of a life-world are themselves the result of socialization processes. I cannot see how these processes can be comprehended without reference to social norms. If this is the case, those rules of interpretation cannot in principle be separated from the rules of social action. Without recourse to social norms, we could explain neither how the "constitutive order" of a life-world arises, nor how it changes. And yet this order is in turn the basis for the individual transformation of norms into actions from which we "read off" what counts as a norm. The analytic separation of rules of interpretation and social norms certainly makes good sense. But neither category of rules can be analyzed independently of the other; both are moments of the complex of social life (1970a:218–29, quoted in McCarthy 1978a:161).

Habermas's intent is to develop a theory which transcends the limits of the interpretative approach and provides a comprehensive and critical approach to sociocultural meanings.[21] A critical theory of society must not only be capable of identifying coercive power relations hidden in cultural meanings (as the critique of ideology), it must also provide for the dissolution of such relations in the very process of interpretation. In this way a critical theory of society must address coercion and unequal social relations with an eye to providing for emancipation from these relations. Without this emancipatory moment, which permits critical reflection on social reality, critical theory would remain abstract and ahistorical

(Habermas, 1973:13ff.). Habermas does not wish to completely reject the contributions of an interpretative approach to the understanding of the social world. What he does question is the ability of the interpretative approach to comprehend the distortions and objectification of a given sociocultural tradition. Such a critical project requires, for Habermas, a concept of reason and rationality which is capable of taking a critical standpoint against given forms of social organization.

Habermas tentatively locates the basis for a critical reason in the a priori organization of communication and speech itself. Before discussing Habermas's proposal for a critical theory based on a general theory of communication, it will be helpful to consider his earlier discussion of the psychoanalytic model of interpretative therapeutics as a model of radical social criticism. In this earlier work, Habermas uses Freudian psycho-analysis as a concrete example and epistemological model for elaborating the idea of critique and as an alternative to the positivist notion of rationality.[22]

As we have seen, Habermas conceives of critical social theory as oriented toward a practical interest in emancipation through critical self-reflection. The idea of critical reflection is, according to Habermas, intimately bound up with the problem of interpretation. In this sense, psychoanalysis is seen as a form of *critical* interpretation. It is a form of interpretation, however, which is capable of going beyond a purely interpretative hermeneutic approach, i.e., of being able to take a critical point of view with regard to a subject's understanding of his/her reality. For example, under contemporary sociopolitical conditions human sub-jects are often not capable of grasping—through self-reflection—their own behavior. Subjective intentions can, in this context, be unreliable and distorted indicators of a human subject's real intent. The possibility of identifying and clarifying an actor's "real" intent is blocked, according to Habermas, through the use of traditional hermeneutic/interpretative techniques. These techniques are premised on the availability of a "public" language and tradition. Habermas perceptively identifies the problems posed by psychologically based distortions in communication and self-understanding (see Habermas, 1970b:207ff.). For example, a schizophrenic's language use may be incomprehensible to others and, in this sense, communication is distorted. The psychic functioning of the individual—which has been disrupted by a variety of situational factors—requires a form of interpretation which rejects the self-understanding of such individuals. Habermas (1971:220) argues that the hermeneutic view is inadequate for "penetrating behind the manifest content" of a subject's alienated and incomprehensible statements. This requires a technique or method which is capable of *explaining* subjective intentions through interpretation—via establishing the structures of determination of those intentions—which are opaque to the actor's understanding. Defined as such, interpretation is directed to the understanding of the way in which the actor misunderstands him/herself through a method which combines explanatory/causal approaches with hermeneutic/interpretative ones.

According to Habermas, the model for combining explanation and understanding is provided by Freudian psychoanalysis. Psychoanalysis is aligned with those interpretative theories which opposed the positivist approach to social explanation. Precisely those factors singled out by the interpretative tradition for analysis, i.e., subjective mental states such as feelings, desires, and thoughts, are the same ones excluded by a positivistic analysis. The positivistic approach is thus incapable of incorporating the concept of the self-reflexive and self-transcending subject. However, the psychoanalytic approach diverges from the interpretative tradition in that it consciously devises procedures for critically evaluating the interpretation offered by a given subject. As noted above, the interpretative approach to social analysis offers no way in which to distinguish "correct" from "incorrect," or "appropriate" from "inappropriate" interpretations. This problem is central for a critical psychoanalysis—for it recognizes that individuals are often influenced by unconscious determinations. Accordingly, the actor's corroboration of the analyst's interpretation does not, according to Habermas, validate its "truthfulness." This is a point neglected by the interpretative tradition. As Bernstein (1976:202) has noted, while the phenomenological tradition is "sensitive to the distortions that can result in social theory when the theorist imposes his own standards and biases on the social actors he is studying, [it is] insensitive to the distortions that can and do result when theories reflect the biases of those investigated."

Habermas's selective appropriation of the metapsychology of psychoanalysis stands in opposition to traditional interpretative sociologies. Although both converge in their attempt to reconstruct past histories, or biographies, the psychoanalytic approach is distinct in its procedures designed to understand the lost or mutilated meanings of utterances or speech. In this sense, psychoanalysis is analogous to a philological analysis of a text—yet different in that it must treat "texts" which not only reveal but also conceal the subject's intentions.[23] For Habermas (1971:217),

> [p]sychoanalytic interpretation . . . is not directed at meaning structures in the dimension of what is consciously intended. The flaws eliminated by its critical labor are not accidental. The ommissions and distortions that it rectifies have a systematic role and function. For the symbolic structures that psychoanalysis seeks to comprehend are corrupted by the impact of *internal conditions*. The mutilations have meaning as such. The meaning of a corrupt text of this sort can be adequately comprehended only after it has become possible to illuminate the meaning of the

corruption itself. This distinguishes the peculiar task of a hermeneutics that cannot be confined to the procedures of philology but rather unites linguistic analysis with the psychological investigation of causal connections.

In another article, "On Systematically Distorted Communication," Habermas (1970b:217) points out that the type of analysis (outlined above) which is capable of "dealing with manifestations of a systematically distorted communication . . . presupposes a theory of communicative competence." Drawing upon the work of his colleague Alfred Lorenzer (1970) on the decoding of patient's distorted self-understanding in terms of an analysis of deformed language games, Habermas (1970b:209–20) reconstructs psychoanalysis as a theory of "systematically distorted communication":

> The fundamental analytic rule introduced by Freud ensures a standard relationship between the physician and his patient, a relationship which meets quasi-experimental conditions. . . . The linguistic material which results from conversations with the patient is classified according to a narrowly circumscribed context of possible double meanings. This context comprises a general interpretation of early-childhood patterns of interaction. Both considerations make it obvious that scenic understanding—in contrast to hermeneutic understanding, or ordinary semantic analysis—cannot be conceived as being a mere application of communicative competence, free from theoretical guidance.

In these points we find the key to Habermas's most recent work. That is, a critical theory of society must articulate a general theory of communicative competence which would include a specification of what a "normal" and "undistorted" model of communication looks like and an understanding of the development of the process by which a subject acquires the ability to communicate in a competent manner (cf., Habermas, 1975b: 184).[24]

HABERMAS'S COMPREHENSIVE THEORY OF COMMUNICATIVE COMPETENCE OR UNIVERSAL PRAGMATICS

In a number of recent articles (not all available in English) Habermas has pursued the problem of distorted communication. Since an understanding of distorted communication must have reference to a theory of undistorted communication and a standard of rationality, Habermas seeks to establish the necessary basis for a critical reason. Indeed, a theory of undistorted communication is necessary to resolve not only the problems of psychoanalytic therapeutics, but, in addition, to overcome the hermeneutic/interpretative tradition's neglect of sociopolitical relations of dominance which are rooted in distortions of communication. In this sense, Habermas's linguistic turn is not a radical departure from the central concerns of his earlier work, but is more appropriately seen as an attempt to further develop the normative and epistemological base of critical theory.

Habermas's concern with a general theory of communication (alternatively referred to as a theory of universal pragmatics or communicative competence) can also be seen in light of his attempt to overcome the "defensive" and pessimistic posture of earlier formulations of critical theory (e.g., Adorno, 1973). Habermas rejects the early critical theorists' alternative claims that critical theory is without a "positive" content. That is, given the suppression of revolutionary possibilities as a result of increased capitalist reification, the aim of a critical philosophy was seen as best confined to self-clarification and the negative critique of the false totality of capitalism (Honneth, 1979:56). While Habermas recognizes the destruction of the classic locus of revolutionary activity (i.e., the proletariat), he avoids the pessimistic conclusions of Adorno regarding the possibility of critical theory contributing to an emancipatory practice. Habermas locates this possibility in the sphere of communicative action. As Honneth (1979:61) puts it:

> The structure of linguistically organized intersubjectivity becomes crucial for critical theory, both from an ethical as well as an epistemological perspective. Through [Habermas's] linguistic turn, critical theory becomes a theory of social communication.

In addition to providing a basis for critical social practice, a general theory of communication is also necessary to provide a clearer understanding *and* justification of a critical social practice. As a theory which claims to be capable of informing an emancipatory practice, Habermas realizes that the basis of such a claim cannot be made on appeals to an objective or formal analysis of knowledge. The critical task facing Habermas—a task which has been debated since Socrates—is the issue of standards of rationality and truthfulness regarding their adequacy for enabling social individuals to make decisions about their life. But then the question arises of how one is to assess or evaluate a standard of rationality. This requires that rational decisions about the adequacy, correctness, or truth of normative standards be made. Accordingly, this is the direction Habermas's recent work has taken. In the face of the positivists' doubts about the possibility of standards of rationality, Habermas has undertaken to devise a replacement for instrumental standards of rationality. Habermas's conceptual strategy is to locate in the basic human activity of communication a possibility of making rational decisions about the truth of norms and values.

The Habermasian project builds upon the work of Chomsky's analysis of linguistic competence and Austin's and Searle's analysis of speech acts. In *Aspects of the Theory of Syntax,* Chomsky (1965) develops his account of linguistic competence, i.e., the ability of the individual to master an abstract set of rules based on an innate language apparatus. Chomsky's theory is not meant to grasp the actual use of speech in concrete situations but is a theory of the a priori existence of an innate language apparatus possessed by each individual. This apparatus, for Chomsky, is a "monological capability," i.e., it is part of each individual organism. Habermas (1970c), in contrast, criticizes this monological conception for neglecting the intersubjective basis of communication. Rejecting the idea of linguistic competence based on an a priori (monological) base, Habermas puts forth a general theory of communicative competence, or theory of universal pragmatics, which is designed to investigate the generic features and general structures present in all communication or every possible speech situation.

This line of reasoning has lead Habermas to a consideration of John Searle's (1969) linguistic philosophy (cf., Austin, 1975). The speech act, as the basic element of every communication, presupposes the ability of each speaker to produce and understand sentences and their relation to the social world. Accordingly, a theory of universal pragmatics "undertakes the systematic reconstruction of general structures that appear in every possible speech situation, that are themselves produced through the performance of specific types of linguistic utterances, and that serve to situate pragmatically the expressions generated by the linguistically competent speaker" (McCarthy, 1978a:276). Implicit in every speech act is a presupposition of the normative base of ideal speech. "The task of universal pragmatics is to identify and reconstruct universal conditions of possible understanding . . . of the general presuppositions of communicative action" (Habermas, 1979a:1).

Every speech act thus contains (implicitly) a claim to validity which can be assessed in ideal speech

> I shall develop the thesis that anyone acting communicatively must, in performing any speech action, raise universal validity claims and suppose that they can be vindicated (or redeemed). Insofar as he wants to participate in a process of reaching understanding, he cannot avoid raising the following validity claims. He claims to be:
>
> a. *Uttering* something understandably;
> b. Giving (the hearer) *something* to understand;
> c. Making *himself* thereby understandable; and
> d. Coming to an understanding with another person.
>
> (From Habermas, 1979a:2.)

The research program aimed at reconstructing the validity basis of speech has been termed universal pragmatics by Habermas.

In the essay "What Is Universal Pragmatics?" Habermas (1979a:1–68) draws the outlines of his reconstruction. In this work he delineates the "system of rules that adult subjects master to the extent that they can fulfill *the conditions for a happy employment of sentences in utterances*, no matter to which particular language the sentences may belong and in which accidental contexts the utterance may be embedded" (1979a:26). Habermas (1971:314) had pointed to the importance of language for critical theory in his inaugural lecture at Frankfurt University in 1965:

> The human interest in autonomy and responsibility is not mere fancy, for it can be aprehended *a priori*. What raises us out of nature is the only thing we can know: *language*. Through its structure autonomy and responsibility are posited for us. Our first sentence expresses unequivocally the intention of universal and unconstrained consensus.

The concern is not with the grammatical rules (syntax, phonetics) for constructing adequate sentences. Although this ability to produce and understand sentences is presupposed by Habermas's concept of universal pragmatics, his central focus is on understanding and situating communicative interaction in relation to the external world. As Habermas puts it:

> By "communicative competence" I understand the ability of a speaker oriented to mutual understanding to embed a well-formed sentence in relations to reality, that is:
> 1. To choose the propositional sentence in such a way that either the truth conditions of the proposition stated or the existential presuppositions of the proposition content mentioned are supposedly fulfilled (so that the hearer can share the knowledge of the speaker [i.e. external reality/truth]);
> 2. To express his intentions in such a way that the linguistic expression represents what is intended (so that the hearer can trust the speaker [i.e. internal reality/sincerity or truthfulness]);
> 3. To perform the speech act in such a way that it conforms to recognized norms or to accepted self-images (so that the hearer can be in accord with the speaker in shared value orientations [i.e. normative reality/rightness]) (1979a:29).

The ability to participate in communicative interaction presupposes the conditions of equality, fairness and the absence of any constraints on communication. Accordingly, communicative competence is grounded in the ideal of the emancipated society:

> The ideal speaking-situation is anticipated with the help of our linguistic means of construction. Through the symmetrical distribution of chance by the choice of and practice of acts of speaking which relate to (a) statements as statements, (b) the relationship of the speaker to his remarks, and (c) the observance or rules, are linguistic-theoretical designations for what we customarily comprehend under the notions of truth, freedom, and justice (Habermas, 1979a:132).

The implication of a universal pragmatics are ultimately related to Habermas's attempt to articulate and ground a conception of rationality and critique.[25] In an unpublished manuscript, McCarthy (1978b:29–30) has succinctly summarized Habermas's intent:

> Habermas attempts to show that truth and rightness claims require discursive justification and thus have to be analyzed in terms of the possibility of rational consensus; that a consensus is rationally motivated only if it is a result of the force of the argument advanced and not of accidental or systematic constraints on communication; that this absence from constraint obtains when the pragmatic structure of communication is such that there is an effective equality of opportunity for the participants to assume dialogue roles; and finally that the requirements for this "ideal speech situation" are connected with conditions for an ideal or pure form of interaction. The outcome of this chain of reasoning is that the idea of the good and just life from which critical theory takes its start is inherent in the notions of truth and rightness and as such is anticipated in every act of speech. Thus *critique need be neither arbitrary nor totally context-dependent; its guiding principles are built into the very structure of discourse, they are grounded in the "fundamental norms of rational speech."*

The preceding discussion of the theory of universal pragmatics might seem remote from a concrete methodology of critical social inquiry. By examining Habermas's general theory of socialization, the link between his theory of communication and his overall program for critical theory will become clearer.

Habermas's interest in the processes of socialization derives from the early critical theorists' concern with the integration of social-psychological concepts with socioeconomic concepts (see Adorno, 1967–68; Marcuse, 1970; Jacoby, 1975). Their interest in the importance of the individual and his/her ego development is connected with the image of an emancipated society as dependent on individuals with autonomous selves. For example, in the *Eclipse of Reason* Horkheimer (1947:105) refects on the point that a totalitarian society cannot tolerate or produce autonomous and morally upright individuals:

> The history of Western civilization could be written in terms of the growth of the ego as the underling sublimates, that is internalizes, the commands of his master who has preceded him in self-discipline . . . [i.e., the] ego of domination, command, and organization.

Habermas (1979a:70–71) recognizes that this emphasis on social-psychological issues must be preserved, especially those psychological studies of ego identity:

> If one considers the normative implications of concepts such as ego strength, dismantling the ego-distant part of the superego, and reducing the domain in which unconscious defense mechanisms function, it becomes clear that psychoanalysis also singles out certain personality structures as ideal. When psychoanalysis is interpreted as a form of language analysis, its normative meaning is exhibited in the fact that the

structural model of ego, id, and superego presupposes unconstrained, pathologically undistorted communication. In psychoanalytic literature these normative implications are, of course, usually rendered explicit in connection with the therapeutic goals of analytic treatment. In the social-psychological works of the *Institut für Sozialforschung* one can show that the basic concepts of psychoanalytic theory could enter integrally into description, hypothesis formation, and measuring instruments precisely because of their normative content. The early studies by Fromm of the sadomasochistic character and by Horkheimer of authority and the family, Adorno's investigation of the mechanisms for the formation of prejudice in authoritarian personalities, and Marcuse's theoretical work on instinct structure and society all follow the same conceptual strategy: *basic psychological and sociological concepts can be interwoven because the perspectives projected in them of an autonomous ego and an emancipated society reciprocally require one another.*

The turn taken by Habermas at this point is not in the direction of Freudian psychoanalysis but toward analytic ego psychology, cognitive developmental psychology, and symbolic interactionist theory of action as necessary extensions of the theoretical and practical projects of emancipatory thought.[26]

Since the continued existence of any society is dependent on the reproduction of its members, Habermas's focus is on developing a framework for understanding how an individual's identity is formed in relation to different forms of social integration. As a part of his work on universal pragmatics, Habermas conceives of the study of individual socialization and ego development in terms of the "rational reconstruction of universal competences":

> Concept formation in sociology is obviously linked up with the everyday concepts in which members of social groups construct the normative reality of their social environment. This suggests developing sociological action theory as a theory that attempts to reconstruct the universal components of the relevant pre-theoretical knowledge of sociological laymen. Sociology would . . . no longer choose its basic concepts conventionally, but develop them with the aim of characterizing the general formal properties of the socialized subject's capability for action, as well as those of action systems. . . . The expression "interactive competence" stands for the assumption that the abilities of socially acting subjects can be investigated from the perspective of a universal—i.e. independent of specific cultures—competence, just as are language and cognition (Habermas, quoted in McCarthy 1978a:335–6).

Habermas's intention is to expand his notion of universal competences to include, in addition to linguistic competence, competence in interaction, cognition, and egological realms as well.

Drawing upon the work of Piaget, Kohlberg, and Loevinger, Habermas construes ego development and socialization as (ideally) a process of acquiring, in stages, linguistic, cognitive, and interactive competences. These processes result (ideally) in the acquisition of increased autonomy for the individual in relation to his/her external world. Although this project is still evolving and is very tentative, Habermas's (1979a:69–94) intent is to provide an understanding of individual autonomy through a reconstruction of the universal competences acquired by the individual in a series of stages. The direction of this ego-formative process leads (ideally) toward the increasing autonomy of the individual. By this Habermas (1979a:74) means

> the independence that the ego acquires through successful problem-solving, and through growing capabilities for problem-solving, in dealing with
> a) The reality of external nature and of a society that can be controlled from a strategic point of view;
> b) The nonobjectified symbolic structure of a partly internalized culture and society; and
> c) The internal nature of culturally interpreted needs, of drives that are not amenable to communication, and of the body.

As Habermas points out, the sociopolitical significance of ego development is enormous—only with the formation of an independent, autonomous, and responsible ego and self-identity can the individual (potentially) free him/herself from the facticity of the given reality.

Although Habermas's interest in a social-psychological perspective is congruent with the early critical theorists' attempts to systematically develop a theory of the mediation between subjective consciousness and objective conditions, his current work represents a significant departure from his predecessors' concerns with the psychic dimension of social existence. The early Frankfurters argued against that sociologistic reductionism in traditional social science and Marxism which obliterates the dialectic between the individual and society. What is missing is an analysis of society's penetration into, and relations with, the psychic structure of the individual. Within orthodox Marxism, the analysis of the subjective dealt primarily with the role and place of the historical individual within *objective* processes (cf., discussion by Jacoby, 1975).

The Frankfurters' original concern with the psychoanalytic study of subjectivity cannot be understood apart from the failure of the European revolutions. As Korsch (1977:128) expressed this concern in his 1920 article "Fundamentals of Socialization":

> In the enormously fateful months after November, 1918, as the political power organizations of the bourgeoisie collapsed and nothing external stood in the way of the transition from capitalism to socialism, the great hour had nonetheless to slip by unseized because the *social-psychological* presuppositions for its utilization were greatly lacking.

It was the concern with the subjective moment of revolution which animated the early critical theorists' appropriation of Freudian psychoanalysis. With the entrance of Erich Fromm into the Institute of Social Research in 1932, the conceptual armament of psychoanalysis was firmly incorporated into the "critical project" and was to inform much of the subsequent research project of the Institute. As Fromm (1978) had first formulated it, the synthesis of Marx and Freud was an extension of Freud's diagnosis of individual psychic pathologies to their root. That is, a critical psychoanalysis indicates how the individual is dialectically embedded and rooted in the social structure. In exposing the falsity of the bourgeois notion of the purely private and autonomous individual or self, a psychoanalytic critical theory is capable of illuminating the "universal in and over the individual" (Marcuse, 1955:52ff.). This is the revolutionary and critical contribution of the psychoanalytic addition to critical theory—to identify the social within the individual. As Marcuse (1955:232) writes in *Eros and Civilization:* "Psychoanalysis elucidates the universal in the individual experience. To that extent, and only to that extent, can psychoanalysis break the reification in which human relations are petrified."

Whereas the early Frankfurt School utilized social-psychological concepts to illuminate prevalent forms of social consciousness (e.g., Adorno, et al., 1950) or, in the case of the later Marcuse (1955, 1972), to provide a positive specification of the biological base of an emancipated society, Habermas's appropriation of the problem of the relation between social processes and ego formation takes a different (though not opposed) direction. Habermas starts from the early Frankfurters' political recognition that the development of an autonomous ego is blocked by an irrational social order and, concomitantly, critical consciousness and an autonomous ego are mutually dependent (see Adorno 1967–68). To this extent, Habermas's identification of the emancipatory cognitive interest of psychoanalysis and his theory of ego development is congruent with the Frankfurt School's view of the potential of psychoanalysis (as a theory of society *and* individual therapy) to lead to a critical theory of society *and* a praxis of liberation. As such Habermas has *not,* as many leftist critics allege, "abandoned the original product of critical theory . . . for a professorial nightmare, a babel of deliberative gobbledygook" (Miller, 1975).

It should be obvious, however, that Habermas's theory of ego development takes critical theory in a distinctly different direction than the earlier members of the Frankfurt School.[27] Whereas, for example, Adorno (1967–68) and Marcuse (1970) ultimately took the position that a totally administered society had all but eliminated the autonomous ego, Habermas devotes his attention—via the model of ego development—to clarifying the question "who is the critical theorist, and from what standpoint does he or she criticize?" (Howard, 1976:177). As part of his larger attempt to rationally reconstruct those universal individual competences necessary to the attainment of an emancipated society, Habermas's recent work represents an advance beyond the pessimistic and negative formulations of the earlier Frankfurters. Whether his persistent attempts to justify the epistemological and normative foundations for critical theory are successful remains to be seen.[28] Indeed, the enormous scope and ambitiousness of Habermas's projected solution to the "riddle of history" is still very, very tentative and programmatic. This is not to absolve Habermas from criticism. There are some obvious problems in his scheme which one must confront. Habermas has yet to provide a satisfactory resolution to the vicious circularity of all attempts to resolve questions of the foundation of critique. More specifically, it seems that his latest atempt—in the model of ego development and identity—contradicts Habermas's hermeneutic emphasis on the situational character of concepts and categories and the critique of all attempts to provide universal/evolutionary perspectives. This is not the time or place to answer these questions, but they are questions which must be answered by critical theory. Habermas's analyses of this subject cannot be neglected by anyone wishing to provide a model of critical social theory capable of informing the construction of a sociopolitical order which is truly emancipatory.

NOTES

1. Cf. the recent work of Anthony Giddens in *Studies in Social and Political Theory*, and Alvin Gouldner in *For Sociology, The Dialectics of Ideology and Technology*, and *The Future of Intellectuals and the Rise of the New Class*. Both theorists similarly point to the necessity of an adequate critical theory of society preserving the empirically rigorous character of the positivist framework for social scientific inquiry.

2. Habermas also mentions the criticisms of positivism developed by Karl Otto-Apel, Paul Feyerabend, Thomas Kuhn, Imre Lakatos and Stephen Toulmin: see his "Postscript" to *Knowledge and Human Interests*.

3 For some useful attempts in this direction see Giddens, 1975 and *SSPT*; Habermas *KHI*; Kolakowski, 1969.

4. For useful accounts of the history of positivism and its influence upon the social sciences see: Kolakowski, 1969; Simon, 1963; Achinsten and Barker, 1969; Gay, 1977; Lenzer, 1975; Radnitzky, 1973; Adorno, et al., 1976; Giddens, 1974; Brown, 1979.

5. Adherence to any one of the positivist attitudes does not imply that one will necessarily adopt the outlook *en toto*. Cf., Giddens's (1975) discussion.

6. See, inter alia, Gardiner, 1959, and Bernstein, 1976, for discussions of the impact of the deductive model upon the social sciences and historical disciplines.

7. For a useful selection of more contemporary versions of logical positivism, see the collection edition edited by Ayer, 1959.

8. It is not surprising that the early logical positivists used the methodological procedures of the established natural sciences as the model for social inquiry. The original members of the Vienna Circle were, on the whole, neither social scientists or philosophers. Rather, as Hempel notes, they "had devoted a large part of their academic studies—often including their doctoral work—to logic and mathematics, to physics, or to a combination of those subjects" (1969:163).

9. See the useful collection of articles translated in Andrew Arato and Eike Gebhardt (eds.), *The Essential Frankfurt School Reader* (1978).

10. The whole of Marx's critique of the categories of bourgeois political economy stands as an important methodological reflection upon the nature of "critique" in social inquiry and, as such, has direct relevance for current methodological controversies. See esp. Marx's *Grundrisse*, 1973:81–111.

11. Cf., Adorno's essay "Subject and Object" in Arato and Gebhardt. *The Essential Frankfurt School Reader*, pp. 497–511.

12. For a clear and reasoned refutation of Popper's views on Marx, see W.A. Suchting, "Marx, Popper and Historicism," 1972.

13. In his autobiography, *Unended Quest*, Popper claims responsibility (credit) for the "death" of logical positivism; see his section, "Who Killed Logical Positivism?" (p. 88).

14. Dick Howard observes that the inability of critical theory to articulate a positive stance was responsible for the pessimism which characterized the Frankfurters' writings. (Howard, 1977:115ff.).

15. Published in 1957, this article appeared in the German edition of *Theory and Practice;* unfortunately it was not included in the English translation. This discussion of Habermas's work draws upon the masterful explication by Thomas McCarthy (1978a; see also McCarthy 1973, 1978b, 1979; and Dallmayr and McCarthy, 1977). McCarthy's exposition—on several points clearer than Habermas himself—is absolutely essential to any serious consideration of Habermas's work or critical theory in general.

16. McCarthy (1978a,b) develops this point.

17. During the past two decades or so, positivistic social science has come under heavy attack from several (often opposing) traditions of social thought. These arguments against the objectivistic presuppositions of positivism have not been ones which argue for the impossibility or worthlessness of the social disciplines. As has been illustrated in the recent work of diverse individuals such as Isaiah Berlin, Charles Taylor, Hanah Pitking, Quentin Skinner, Alasdair MacIntyre, Herbert Blumer, Erving Goffman, Aaron Cicourel, Maurice Natanson, John O'Neill, etc. the common point of departure is the recognition that humans are self-interpreting beings and these interpretations are constitutive of the social world we wish to understand. The point to be made is that an adequate and comprehensive analysis of social phenomena must have reference to the understanding of reality as it is experienced and interpreted by human actors in everyday life. This is not to argue that the methods of causal analysis must be completely replaced by those of interpretative understanding. As Habermas takes great care to point out, the matter does not involve the exclusive choice of one methodological procedure over the other. The point is to bring the two approaches under one roof in which both procedures are brought together in a new form. (Cf., McCarthy's [1978a:140ff.] discussion of these points.)

18. A consequence of positivistic notions of objectivity and the methodological dichotomies of fact and value, and of description and evaluation, is that the theoretical process itself is left unexamined. This is the meaning of the charge that positivism is unreflective: the (positivist) theorist has no interest in (nor is it important) the understanding of the grounds of theorizing itself. Positivism is concerned *not* with the intersubjective ground of theory itself but with how a theoretical proposition is to be empirically validated. The problem of the source of knowledge is defined out of existence by the positivist; social theory is thus cut adrift from philosophy and epistemology. The positivist is left without any grounds for evaluating and assessing his/her roots in the sociocultural world, the purpose of knowledge, and the commitment of the theorist.

19. Anthony Giddens has made a similar point in his recent work *Studies in Social and Political Theory* (1977). As he puts it, the reflection on the conditions under which social life takes place involves a recognition of:

the degree of "permeability" of the boundary between the knowledge claimed by professional investigators as the product of esoteric expertise and that applied by lay actors in their day to day lives. The cumulation of nomological knowledge in natural science typically occurs within rather clear parameters separating scientists and laymen, that broadly speaking are accepted by both sides, although there may be some degree of controversy over how far scientific knowledge can or should be "popularized" and made accessible to the lay population. But the boundaries between "expert" and "lay" knowledge in the social sciences are unlikely to be as clear-cut as they have become in natural science (nor is it desirable that they should be so). This is because "expertise" in the world of social relations is not incidental to social life, but is the very medium of its orderliness. The necessary intersubjectivity of the social world makes it "our world" in a way that has no parallel in the relation of human beings to nature, where knowledge is certainly routinely used in a transformative way, but where that knowledge is not part of the conditions of existence of the universe of object and events to which it relates. (*SSPT*:27)

20. How Habermas intends to positively accomplish this task is found in his communications theory and theory of social evolution—to be discussed below.

21. Against more sophisticated versions of the hermeneutic/interpretative approach (viz., Gadamer), which draw out the sociohistorical dimension of the process of understanding in order to avoid an ahistorical conception of social inquiry, Habermas identifies a similar inadequacy. While Gadamer's account of hermeneutic reflection does not conceptualize meaning as constituted merely by individuals, it tends to lose sight of the point that meanings can also function to occlude the understanding of the institutional structure from which they emerge. To the extent that the hermeneutic approach limits itself to understanding obtained through a dialogue between the interpreter and social actor, it is incapable of treating the dialogue as a process which may conceal and distort oppressive relations rooted in, e.g., a system of hierarchical class relations.

22. The long and controversial relationship between Freudianism, psychoanalysis and critical theory will not be discussed here. For useful discussions see Jay (1973), Jacoby (1975), and Robinson (1969). Nor will I treat the adequacy of Habermas's interpretation of Freud's own work; for discussion of this point see McIntosh (1977); Nichols (1972). For a discussion of psychoanalysis and its relation to the hermeneutic/interpretative tradition, see Ricoeur (1970).

23. Freud (1966:176–8) conceived of the psychoanalytic interpretative process as very similar to philological analysis.

24. I will not discuss the objections which have been raised to Habermas's utilization of psychoanalysis as a model for critical theory which can be applied to the analysis of reality with a practical intent. The center of the debate concerns the extension of the therapeutic relationship in psychoanalysis to the practical critique of society which is aimed at the radical transformation of human existence. (Cf., Bernstein 1976; Dallmayr 1972a; McCarthy, 1978a for discussion of this point.)

25. It also serves as the base for his theory of socialization and theory of social evolution —discussed below. See especially Habermas, "History and Evolution" (1979b).

26. See his essays "Moral Development and Ego Identity" and "Historical Materialism and the Development of Normative Structures" in *Communication and the Evolution of Society* (1979a).

27. Habermas's essay "Moral Development and Ego Identity"—originally delivered as a commemorative address marking the fiftieth anniversary of the founding of the Institute for Social Research—begins by situating his position in relation to the original Frankfurt formulations of the "critical project."

28. In addition to McCarthy's (1978a) masterful work on Habermas, cf., the following critical discussions of Habermas's recent work: Whitebook (1979), Cohen (1979), Honneth (1979), Schmidt (1979), Sensat (1979), and Hohendahl (1979).

REFERENCES

Achinsten, Peter, and Barker, Stephen
1969   The Legacy of Logical Positivism. Baltimore: John Hopkins University Press.
Adorno, Theodor
1967–8 ''Sociology and psychology'' (2 parts). New Left Review Nos. 46 & 47.
1972   ''Society.'' In M. Horkheimer and T. Adorno (eds.), Aspects of Sociology, Boston: Beacon Press.
1973   Negative Dialectics. New York: Seabury Press.
1976   ''On the logic of the social sciences'' In T. Adorno, et al. (eds.), The Positivist Dispute in German Sociology. London: Heinemann.
1978   ''Subject and object.'' In A. Arato and E. Gebhardt (eds.), The Essential Frankfurt School Reader. New York: Urizen Books.
Adorno, Theodor W., Else Frenkel-Brunswick, Daniel J. Levinson, and Nevitt Sanford
1950   The Authoritarian Personality. New York: Harper & Row.
Arato, Andrew, and Gebhardt, Eike (eds.)
1978   The Essential Frankfurt Reader. New York: Urizen Books.
Arendt, Hannah
1959   The Human Condition. Garden City, N.Y.: Doubleday.
Austin, J. L.
1975   How to Do Things With Words, 2nd ed. Cambridge, Mass.: Harvard University Press.
Ayer, A. J. (ed.)
1959   Logical Positivism. New York: Harper & Row.
Bernstein, Richard
1971   Praxis and Action. Philadelphia: University of Pennsylvania Press.
1976   The Reconstruction of Social and Political Theory. New York: Harcourt Brace Jovanovich.
Blalock, Hubert
1969   Theory Construction. Englewood Cliffs, N.J.: Prentice-Hall.
Blum, Alan, et al.
1974   On the Beginning of Social Inquiry. Boston: Routledge & Kegan Paul.
Brodbeck, May
1968   ''Explanation, prediction and 'Imperfect' knowledge.'' In May Brodbeck, (ed.), Readings in the Philosophy of the Social Sciences. New York: Macmillan.
Chomsky, Noam
1965   Aspects of the Theory of Syntax. New York: Cambridge University Press.
Cohen, Jean
1979   ''Why more political theory.'' Telos No. 40.
Dallmayr, Fred, and McCarthy, Thomas (eds.)
1977   Understanding and Social Inquiry. Notre Dame, Ind.: University of Notre Dame Press.
Fromm, Erich
1978   ''The method and function of an analytical social psychology: notes in psycho-analysis and historical materialism.'' In A. Arato and E. Gebhardt (eds.), The Essential Frankfurt School Reader. New York: Urizen Books.
Gadamer, Hans-Georg
1975   Truth and Method. New York: Seabury Press.
Gardiner, Patrick (ed.)
1959   Theories of History. New York: Free Press.
Gay, Peter
1977   The Enlightenment. New York: Norton.

Giddens, Anthony
    1974   (ed.) Positivism and Sociology. London: Heinemann.
    1976   New Rules of Sociological Method. London: Hutchinson.
    1977   Studies in Social and Political Theory. London: Hutchinson.
Gouldner, Alvin
    1973   For Sociology: Renewal and Critique in Sociology Today. New York: Basic
            Books.
    1976   Dialectic of Ideology and Technology. New York: Seabury Press.
    1979   The Future of Intellectual and the Rise of the New Class. New York: Seabury
            Press.
Habermas, Jürgen
    1970a Zur Logik der Sozialwissenschaften. Frankfurt: Suhrkamp.
    1970b "On systematically distorted communication." Inquiry No. 13.
    1970c "Towards a Theory of Communicative Competence." Inquiry No. 13.
    1971   Knowledge and Human Interests. Boston: Beacon Press.
    1973   Theory and Practice. Boston: Beacon Press.
    1975a Legitimation Crisis. Boston: Beacon Press.
    1975b "A postscript to Knowledge and Human Interests." Philosophy of the Social
            Sciences No. 3.
    1976   "The analytical theory of science and dialectics." In T. Adorno, et al. (eds.), The
            Positivist Dispute in German Sociology. London: Heinemann.
    1979a Communication and the Evolution of Society. Boston: Beacon Press.
    1979b "History and evolution." Telos No. 39.
Heller, Agnes
    1978   "The Positivist Dispute as a turning point in German post-war theory." New
            German Critique No. 15.
Hempel, Carl
    1965   Aspects of Scientific Explanation. New York: Free Press. .
    1969   "Logical Positivism and the Social Sciences." In S. Barker and P. Achinstein (eds.).
            The Legacy of Logical Positivism. Baltimore: John Hopkins University Press.
Hohendahl, Peter
    1979   "Critical theory, public sphere and culture." New German Critique No. 16.
Honneth, Axel
    1979   "Communication and reconcilliation." Telos No. 39.
Horkheimer, Max
    1947   Eclipse of Reason. New York: Columbia University Press.
    1972   Critical Theory. New York: Herder & Herder.
Horkheimer, Max, and Adorno, Theodor
    1972   The Dialectic of Enlightenment. New York: Herder & Herder.
Howard, Dick
    1976   " 'Moral development and ego identity': A clarification." Telos No. 27.
    1977   The Marxian Legacy. New York: Urizen.
Jacoby, Russell
    1975   Social Amnesia: A Critique of Contemporary Psychology from Adler to Laing.
            Boston: Beacon Press.
Jay, Martin
    1973   The Dialectical Imagination. Boston: Little Brown.
    1974   "The Frankfurt critique of Mannheim." Telos No. 20
Kolakowski, Leszek
    1969   The Alienation of Reason. Garden City, N.Y.: Doubleday.
Korsch, Karl
    1977   Karl Korsch: Revolutionary Theory. Austin: University of Texas Press.

Lenin, V. I.
1965   Materialism and Empirio-Criticism. New York: International Publs.
Lenzer, Gertrude (ed.)
1975   Auguste Comte and Positivism. New York: Harper & Row.
Lorenzer, Alfred
1970   Symbol und Verstehen im Psychoanalytischen Prozess. Frankfurt: Suhrkamp.
Marcuse, Herbert
1968   Negations: Essays in Critical Theory. Boston: Beacon Press.
1970   "The obsolescence of the Freudian concept of man." In Five Lectures. Boston: Beacon Press.
1972   Counterrevolution and Revolt. Boston: Beacon Press.
Merton, Robert
1968   Social Theory and Social Structure. New York: Free Press.
McCarthy, Thomas
1973   "On misunderstanding understanding." Theory and Decision No. 3.
1978a The Critical Theory of Jürgen Habermas. Cambridge, Mass. M.I.T. Press.
1978b "On changing relations of theory to practice in the work of Jürgen Habermas." (Unpublished manuscript.)
1979   Translator's Introduction, to J. Habermas, Communication and the Evolution of Society. Boston: Beacon Press.
McIntosh, Donald
1977   "Habermas on Freud." Social Research 44:3
Miller, James
1975   "Essay review of Habermas's *Legitimation Crisis*." Telos No. 25.
Nagel, Ernest
1961   The Structure of Science. New York: Harcourt Brace Jovanovich.
Nichols, Christopher
1972   "Science or reflection: Habermas on Freud." Philosophy of the Social Sciences 2:3.
Parsons, Talcott
1950   "The prospects of sociological theory." American Sociological Review 15.
Popper, Karl
1957   The Poverty of Historicism. New York: Harper & Row.
1962   The Open Society and Its Enemies. New York: Harper & Row.
1968   The Logic of Scientific Discovery. London: Routledge & Kegan Paul.
1969   Conjectures and Refutations. London: Routledge & Kegan Paul.
1972   Objective Knowledge. New York: Oxford University Press.
1978   Unended Quest: An Intellectual Biography. London: Fontana.
Radnitzky, Gerard
1973   Contemporary Schools of Metascience. Chicago: Regnery.
Ricoeur, Paul
1970   Freud and Philosophy. New Haven, Conn.: Yale University Press.
1971   "The model of the text." Social Research 38:4.
Robinson, Paul
1969   The Freudian Left. New York: Harper & Row.
Searle, John
1969   Speech Acts. New York: Cambridge University Press.
Sensat, Julius
1979   Habermas and Marxism: An Appraisal. Beverly Hills, Calif.: Sage Publns.
Simon, W.
1963   European Positivism in the 19th Century. Ithaca, N.Y.: Cornell University Press.

Smelser, Neil
    1968   Essays in Sociological Explanation. Englewood Cliffs, N.J.: Prentice-Hall.
    1969   "Some personal thoughts on the pursuit of sociological problems." Sociological
           Inquiry No. 39.
Suchting, W.A.
    1972   "Marx, Popper and historicism." Inquiry 15.
Wellmer, Albrecht
    1971   Critical Theory of Society. New York: Herder & Herder.
Whitebook, Joel
    1979   "The problem of nature in Habermas." Telos No. 40.
Wittgenstein, Ludwig
    1961   Tractatus Logico-Philosophicus. London: Routledge & Kegan Paul.
Zetterberg, Hans
    1965   On Theory and Verification in Sociology, 3rd ed. Totowa, N.J.: Bedminster Press.

THE TRANSMUTATION OF WEBER'S *STAND* IN AMERICAN SOCIOLOGY AND ITS SOCIAL ROOTS

Morton G. Wenger

The analyses of the distribution of power in societies which Max Weber presents in *Wirtschaft und Gesellschaft* exhibit prodigious conceptual fertility. With the exception of Weber's provocative methodological stance, the comment they occasion and the subsequent development they engender are unparalleled among the theorist's many contributions. The idea of a "tripartite" model of social stratification, its lineal descendant of status crystallization/inconsistency and the emphasis on "lifestyle" are only the first among many offshoots of this analytical reconstruction of social inequality. In American sociology, Weber's analysis has formed the cutting edge of a comprehensive attack on Marxist inequality theory which is typically portrayed as relatively mechanistic, oversimplified, materialistic and history-bound. Cox (1950), Pfautz and Duncan (1950), Zeitlin (1967, 1968, 1973), and Pease et al. (1970) have rejected this in-

Current Perspectives in Social Theory, volume 1, 1980, pages 357–378.

terpretation of Marxist theory with varying degrees of specificity. In the process, however, they, like the theorists they criticize, tended to systematically misinterpret Weber himself. The question is one of whether Weber's diverse statements about inequality really form an incantation with which the ghost of Marx may be banished or whether, more accurately, this use of Weber is an artifact of his interpreters' ideological stance.

The matter of conceptual paternity raised here has contributory as well as critical aspects. Although the task of refuting the claims of a wide variety of theoretical statements of "descent" from Weber is significant as such, it stands beside a more intriguing and ultimately more productive matter. If Weber's own position only partially encompasses the mass of the putative deductions of his readers, the essential form and significance of the original work thus remain undelineated and unrealized. Furthermore, the disentanglement of Weber from his self-proclaimed heirs requires metatheoretical elaboration. If a widespread theoretical tendency comes into being, flourishes, and attains conceptual hegemony in a major sociological tradition, then explanation is required. Among other things this involves a comparative and critical portrayal of the variant readings of Weber and an estimation of their actual affinity with the theorist's own positions. The tactic by which this may be achieved involves a textual and contextual examination of the pivotal concept in Weber's discussions of inequality in society: that of *Stand*. (Henceforward, *Stand* will be used to denote Weber's own usage, as opposed to its subsequent derivatives.)

STAND AS "STATUS GROUP"

The starting point of statements defining Weber's position on the *Stand* is a brief passage in *Economy and Society* wherein Weber (Gerth and Mills, 1946:286–7) notes:

> In contrast to classes, *status groups* are normally communities. They are, however, often of an amorphous kind. In contrast to the purely economically determined "class situation" we wish to designate as "status situation" every typical component of the life fate of men that is determined by a specific, positive or negative, social estimation of *honor*. This honor may be connected with any quality shared by a plurality, and, of course, it can be knit to a class situation: class distinctions are linked in the most varied ways with status distinctions.

While this is Weber's central statement on *Stand*, it is preceded and followed by intricate and cautious qualifications. These *caveats* are typical of Weber's subtle intellectual style. The establishment of limiting conditions for the deployment of his ideas comes to adumbrate Weber's concepts as much as does the definitional statement itself. As will be demonstrated, the common inattention to the context in which the concept of *Stand* is developed is a precondition for its exclusive interpretation as "status group"; taken as part of a larger fabric, the concept *cannot* be so portrayed. In any case, as "status group," *Stand* has been seen to have several salient and related characteristics which can be summarized as "looseness," "middleness," and "progressiveness." To the extent that they may be unraveled, each of these highly intertwined aspects of status group requires individual attention.

It has long been an aspect of mainstream doctrine in the study of social stratification that the succession of the social organizational forms which institutionalize inequality shows progressive development. In other words, things are getting better all the time. A trans-social and trans-historical evolutionary process is posited wherein movement takes place from systems of social impermeability to systems of social mobility. Davis (1949), in an early and classic work, identifies this epochal process as moving from caste, to estate, to class. (This will be of further interest in later discussion.) While noting the violence his own reading does to Weber, (sharing it with unnamed "recent sociologists"), and assigning its necessity to the lagged nature of historical development, Bottomore (1966) proceeds to tack "status group" on to this succession of inequality structures. By so doing, "status groups" are simultaneously imbued with the mission of progress, they transcend class, and they come to represent the attainment of a previously unparalleled human freedom. Furthermore, not only is class transcended, it is relegated to the dustbin of history. If this view of "status group" were confined to a single theorist, it would scarcely justify the attention already paid to it. Bottomore's view, however, is only the lucid summarization of a cohesive and ubiquitous theoretical tendency.

It cannot be overemphasized that if permeability is the definitive structural aspect of status groups, the replacement of class as a theoretical touchstone is "status group's" raison d'être. Intimately tied with concepts of "new middle classes" and the proletariat *embourgeoisié*, status groups come to play the role of the material carriers of "inequality without social stratification," as Wrong (1964) styles it. Rinehart (1971:149–62) has noted the related emergence of a perspective he labels, after Ossowski (1963, 1969), "non-egalitarian classlessness," the three definitive parts of which he perceives as:

> (a) a continuum of persons possessing minutely different amounts of prestige, (b) a series of status groups hierarchically arranged, (c) a vast middle class which includes a large segment of the working class (1971:149).

"Non-egalitarian classlessness" represents a distillation of the massive assault on class as an analytical tool which perhaps is best summarized in

Nisbet's (1959) "The Decline and Fall of Social Class." However, "non-egalitarian classlessness" (as a perspective on social inequality) is not always equivalent to the conventional rendering of "status group." As is evident in Riesman (1955), Birnbaum (1969), Shostak (1969), Coleman and Neugarten (1971), and others, the "middle" is occasionally seen as an undifferentiated or homogeneous mass (i.e., without status "communities"). This viewpoint denies the adequacy of class analysis, but it provides no constructive alternative. Indeed, while replacing "class," it nonetheless runs up against another form of social (dis)organization with which American sociology has been uneasy, i.e., "mass society." The model of a vast and atomized middle with tastes, values, and politics gleaned from the mass media is unlikely to have intrinsic appeal for a sociology which still pays homage to de Tocqueville, Simmel, and Durkheim. As a result, any replacement of "class" by "mass" is a trade-off of minor consolation. As an alternative, the ability of "status group" to negate *both* mass *and* class virtually guarantees its eventual creation/discovery. It is a final solution to the problems of Western sociology and, by its adherents' hopeful extension, Western society itself.

The statements aligning the "middle" of advanced capitalist societies with the Weberian concept of status group are not equally clear. Mayer (1963), Berger (1960), and Wilensky (1960) represent marginal cases wherein a middle mass is perceived, but one wherein significant variation exists as to life style *cum* consumption style. Mayer refers to these differences as "symbolic *minutiae*," but along with Wilensky he subsequently asserts the heightening significance of such differences in the face of "class" or economic/occupational homogeneity. It is a very small step from these transitional cases to well-developed "status group" positions like that of Bensman (1972), wherein it is argued that there exist vast numbers of "status communities" based upon relatively narrow sets of values. Similar arguments are to be found in Dobriner (1963), and, to a lesser extent, Martindale (1960), while Stone and Form (1953) represent an unusual variation on this theme, arguing that "communal" status *groups* exist at the "top" and "bottom" of society, but that status *aggregates* hold the "middle" ground. This is more faithful to Weber's own conception of *Stand*, and it emphasizes the role of self-consciousness in the structure and function of status group, i.e., the replacement of class as an operative concept in advanced capitalist societies due to the postulated lack of proletarian consciousness.

The conceptual evolution of status group as an orienting concept in contemporary stratification theory exhibits several facets. It develops against a background of intellectual hostility to Marxism and a quest for "classical" legitimacy. Further, the concept is the sophisticated carrier of a long tradition arguing the increasing "classlessness" of American society, which is then seen as typical of all "developed" or "modern" societies.[1] This transhistorical movement toward more open inequality structures is posited as empirically present in the vast "middles" to which wide sociological attention has been paid. In an overall ideological atmosphere of "evolutionary liberalism," such a phenomenon must be seen as de facto progressive. That is, from this general viewpoint, inequality and differentiation are evaluated as functionally necessary, but stratification is perceived as a social evil and little more than a cultural survival. As a result, the proposed historical movement toward more open inequality structures comes to be identified with the development of status orders and, in turn, socially manifest in status groups. Bottomore's (1966) historical model formalizes this elision, but it is present in rudimentary form throughout all the works cited here. Whereas in empirical reality the issues of structural permeability and progress may be analytically separated, in the present theoretical context one implies the other. Progress itself is announced by the development of status groups; they are by their nature a further extension of human freedom. As Bensman (1972) makes explicit and others suggest, membership in status groups contains a volitional element; it is a triumph over the material constraints of ascribed social position.

Here, as in any mature intellectual tradition, there is coherence among basic axioms. Thus, while "looseness," "progressiveness," and "middleness" are seldom bracketed or treated self-consciously, they nonetheless are the bedrock upon which "non-egalitarian classlessness" rests. Rinehart's (1971) reconstruction makes this clear. The unasked and thus answered question is that which inquires whether the leading concept about which this tradition orbits—status group—is what it claims to be. Are status group and *Stand* congruent concepts? The text of *Wirtschaft und Gesellschaft* can provide an answer, as does a body of previous literature which is more literal in its deployment of *Stand* and which, not coincidentally, has little intellectual capital invested in the larger model of nonegalitarian classlessness. This opposed exegetical tradition emphasizes a major contribution by Weber which is obscured by his forced investiture as the patriarch of Ross, Small, and Warner—to wit, an understanding of the internal dynamics of inequality structures.

STAND AS ESTATE

The textual grounds for rejecting the status group interpretation of *Stand* and replacing it by "estate" are immediate and uncomplicated. They include the identity of the social "strata" or sectors which Weber uses as examples and data; the mechanisms by which *Staende* are seen to develop; the social closure which such development is taken to indicate; and the place Weber assigns *Staende* within the broad sweep of history. On each of these grounds, Weber's position is diametrically opposed to the status group formulation . Rather then being the volitional end product of individuals occupying a "middle," *Stand* is a conscious creation of elites acting as "classes"; instead of representing a movement toward greater permeability of inequality structures, it represents a higher degree of stratification. Further, it is subepochal, not transepochal, i.e., it does not represent the transhistorical unfolding of an evolutionary or developmental structure but instead describes tendencies implicit in any given social order. *Stand* is the outcome of social, and not historical, imperatives. As an obvious consequence of this, within the value system of liberalism, *Stand* is a retrogressive, and not a progressive, social outcome.

In the several discussions of *Stand* which Weber presents, a span of social types are used as illustrations. In speaking of the supramarket nature of *Staende,* Weber (Wittich and Roth, 1968:928) asserts that "slaves are not . . . a 'class' in the technical sense of the term. They are . . . a *Stand.*" At another point, Weber (Gerth and Mills, 1946:192) refers to a *Stand* rejecting of "parvenus" and consisting of members who "have never besmirched its [the group's] honor by their own economic labor." Speaking of the development of *Staende* in America, Weber (Gerth and Mills, 1946:188) lists the "First Families of Virginia" and the descendants of the Pilgrims and/or the Knickerbockers as the most likely candidates for elevation to the status of *Stand.* Similarly, when describing social tendencies at work in the then-contemporary Untied States, Weber alludes to the increasingly "precarious camaraderie" of "American gentlemen" toward their clerks. In this Weber is as unlike Mayer (1963) as is possible; he (Weber) sees an increase in social distance over time with egalitarianism a vanishing relic of the American past. The discussions of emerging American "high society" and "the street" in the context of Prussian dueling circles is yet another instance of the social situations where Weber applies the concept of *Stand.* Similarly, when speaking of the social extremes of these elite sectors, Weber refers to Calderon's peasantry and the aforementioned slaves (Gerth and Mills, 1946:192). It requires a lofty social perspective to amalgamate these historical strata into a "middle," old or new. It is yet more difficult to present these *Staende* as equivalent to a middle class largely composed of affluent proletarians, whether of blue or white collar—those most frequently subsumed under the category of "status group."

There are two subtly distinguishable but interwoven conceptual trends active here. The first and more straightforward embodies the issue of the applicability of *Stand* to the middle sector of modern societies. The second involves the more intricate matter of the development of *Staende.*

This, in turn, requires the identification of the "class range" of the phenomenon and the social activity by which it is created. As a further involution, an understanding of the preceding is itself a precondition for the evaluation of the degree to which the emergence of *Staende* represents a "progressive" development. By proceeding in this manner, the final piece of the puzzle is put in place—the actual significance of Weber's analysis of *Stand* for a model of the historical development of inequality structures.

Heberle (1959) attempts to reconcile the relationship between *Staende* and classes by establishing the two social phenomena as independent but historically overlapping. This is a partial, but not a complete, step to the unraveling of the Gordian knot anti-class analysis has tied. Although Heberle correctly indicates that the validity of the concepts of class and *Stand* is a matter to be resolved only in terms of particular societies at particular moments in history, he does not reveal the relationship between class and *Stand* to be anything more than one of temporal coincidence. Any relationship between class amd *Stand* is seen to be historical, not social. Pfautz and Duncan (1950) go a good deal beyond this in their astute examination of Weber on *Stand*. In passing, they construct arguments closely paralleling in content, if not form, those presented here (Pfautz and Duncan, 1970:212):

> The "upper-upper" and the "lower-lower" classes are more nearly, in Weber's terms, "status groups" than "social classes." The concept of "closure," which is crucial for the structure of status groups, would seem to have little meaning relative to the "middle" classes; whereas the estate-tendencies at the extremes of the social class configuration as well as the "communal" character of the upper-uppers and the lower-lowers are obvious from the data at hand.

It should be recalled that one of the defects commonly assigned to the concept of class by non- and anti-Marxist analysts has been its perceived failure to come into being as a sociopolitical reality in advanced capitalist societies. In other words, classes have not shown class consciousness. How then do *estates* originate? Around what mutuality does their closure coalesce? While Weber was seen to argue that *Staende* are *of necessity* groups, inequality groups are *not* of necessity *Staende*. Further, as Cox (1950) informs us, Weber did *not* say that classes *could not* become groups. Indeed, a substantial portion of Weber's discussion of "class" deals with the conditions under which class *may* become the basis for "communal action." This retroactively illuminates the relationship between *Stand* and "class," while simultaneously revealing the social origins of *Staende*, i.e., *Staende* grow out of classes. They are not "merely" classes, they are already self-conscious classes which have undergone further closure and thus represent classes "at a higher level."

They are based *in* the economic order, but they transcend it. This complex relationship between class and *Stand* is the source of Weber's many warnings about the intertwining of the two "modes of the distribution of power."

The power of the "marketplace," which Weber (Gerth and Mills, 1946: 186–187) styles as "purely economic," is only one system of super- and subordination. When power comes to rest on deference, esteem, prestige, respect, and/or honor—as it does in an estate system—by definition it resorts to symbolic displays ("style of life") to actualize itself. There is tangential and direct reference to this in statements by Weber that have already been cited, e.g., the allusions to the "the street," lineage, and behavioral "conventions." Weber goes beyond this description to trace the conditions which allow for the development *Staende,* and thence to a description of the means by which they are constructed. The "class" origin of *Staende* is confirmed when Weber suggests that it is the economic conditions of a society that determine the possibilities of estate formation (Gerth and Mills, 1946:193–4). More precisely, monopoly, technological stagnation, and the decline of the entrepreneurial ethic are all harbingers of the emergence of estates. Weber sees this as a potential for any stable economic order ("epochs and countries"). This is of extraordinary consequence for the refutation of the view of status group as the acme of historical development. For Weber then, estate tendencies exist in any society.

It is obvious that this view is destructive of the view of *Staende* as representing a highly permeable inequality structure. In addition, this model of the dynamics of social inequality rather neatly rejects the notion of transhistorical progress itself at the same time that it deprives it of its putative carrier, *Stand.* Cox (1950:226), albeit critically, indicates this when he characterizes Weber's conception of social orders "not as moving from a condition of stratification to that of atomized social status but *vice versa.*" In passing, this serves to clarify the defect in Heberle's (1959) view of the relationship between class and *Stand.* Heberle's picture of nineteenth- and twentieth-century European society as a mélange of the two forms of inequality structure is descriptively correct, but analytically deficient. His implied acceptance of transhistorical progression leads him to see the societies in question as caught on the cusp of transition from one all-encompassing macrosocial form to the next. A deduction from this would be that given time, only "classes" would remain. This is, of course, precisely contrary to Weber's developmental but non-teleological model. In Weber's view, the nineteenth century represents a period of overlap between the remaining estates of land-based "feudalism" (which itself becomes a more tenuous concept as Bloch's [1964] analysis suggests) and the emerging classes of industrial capitalism. To this point, there is no difference between Heberle and Weber. However,

Weber's analyses of nineteenth-century America suggest quite different conclusions than those Heberle proposes. An extension of Heberle's position would seem to suggest an increasingly ascendant class order replacing a concomitantly declining estate order—ultimately leaving the class order standing alone. This view of estates as historically unilinear rather than multilinear repetitive phenomena diverges from the outcome discernible in Weber's stance. In a model such as Weber's, a *particular* estate order (land-based feudalism) disappears while another (wage labor–based capitalism) may come into being even though for an *indefinite period* a "class" order exists. This sophisticated cyclicalism is consistent with that present in Weber's analyses of charisma and institutionalization as well as being harmonious with the fashion among German historiographers of the time. It also does no violence to Weber's antievolutionism; in fact, it affirms it.

A number of the loose ends present in the use of *Stand* have been tidied up; a number still remain. Primary, *Stand* has been restored to its proper status as a nonprogressive, nonpermeable, and trans-social but *not* trans-historical phenomenon. In the process, the separation of "status group" from *Stand* is achieved, and "nonegalitarian classlessness" is denied its self-proclaimed paternity. This is an accomplishment, but largely a negative or critical one. It still leaves the question of the *process by which Staende* comes into being. Associated with this are the grounds for identifying *Staende*, not with the associational tendencies of amorphous middles, but with the class interests of already self-conscious elites. While observable in Weber's choice of illustrations, this aspect of the dynamics of *Stand* still demands explication.

At their root, *Staende* are self-creating phenomena. The analyses of Bloch (1964), Mayhew (1968), and Leach (1967) on feudalism, ascription, and endogamy are all confirmatory of this, although they touch on Weber only peripherally. Weber sees classes in their "primitive" forms as developing organically out of the interactions of a vast and abstract "market." *Staende*, emerging as they do from already communal class situations, are volitional creations. This has significance in and of itself, but it also refers to the implications of closure for impermeability. As was noted, the "status group" formulation, especially in more developed works (cf., Bensman, 1972), on occasion acknowledges or even emphasizes the volitional element implicit in the concept of *Stand*, but only in a limited manner. *Individual* membership choice is seen as the functional means of entry into the "status community" and, as a logical consequence, it is seen as an intragenerational rather than intergenerational phenomenon. This deviates from Weber's own position, although it resonates exquisitely with the "voluntaristic nominalism" (Hinkle and Hinkle, 1954) which has long typified American sociology.

In speaking of the life-style expectations of estates, Weber links these to "restrictions on social intercourse" (Gerth and Mills, 1946:187–188). This is consistent with both the status group and estate uses of *Stand*. However, a parting of the ways occurs when reference is made to the endogamous nature of *Staende*. Indeed, Weber confines the term *Stand* to social strata exhibiting characteristics such as in-marriage (Gerth and Mills, 1946:188):

> As soon as there is not a mere individual and socially irrelevant imitation of another style of life, but an agreed-upon communal action of this closing character, the "status" development is under way.

The central concept which identifies *Stand* as the creation of an already self-aware elite is that of "usurpation." Weber brings it to bear in the context of his discussion of the F.F.V., Knickerbockers, and other such symbolic displays (Gerth and Mills, 1946:188):

> all these elements usurp "status" honor. The development of status is essentially a question of stratification resting upon usurpation. Such usurpation is the normal origin of almost all status honor. But the road from this purely conventional situation to legal privilege, positive or negative, is easily traveled as soon as a certain stratification of the social order has in fact been "lived in" and has achieved stability by virtue of a stable distribution of economic power.

Not only does the reference to "legal privilege" attest to the estate nature of *Staende,* it also serves to present *Stand* as a ploy or stratagem of a group which already dominates by more instrumental means, that is, which is dominant within a class order. This is also discernable in Weber's brief statement subsuming professions (sometimes translated as "occupational groups") under the heading of *Stand* (Gerth and Mills, 1946:193). In this aside, Weber identifies the symbolic displays/style of life of this social sector as the key to their existence. The monopolization of knowledge, skill, and technique which is the basis of professions rests upon the same type of moral, conventional, and legal order upon which rest *Staende* as a whole.[2] The negatively evaluated social antitheses of the precipitating *Staende* (i.e., nonelites) are excluded by the actions of an already powerful elite, not by their own activities, as in a class/market situation. For Weber, "classes" in their primitive form tend to emerge out of the "mass" interplay of social actors; they are a manifestation of mass action. Through the totality of the process of individuals pursuing their own interests, Weber asserts, class situations sort themselves out as a "natural" outcome of interactions in "markets." In contrast to this, estate formation comes about as a result of intended "social"—not "mass"—action. On this basis rests the significance of the concept of "ursurpation." It represents social action (even "rational" action) on the part of already existing and self-aware social collectivities, i.e., "classes for themselves," to further their political, economic, and social ends.

As Weber implies in his analyses of authority as a phenomenon and by his development of authority as a concept, the advantages to ruling classes of the transition from fluid, precarious economic/instrumental dominance to partially self-enforcing systems of psychic domination are obvious. Indeed, Habermas's (1975) recent work on "legitimation crises" demonstrates by extension the importance of "ideological hegemony." Weber's great student, Lukacs (1971), also lends credence to this position by emphasizing the centrality of "false" as opposed to "class" consciousness for revolutionary theory and practice. Legal privilege, deference, prohibitive ritual display and their many manifestations are means of domination which are exercises in the establishment of legitimacy. The key point here is that they come into being as a result of *already* existing relations of super- and subordination. They are their realization at a higher level—the level of *Staende* as opposed to that of *Klasse*—and it is this distinction that motivates Weber's subtle analysis.

It should be noted that the contradictions present in the "Warnerized" Weber have been obvious even to its adherents or sympathizers. Bottomore (1966:25) speaks of the "nobility, the scholarly professions, and the high officials" of "pre-capitalist" society as corresponding to Weber's *Staende*. He then goes on to qualify his damaging statement by restating the applicability of *Stand* to the "new middle class." However, Bottomore provides neither empirical nor textual substantiation of his assertion. Bendix (1960:85) is also sensitive to this equation:

> I believe that "status group" is an adequate translation of *Stand*. In medieval society its original meaning was "estate." However, Weber's use of the term includes all instances of cohesive social groups with their subcultures and their exclusion of outsiders.

The major defect in this assertion is that *Weber* does not address himself to "all . . . cohesive social groups," but confines himself to political / economic orders and/or relationships *of a particular kind*, i.e., historically mature or maturing class systems and their characteristic social segments (the F.F.V., Knickerbockers, and Junkers). It can be argued at the level of material–theoretical interests that the self-conscious replacement of "estate" with "status group" is necessary to many of Bendix's interpretations of Weber. Like Bottomore, he presents no textual analysis to support his assertion, which appears in a footnote. In a later footnote to a discussion of patrimonialism, this is again an issue (Bendix, 1960: 361):

> *Staatssoziologie* . . . I use the term "estate" here since in the present context Weber referred to "medieval estates" rather than more broadly to status groups.

Weber himself is mute on such a distinction. His references to the America of *his* day in terms of *Stand* militate against the Bendix–Bottomore position. The "two *Stand*" solution to the problems of conventional reconstructions of Weber on inequality acts by fiat, not by evidence. It is a poorly supported attempt to transform the historical specifics of Weber's discussions of two different estate systems into general theoretical distinctions.

Weber's use of the term *Stand* in the context of feudalism takes place, as Bendix was seen to note, within the parameters of the more limited phenomenon of the *Standestaat,* or that which Wittich and Roth (1968) label the "polity of estates." This political form represents the social development of estates to the point of institutionalizaton, i.e., the legal formalization of their already material and social domination. Weber (1968:1086) makes this clear when he states that:

> fief-holders and other power-holders . . . consociate with one another for the purpose of a concrete action which would not be possible without this collaboration. The existence of a *Standestaat* merely indicates that this system of alliances, which was unavoidable because of the contractual guarantee of all rights and duties and because of the resulting inelasticity, has developed into a chronic condition, which under certain circumstances was legally prepetuated through an explicit association.

This is self-consciously a discussion by Weber of a mature estate system; it contrasts only in historical detail with Weber's earlier cited discussions of nineteenth-century America. The formation of estates in America was largely inchoate; being poorly developed it showed less closure, and, most significantly, the absence of legal privilege. This does not represent an assertion by Weber of the existence of two *types* of *Staende,* but rather of two specific instances at different points in their development. The perception of the medieval case as the more mature of the two manifestations of the general social form is evident when Weber (1968:1087) talks about the economic forces which brought forth social closure out of individual independence among fief-holders; the financial requirements of the military and administrative structures of emerging nation-states. Weber saw the changing economic structure of feudalism, especially the rising money economy, as mandating the formalization of political relationships among the power-holding estate members. As he puts it (Weber, 1968: 1087):

> the frequent conclusion of new agreements was unavoidable, eventually requiring a consociation of the individual power-holders in the form of a corporative assembly. This very association either included the prince or turned privileged persons into "Estates," and thus changed the mere agreed-upon action of the various power-holders and the temporary associations into a permanent political structure.

What Weber is talking about in the medieval case is the politics of well-developed estates, estates so far advanced that they institutionalize their own power, i.e., they *overtly* "establish" their own already-existing social, political, and economic domination.

In the then-contemporary American case, estates were in the process of early coalescence. As was fashionable among European intellectuals, Weber was using the American case as a "laboratory" for *Staende*, a situation where to a considerable extent a society was being constructed from the beginning. The discussions of *Stand* in such a context portray a more flexible instance. This is not, however, the result of a different *type* of phenomenon, but rather of a contrast between more mature and less mature manifestations of the same social process. In contrast, Bendix, Bottomore, and others show no such internal consistency; indeed, their position deploys no supportive evidence at all. In the face of this, the origins of the 'two *Stand*' solution to the problem of status group must be sought not in Weber, but in his readers. The sociotheoretical origins of the transformation of *Stand* into status group are somewhat less complex than the issues which they engender.

THE SOCIOTHEORETICAL ORIGINS OF "STATUS GROUP"

The development of "status group" and its homage to the work of Max Weber is a response to both theoretical and social imperatives. Whether these are empirically separable or not, they are at least metatheoretically divisible. There is no mystery to the immediate theoretical constraints which bring "status group" forth, subsume it under a broader perspective of "non-egalitarian classlessness," and attribute it to Weber. Taken as a whole, this theoretical construction represents an internally consistent alternative to a Marxian class analysis—a tradition which has been treated with hostility and dismissed without hearing almost from the inception of American sociology. As was already noted, the more palatable alternative at issue here, "status group," has the added virtue of negating the equally unattractive option which posits an atomized or "mass" society consisting of anomic social actors unaffiliated with classes, or any other social collectivity. Its (questionable) claim to a European/classical heritage completes its irresistible intellectual charms. These matters of the mind are rooted in turn in the material conditions of American society and the nature of American academia and academics. Dahrendorf (1959:6–7), who categorically states that Weber's *Staende* are estates, disdains the whole concept of status group, which he equates with the bastard construction of "Mittelstand." Dahrendorf (1959:7) wryly observes that the interpretation of *Stand* as "status" is one example of the exigencies of translations—and of their creativity. By the very fact of misleading they can create terms that acquire a life of their own.

Neither Reinhard Bendix, Guenther Roth, nor Hans Gerth is unfamiliar with the German language. To assign such a weighty "error" or to engage in "creative" translation as Dahrendorf does begs the question of the sources of this creativity. Helpfully, the concept of *Mittelstand,* which in German social thought corresponds in origin and form to "status group," has drawn comment outside of sociology.

In Schorske's (1970:20–5) critique of Herman Lebovic's incisive work, there is the following:

> In Lebovic's title, *Social Conservatism and the Middle Classes in Germany, 1914–1933,* the term "middle classes" needs clarification. The word which the author would have used, had our language a clear equivalent for it, is *"Mittelstand."* The term means "middle estate," implying status in a feudal, hierarchical order, as distinct from "class," which refers to position in a socio-economic order.

This is as yet inconclusive for the current argument. However, Schorske (1970:20) goes on to deliver a critical analysis of the *social* sources of the *concept* of *Mittelstand.*

> Yet *"Mittelstand,"* for all its feudal ring, is not a truly feudal term. It arose in the nineteenth century, and was developed by conservative social theorists to apply to the pre-industrial artisans, shopkeepers, peasants, etc., threatened by the new industrial capitalism. The term expressed both nostalgia for the lost privileges and rights of medieval guildsmen, and a claim to status independent of wealth. Above all the concept of "estate" offered a psychological refuge—though no economic defense—against the two modern classes which were squeezing the industrial middle class between them: big capital and big labor.

It is somewhat ironic that Schorske, a social historian with no particular Weberian ax to grind, provides the most trenchant insight into the social sources of the "Warnerized" reading of Weber's *Stand.* While Schorske speaks to the specifics of the intellectual origins of *Mittelstand* and its roots in the desperation of declining medieval estates in Germany, he might as easily be talking of the well-springs of the concept of "status group" which, it should be noted, is itself merely "middle class" raised to a more abstract level. The social history being written by Warner, his colleagues, and his social anthropological fellow travelers in the 1930s and 1940s was a story of the decline and fall of small-town and small-city America in the face of monopolistic tendencies in American finance, industry, and distribution. The concentration of the populace of nineteenth-century America into vast megalopolitan centers, its incorporation into the rationalized, demystified social relations of Taylorized wage labor, the ongoing centralization of finance into gigantic national or transnational banks, and the evolution of vast commercial enterprises which rapidly eliminated all but a few vestiges of individual entrepreneurial activity, all composed the wildly proliferating social thicket the shadow of which was "eclipsing" (as Stein styled it) the image of "community" which the Warnerians wished to preserve. As is so often the case in social theory, even as it is in social reality, that which is sought is found, although more often at the level of socially conditioned perception than in the realm of material reality. The transmutation of the primal element of social class was fascinating. The denial of the social results of capitalism and all it portended was accomplished by a set of clearly identifiable steps: first, the large national centers from which capitalist social relations spread outward were ignored; second, places where precapitalist or primitive capitalist enterprise continued to exist were selected; third, the peculiar social relations which were extant in such areas were considered; but fourth, those social relations were themselves ideologically mystified.

The pictures drawn by the students of American community were, as a general rule, as reflective of the reality of American social relations as were Norman Rockwell's. Not only was small-town capitalism venerated, it was also cast in terms of its own ideology—that of a kind of Jeffersonian classlessness, the transparency of which had long before been pierced by de Tocqueville's skeptical aristocratic eye. It was the self-denial and minimization of class relations in nonmetropolitan America that are mirrored in the Warnerian view of class *gradation,* in which all were supposedly equal in fundamental ways, differing only as to their place in the smooth, even distribution of prestige, which itself was seen as only loosely linked to the realities of class and capital. Just as Schorske saw a major distortion in the context of *Mittelstand,* so too does the view of the class structure of early capitalism presented by the early students of "community" represent a fundamental misperception. Not only was an atypical and vanishing segment of a total society selected as a universal model for class structure, but even that segment was miscast. More recent work in the model of Thernstrom's (1964) pioneering activities has demonstrated the way in which class relations dominated and divided the early America of small towns and small cities. Yet, the rapid transition from predominantly individual ownership of the means of agricultural and craft production to a somewhat primitively centralized corporate ownership in the mid-nineteenth century brought with it an ideology of denial which persisted unto the time of Warner and beyond. It is this "precarious camaraderie" of bogus democratism which Weber was seen to observe at the earlier point in this exposition, and which was later embodied in Warner's classless society.

In essence, the social changes brought about by the decline of the

peculiar forms of "yeoman" agriculture and craft production, which predominated in the United States in the early nineteenth century plants the
seeds of an ideological development which flower in the social sciences a
hundred years later. What is most interesting in the context of this paper
is the way in which Max Weber's ghost is recurrently involved in this
development. It should be realized that the overall evaluative stance of
the students of small-town, entrepreneurial, farm, and craft America was
mournful. Although Warner and his emulators succeeded in many ways in
presenting the legitimating ideology of a unique epoch in American history, they could not prevent the material erosion of the social relations
which they cherished and which that ideology obfuscated. As with most
historical developments, there were more, as well as less, radical analyses
of the origins of the decline of premonopoly capitalistic America. The
Lynds' (1929, 1937) analyses did touch on the supplantive process of
modern class relations and began to place the onus of destruction on
capitalism as a system. Of particular relevance here is the work of
Bensman (with Vidich, 1960) and more importantly Mills who, it goes
without saying, had no small role in the promulgation of Weberian analyses in the United States. A fascinating insight into the evolution of Mills'
thought, and the sources of his early affinity for Weber, are to be found in
an article which appears in the same year, 1946, as does his cotranslation
with Gerth of Weber's seminal work. In this article Mills begins his critique of capitalism from a uniquely American perspective: that of the
destroyer of an America which was, for the vast bulk of its European
population after 1948, and for all of its non-European population always,
as mystical as Baum's Oz. The Mills of 1946 begins a critique which goes
on to *White Collar, The Power Elite,* and beyond, but it starts from an
assumption of the ubiquity and reality of small-town democracy which is
no different and no less fictitious than poorly developed and evolving
class relations of emergent capitalism in the United States that "status
group" grows and, as Schorske instructs us, it is from similar sources that
the false concept of *Mittlestand* evolves. The work of Weber on capitalism is replete with concerns similar to those voiced by Mills, Warner, and
the others—the decline of traditional society, the "demystification of the
world," and a decline of honor in capitalist society. The description of the
social origins of American sociology that Hinkle and Hinkle (1954) provide is not entirely inappropriate as a description of the background of
Weber himself.

An affinity of this magnitude could not remain long unrequited. Just as
Mittelstand plays a particular ideological function for a dying class segment in nineteenth-century America, so too does the concept of "status
group" salvage the psychological lot of another social sector with its *own*
roots in a declining transitional early capitalist social order, i.e., the

stratum of small-town, quasiclerical, liberal thinkers that gave (give?) American sociology its distinctive flavor.

The parallel between the "conservative theorists" of nineteenth-century Germany and the early Mills who laments the decline of the old "middle class" in the face of advancing capitalism is an important one. The inheritors of a rapidly evanescing class order seem to respond in a relatively uniform manner to that disappearance regardless of national tradition. Weber constructs his model of inequality relations at the very time that the rise of imperial Germany renders many of them obsolete. In the United States it is significant that the bulk of these studies also emerges at the point where capitalist social relations begin their metamorphosis. For a last similarity, there is the doubly suggestive picture of the ideal-typical intellectual struggling against the crass pressures of the "economic" order to be seen in Bendix and Roth's (1971) portrait of Weber. This is significant in that it corroborates the "nested" intellectual *and* social bases upon which status group rests: an image of Weber, an image of the scholarly "estate," and a translation which reverberates in several tones with both. Warner's (1949a, 1949b) concern for the nature of small town America and his generalization of its structure to a rapidly changing urban/industrial society completes the sociotheoretical genealogy of "status group." As was noted, the cosmic egg from which this tradition grows is an academic sociology rooted in and reflecting the interest of a social stratum threatened by the emergence of twentieth-century America; it attaches itself to a bogus concept emerging from an historical Germany of similar contradictions, asserts a dubious claim to Weberian paternity on the basis of "creative" translation, and is promulgated as an alternative to a class analysis alleged to be historically bound.

CONCLUDING OBSERVATIONS

Reconstructuring *Stand* has certain benefits at the theoretical level. By moving the interpretation of the concept further from Warner and closer to Weber, a new edge is provided for an old tool of social analysis. That is, by using Weber for its own ends, modern stratification theory has been forced to ignore some of the more suggestive aspects of Weber's rich and unique analysis. If the process of social closure of collectivities is fully grasped as Weber has modeled it (albeit in fragmentary form in his empirical discussions in *Economy and Society*), the questions that may be raised and perhaps even answered are many and important. If classes undergo alteration into estates, and then into castes, under what conditions does this occur? Much earlier, Weber was seen to argue that conditions of social "stability" encourage such development. Does this mean that capitalism, with its inherent instability, i.e., its growth orientation, is immune to such development? What then may be made of the work of Domhoff (1967, 1971) and Baltzell (1958, 1964)? The emergence of a self-conscious bourgeoisie, its construction of a special culture and con-comitant usurpation of "status honor," the emergence and solidification of class-specific legal treatment and privilege, are all empirical realities which can be profitably considered from a more orthodox Weberian perspective. The pioneering work of Laumann (1966, 1973) and sub-sequent studies of the limits on interclass social intercourse, becomes theoretically meaningful at this point. Even the work of Lukacs, Weber's greatest student regardless of his "loss" to Marxism, becomes more provocative in light of a corrected *Stand* concept. Lukacs has suggested that the consciousness of classes is unique and not a general sociological category. For him, the sociopolitical consciousness of the bourgeoisie is a separate category from that of the proletariat. If bourgeois consciousness (ideology for Lukacs) moves a total class structure toward solidification through the process of usurpation, does this mean that proletarian con-sciousness counters such a process? Can the process take place in a situation of overt class conflict or does it require some sort of class accommodation, even through imperialism, national chauvinism, labor aristocracy, or some other process? By raising these issues, Weber's insights cast new light on many questions which have historically troubled Marxists. Indeed, class analysis is not threatened by such a development; it is broadened and deepened. At the metatheoretical level, equally pro-vocative questions arise. The tie between "class consciousness" as a general concept and *Stand* is a doubly recurred one. The justification given by its adherents for the supplanting of "class" as a concept with that of "status group" is that in the absence of "class consciousness," class is a nominal rather than a real category. This both ignores Weber's notion of "life-chances" and shows a curious relationship to the empirical connection of estate-tendencies and "class consciousness," as the latter differentially exists in contending classes. These are all matters beyond the scope of this work; however, the key point is that unless Weber's concept of *Stand* is recast in its fuller form, such crucial questions cannot be raised.

It should be noted that the preceding comments merely justify the severance of *Stand* from the common construction of "status group" on utilitarian grounds. They do not address the question of the potential independent value of a concept of "status group" purged of its question-able reliance on Weber's work. As Dahrendorf (1959) was seen to ob-serve, such concepts take on a life of their own and thus may be worthy of independent preservation. While they are not what they claim to be, they do exist. Although "status group" has had an unquestionably ideological career, in its less ambitious formulations (e.g., Bensman, 1972) it shows interesting characteristics. Further, it is unquestionably the case that Weber does treat *Stand* in a much broader meaning than "estate." However, by minimizing the perhaps greater significance of the estate usage, the general concept becomes sterile and confused. It thus becomes difficult to determine whether Weber is "wrong" in one usage and "right" in another as long as it is argued that there is only one usage. In terms of sheer mass, Weber gives as much space to the estate use as to the general typological form. Yet, as has been noted, the latter is relegated to footnotes while the former becomes the basis for a vast intellectual edifice. While it is beyond the scope of this particular paper to elaborate on these assertions in detail, several final recommendations should be proposed. It is unquestionable that systematization of the multiple uses of "status group" discussed in the early parts of this paper is required. Second, assuming this has been accomplished, a partitioning of "ideological" and "scientific" components within these uses would be equally necessary. Following this, the question might be raised as to whether the conventional reading of "status group" is a phenomenon of primary interest to those studying inequality structures or, rather, whether it is a serendipitous development which might be more germane to students of "community." Although the answer to the last question may seem to be implied in the asking, the issue is not quite so clear-cut. One final point that *is* clear is that further use of Weber's concept of *Stand* as it is conventionally rendered is a procedure which should be undertaken with caution.

ACKNOWLEDGMENTS

This article is a revision and amalgamation of two earlier papers, one presented at the 1977 meetings of the American Sociological Association and the other given at the Symposia and Colloquia on Max Weber, University of Wisconsin–Milwaukee, 1977. I thank Gary Howe and my collegue David Ashley for their comments on this paper. Of course, I alone am responsible for its contents.

NOTES

1. See Charles Page (1969) for the definitive summary of the roots of this theoretical tendency in American sociology.

2. Leach (1967) labels the conventional use made of Weber on professions/occupations in this context the "degenerate Max Weber view."

REFERENCES

Baltzell, E. Digby
  1958   Philadelphia Gentlemen: The Making of a National Upper Class. New York: Free
          Press.
  1964   The Protestant Establishment: Aristocracy and Class in America. New York:
          Random House.

Bendix, Reinhard
    1960   Max Weber: An Intellectual Protrait. Garden City, New York: Anchor Books.
Bendix, Reinhard, and Guenther Roth
    1971   Scholarship and Partisanship: Essays on Max Weber. Berkeley: University of
           California Press.
Bensman, Joseph
    1972   "Status communities in an urban society: the musical communty." Pp. 113–30 in
           Holger R. Stub (ed.), Status Communties in Modern Society. Hinsdale, Ill.:
           Dryden Press.
Berger, Bennett M.
    1960   Working-Class Suburb. Berkeley: University of California Press.
Birnbaum, Norman
    1969   The Crisis of Industrial Society. New York: Oxford Univeritsy Press.
Bloch, Marc
    1964   "Feudalism as a type of society." In Feudal Society, Vol. 2, tr. by L. A. Manyon.
           Chicago: University of Chicago Press.
Bottomore, T.B.
    1966   Classes in Modern Society. New York: Random House.
Coleman, Richard P., and Bernice L. Neugarten
    1971   Social Status in the City. San Francisco: Jossey-Bass.
Cox, Oliver C.
    1950   "Max Weber on social stratification: a critique." American Sociological Review
           15:223–7.
Dahrendorf, Ralf
    1959   Class and Class Conflict in Industrial Society. Stanford, Calif.: Stanford University
           Press.
Davis, Kingsley
    1949   Human Society. New York: Macmillan.
Dobriner, William M.
    1963   Class in Suburbia. Englewood Cliffs, N.J.: Prentice-Hall.
Domhoff, G. William
    1967   Who Rules America? Englewood Cliffs, N.J.: Prentice-Hall.
    1971   The Higher Circles: The Governing Class in America. New York: Vintage Books
           (Random House).
Gerth, H.H., and C. Wright Mills (eds.)
    1946   From Max Weber: Essays in Sociology. New York: Oxford University Press.
Habermas, Jürgen
    1975   Legitimation Crisis. Boston: Beacon Press.
Heberle, Rudolf
    1959   "Recovery of class theory." American Sociological Review 2:18–24.
Hinkle, Roscoe C., Jr., and Gisela J. Hinkle
    1954   The Development of Modern Sociology. New York: Random House.
Laumann, Edward O.
    1966   Prestige and Association in an Urban Community. Indianapolis, Ind.: Bobbs-
           Merrill.
    1973   Bonds of Pluralism. New York: Wiley.
Leach, Edmund R.
    1967   "Caste, class and slavery: the taxonomic problem." In Anthony de Reuck and
           Julie Knight (eds.), Caste and Race: Comparative Approaches, London: Churchill.
Lukacs, Georg
    1971   History and Class Consciousness. Cambridge, Mass.: M.I.T. Press.

Lynd, Robert S., and Helen M. Lynd.
  1929 Middletown. New York: Harcourt Brace Jovanovich.
  1937 Middletown in Transition. New York: Harcourt Brace Jovanovich.
Martindale, Don
  1960 The Nature and Types of Sociological Theory. Cambridge, Mass.: Riverside.
Mayer, Kurt B.
  1963 "The changing shape of the American class structure." Social Research 30:458–68.
Mayhew, Leon
  1968 "Ascription in modern societies." Sociological Inquiry 38.
Mills, C. Wright
  1946 "The middle classes in middle-sized cities: the stratification and political position of small business and white collar strata." American Sociological Review 11:520–9.
  1951 White Collar. New York: Oxford University Press.
Nisbet, Robert A.
  1959 "The decline and fall of social class." Pacific Sociological Review 2:11–7.
Ossowski, Stanislaw
  1963 Class Structure in the Social Consciousness. New York: Free Press.
  1969 "Non-egalitarian classlessness: similarities in interpreting mutually opposed systems." In Celia Heller (ed.), Structured Social Inequality. New York: Macmillan.
Page, Charles
  1969 Class and American Sociology. New York: Schocken.
Pease, John, William H. Form, and Joan Huber Rytina
  1970 "Ideological currents in American stratification literature." The American Sociologist 127–37.
Pfautz, Harold W., and Otis Dudley Duncan
  1950 "A critical evaluation of Warner's work in community stratification." American Sociological Review 15:205–15.
Riesman, David (with Howard Roseborough)
  1955 "Careers and consumer behavior." In Lincoln H. Clark (ed.), Consumer Behavior, Vol. II. New York: New York University Press.
Rinehart, James W.
  1971 "Affluence and the embourgeoisement of the working class: a critical look." Social Problems 19:149–62.
Schorske, Carl E.
  1970 "Weimar and the intellectuals: II" The New York Review of Books (May):20–5.
Shostak, Arthur B.
  1969 Blue Collar Life. New York: Random House.
Stein, Maurice R.
  1960 The Eclipse of Community: An Interpretation of American Studies. Princeton, N.J.: Princeton University Press.
  1953 "Instabilities in status: the problem of hierarchy in the community study of status arrangements." American Sociological Review 18:149–62.
Thernstrom, Stephan
  1964 Poverty and Progress: Social Mobility in a Nineteenth Century City. Cambridge, Mass.: Harvard University Press.
Vidich, Arthur J., and Joseph Bensman
  1960 Small Town in Mass Society: Class, Power and Religion in a Rural Community. Garden City, N.Y.: Doubleday.

Warner, W. Lloyd, Marchia Meeker, and Kenneth Eells.
   1949a Social Class in America. New York: Science Research Associates.
   1949b Democracy in Jonesville. New York: Harper & Row.
Weber, Max
   1968 Economy and Society, Vols. 1–3, Guenther Roth and Claus Wittich (eds.). Totowa,
       N.J.: Bedminster Press.
Wilensky, Harold L.
   1960 "Work, careers and social integration." International Social Science Journal
       12:543–60.
Wittich, Claus, and Guenther Roth (eds.)
   1968 Max Weber, Economy and Society. Totowa, N.J.: Bedminster Press.
Wrong, Dennis H.
   1949 "Social inequality without social stratification." The Canadian Review of Soci-
       ology and Anthropology 1: 5–16.
Zeitlin, Irving
   1967 Marxism: A Re-examination. New York: Van Nostrand.
   1968 Ideology and the Development of Sociological Theory. Englewood Cliffs, N.J.:
       Prentice-Hall.
   1973 Rethinking Sociology: A Critique of Contemporary Theory. Englewood Cliffs,
       N.J.: Prentice-Hall.